Gerd Hurm is Professor of American Literature and Director of the Center for American Studies at the University of Trier, Germany. He has published widely in the fields of urban, media, and gender studies, with a particular focus on American political rhetoric, realist and modernist discourses, and on post-World War II American arts and culture. He is currently researching the photography, aesthetics and curatorial politics of Edward Steichen.

Anke Reitz is a photography curator at the Centre national de l'audiovisuel (CNA) in Luxembourg and is in charge of the CNA's Steichen Collections *The Family of Man* and *The Bitter Years*. She has written on art history and visual communication and lately her focus has been on audiovisual arts, photographic history and conservation, as well as art mediation.

Shamoon Zamir is Associate Professor of Literature and Visual Studies and Director of Akkasah: Center for Photography at New York University Abu Dhabi. He works on American literature, photography and intellectual history. He is the author of *The Gift of the Face: Portraiture and Time in Edward S. Curtis's The North American Indian* (2014). He is also co-editor of *The Photobook* (I.B.Tauris, 2012).

I0802681

'This anthology of contemporary essays and historical sources is an important contribution to the growing field of exhibition history. Through critical reevaluation of *The Family of Man* and analyses of its international reception, the book breaks new ground with varied accounts of the show's place in postwar culture and detailed discussion of its curatorial construction and modes of presentation.'

– **Bruce Altshuler**, Director, Program in Museum Studies, New York University

'Of exhibitions of photography, *The Family of Man* is the one most deserving of renewed critical reflection and assessment. This volume offers exactly that, providing new perspectives and information in an effort to make us think again about what we imagined we already knew. Anyone interested in photography's history and creative possibilities will want to read it.'

– **Geoffrey Batchen**, Victoria University of Wellington, New Zealand

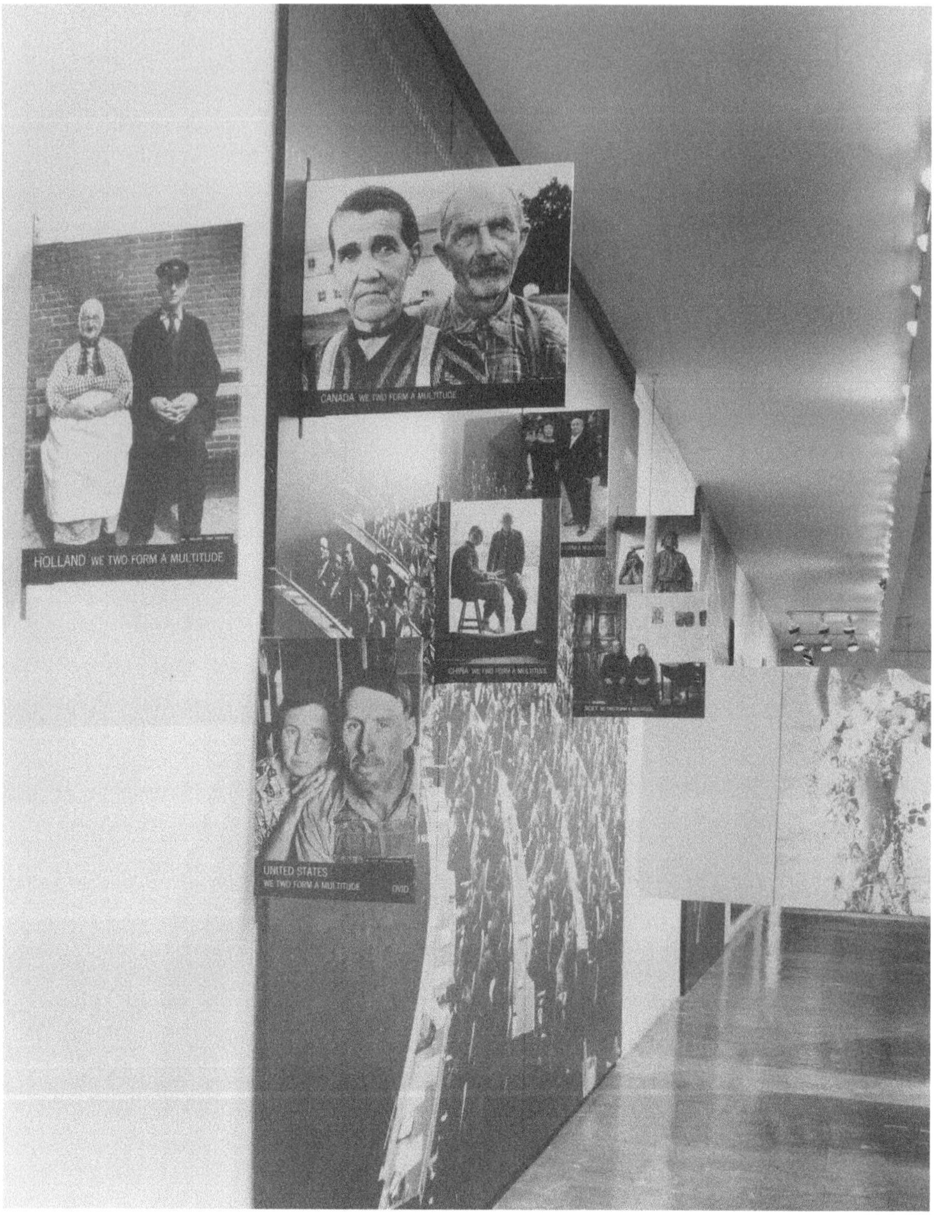

Rolf Petersen, installation view of *The Family of Man* at the Museum of Modern Art, New York City, 1955.

THE FAMILY OF MAN REVISITED

Photography in a Global Age

Edited by
Gerd Hurm
Anke Reitz
Shamoon Zamir

Routledge
Taylor & Francis Group
LONDON AND NEW YORK

First published 2018 by I.B. Tauris

Published 2020 by Routledge
2 Park Square, Milton Park, Abingdon, Oxon OX14 4RN
605 Third Avenue, New York, NY 10017

Routledge is an imprint of the Taylor & Francis Group, an informa business

A full CIP record for this book is available from the British Library
A full CIP record is available from the Library of Congress

Library of Congress Catalog Card Number: available

Typeset by Free Range Book Design & Production Limited

ISBN 13: 978-1-7845-3966-5 (hbk)
ISBN 13: 978-1-7845-3967-2 (pbk)

Dedicated to

Jean Back

Contents

List of Illustrations

Introduction

The Family of Man Revisited

Shamoon Zamir and Gerd Hurm

The Family of Man (1955) is, by a very long measure, the most widely seen exhibition in the history of photography. The book of the exhibition is also the most commercially successful photobook of all time. Close to 500 images from 68 countries were selected from millions reviewed, and staged as an unfolding thematic sequence through a radically immersive and interactive design (see illustrations 1 and 2). Conceived, curated and designed by Edward Steichen in the early years of the Cold War, the exhibition affirmed a common human identity and fate against the continuing political and cultural divisions that shaped World War II, and that persisted or were reconfigured after it. This commonality was figured in particular as a response to the threat of nuclear annihilation that had transformed all nations into what Wendell Willkie some years earlier had referred to as 'one world'[1]: the photographs showed what Steichen described as 'the gamut of life from birth to death with emphasis on the daily relationships of man to himself, to his family, to the community and to the world we live in'. The images shared a focus, in other words, on 'the everydayness of life' and 'the essential onenesss of mankind throughout the world'. But it was a towering colour transparency of an atomic explosion, the only full colour image in the entire show, that was the photograph that anchored *The Family of Man* most explicitly to its immediate historical context (see illustrations 42 and 43).[2] The exhibition opened at the Museum of Modern Art (MoMA) in New York on 25 January 1955 and ran until 8 May. Steichen and MoMA had always planned for a version of the exhibition to travel internationally as well as within the United States. However, the unprecedented success of the show attracted the attention of the United States Information Agency (USIA) which incorporated it into its programme of cultural propaganda and helped devise for it a remarkably ambitious international itinerary in addition to its national circulation. By the time its global tour came to an end in 1965, *The Family of Man* had been seen by more than nine million people in 48 countries all over the world.[3] The book of the exhibition was similarly successful: still in print, it has sold several million copies.

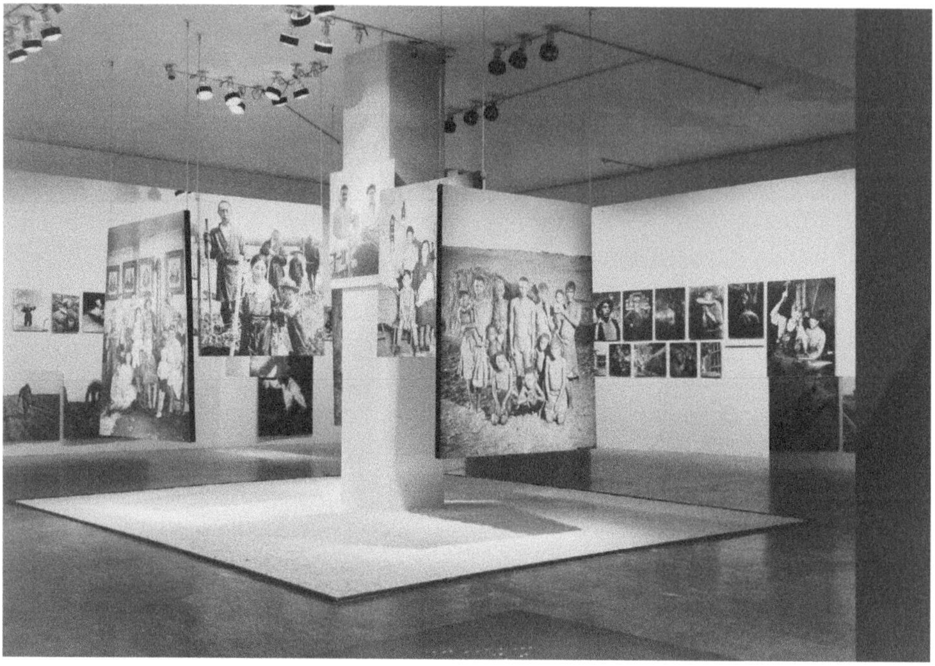

1 *The Family of Man* at the Museum of Modern Art, New York City.

The popular response to *The Family of Man* indicates that the exhibition did cultural work that people found relevant on an unprecedented scale in the post-war world; it also suggests a near universal acceptance of the show's particular articulation of humanism and a confirmation of its faith in photography as a medium uniquely able to communicate across cultures and time.

In stark contrast, though with some notable exceptions, the critical response has characterized Steichen's project largely as historically, politically and aesthetically naïve, and as emotionally immature. A number of commentators writing in the 1950s offered variations on this assessment but it was Roland Barthes's short 1957essay on the Paris version of the exhibition, 'The Great Family of Man', that most influentially set the terms in which the exhibition has been evaluated consistently ever since.[4] For Barthes, Steichen replaces the claims of politics and difference with a sentimental myth of human sameness, thereby substituting Nature for 'the determining weight of History' – 'determining' because for Barthes it is only history and not nature that gives meaning to human existence. Those critics who have paid greater attention than Barthes to the cultural and historical contexts of *The Family of Man* in the United States have extended the logic of his analysis and argued that the exhibition's bourgeois myth of the human and its middlebrow aesthetics were perfect vehicles for an American ideology geared towards domestic social conservatism and Cold War cultural hegemony. Implicit in Barthes's critique and in those that have followed in his

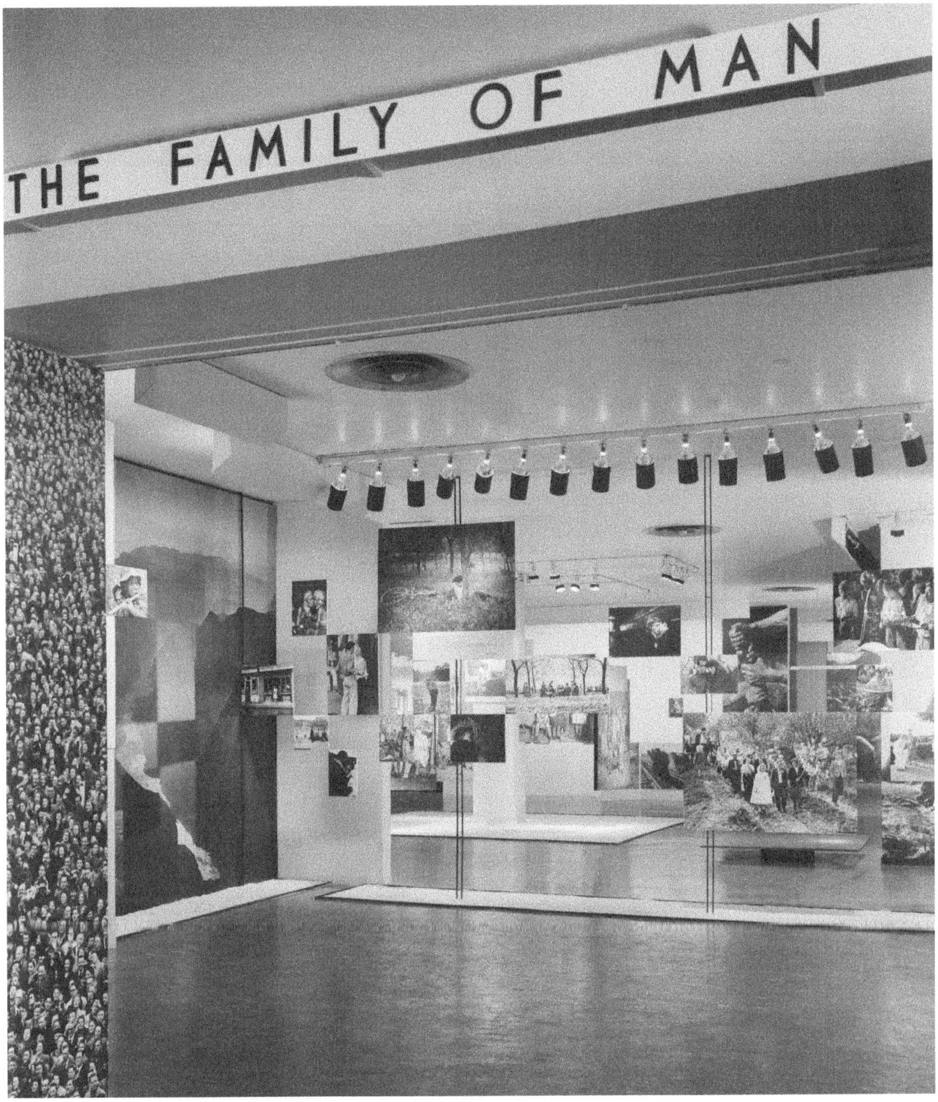

2 *The Family of Man* at the Museum of Modern Art, New York City.

footsteps is, of course, a distrust of, and occasionally even open contempt for, both the popular response to the exhibition and the widespread appeal of its aesthetic.

Without being sanguine, the essays collected in the present volume share the conviction that the critiques of *The Family of Man* conducted in the name of history have, in fact, emptied the exhibition, and also the popular response to it, of their own historicity. The essays try to retrieve and to understand anew the sense of cultural and social urgency, what one might call the crisis content, that drove both Steichen's project and the global audience's response to it. They do so by exploring new cultural contexts for the exhibition and by undertaking new and detailed formal and conceptual analyses of it.

These new interpretations include fresh perspectives on the American and the Cold War locations of *The Family of Man*, as well as critical engagements with Barthes that reframe the debate about the exhibition and move us towards more capacious and complex readings. But at the heart of this book is a series of attempts to think about the formal and visual aspects of the exhibition in new ways and in unprecedented detail, and with a focus on Europe and its experience of Steichen's project.

Germany provides a case study of the exhibition's international reception and additional perspectives are drawn from Poland and Luxembourg. A remarkable collection of previously unknown or untranslated archival material is included in this volume and examined for the first time in its contributions: commentaries by philosopher and cultural theorist Max Horkheimer and novelist Wolfgang Koeppen, letters from photographer August Sander expressing a practitioner's sense of Steichen's achievement, as well as a uniquely detailed survey of audience responses to the show in Munich in 1958. The book also presents for the first time in English a translation of *Komentarze do fotografii: The Family of Man* (1962), a sequence of poems based on selected photographs from the exhibition by Polish poet, novelist, critic and translator Witold Wirpsza.[5]

Horkheimer's '*The Family of Man* – Wir Alle' is the text of his address at the opening of *The Family of Man* in Frankfurt on 25 October 1958; it was delivered only a year after Barthes published his critique of the exhibition, but offers a very different assessment to Barthes's. Horkheimer was, of course, one of the founders of the Frankfurt School and, along with Theodor Adorno, Walter Benjamin and Herbert Marcuse, one of the leading exponents of critical theory. Given this group's well-known critiques of middlebrow aesthetics, popular culture and bourgeois ideology, Horkheimer's spirited and philosophical defence of the aesthetics and humanism of Steichen's show is both unexpected and a radical counterpoint to Barthes. Horkheimer accepts the exhibition as 'a symbol of common bonds among human beings' but reads it through the tradition of Kantian philosophy and its affinities with the American philosophical tradition, arguing that the exhibition explores above all 'the identity of human beings in their non-identity'. Horkheimer's emphasis is, in other words, on the exhibition's ability to sustain a mutually supportive dialectic of difference and sameness and not on the erasure of difference; his address offers a nuanced and suggestive set of reflections on the relationship between idea and reality, thought and image, and the importance of 'the knowledge of ephemeral things' made available uniquely by photography. For

Horkheimer, Steichen's exhibit offers nothing less than 'a new way of looking at things that we will never forget'.

Unlike his colleagues and friends Walter Benjamin, Theodor Adorno and Siegfried Kracauer, Horkheimer is not known for any substantial engagement with photography. Yet, only a year and a half after the Frankfurt opening of *The Family of Man* he delivered another address on photography (on the occasion of the centennial of the Adox photochemical factory). Here Horkheimer develops issues touched upon in his reflections on Steichen's exhibition: the interactions between image and concept and between image and reason. Horkheimer's thinking on photography is clearly influenced by the work of his friend Kracauer whose own thoughts on the interplay between photographic image, reality and reason, and whose invocation of *The Family of Man* as an exemplary embodiment of photography's ability to redeem physical reality and to reveal the common world, appeared the same year in his *Theory of Film* (1960).[6] As Janine Marchessault has noted, while there can be little doubt that the USIA used Steichen's exhibition for its own political ends, for Kracauer *The Family of Man* 'foregrounded an emancipatory intercultural communication'.[7] Kracauer argued that the 'photographic media' were best placed 'to record the material aspects of daily common life in many places', and it was this that made them the vehicles for 'rendering visible' the slow emergence of a human commonality across the world. It was *The Family of Man*'s ability to capture this commonality through concrete forms that explained for Kracauer 'the world-wide response to Edward Steichen's exhibition'.[8]

The texts of both of Horkheimer's addresses are presented for the first time in English in this book. Also included is Horkheimer's letter accepting the invitation to open *The Family of Man* in Frankfurt in which he indicates his willingness to temporarily come out of effective retirement because of his enthusiasm for the exhibition. These texts have never before been discussed in relation to *The Family of Man*, nor to Horkheimer's own thought and career. They allow us to grasp the historical meanings of Steichen's exhibition in ways entirely different from the approach established by Barthes and continued by his followers, and they open up and re-energize contemporary considerations of the exhibition as well as of the role of humanist photography. A number of contributions to this volume engage with different aspects of Horkheimer's thoughts on *The Family of Man.* The most detailed examination of Horkheimer's address is offered by Martin Jay, a leading scholar of both the Frankfurt School and of visual culture, who places them in the context of Horkheimer's thought and the work of his German colleagues. Jay emphasizes that Horkheimer's reliance on Kant positions the text as something of an unexpected anomaly within his oeuvre; Horkeimer's bringing together of European and American traditions of philosophical thought also provides an original critical framing of *The Family of Man*.

Wolfgang Koeppen, one of the foremost German novelists of the post-war era, offers an enthusiastic, impressionistic rather than philosophical response to *The Family of Man* in a review of the exhibition for the *Süddeutsche Zeitung*, a Munich newspaper (21 November 1955). Koeppen is best known for his three mid-century novels exploring with an unflinching gaze the recent past and present realities of post-1945 Germany: *Pigeons on the Grass* (1951), *The Hothouse* (1953) and *Death*

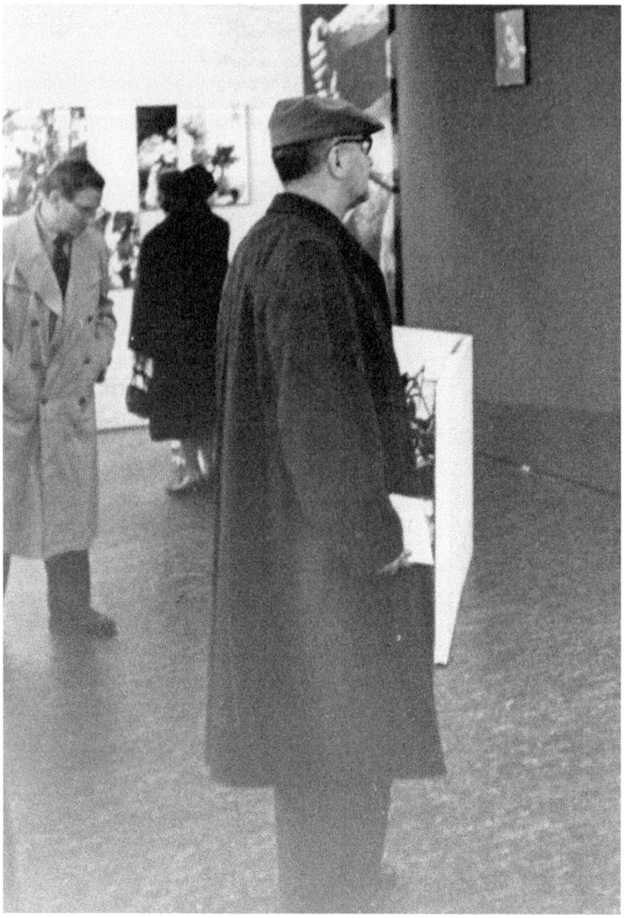

3 Bertolt Brecht visiting *The Family of Man* at Hochschule für bildende Künste, Berlin, 1955.

in Rome (1954). These novels form a trilogy that interrogates the historical amnesia, the denial of history, that characterized much of German society after the war, and it is their combination of a committed political stance and a radical aesthetics derived from a wide engagement with modernist literature that made these works inspirations for many of the writers who emerged in Germany in the 1960s, including Günter Grass. Given his commitment to history and to radical form, Koeppen's assessment of *The Family of Man* goes as much against the grain of the broad critical consensus about the exhibition as Horkheimer's. Koeppen characterizes the exhibition as 'a *comédie humaine*, written by the photographic lens [...] exactly as it was in Balzac, both drama and tragedy'. Where others have seen only sentimental optimism in the exhibition, Koeppen proposes that 'melancholy' is its defining note, and he aligns Steichen's project with the critical realism of contemporary fiction: 'the photographs in this exhibition [...] are irrefutable proof of the truthfulness and the correct direction of contemporary literature, because a lens that sees only what is there contradicts by what it captures the attacks against the modern novel, as they have recently been made by *Life* magazine and everywhere in Germany, the accusation that fiction represents the world too gloomily and thus is untrue'. Koeppen's review of *The Family of Man* is engaged with a way into the exhibition in this volume in particular by Werner Sollors, among the leading authorities on ethnicity, race and culture in the United States, and also the author of a major recent study of German culture in the aftermath of World War II. Sollors turns to Koeppen in a series of open-ended reflections on *The Family of Man* that help map succinctly a wide range of critical issues that remain relevant to ongoing considerations of the exhibition.

The Family of Man was not exhibited in the German Democratic Republic (the US in fact did not recognize the GDR), but the show toured the Federal Republic of Germany before the wall dividing East and West was built, and at a time when it was still possible for visitors from the East to visit the West. One visitor was Bertolt Brecht. According to an 'Operations Memorandum' sent by the United States Information Service (as the USIA was referred to overseas) from Bonn to the Washington head office (10 January 1956), Brecht, 'famous East-zone pro-communist playwright', was photographed by a 'Berlin student' while visiting the show (see illustration 3).[9] We do not know what Brecht made of the exhibition, but we do know that he kept a catalogue of *The Family of Man* in his library.[10] His own photobook, *Kriegsfibel* (*War Primer*), was published only a few weeks after the visit.[11] In preparation since 1940, the book presented images taken from magazines and newspapers, many of them, as in *The Family of Man*, from *Life* magazine, with each image accompanied by a short, four-line poem, the text providing ironic and biting commentaries on the politics and human experience of war. At first sight there seems to be little in common between Steichen's and Brecht's projects. The sense of history and of political critique in the latter is precisely what is found lacking by so many in the celebration of human commonality in *The Family of Man*. But Steichen himself had lived through two world wars, serving as an aerial photographer in the first and as the head of the photography unit for the Navy in the second, and *The Family of Man* took shape as an idea and an exhibition in large part during the years in which the United States was embroiled in the brutal war in Korea. In the 1940s and early 1950s, Steichen had tried to show the realities of war by curating a series of exhibitions, but felt that these had failed to effectively nurture in the audience a properly critical consciousness about the horrors and consequences of armed conflict:

> Although I had presented war in all its grimness in three exhibitions [wrote Steichen in his autobiography], I had failed to accomplish my mission. I had not incited people into taking open and united action against war itself. This failure made me take stock of my fundamental idea. What was wrong? I came to the conclusion that I had been working from a negative approach, that what was needed was a positive statement on what a wonderful thing life was, how marvelous people were, and, above all, how alike people were in all parts of the world.[12]

The exhibitions were *Road to Victory* (1942), *Power in the Pacific* (1945) and *Korea: The Impact of War in Photographs* (1951).[13] Steichen stated that *The Family of Man* 'had its genesis' in these exhibitions (though elsewhere he also notes other moments of origin). While the first two of the three were very much part of the war effort, intended to boost national morale as much as to show war, the exhibition on Korea was less constrained by a local political agenda. Steichen, inspired in part by David Douglas Duncan's *This is War* (1950), which he considered 'the most forceful indictment of the subject ever put forth by photography', 'had banked particularly' on the Korea exhibit 'to make a thought-provoking impression on the world, for this war had undergone a more realistic photographic interpretation than any other'. But Steichen was disappointed by what he perceived to be the reception of the exhibition: 'People flocked in great numbers to see it. They found some pictures revolting, some deeply moving. There were even tears shed, but that was as far as it went. They left the exhibition and promptly forgot it.'

The first phase of planning for *The Family of Man* began while Steichen was working on the Korea exhibit and while that exhibit was on show at MoMA, and *The Family of Man* was designed clearly as a sort of counterpoint and alternative to the war exhibits, an attempt to engage people by showing them not the horror of war but what is lost in war – what in fact would be irretrievably lost in a third, nuclear world war. And here we find that the distance between Brecht, 'famous East-zone pro-communist playwright', and Steichen, the liberal humanist, may not be quite as great as may be suggested by only a casual comparison of *Kriegsfibel* and *The Family of Man*. The publication of Brecht's book came with an announcement that a companion volume, *Friedensfibel* (*Peace Primer*) was intended for future publication. Brecht, like Steichen, appears then to have wanted to move beyond war, what Steichen referred to as negativity, towards an engagement with alternative, more positive aspects of life. Brecht never completed this project, but the back cover of *Kriegsfibel* carried a preliminary image from it (see illustration 4). In motif and set-up it strongly resembles the photo of first-year medical students, earnest young women and men in a packed, tiered lecture hall, by Alfred Eisenstaedt, taken from a 1948 *Life* magazine story on Charles University in Prague and included in the section devoted to education in *The Family of Man*. Brecht must have been surprised and intrigued to find that an image similar to the one he had chosen for his own project had been used by Steichen (see illustration 5).[14]

This brief comparison with Brecht, as much as the commentaries by Horkheimer and Koeppen, as well as Kracauer, should serve as cautions against too-easy characterizations of *The Family of Man* as only American Cold War propaganda, or as an embodiment of bourgeois ideology. But if German responses to and contexts for Steichen's exhibition enable us to take a fresh look at the cultural and social politics of the show, they can also encourage us similarly to re-examine the exhibition's formal aspects and the impact these had at least on some visitors in the 1950s. Koeppen's review suggests some possible framings in this regard for *The Family of Man*'s image work, but the reaction of another German artist, Gerhard Richter, conveys more immediately the sense of excitement and possibility experienced in the encounter with Steichen's show.

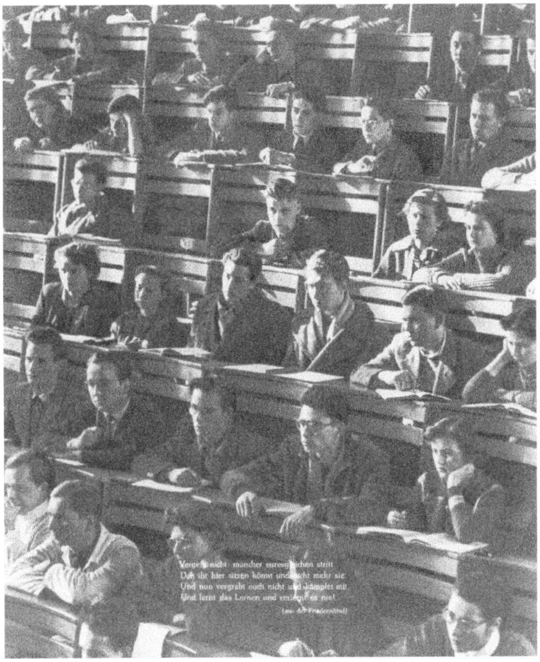

4 Back cover: Bertolt Brecht, *Kriegsfibel* (1955).

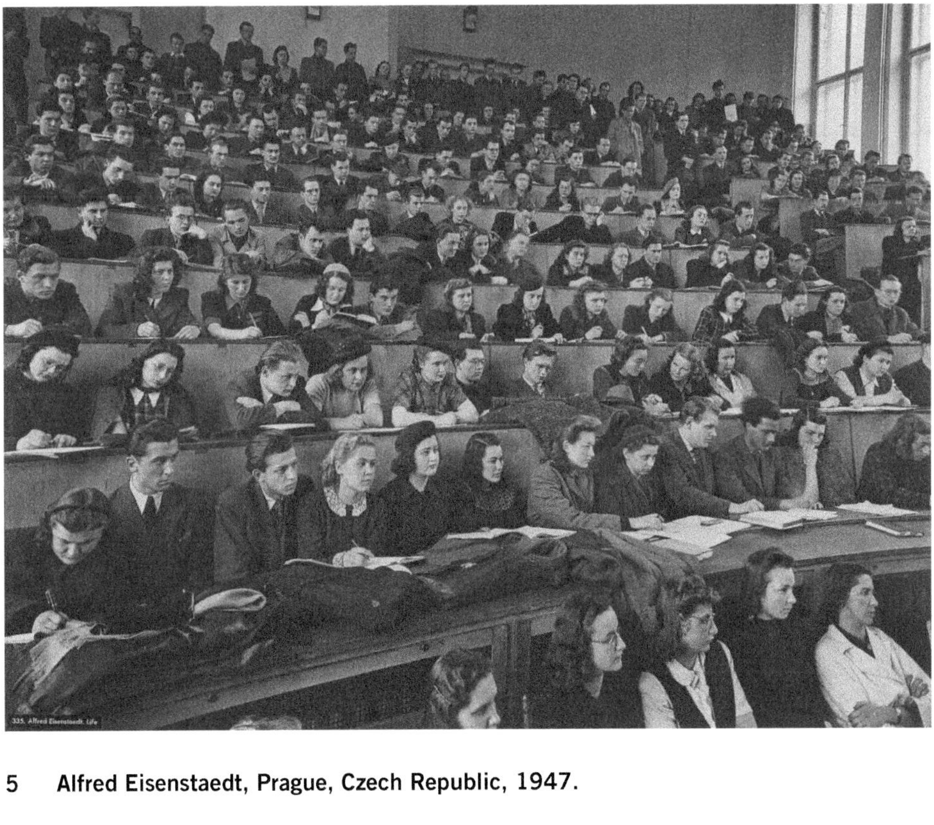

5 Alfred Eisenstaedt, Prague, Czech Republic, 1947.

Richter, like Brecht, saw the show in Berlin in 1955. Unlike Brecht, he was then an artist at the very start of his career, but like Brecht, a visitor from the East. Speaking of how 'terrible' life was in the East, and how restricted personal freedom was, he recalls that there was 'the possibility to go every year at least twice to West Berlin' to see 'movies and exhibitions'. It was on one such trip that he saw *The Family of Man*: 'This was a real shock for me, this show [...] to see these pictures, because I knew only paintings [...] they showed so much and they told so much these pictures, these photographs, told so much about modern life, my life.' Richter dates his own interest in photography from this moment when he encountered Steichen's exhibition because it showed him the 'power' of photography and 'what photography can do'. These comments are from a conversation between Richter and Nicholas Serota, the director of the Tate Gallery in the UK, on the occasion of Richter's major exhibition *Panorama* (6 October 2011–8 January 2012). At this point in the conversation Serota says, 'To see *The Family of Man* was to understand how a photograph could capture a moment or a place or an image.' The statement is clearly intended more as a question than as an affirmation of an assessment accepted by Serota himself, and Richter responds, 'Yes. This was really new.'[15] In a more recent personal note to the editors, Richter reiterates that he was 'deeply impressed' by the exhibition and looked at the pictures in amazement.[16]

Richter went on to make extensive and varied use of photography in his own work, including the use of photographs as bases for paintings. His acknowledgement of the role of *The Family of Man* in impelling and shaping this engagement with photography, coming as it does from one of the most innovative and diverse artists of post-war Europe, opens a way of understanding the genealogy of Steichen's exhibition design as something other than the bastardization of American and European highbrow modernism into middlebrow kitsch. Herbert Bayer, a Bauhaus exile in America, helped Steichen design both *Road to Victory* and *Power in the Pacific*; he had actually left MoMA by the time Steichen began work on the layout of *The Family of Man*, but Bayer's ideas about exhibition design and the experience of working with him clearly shaped the final design of *The Family of Man* in very significant ways. But while Bayer's influence has been widely acknowledged in accounts of the exhibition, Steichen's own deep and personal familiarity with the works of Rodin, Matisse, Picasso, Brancusi and other figures of the early twentieth-century avant-garde, as well as his partnership with Alfred Stieglitz in introducing modernist art to America and in developing innovative exhibition techniques at the New York Gallery 291, have been less frequently noted as contexts relevant to an understanding of *The Family of Man*. Gerd Hurm's contribution begins to map out some of these contexts. The conception of *The Family of Man* thus need not be tied exclusively to a 1950s Cold War framework. The possibility of an ambitious exhibition of photography organized around a central theme had in fact been on Steichen's mind since the late 1930s. Wayne Miller recalled that Steichen 'hoped to use the Grand Central Station [...] where all the people going back and forth from work could see it, in the heart of Manhattan'.[17]

In Richter's recollections of *The Family of Man* from the second decade of the twenty-first century, one can still catch the surprise and sense of invigoration of his youthful encounter with the exhibition, even though more than 50 years had by then passed since his visit to the show. Those who reviewed *The Family of Man* professionally in newspapers and magazines while the exhibition was on tour in America and in cities around the world have left us with one kind of record of what it meant to see Steichen's show in its various iterations. But the available literature on *The Family of Man* provides us with no account based on first-hand testimony of what 'ordinary visitors' or the 'general public' experienced when they went to the exhibition. Sollors' contribution to this book includes glimpses of his own visit to the exhibition in Frankfurt in 1958 – a unique instance of such testimony in the literature as far as we are aware. But Sollors was only 14 years old when he saw *The Family of Man*, and his memories of the experience are necessarily broad and fleeting. The dearth of such first-hand accounts is regrettable because the audience response to *The Family of Man* is one of the most important and also perhaps the least examined aspects of the phenomenon the exhibition became. We know that millions of individuals went to the see the exhibition all over the world, but what did they think when they saw it and what did they experience as they walked through it – in Kabul, Johannesburg, Djakarta or Caracas? Even if we restrict our attention to the United States and Europe, the force of this question is no less compelling. What would it have meant to visit the exhibition in cities still in ruins after the war and divided across East and West geopolitical blocs, rather than in American cities untouched by the immediate violence of war? Newspaper reports, which are overwhelmingly positive, give us an idea of the exhibition's reception around the world but very often these reports do little more than repeat or elaborate on the press releases prepared by the USIA or MoMA. And in any case the journalistic archive cannot be taken as a faithful record of public opinion and experience. The USIA's own records are not as extensive as one would wish for; they are uneven in their coverage of the many international locations, and press clippings that can be accessed elsewhere make up a significant proportion of these records.

It is not surprising then that only a few scholars have pursued the question of audience response in relation to *The Family of Man*. They have done so by either approaching the issue in broad conceptual terms or by placing the exhibition in the cultural and historical contexts of a particular country in the 1950s. Blake Stimson is the critic who has most clearly and eloquently placed the question of *The Family of Man*'s global reception at the forefront of discussions about the exhibition. Stimson's own answer is very broad, resting as it does on a claim for an international need for affinity and identification in the post-World War II world, and framed as it is within an account of cosmopolitan modernity dating back to the time of Hegel and Goethe.[18] There have been other, brief accounts of *The Family of Man* in Tokyo, Johannesburg, Moscow and Guatemala City that have paid greater attention to the specificities of particular locations; but Eric Sandeen's chapter on the exhibition at the Moscow Fair (in the final chapter of his ground-breaking *Picturing an Exhibition* (1995), still the only book-length study devoted to the exhibition), and Sarah James's more recent chapter on the show in the context of Weimar and post-war Germany are the only sufficiently detailed and thorough examinations of *The Family of Man* outside of its United States contexts. Although elements of audience response are noted by both

Sandeen and James, their analyses rely primarily on cultural and historical contexts for understanding the international meanings of the exhibition.[19]

There is, however, a document that offers a uniquely detailed access to visitors' responses to and experiences of *The Family of Man*. The Office of Public Affairs of the United States Embassy in Germany prepared meticulous and extensive reports on the various exhibitions sponsored by the American government as part of its international cultural programming after the war. When *The Family of Man* came to Munich between 19 November and 18 December 1955, the Office of Public Affairs commissioned DIVO, a respected German opinion survey organization, to prepare a report on the audience response to the exhibition. DIVO conducted 700 interviews: 298 exit interviews and then 472 home interviews a few days later in order to ascertain whether and in what ways their assessment of the exhibition had changed after visitors had time to reflect. The questions asked and the data gathered were extensive. The questions as well as the interviewees' responses, often with direct quotations, are recorded and analysed in a carefully prepared 87-page report. This report is one of only two documents of its kind relating to *The Family of Man* so far discovered (the other is a similar, though less thorough survey of audience responses from Mexico City). These reports have not previously been examined in the literature on the exhibition and the Munich report is presented here for the first time in the form of a critical summary and analysis (see Zamir's chapter on Munich).

The Munich report provides a breakdown of the people interviewed by social class and educational attainment. One of the surprising facts noted in the report is that people with above average and advanced levels of education made up a higher percentage of the visitors than for other cultural events sponsored in Germany by the United States government. Whatever his or her social and educational standing, almost every single visitor reacted with enthusiasm to the exhibition (those who expressed any reservations at all were in a very small minority). The questions asked were framed in such a way that they allowed the visitors to register their responses to *The Family of Man* both as a humanist proposal and as a visual environment, to the role of America and its cultural policies in Europe, even to individual photographs. What emerges from these responses is a remarkable degree of consensus and match between popular understanding and the analyses of intellectuals and artists like Horkheimer, Koeppen, Kracauer and Richter. The new German materials presented in this book can be seen then, when taken together, to challenge the oppositions between high art and low, populist emotion and critical reason, mass psychology and radical politics that underlie, implicitly or explicitly, the critiques of Steichen's work epitomized by Barthes, and that have been a commonplace of discourse about American culture, from Clement Greenberg's 'Avant-Garde and Kitsch' (1939) and Dwight MacDonald's return to the theme in 'Masscult and Midcult' (1960), up to now.[20]

One of the most noteworthy features of the Munich survey is that it allows us to identify the image groups and the individual photographs which most appealed to, or left the deepest impressions on, the visitors. As a result, the survey can be used to map to some degree at least the flow and structure of the viewers' attention and engagement as they move through the exhibition. And as the summary presented in this book makes clear, some of the images that most affected the visitors come as surprises.

Witold Wirpsza's *Commentaries on Photographs* also focuses on individual photographs. Where Horkheimer and Koeppen use the exhibition to reflect on the nature and power of photography as a medium, Wirpsza explores the concrete examples of what Horkheimer refers to as the ephemeral dimensions of physical reality. *Commentaries* consists of 13 poems, each taking a particular image as its point of departure, with the series framed by a poetic prologue and epilogue. Wirpsza writes from a very different cultural and political location than his West German contemporaries. Wirpsza, who was also a major translator of German (he translated Mann, Bloch and Schiller among others), emigrated to Germany in 1970. But he lived until then under the communist regime in Poland. His poems on *The Family of Man* were published in 1962 and he must have seen the exhibition when it toured various Polish cities from September 1959 to August 1960. Up to this point, Wirpsza's writing was marked by a leaning towards socialist realism, but he had started to move towards greater lyrical experimentation, and *Commentaries* signals this shift. Wirpsza is interested less in exploring or supporting the larger philosophical and social meanings of *The Family of Man* than in what the exhibition makes evident about the nature of photography. His poetic sequence is an important text of Polish modernism and its publication here for the first time in English and in its entirety in a translation by Benjamin Paloff, who also provides an introduction to the work, is itself a significant literary event.

The kind of close attention Wirpsza brings to bear on particular images is rare in the critical writings on *The Family of Man*. Given how much has been written about the exhibition, this claim may seem improbable, even absurd. But it is nevertheless the case that there are few critical accounts that provide truly sustained engagements with particular images or image sequences, or with the viewer's experience of the complex, three-dimensional visual spaces of the exhibition. This critical lack is compounded by the fact that almost everyone who has written on *The Family of Man*, excepting the early reviewers, has done so without actually having seen the exhibition. The main visual resource for understanding Steichen's project has been the book of the exhibition. The book inflects the meanings and interactions of the photographs in ways quite different from the exhibition, and in a number of cases the book can be said to significantly distort them. Even where it is faithful to the exhibition, the experience of the book is very different to the experience of walking through Steichen's radical exhibition layout.[21] Those who have tried to reimagine this layout and the kinds of impact it might have had on the audience (most compellingly Fred Turner) have had to rely on Sandeen's description of it and on the installation photographs of the MoMA version (richly documented) and of international locations (where the visual documentation is usually sketchy or non-existent).[22] However, a version of *The Family of Man* that comes very close to reproducing one of the original European versions of the exhibit has been on permanent display at Clervaux Castle in Luxembourg, under the auspices of the Centre national de l'audiovisuel, since 1994 (see illustration 6).

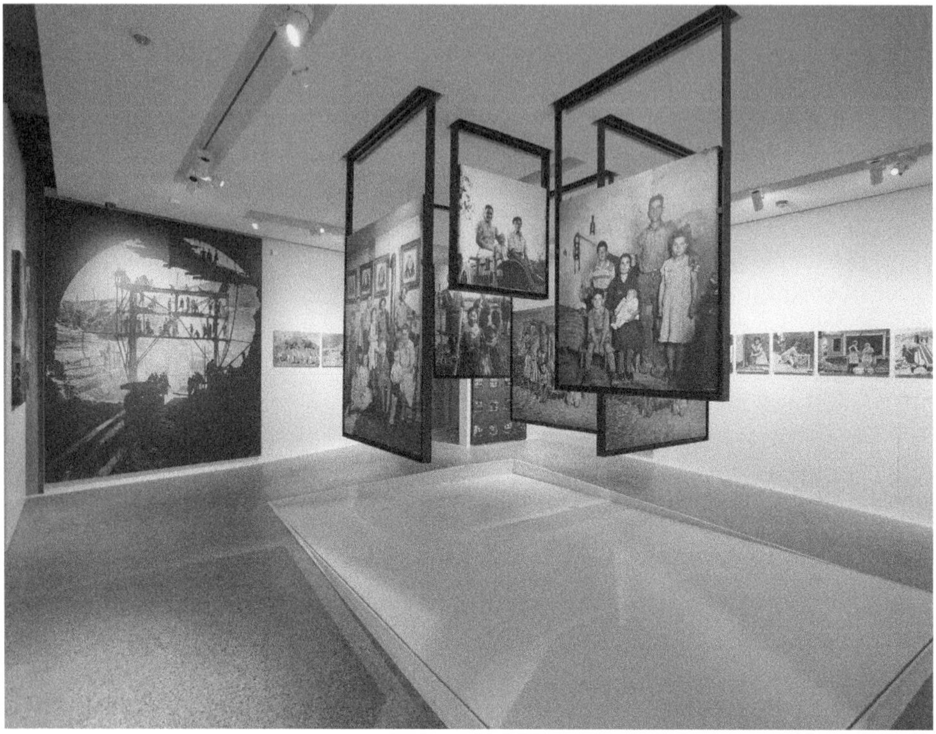

6 *The Family of Man* installation at Clervaux Castle. Theme 'Family of Man: central theme pictures'.

The exhibit was listed on the UNESCO Memory of the World register in 2003 and all of the original prints were restored and the exhibition space renovated in 2013. Steichen was born in Luxembourg and, at his request, the US government donated a complete overseas copy of *The Family of Man* to the country after the exhibition had completed its international tour.

If it is surprising that there are few close readings of the images in *The Family of Man*, it is equally surprising that almost no use has been made of the Clervaux installation as a resource for thinking about the exhibition. The permanent display in Luxembourg provides unique access to a gallery experience that comes close to the original experience of Steichen's exhibition, at least in its travelling versions, and as such it is also invaluable for anyone interested in the histories of photography and exhibition design. Nearly all the essays in this book are informed by at least one, sometimes several visits to Clervaux. All the essays, save Martin Jay's commentary on Horkheimer and Paloff's translation, have their origin in a conference on *The Family of Man* held at Clervaux in 2015, and a number of them offer substantial engagements with the visual forms and dynamics of Steichen's exhibition design.[23]

Shamoon Zamir's chapter on the installation of *The Family of Man* at MoMA examines selected image sequences and the webs of interactions they set in motion across various rooms; he reconstructs in this way, and in far greater detail than in previous criticism, the particularities of the exhibition experience, not only to distinguish it from the book but to make clear why the differences matter to our understanding of Steichen's project. It is part of Zamir's argument that the concept of family as it is engaged in the exhibition has been misconstrued as a withdrawal from politics and history into the private realm; he proposes instead that the narrative of the exhibition moves from the private to the public realm, from an idea of the family based on descent to one based on consent and embodied in the global collectivity of the United Nations. Kerstin Schmidt builds upon her previous scholarship on photography and location, and on recent works on the philosophies of place, to develop a conceptual framework for a critical reading of space and place in the exhibition design of *The Family of Man*. Like Zamir, she considers ways in which the exhibition engaged the viewer in active, dynamic and relational modes of perception, experience and thought. Ulrike Gehring constructs an unexpected dialogue between post-World War II American art and Steichen's exhibition design, focusing in particular on what she sees as structural analogies between Steichen's narrative concept and the art of the 1950s. As noted above, most of the contributors to this volume draw upon visits to Clervaux. Anke Reitz, who is responsible for *The Family of Man* at Clervaux, provides an account of the Luxembourg installation that allows us to see the exhibition from a curator's point of view and to understand how the relationship with Steichen's original design is negotiated by the exhibition's contemporary European reconstruction.

Gehring's essay shares with Zamir and Schmidt an effort to examine anew the visual aspects of *The Family of Man*, but it also contributes to a focus on new American contexts for understanding Steichen's exhibition. Miles Orvell examines one image, the hydrogen bomb explosion, in detail, contextualizing it deftly and richly within American culture's coming to terms with the realities of nuclear weaponry after World War II. Orvell too goes against critical consensus and argues that it is precisely history – the advent of the hydrogen bomb in 1945 – that is central to the logic of the exhibition, if not in the same way in the book of the exhibition. Eric Sandeen places Steichen's multi-year effort in assembling the photographs for *The Family of Man* in the context of other efforts to create anthologies that functioned as cultural texts for large American audiences during the second third of the twentieth century. He focuses in particular on the poet Carl Sandburg's interwar career, and on his relationship to Steichen, his brother-in-law. This is an account that further helps locate *The Family of Man* within the history of American cultural thought and practice, and helps us better understand some of the philosophical underpinnings of Steichen's project .

Two essays frame in broad and different ways the issues and debates examined in this collection. Gerd Hurm's essay launches the volume with a sustained critique of Barthes that turns out to be a wide-ranging reorientation of accepted ideological characterizations and historical contextualizations of *The Family of Man*. Hurm's contribution is helpful not only because it effectively clears the critical ground for fresh approaches, but also because it directs our attention to earlier phases in Steichen's curatorial career as contexts relevant to a proper understanding of his 1955 exhibition. The other essay that undertakes a conceptual reframing of critical approaches to *The Family of Man* is by Winfried Fluck. Fluck examines the visual logic that underlies the exhibition; he proposes an ongoing interactive transfer between picture and spectator, and, more specifically, between picture (*Bild*) and image (*Vorstellung*), arguing that the two are never identical and that the gap between the two acts as an imaginary space for the spectator that is not 'visible' in the photograph itself. Fluck's model of an active spectatorship constructed by *The Family of Man*, and his placing of this spectatorship in the context of mid-century liberalism, links his work to that of Zamir and Schmidt, as well as to other recent contributions to the ongoing study of Steichen's exhibition.

Steichen's project emerges from the new readings presented here not as a redeemed ideal humanism but as a richly contradictory work addressing its own time more complexly than the broad critical consensus about it has acknowledged; it also emerges as a work able to engage with the early twenty-first century and its global concerns in surprisingly relevant ways.

The unprecedented horror of World War II and the divided world that emerged in the years after the war provided the immediate impetus for Steichen's conception of *The Family of Man*. Much of the criticism that have been levelled at Steichen has focused on the apparent naivety of his conception, of its simple-minded response to the intractable political and cultural complexities of the world. It is also the case that, with the collapse of the Soviet Union, the dismantling of the Berlin Wall and so the supposed end of the Cold War, many of the historical questions and dilemmas that shaped *The Family of Man* have, for a time at least, seemed less urgent than they did to Steichen and to the worldwide audiences in the 1950s. But we find ourselves today once again in a world in which nationalist self-enclosure and cultural intolerance are on the rise, the future of the experiment that is the European Union is in some doubt, and proliferating wars and economic hardship have set in motion vast flows of refugees and migrants across the globe. It seems, then, appropriate and necessary, and also regrettable, to be reflecting again on the questions that were asked by *The Family of Man* at mid-century.

If the question of humanity's common fate in the face of political (and now environmental) catastrophe has taken on an urgency that Steichen and his immediate audience had hoped would never happen again, there have also been shifts in cultural thinking that encourage a reassessment of *The Family of Man* at the present time. With the waning of excessively ideological and social constructivists readings in the arts, and especially in photography, aesthetics, ethics and the relationships of the two are returning to the fore of discussions in new ways; equally, the claims of humanism and universalism are open to new debates, not only in ethical philosophy, but also in anthropology and biology.

Clearly, most of the contributions to this book are, in different ways and to different degrees, responsive to these cultural and political reorientations. But this is not to suggest that they share any one common critical or ideological ground. It is, however, the case that we as editors have been motivated by a number of shared cultural and critical perspectives in bringing together all of the new engagements with *The Family of Man* that make up this volume. We find an affinity with Rita Felski's realization that

> there is a dawning sense among literary and cultural critics that a shape of thought has grown old. We know only too well the well-oiled machine of ideology critique, the x-ray gaze of symptomatic reading, the smoothly rehearsed moves that add up to a hermeneutics of suspicion. Ideas that seemed revelatory thirty years ago – the decentered subject! The social construction of reality! – have dwindled into shopworn slogans; defamiliarizing has lapsed into doxa, no less dogged and often as dogmatic as the certainties it sought to disrupt.[24]

Felski's focus is on literature and literary studies but her reflections are widely applicable to other arts. Susie Linfield has spoken out similarly with force and clarity against the state of photography criticism. Reminding her readers of the intimate and necessary connection between emotion, pleasure, love and critical reason in the best writings on the arts (in Edmund Wilson's writings on literature or Pauline Kael's on film, for instance), she notes that critics of photography

> view emotional responses [...] not as something to be experienced and understood but, rather, as an enemy to be vigilantly guarded against. For these writers, criticism is a prophylactic against the virus of sentiment, and pleasure is denounced as self-indulgent [...] Rather than enter into what [Alfred] Kazin called a 'community of interest' with their chosen subject, these critics come armed to the teeth against it.[25]

When *The Family of Man* was shown at the Corcoran Gallery in Washington, DC, it was billed as 'the exhibition you see with your heart'.[26] Steichen may or may not have had a hand in this characterization, but there can be no doubt that he would have fully agreed that the emotions have a central role to play in *The Family of Man*. But it is also the case that Steichen's often breezy and folksy articulations of the motivations and meanings of his exhibition ('what a wonderful thing life was, how marvelous people were'), as much as Sandburg's saccharine and inflated prologue to the book of the exhibition ('A camera testament, a drama of the grand canyon of humanity, an epic woven of fun, mystery and holiness'), have got in the way of a properly nuanced and just understanding of these motivations and meanings. Too often critics have been unable to separate Steichen's and Sandburg's promotional statements from the exhibition itself; they read the exhibition through the clouded lens of authorial rhetoric and bluster. We hope that the materials gathered in this book will help redirect attention to the exhibition as an art object with its own agency, and to the work that *The Family of Man* did in the 1950s – and continues to do at Clervaux today.

HERE'S A GUIDE TO THE FAMILY OF MAN

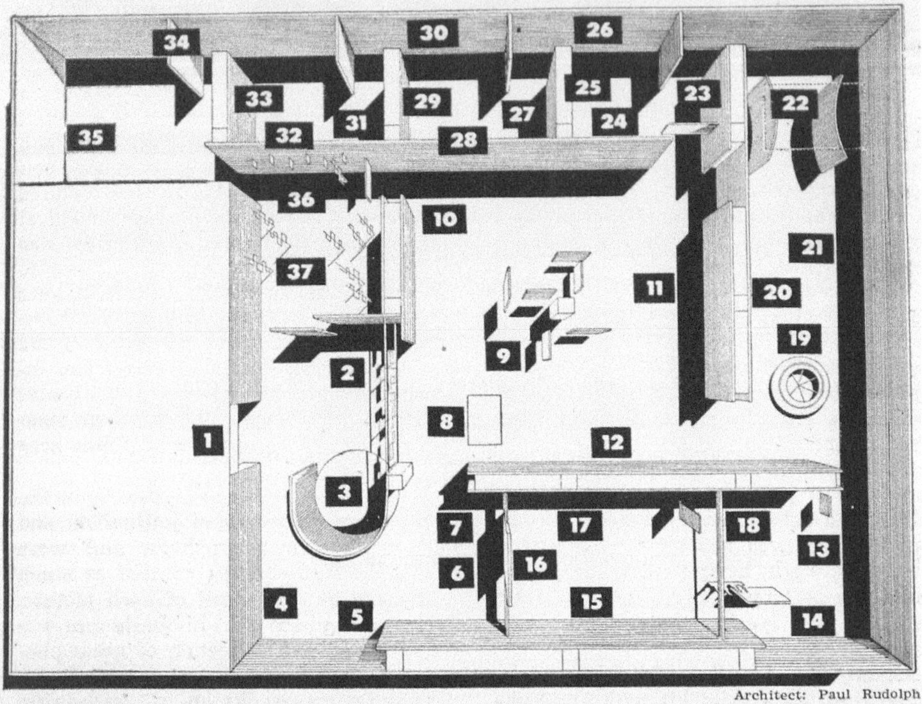

Architect: Paul Rudolph

Steichen's photographic tribute to humanity is so huge and covers such a wide scope that it requires new approaches to organization and display. The architect's drawing above shows how some of the problems were solved. Groups of related pictures are indicated by number in approximately the order they are seen by a visitor walking through the exhibition: **1** entrance arch, **2** lovers, **3** childbirth, **4** mothers and children, **5** children playing, **6** disturbed children, **7** fathers and sons, **8** photograph displayed on the floor, **9** "family of man" central theme pictures, **10** agriculture, **11** labor, **12** household and office work, **13** eating, **14** folk-singing, **15** dancing, **16** music, **17** drinking, **18** playing, **19** ring-around-the-rosy stand, **20** learning, thinking, and teaching, **21** human relations, **22** death, **23** loneliness, **24** grief, pity, **25** dreamers, **26** religion, **27** hard times and famine, **28** man's inhumanity to man, **29** rebels, **30** youth, **31** justice, **32** public debate, **33** faces of war, **34** dead soldier, **35** illuminated transparency of H-bomb explosion, **36** UN, and **37** children.

7 **Floor plan and synopsis of *The Family of Man*, Museum of Modern Art, New York City, 1955.**

Notes

1 Wendell Wilkie, *One World* (New York: Simon and Schuester, 1943).

2 Edward Steichen, introduction to *The Family of Man* (New York: Museum of Modern Art, 1955), n.p. Though the bomb image has been referred to repeatedly as the *only* colour photograph in the exhibition, archival evidence from a range of documents suggests that there were other images in the exhibition that were tinted, and that the walls and panels also made use of different colours for structural and emotional effects. The picture of the hydrogen bomb explosion was famously missing from the book of the exhibition, but there were several other differences between the book and the exhibition. These and other revisions to widely accepted facts about *The Family of Man* will be presented in more detail in a monographic study of the exhibition by Shamoon Zamir.

3 The information on the international attendance is based on an itinerary of the exhibition compiled from various archival sources by the Centre national de l'audiovisuel (CNA), Luxembourg, and shared by the collection's curator, Anke Reitz.

4 Roland Barthes, 'The Great Family of Man', in Barthes, *Mythologies*, trans. Anette Lavers (1957; New York: Hill and Wang, 1972), 100–2. Roland Barthes, 'La grande famille des hommes', *Mythologies* (Paris: Seuil, 1957), 173–6

5 The editors are grateful to Werner Sollors for his discovery of the Wirpsza poems.

6 Siegfried Kracauer, *Theory of Film: The Redemption of Physical Reality* (1960; Princeton, NJ: Princeton University Press, 1997), 309–11.

7 Janine Marchessault, 'Manufacturing Humanism: Steichen/ Burtynsky', *Prefix Photo* 15 (2007): 56.

8 Kracauer, *Theory of Film*, 310.

9 The dispatch and memorandum, and also the photograph of Brecht, are in Box 1, Photographs and Clippings relating to *The Family of Man* exhibition, 1955–1956, Records of the US Information Agency, Record Group 306-FM, National Archives at College Park, College Park, MD.

10 Erdmut Wizisla, Helgrid Streidt and Heidrun Loeper (eds), *Die Bibliothek Bertolt Brechts: Ein kommentiertes Verzeichnis* (Frankfurt am Main: Suhrkamp Verlag, 2007), 24. Brecht's copy of *The Family of Man* book is now unfortunately missing from his library. Our thanks to Erdmut Wizisla, the head of the Brecht Archive, for assisting us with this information (personal communication, 4 October 2016).

11 Berlin: Eulenspiegel, 1955.

12 Edward Steichen, *A Life in Photography* (New York: Doubleday, 1963), n.p. See chap. 13, 'The Museum of Modern Art and *The Family of Man*'. The other quotations from Steichen that follow in the next paragraph are also taken from this chapter.

13 *Road to Victory*, 21 May–4 October 1942; *Power in the Pacific: Battle Photographs of Our Navy in Action on the Sea and in the Sky*, 23 January–20 March 1945; *Korea: The Impact of War in Photographs*, 13 February–22 April 1951. Installation shots of these exhibitions and of *The Family of Man*, as well as master lists of photographs and press releases relating to each, are available on the MoMA website, http://www.moma.org/calendar/exhibitions/history?locale=en&utf8= &q=Pacific&sort_date=relevance&constituent_id=&mde_type=All&begin_date=1929&end_date=now&page=&direction= (accessed 19 September 2016).

14 The image can be found in Steichen, *The Family of Man*, 121.

15 The video and transcript of the conversation between Richter and Serota (dated 11 October 2011) can be found at: www.tate.org.uk/context-comment/video/gerhard-richter-panorama (accessed 18 July 2016). The last comment by Richter is wrongly transcribed as 'Yes, that's what we knew.' According to Greg

Allen, there is no other mention of *The Family of Man* in the writings by or about Richter. Allen also notes that in the biographical conversation recorded by Robb Storr, Richter does say he received copies of *Magnum* magazine from his aunt in West Germany every month. See http://greg.org/archive/2011/10/21/gerhard_richter_on_the_family_of_man.html (accessed 19 September 2016). For Richter's access to *Magnum*, see https://www.gerhard-richter.com/en/biography/the-dresden-years-3 (accessed 19 September 2016).

16 Gerhard Richter to Gerd Hurm, e-mail, 17 May 2016.

17 In 1938, Steichen had seen an exhibition with FSA photos in Grand Central Palace in New York. He became the first to champion FSA documentary pictures in the prestigious *U.S. Camera Annual*. John Raeburn, *A Staggering Revolution: A Cultural History of Thirties Photography* (Urbana: University of Illinois Press, 2006), 106. Several FSA photos would later be included in *The Family of Man*.

18 Blake Stimson, 'Photographic Being and *The Family of Man*', chap. 1 of Stimson's *The Pivot of the World: Photography and its Nation* (Cambridge, MA: MIT Press, 2006), 59–104.

19 Eric Sandeen, *Picturing an Exhibition: The Family of Man in 1950s America* (Albuquerque: University of New Mexico Press, 1995); Sarah E. James, *Common Ground: German Photographic Cultures Across the Iron Curtain* (New Haven, CT: Yale University Press, 2013). For the reception of the exhibition in Tokyo, Johannesburg and Guatemala City, see respectively: John O'Brien, 'The Nuclear Family of Man', *Asia-Pacific Journal* 6, no. 7 (2008): 1–13; Tamar Garb, 'Rethinking Sekula from the Global South: Humanist Photography Revisted', *Grey Room* 55 (Spring 2014): 34–57; Eric J. Sandeen, '*The Family of Man* in Guatemala', *Visual Studies* 30, no. 2 (2015): 123–30. For Moscow, see also Louis Kaplan, 'Photo Globe: The Family of Man and the Global Rhetoric of Photography', in Kaplan, *American Exposures: Photography and Community in the Twentieth Century* (Minneapolis: University of Minnesota Press, 2005), 69–76.

20 Clement Greenberg, 'Avant-Garde and Kitsch', *Partisan Review* 6, no. 5 (1939): 34–49; Dwight MacDonald, 'Masscult and Midcult', *Partisan Review* 27, no. 2 (1960): 203–33.

21 Though the book cover claimed there were 503 images in the show and that all were reproduced in the book, this was incorrect on both counts, though it is one of many facts about the exhibition that has been endlessly repeated (see also note 2 above on the hydrogen bomb image and the issue of colour). Images other than the bomb image were also excluded from the book and new ones added. The book appeared in different formats and there were also differences between each version. The paperback version of the book, which originally sold for $1 and was by far the most widely available edition, has only 481 images (if we count the Peruvian flute player as one even though repeated five times), and if we count Ruth Orkin's six-image sequence of the children playing cards as one (as it was counted at MoMA). The cloth edition has two fewer images: the end papers do not have the image from the Lick observatory or the breaking wave of the paperback at the start and end (so 479 images). The deluxe edition, however, excluding the portfolio of installation shots at the end (which includes a shot of the bomb transparency in black and white), has one more image than the paperback: Pat English's image of the British crowd is repeated as end papers at the book's start and end (so 482 images).

22 Fred Turner, *The Democratic Surround: Multimedia and American Liberalism from World War II to the Psychedelic Sixties* (Chicago: University of Chicago Press, 2015).

23 '*The Family of Man* in the 21st Century: Reassessing an Epochal Exhibition', 19–20 June 2015, Clervaux Castle, Clervaux, Luxembourg. The conference was organized by the editors of the present volume and supported by the Centre national de l'audiovisuel, Luxembourg, the Center for American Studies at the University of Trier, and Akkasah: Center for Photography at New York University Abu Dhabi. Due to unforeseen circumstances, Miles Orvell and Ulrike Gehring were unable to participate but both were very much part of the original planning and conception of the conference. Gehring's paper was presented in her absence by Hurm. Video recordings from the conference can be accessed at http://steichencollections-cna.lu/fra/documentations/1_the-family-of-man-in-the-21st-century (accessed 17 March 2017).

24 Rita Felski, *The Uses of Literature* (Oxford: Blackwell, 2008), 1. See also Felski's *The Limits of Critique* (Chicago: University of Chicago Press, 2015).

25 Susie Linfield, *The Cruel Radiance: Photography and Political Violence* (Chicago: University of Chicago Press, 2010), 4–5.

26 Quoted in Sandeen, '*The Family of Man* in Guatemala', 124.

1 Reassessing Roland Barthes's Myth of *The Family of Man*

Gerd Hurm

> I went on to say how persuasive I had always found Barthes's eloquent argument – until I chanced upon the published book version of *The Family of Man*. Barthes had [...] missed the real drama of the exhibit [...] From the middle of the volume onward, page after page juxtaposes scenes in America with scenes in South Africa, Eastern Europe, and Asia, endorsing literacy, voting rights, and human rights generally. Far from accepting a repressive status quo in the name of universal values, the exhibit was actually doing the opposite: promoting an activist agenda of social change, aimed squarely against forces of political and economic oppression around the world. Barthes may have had his fill at the start and walked out without even seeing these rooms in the exhibit; or he saw, but failed to comprehend their political point.
>
> David Damrosch (2000)[1]

> [...] in Barthes's text the curator emerges as an omnipotent author, while the spectator becomes an impotent reader and viewer. Anxious that the viewers might recognize a multiplicity, Barthes calls upon them to acknowledge it as unity. However [...] a photography exhibition cannot be reduced to the voice of the curator. Dominant as he may have been, Steichen's voice is but one possible voice among many others in the exhibition, and even this voice itself is multiple, split, and rife with contradictions, let alone the voices emerging from the photographs themselves.
>
> Ariella Azoulay (2013)[2]

Roland Barthes is unquestionably the most influential critic of Edward Steichen's *The Family of Man*. His devastating account of the 1956 Paris version of the exhibition shaped the exhibit's 'intellectual reception' and 'set the tone for critiques that followed it'.[3] The interpretation in his short review, 'The Great Family of Man', was given extra weight as it came to be seen as one of the central pieces of his ground-breaking

Mythologies.[4] In the decades following its publication, *Mythologies* acquired the status of a postmodern cultural studies classic. Barthes's reading of *The Family of Man* was therefore also discussed frequently in contexts not directly related to photography criticism and hence acquired additional credibility and authority. More than 60 years after its initial publication, Barthes's review has kept its position as a key reference point for *The Family of Man* in both the academic and the popular field.[5]

Over the years, however, a host of criticisms have substantially challenged the accuracy and validity of the account given of *The Family of Man* in Barthes's *Mythologies*. Like David Damrosch, many scholars have raised the question of why Barthes obviously failed to see 'what was before his eyes'.[6] In 2006, Jacqueline Guittard even went so far as to suggest that Roland Barthes might not have visited the Paris exhibition at all.[7] While such speculations in all likelihood cannot be verified – whether Barthes did not see the exhibition at all or whether he saw it only in parts, as Damrosch insinuated; whether he reviewed the show on the basis of one of the catalogue versions or only on the basis of the French exhibition leaflets[8] – the critical thrust underlying the suspicions needs to be addressed. Clearly, the account Barthes gives of Steichen's exhibition is not a completely trustworthy one and therefore his 'well worded indictment'[9] needs to be revisited and examined critically.

One of the reasons why Barthes's essay 'The Great Family of Man' continues to loom large in Steichen criticism, despite reservations about its reliability, is that the contested points have appeared in piecemeal fashion, in scattered places and also in languages other than English.[10] In this chapter, I will therefore summarize previously voiced challenges as well as add new facets to its critique. I intend to highlight the omissions and errors in Barthes's review, its open and hidden incongruities, and historicize the universalizing stance of its specific French post-war perspective. I thereby hope to generate fresh insights for critics and viewers alike in assessing the complex message of roughly 500 photos by some 270 photographers that constitute *The Family of Man*.

***

Originally published in *Lettres nouvelles* in March 1956, the essay 'The Great Family of Man' applies, in exemplary fashion, the strategy of demystification which Roland Barthes developed in his paradigm-setting volume *Mythologies*. In the following paragraphs, several longer quotations from Barthes's review will be presented to ensure that the specific formulations of his argument rather than second-hand summaries will be the focus of the analysis.

Barthes's main point, repeated in variations throughout the essay, is that historical change and diversity are reduced in Steichen's exhibition to a monolithic, depoliticized message. The key passage, quoted frequently by critics, reads as follows:

> Everything here, the content and appeal of the pictures, the discourse which justifies them, aims to suppress the determining weight of History: we are held back at the surface of an identity, prevented precisely by sentimentality

> from penetrating into this ulterior zone of human behaviour where historical alienation introduces some 'differences' which we shall here quite simply call 'injustices'. (101)

The problematic shift in *The Family of Man*, for Barthes, lies in sentimentalizing and naturalizing the photos instead of presenting them as critical 'signs of an historical writing' (102). The exhibition thus participates generally in the conservative mythmaking strategy of bourgeois ideology which Barthes attacked in his essays in *Mythologies*:

> This myth of the human 'condition' rests on a very old mystification, which always consists in placing Nature at the bottom of History. Any classic humanism postulates that in scratching the history of men a little, the relativity of their institutions or the superficial diversity of their skins [...] one very quickly reaches the solid rock of a universal human nature. (101)

Barthes instead claims to promote with his own critique a radical stance: 'Progressive humanism [...] must always remember to reverse the terms of this very old imposture, constantly to scour nature, its "laws" and its "limits" in order to discover History there, and at last to establish Nature itself as historical' (101).[11]

The unearthing of historical particulars, for Barthes, is one of the key strategies to promote such a 'progressive humanism' (101). As Jonathan Culler has argued, Barthes's 'novelistic eye for details' can be seen to lie at the root of such a critical practice.[12] Barthes's review consequently invokes concrete historical incidents and raises the question of what specific underprivileged groups would 'think of *The Great Family of Man*' (101). It addresses recent cases of racist violence (the African-American youth 'Emmet [sic] Till') and striking local instances of capitalist exploitation ('the North African workers of the Goutte d'Or district in Paris' (102)).[13] Barthes argues that Steichen's exhibition, with its moralizing and sentimentalizing stance, conceals such historical 'injustices' (101). In addition, the homogenizing strategy evident in *The Family of Man* obscures the possibility of political change and produces the impression of an 'immobility of the world' (102). In general terms, the exhibition denies for Barthes, who explicitly references Karl Marx on this point, the key insight that most natural objects contain 'a political trace' (143). Barthes elaborates on this idea in his theoretical reflections in *Mythologies*: 'In passing from history to nature, myth [...] abolishes the complexity of human acts, it gives them the simplicity of essences, it does away with all dialectics, with any going back beyond what is immediately visible, it organizes a world which is without contradictions' (143).

Barthes's interpretation proved highly influential, particularly after the translation of his *Mythologies* into English in 1972. Susan Sontag, for instance, used parts of his position verbatim in her 1977 classic *On Photography*, repeating the quintessential claim that '*The Family of Man* denies the determining weight of history.'[14] Other critics subsequently praised Barthes's review for its critical thrust and lauded it as a 'small masterpiece' of 'discursive deflation'.[15] In some instances, Barthes's 'eloquent argument'[16] even came to completely replace the critical engagement with the exhibition photos:

> Roland Barthes' astringent analysis of an American exhibition of photographs ('The Great Family of Man') has remained for the last thirty-odd years a touchstone for anti-humanist demystifications of humanist discourses. Who could deny that an exhibition of that sort (I've never seen it, but I take Barthes' word for it) directs us to a 'myth of human "community", which serves as an alibi to a large part of our humanism'?[17]

***

One of the most severe criticisms launched at Barthes was that his essay used the same universalizing strategy which he himself had criticized as a major defect in Steichen's exhibition. Damrosch highlights this contradictory attitude:

> [Barthes's] mistake was to present his reading as the whole truth and nothing but the truth, as though the exhibit had an essence, an inherent meaning that persisted unchanged as it moved from one cultural-political sphere into another and very different arena across the Atlantic. Thus Barthes himself universalized the exhibit's nature and meaning [...] – an ironic result, in view of his ongoing efforts to deconstruct essentialist and universalizing approaches to cultural artifacts.[18]

This broad challenge to Barthes's own mythmaking attempt for the Paris exhibition clearly is important. However, it is also crucial to look at the ways in which Barthes deliberately employs exclusively French positions and materials to discredit Steichen's project at large.

Barthes's attitude towards the altered French exhibition title is particularly telling. Barthes announces in the beginning his awareness that it is only the Paris version which is called 'The Great Family of Man', whereas the 'original title' of the American project simply consisted of the plain phrase *The Family of Man* (100). He then grants that the epithet 'great' in the French title has the effect of 'amply' moralizing and sentimentalizing the exhibition (100). Yet despite this insight, Barthes does not distinguish in the remainder of the essay between the connotation of the French title and the original concept developed by Steichen. Significantly, in both instances in which Barthes criticizes the American exhibition for its lack of historical specificity in addressing contemporary forms of 'alienation' and injustice, he consciously evokes the ironic connotations of the sentimentalizing French title: 'but why not ask the parents of Emmet [sic] Till, the young Negro assassinated by the Whites what they think of *The Great Family of Man*?' (101) and 'let us also ask the North African workers of the Goutte d'Or district in Paris what they think of *The Great Family of Man*' (102).[19]

In similar fashion, Barthes also does not refer to or take issue with Edward Steichen's or Carl Sandburg's accompanying exhibition texts. Instead, he quotes an interpretation of *The Family of Man* by the French author André Chamson in a Paris exhibition brochure. It is a unique French source, then, which Barthes uses to insinuate that 'God is re-introduced into our Exhibition' and that religion establishes a sentimental frame for the exhibition: 'this look over the human condition must somewhat resemble the benevolent gaze of God on our absurd and sublime ant-hill' (100). Chamson's lines are subsequently used by Barthes to ascribe a 'pietistic intention' (100) to Steichen's installation. Finally, in the concluding section of the essay, Chamson's reference to 'God' is invoked again in aligning rhetorically the choice of photographs with an 'Adamism' (102) attributed to the original American project. However, Steichen, his biographer Penelope Niven explains, 'never cared for rituals or ministers' and harboured a 'lifelong distaste' for 'organized religion'.[20]

***

Barthes's account of the Paris version is certainly problematic, as Damrosch was first to point out, by imposing a French bias on the overall conception of the exhibition.[21] In addition to this more general criticism, it is also important to note that Barthes simply overlooks or omits specific French instances of 'perfectly historical' (102) photos in *The Family of Man*. In several places, Barthes misses the exhibition's topical interventions in contemporary French politics that he saw as the hallmark of a progressive humanist project. In one of the most striking absences in his review, Barthes fails to comment on French women voting in a photo by Dmitri Kessel (176; see illustration 8). Just about a decade prior to the Paris exhibition, in 1944, French women had received for the first time the right to cast their votes. Barthes himself would have been affected personally by this decision as the woman shown in the picture must have been approximately of the same generation as his own mother. Still, he remains silent on this specific sign of 'historical writing' (102) which empowered French women in the 1940s and 1950s.[22]

This focus on women's rights in the exhibition was hard to miss. It was not just French women who were seen enacting and celebrating the right to vote for the first time in the twentieth century, but also Turkish, Japanese and Chinese female voters (176–7). Steichen himself explained that this striking montage of ballot box photos did not make it into the exhibition by accident, but was to document explicitly his pride in the historical success of the suffragist efforts: 'All the pictures showed women voting along with their men-folk [...] a step towards a universal human right that has been taken in my lifetime.'[23] It is a key contradiction in Barthes's interpretation that he does not comment on the improvement in the political status of women in *The Family of Man* as he himself explicitly takes on the role of an advocate for women's rights in his essay. He complains that the exhibition fails to address the historical specificity in the role of women and mothers: 'Whether or not the child is born with ease or difficulty, whether or not his birth causes suffering to his mother, whether or not he is threatened by a high mortality rate, whether or not such and such a type of future is open to him: this is what your Exhibitions should be telling people.' (102)

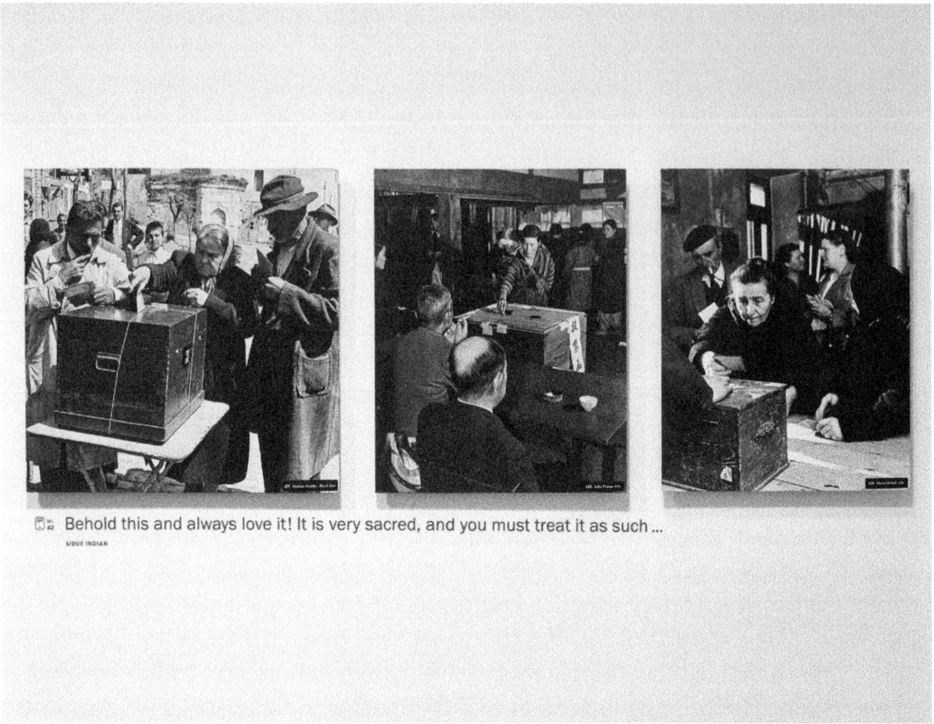

8 *The Family of Man* installation at Clervaux Castle. Theme 'Justice': (from left to right) Herman Kreider, John Florea and Dmitri Kessel.

Barthes also completely misses the specific historical connotations of the phrase 'the family of man'. He is the first in a long line of critics who fail to see the relation of the expression to the progressive political context of one of the most significant American women's rights texts, the 'Declaration of Sentiments'.[24] As introduced to suffragist discourse by its author Elizabeth Cady Stanton, 'the family of man' substantially redefines the status and role of women.[25] At the 1848 Seneca Falls convention, Stanton rhetorically transformed the 'beautiful earth' into the 'home' for both women and men and thus made the discourse of domesticity serve as a potent tool for the empowerment of women.[26] Brian Norman has stressed the larger political implications of this emancipatory shift in Stanton's rhetoric:

> The re-vision also draws on familial discourse in order to provide women an entry point into state language and to include the whole family of the citizenry. Whereas the original Declaration imagines a universal model of People that can 'dissolve the political bands' between them when necessary, the re-vision draws on the language of humanity as 'the family of man' (139), which

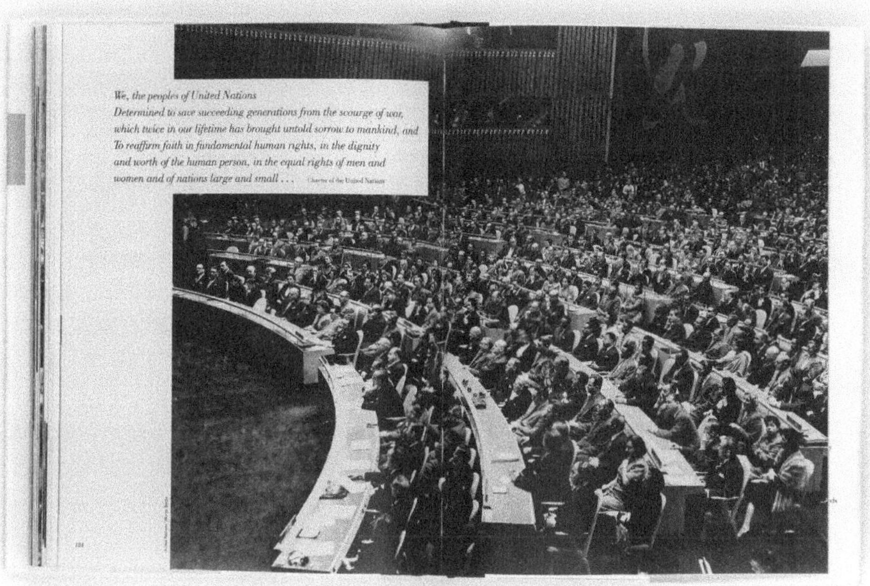

9 Pages 184–5 extracted from *The Family of Man: 60th Anniversary Edition.*

> includes gendered factions. Though the familial imagination is conspicuously silent on matters of racial difference, the Declaration of Sentiment's insertion of a particular group into a universalist founding document opens the possibility for other excluded factions to follow suit, even if it fails to do that work itself.[27]

Steichen's exhibition explicitly pays tribute to the continuation of this historical progress on women's rights in the twentieth century. By turning Maria Bordy's image of the U.N. General Assembly (184) in the final section into the exhibit's largest photo, the UN Charter's textual montage of 'the equal rights of men and women' (184) is given added prominence (see illustration 9). Indeed, when reviewing the exhibition in New York in 1955, Eleanor Roosevelt publicly praised Steichen for captioning the 'entire exhibition' with these key words from the UN Charter.[28] A leading human rights activist herself, Roosevelt had presided over the draft of the UN Charter and had only recently foregrounded Elizabeth Cady Stanton's significant role in the fight for equal rights in her book *Ladies of Courage* (1954).

The phrase 'the family of man', then, does not inadvertently suggest a stereotypical gender position, only 'too evident in the exhibition's title'.[29] It may instead be linked in its connotations to the radical transnational efforts of suffragists and abolitionists in their fight against historical forms of gender and race oppression. Discussing one of the crucial political seeds for his project, Steichen himself revealed that a progressive domestic education by an 'outspoken mother'[30] imbued him with his enlightened stance in *The Family of Man*:

> Once, when I was about ten years old, I came home from school, and as I was entering the door of her [Marie Kemp Steichen's] millinery shop, I turned back and shouted into the street, 'You dirty little kike!' My mother called me over to the counter where she was serving customers and asked me what it was that I had called out. With innocent frankness, I repeated the insulting remark. She requested the customers to excuse her, locked the door of the shop, and took me upstairs to our apartment. There, she talked to me quietly and earnestly for a long, long time, explaining that all people were alike regardless of race, creed, or color. She talked about the evils of bigotry and intolerance. This was possibly the most important single moment in my growth toward manhood, and it was certainly on that day the seed was sown that, sixty-six years later, grew into an exhibition called *The Family of Man*.[31]

The progressive education by Mary Kemp Steichen, a strong and independent Luxembourg-born businesswoman, was important for Edward Steichen.[32] It became even more decisive through the radical family impulses Steichen received from the suffragist and socialist positions championed by his sister Lilian. It was Lilian Steichen – who studied with Thorstein Veblen in Chicago, who read Karl Marx and who translated German socialist tracts into English – who made her older brother Edward attend the Socialist International Congress in Stuttgart and photograph its leaders in 1907.[33] Among other concerns, the question of women's voting rights was then central to the socialist Stuttgart agenda. At the same time, in suffragist talks to Milwaukee women's groups Lilian praised Abraham Lincoln 'as an example of the true spirit of socialism'.[34] Lilian's 'political involvement as a suffragette'[35] occurs long before her future husband Carl Sandburg wrote the Pulitzer-winning biography of Abraham Lincoln and incorporated the reference to 'the family of man' in his 1936 poem 'The People, Yes'.[36]

In the Steichen family context then, the Lincoln quotation of 'the family of man' appears in a distinct political light. It certainly did not evoke chiefly the association of zoology and an essentialist nature which Barthes attributes to the exhibition title. In this instance, it is Barthes himself who suggestively naturalizes and de-politicizes the Stanton phrase in the opening paragraph of his essay:

> So what could originally pass for a phrase belonging to zoology, keeping only the similarity in behaviour, the unity of a species, is here amply moralized and sentimentalized. We are at the outset directed to this ambiguous myth

> of the human 'community,' which serves as an alibi to a large part of our humanism.
>
> This myth functions in two stages: first the difference between human morphologies is asserted, exoticism is insistently stressed, the infinite variations of the species, the diversity in skins, skulls and customs are made manifest, the image of Babel is complacently projected over that of the world. Then, from this pluralism, a type of unity is magically produced: man is born, works, laughs and dies everywhere in the same way; and if there still remains in these actions some ethnic peculiarity, at least one hints that there is underlying each one an identical 'nature', that their diversity is only formal and does not belie the existence of a common mould. (100)

Steichen's use of the quotation, however, is clearly intended to be political. Given the larger suffragist and feminist family context, it may not come as a big surprise that Steichen was known to communicate progressive positions on female emancipation early in his career.[37] His pronounced interest in women's rights also explains the presence of another controversial contemporary photo in *The Family of Man* that questioned stereotypical gender representations in 1950s France. Again, Roland Barthes does not deal with the particulars of Nat Farbman's portrait of Yvonne Chevallier (1952). With the inclusion of this crucial French icon, Ariella Azoulay notes, Steichen consciously challenged conservative gender conceptions:

> In the context of the exhibition, but also in that of women's civil status at that time, Steichen's choice to place the image of a woman accused of murder as a claimant is a courageous one. Considering the oppression of women and their subjugation to the marriage contract, justice requires more than a written law.[38]

***

The most blatant sign of 'historical writing' (102), ignored by Barthes's review, is the central counterpoint of a hydrogen bomb explosion in the exhibition (see illustrations 43, 44). Steichen had placed the photo deliberately at the climactic end of *The Family of Man*. The shocking image of the hydrogen bomb was to reaffirm its overall pacifist message and to admonish humanity about the possibility of annihilation in a future war.[39] In retrospect, Barthes's exclusion of the bomb image from his review – given its huge impact on Steichen criticism – was highly consequential for the early scholarly assessments of the exhibition. In Paris, Barthes could have seen the bomb image that was not available subsequently to most critics who had to rely on the exhibition catalogue. For reasons still not clear today, the hydrogen bomb image was not reproduced in most versions of the catalogue and thus the key counterpoint to the exhibition's affirmative stance was lost.[40] In his ground-breaking monograph *Picturing an Exhibition*, Eric Sandeen was the first scholar to highlight the grave consequences for the exhibition's catalogue-based reception in the first 40 years:

> The exhibition spoke directly to the audience of 1955 and was destroyed. The book, designed to commemorate the look of the exhibition [...] had lost the reading that tied Steichen's work most closely to its audience. The bomb was not there [...] Since the bomb was represented in all of the traveling versions of the exhibition, it cannot be that Steichen was retreating from his view [...] In any case, the bomb was left out. The decision that brought *The Family of Man* its millions of sales lay it open to criticism, particularly as viewers became more familiar with this retelling than with Steichen's original statement. In fact, one can look in vain through contemporary criticisms of Steichen's work for any recognition that there had been a nuclear argument in the arrangement of the photographs just before the invocation of the United Nations.[41]

Barthes's failure to mention the image of the bomb clearly goes against the interventionist stance he himself had voiced in his review with regards to Emmett Till or the workers of the Goutte d'Or. The dangers of nuclear warfare were openly discussed by the French public in the mid-1950s. In March 1955, for instance, the French Socialist Party protested against a French nuclear armament programme.[42]

Significantly, Barthes also fails to notice and discuss an important quotation by Bertrand Russell which was placed next to the room with the image of the hydrogen bomb in the exhibition (see illustration 10).[43] On 23 December 1954, the BBC had aired Russell's talk 'Man's Peril from the Hydrogen Bomb'. Russell's stark annihilation warning was incorporated at the last minute into *The Family of Man*:

> [...] the best authorities are unanimous in saying that a war with H-bombs might possibly put an end to the human race [...] there will be universal death, sudden only for a minority, but for the majority a slow torture of disease and disintegration. (179)[44]

A development which Steichen could not foresee was that his inclusion of the Russell quotation would be given additional political significance. By the time that *The Family of Man* went on the road globally, the quoted passage made it into the highly contested Russell–Einstein Manifesto, published on 9 July 1955. One of the signers and a leading figure behind the publication of the manifesto was the French scientist Frédéric Joliot-Curie.[45] A highly controversial physicist, Joliot-Curie, a Nobel Prize winner and a vocal member of the French Communist Party, had been in the centre of public debate, especially after his expulsion from the Atomic Energy Commission in the early 1950s. When Barthes reviewed the Paris exhibition early in 1956, he could have strengthened the exhibition's critical intervention in nuclear politics and could have sided with Joliot-Curie, Russell, Einstein, Steichen and other critical minds in opposing the threat of atomic weapons. As the issue of nuclear armament was highly controversial in the United States, Steichen had taken a risk by including the image of the bomb, by quoting Bertrand Russell and by including a photo of Robert Oppenheimer (125).[46] Barthes, however, remained silent on this politically hot issue.

***

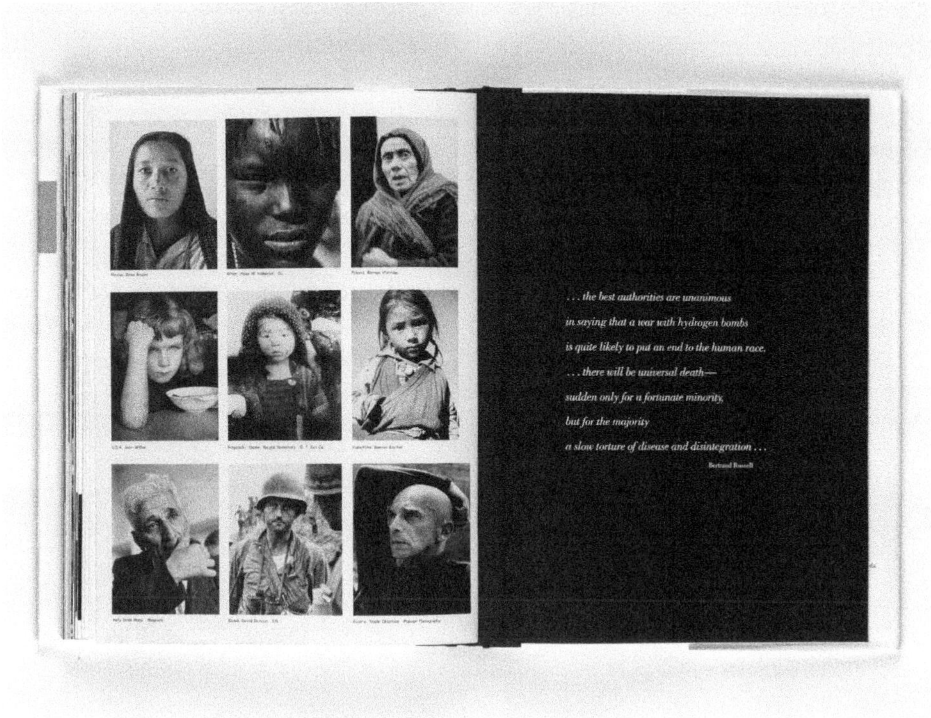

10 Pages 178–9 extracted from *The Family of Man: 60th Anniversary Edition.*

The neglect of Bertrand Russell's warning highlights another major blind spot in Barthes's review. Barthes does not discuss the great diversity of quotations which were juxtaposed with the photos. The exhibition included passages of both oral and written origins, from a great variety of cultures, religions and historical periods. Barthes obscures this multiplicity of voices and sources. He argues that all 'these quotations' define 'an eternal wisdom' and that they serve the purpose of concealing 'the determining weight of History' (101). His summative account turns the diversity of materials into an ahistorical stance that primarily expresses Steichen's essentialism:

> The pietistic intention is underlined by the quotations which accompany each chapter of the Exhibition: these quotations often are 'primitive' proverbs or verses from the Old Testament. They all define an eternal wisdom, a class of assertions which escape History: *'The Earth is a Mother who never dies, Eat bread and salt and speak the truth etc.'* This is the reign of gnomic truths, the meeting of all the ages of humanity at the most neutral point of their nature, the point where the obviousness of the truism has no longer any value except in the realm of a purely 'poetic' language. (101)

Clearly, Bertrand Russell's critical stance could not be subsumed under this heading. Nor could the contemporary quotations from works by Albert Einstein or Anne Frank (156–7, 162–3). It is also not accurate to claim that the montage of text fragments and proverbial expressions 'accompany each chapter of the Exhibition' (101). There were evidently no visible chapters structuring the open flow of the exhibition and the quotations were not used to mark or caption thematically any such section in the exhibition.

Contrary to what Barthes claimed, Dorothy Norman, the human rights activist who suggested the texts to Edward Steichen, had also chosen quotations from some of the most provocative modernist authors such as James Joyce (7) and had also included a statement by radical atheist thinkers such as Thomas Paine (121).[47] A quotation by one of the most then-controversial mid-century American writers, Lillian Smith, was also featured prominently. Smith was known mainly through the outrage surrounding her anti-racist novel *Strange Fruit* (1944). The title, with its allusion to a song by Billie Holiday, carried associations of the brutal practice of lynching.[48] Barthes, who complained that a discussion of Emmett Till was missing, simply failed to note that *The*

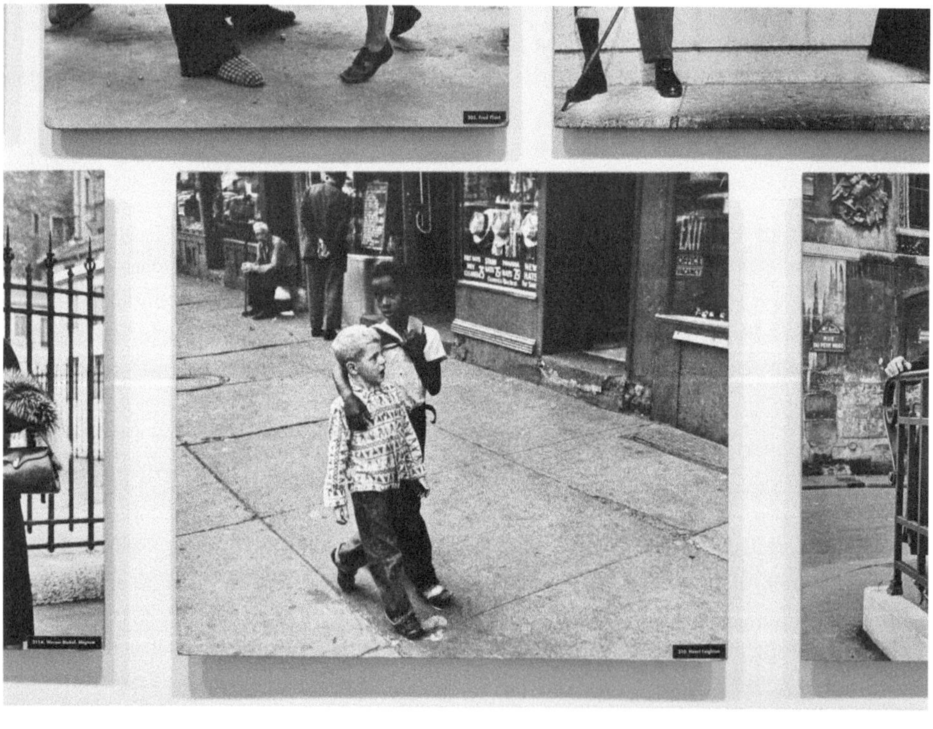

11 ***The Family of Man*** **installation at Clervaux Castle. Theme 'Human Relations': Henri Leighton.**

Family of Man included an obvious reference to racist violence. Indeed, Smith had just augmented her reputation as an engaged writer by publishing in 1955 a volume entitled *Now is the Time* in which she advanced the urgency of civil rights protest.[49] In 1956, when the exhibition reached Paris, Barthes, rather than complaining about a missing allusion to racist practices via Emmett Till, could have pointed to the presence of Lillian Smith in the exhibition.[50]

The inclusion of Lillian Smith in *The Family of Man* is in line with Steichen's general stance on racial politics. John Roberts has generally pointed out that the treatment of African Americans by Edward Steichen in *The Family of Man* in this problematic 'period of violent anti-leftism and racism in the USA' was to be considered 'progressive'. Roberts highlights that at a time 'when the representation of black peoples in the illustrated magazines as other than victims or "primitives" was practically non-existent, Steichen includes a number of non-stereotypical images of black Americans at work and play'.[51] In challenging and subverting the particularities of racial stereotyping in American society, Steichen's exhibition can be seen to demystify mainstream discourses on social and ethnic relations (see illustration 11).

***

The least explicable absence in Barthes's review of a photo exhibition is any discussion of the actual photos shown in the exhibition. As Jacqueline Guittard has noted, Barthes's review does not discuss a single photo. Significantly, his reference to Emmett Till and to the Goutte d'Or workers is not to photographs.[52] He also does not mention individual photographers, even though some of the most critical and controversial of twentieth-century photographers were featured in *The Family of Man*. In particular, the work of August Sander, which was important for Barthes's other texts on photography, is completely ignored. As Sarah James has pointed out, Sander's *Antlitz der Zeit* (1929), in its ambitious portrait of society, clearly provided a 'precedent for Steichen's exhibition' and its attempt at a photographic totality.[53] In instances in which Barthes is explicitly discussing 'the failure of photography' (101) in his review, he is not addressing the particulars of *The Family of Man*, but is repeating well-known Brechtian doubts about the medium at large.[54]

Barthes's disregard for individual photos and photographers is matched by his complete silence on their unconventional form of presentation. It is precisely Steichen's pioneering montage of photos which has been in the centre of the most important revisionist accounts of *The Family of Man* in recent years. Interpretations by Eric Sandeen, Blake Stimson, Sarah James and Fred Turner have stressed multiplicity and diversity as a deliberate effect of its modernist exhibition architecture.[55] Turner even suggested for Steichen's project that an 'antiauthoritarian politics' may be seen 'behind its design'.[56] Steichen's show, in his eyes, 'became less a vehicle for a single message than a three-dimensional arena in which visitors could practice acts of mutual recognition, choice, and empathy – the core perceptual and affective skills on which democracy depended'.[57]

Its modernist form of presentation is central to the exhibition's progressive message. The open montage aesthetic of *The Family of Man* was the climactic result of Edward Steichen's lifelong experience as an avant-garde curator.[58] Around the turn of the century, Steichen had already initiated radically new forms of presentations for photographs and paintings: he himself had suggested to Stieglitz the founding of 291, the central venue for innovative art exhibitions in New York. Subsequently, he conceived and designed the pioneering gallery space at 291 as a forerunner of the white cube.[59] In it, he curated some of the most controversial exhibitions of early modernist art, introducing to American culture contested European artists such as Auguste Rodin, Henri Matisse, Paul Cezanne, Constantin Brancusi and Pablo Picasso. Steichen's cutting-edge presentations significantly predate the 1913 avant-garde landmark of the New York Armory show.[60] Alfred Stieglitz noted that the 1908 Matisse exhibition in 291, procured and organized by Steichen, marked 'the real introduction of modern art to America'.[61] In one of his most radical installation contributions to 291, in 1915 Steichen placed the object trouvé of a wasp nest next to African reliquary figures and cubist works by Pablo Picasso and Georges Braque (see illustration 12).[62]

In 1938, when New Deal documentary photographs from the Farm Security Administration (FSA) were exhibited for the first time in New York's Grand Central Palace, Steichen again had the impulse to push the curatorial limits of the medium and developed the idea of a huge photographic theme show.[63] As one of the first attempts at using text and FSA photos in critical montage fashion in the 1930s, he single-handedly prepared an edition of 41 photos by Dorothea Lange, Walker Evans,

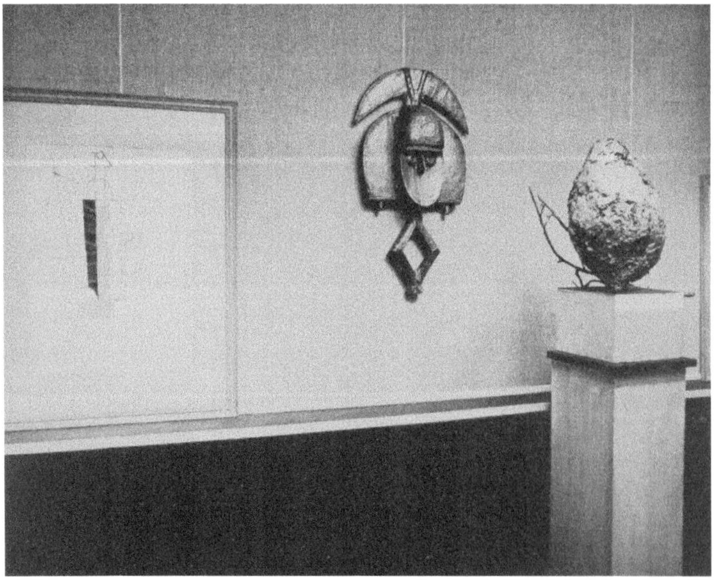

12 Detail from Picasso-Braque exhibition at 291 (1915), photographed by Alfred Stieglitz.

Russell Lee and others for the prestigious journal *U.S. Camera Annual 1939*.[64] For the first time, a wide variety of FSA photos where shown to a national audience in a progressive art context.[65] Documenting Steichen's long-standing efforts to promote novel trends in photography, several of these New Deal photographs would eventually be included in *The Family of Man* (150–1).

The often voiced criticism, that Steichen, as a 'functionary of conservative cultural forces'[66] and 'middlebrow American' realist,[67] had nothing but a naïvely sentimental Cold War message to offer in *The Family of Man* does not take into account his experience with experimental art positions and avant-garde presentations from the beginning of his curatorial career. If Steichen had Bauhaus-trained interior designers such as Herbert Bayer and Paul Rudolph assist him with his huge theme shows it was not because Steichen was unfamiliar with the formal challenges of his projects.[68] Steichen stressed that his theme exhibitions were best understood as an innovative genre unto itself. In its progressive set-up, viewers were to be given democratic agency. Steichen elaborated on the idea behind *The Family of Man* in his 1963 volume *A Life in Photography*:

> In the cinema and television, the image is revealed at a pace set by the director. In the exhibition gallery, the visitor sets his own pace. He can go forward and then retreat or hurry along according to his own impulse and mood as these are stimulated by the exhibition. In the creation of such an exhibition, resources are brought into play that are not available elsewhere. The contrast in scale of images, the shifting of focal points, the intriguing perspective of long- and short-range visibility with the images to come being glimpsed beyond the images at hand – all these permit the spectator an active participation that no other form of visual communication can give.[69]

Given the specific theoretical focus in *Mythologies*, in which Barthes applied Saussurean structuralist discourse to the interpretation of everyday culture, it appears especially puzzling that Barthes fails to note Steichen's proto-structuralist aesthetic. Each photo in Steichen's concept only achieves meaning in the montage context of another photo. The structures of juxtaposition ultimately determine the message in *The Family of Man*.[70] Barthes, however, does not address this multiplicity and openness of meaning generated by Steichen's ingenious exhibition architecture.[71]

The form of presentation, which in Barthes's words suppressed 'History', should then be assessed in very different terms. Ariella Azoulay has pointed out that the radical juxtaposition of images with their striking absence of historical information may be interpreted in diametrically opposed fashions to the dominant trend started by Barthes:

> Although all the photographs in the catalog and exhibition are unaccompanied by information to help us know more about the concrete photographed situation, they are not stripped of history. Presented this way, these images are more malleable for the curator, and more enigmatic: a Rorschach test of sorts

> for the viewers, who are invited to make the photographs speak or project onto them their own thoughts and experiences. However, malleable as they may be, they could not be turned into clay in the hand of a single creator. They bear traces of an encounter of multiple participants and they – whether subjects or viewers – cannot be entirely subjected to any single person's intention. This lack of information is precisely what turns the exhibition into the utter opposite of the implication made by the common argument against it and its viewers, that the public likes to be spoon-fed.[72]

Finally, Barthes's implicit critique of the cyclical routines of 'everydayness' (4) in *The Family of Man* as essentially conservative may be related to a bias in Marxist discourse and the impact of ideas by Bertolt Brecht at this point in his career.[73] As Rita Felski has shown at large, the underlying impulse in Marxist demystifications of everyday culture is highly problematic.[74] Felski has called attention to the customary, yet misleading association of routine in Marxist thought with repressive forms of discourse.[75] Cyclical forms, however, need not inevitably be identified with a reactionary, ahistorical essentialism, but can be shown to possess a progressive potential:

> The temporality of everyday life is internally complex: it combines repetition and linearity, recurrence with forward movement. The everyday cannot be opposed to the realm of history, but is rather the very means by which history is actualised and made real. Thus repetition is not an anachronism in a world of constant flux, but an essential element of the experience of modernity.[76]

Barthes's demystification strategy in *Mythologies*, his reading of everydayness in *The Family of Man*, however, generally reflects the bias of the linear teleology to be found in the Marxist grand narrative of history.[77] Without a hint of irony, Barthes claims in *Mythologies* that 'revolution excludes myth' and that 'revolutionary language proper cannot be mythical' (146). Obviously, Barthes's response to the forms of everydayness found in the exhibition needs to be historicized within the context of 1950s Marxist discourses. Barthes's view that *The Family of Man* reduces history to a regressive essentialism is challenged by other critical theorists of the period.

At about the same time Frankfurt School thinkers Siegfried Kracauer and Max Horkheimer stressed the future-oriented dimension and progressive potential of Steichen's exhibition. It has already been pointed out that Kracauer, for instance, detected an 'emancipatory' potential in the 'intercultural communication' in *The Family of Man*.[78] Horkheimer, similarly, in his 1958 Frankfurt opening address, notes the great potential of the exhibition's progressive form of humanism. For Horkheimer, the show is 'representative of all the forces that are now counteracting the [...] regressive movements that have occurred in Europe in recent years'. Horkheimer also highlights the power of Steichen's images in generating new ways of seeing:

> The individual photographs claim to be not so much aesthetic objects as discoveries. They show what everyone sees without becoming aware of it. By directing the gaze at the familiar unfamiliar, they help those who look at them to gain a new, subtler relationship with things. For anyone who has once learned to see objects in this way, the senses are no longer simply functional; they are strangely altered and sharpened. In future he will see more vividly, and in a greater variety of ways than before. Indeed, this is what the exhibition has in common with real artists: it provides us with a new way of looking at things that we will never forget, of however little practical use it may be.[79]

In Horkheimer's eyes, the aesthetic power of the exhibition may be seen to anticipate a new kind of human community which is to evolve in the future:

> Their interrelatedness, which was not established consciously but which yet exists nevertheless, tells us that individual human beings within one group and one community of people in relation to another, should support each other rather than torment each other and work together to the best of their ability to bring about a mode of existence based on reason with which everyone can be satisfied. And which is certainly possible. The photos aim to encourage human beings to find happiness in the awareness that they can only be happy when individuals cease to suffer from misfortune or disaster that could have been averted through the efforts of all people. They aim to help bring about such a consciousness.[80]

To conclude, measured against the standards developed by Roland Barthes in his review, his critical practice in 'The Great Family of Man' falls short of its own claims. As Damrosch noted correctly, Barthes universalizes his critique where he should reflect his own cultural and historical bias. Barthes also fails to discuss topical references and allusions which he otherwise claims to be central for an emancipatory humanist position. Indeed, if one uses Barthes's yardstick for a progressive critique, then Steichen's *The Family of Man* clearly needs to be put into this category. There is no use in speculating why Barthes consigns the exhibition in contradictory fashion to a 'repressive'[81] form of humanism. But Damrosch was clearly correct in observing that in this instance Barthes 'failed to see what was before his eyes'.[82]

Notes

1 David Damrosch, *Meetings of the Mind* (Princeton, NJ: Princeton University Press, 2000), 58. I would like to thank Steven Alford, Suzanne Ferriss, Hedwig Hinzmann and Danielle Weider for their help in preparing this chapter.

2 Ariella Azoulay, '*The Family of Man*: A Visual Universal Declaration of Human Rights', in *The Human Snapshot*, ed. Thomas Keenan and Tirdad Zolghadr (Feldmeilen: LUMA Foundation, 2013), 31.

3 Ibid., 30.

4 Roger Célestin calls it 'one of the most famous essays in *Mythologies*'. *Cannibals to Radicals: Figures and Limits of Exoticism* (Minneapolis: University of Minnesota Press, 1996), 146. Roland Barthes, *Mythologies* (Paris: Seuil, 1957). All references to the essay are from the translation by Annette Lavers, 'The Great Family of Man' (New York: Hill and Wang, 1972), 100–2. All further references to this work will be cited in the text.

5 For a compact, general account of the reception, see Monique Berlier, '*The Family of Man*: Readings of an Exhibition', in *Picturing the Past: Media, History & Photography*, ed. Bonnie Brennen and Hanno Hardt (Urbana: University of Illinois Press, 1999), 206–24. The German Wikipedia entry in 2014, for instance, consisted primarily of a summary of Barthes's argument. See also my essay, 'Die Rhetorik des Details: Barthes, Brecht und die epochale Fotoausstellung *The Family of Man*', in *grenzen & gestaltung. Figuren der Unterscheidung und Überschreitung in Literatur und Sprache*, ed. Nikolas Immer, Stefani Kugler and Nikolaus Ruge (Trier: WVT, 2015), 323–31, 326.

6 Damrosch, *Meetings of the Mind*, 59. Eric J. Sandeen was among the first to present a large-scale correction of misleading assumptions about the exhibition. *Picturing an Exhibition: The Family of Man and 1950s America* (Albuquerque: University of New Mexico Press, 1995).

7 Jacqueline Guittard, 'Impressions photographiques: les Mythologies de Roland Barthes', *Littérature* 143 (2006): 130. In 2005, Rosch Krieps, too, raised doubts as to whether Barthes had actually seen the exhibition. *Humanheit: The Family of Man richtig verstehen* (Dudelange: Centre de Documentation sur les Migrations Humaines, 2005), 99. It was Guittard who first provided a detailed list of evident omissions and incongruities to back her suspicion.

8 Damrosch, *Meetings of the Mind*, 58. Guittard, 'Impressions photographiques', 133.

9 Sarah James, *Common Ground: German Photographic Cultures Across the Iron Curtain* (New Haven, CT: Yale University Press, 2013), 55.

10 The 1958 interpretation of *The Family of Man* by Max Horkheimer, for instance, which offers in many aspects a reading diametrically opposite to that of Barthes, has been in print in German for more than a quarter of a century, but has not been discussed in criticism of *The Family of Man*. For a first discussion, see my essay 'Die Rhetorik des Details', 323–31.

11 It is important to note that Barthes does not challenge humanism at large in his essay in 1956, as has often been erroneously claimed, but that he distinguishes between two forms of humanism: an affirmative and a critical one. James, *Common Ground*, 55.

12 Jonathan Culler, *Barthes: A Very Short Introduction* (Oxford: Oxford University Press, 2002), 40.

13 Cindy I-Fen Cheng wrote, 'For Barthes, the death of fourteen-year-old Emmett Till was noteworthy precisely because it brought into view the deep racial divide in Mississippi during the 1950s [...] In this understanding, a death's history, not its essence, distinguished it and made it worth mentioning. The recognition of death's particularities could in this way help transform the immobile and ahistorical world of *The Family of Man* into a mobile and historically relevant one.' *Citizens of Asian America: Democracy and Race during the Cold War* (New York: New York University Press, 2013), 199.

14 Susan Sontag, *On Photography* (London: Penguin 1977), 33.

15 Abigail Solomon-Godeau, '*The Family of Man*: Refurbishing Humanism for a Postmodern Age', in *The Family of Man 1955–2001: Humanism and Postmodernism. A Reappraisal of the Photo Exhibition by Edward Steichen*, ed. Jean Back and Viktoria Schmidt-Linsenhoff (Marburg: Jonas Verlag, 2004), 28–55, 31.

16 Damrosch, *Meetings of the Mind*, 58.

17 Bob Chase, 'History and Poststructuralism: Hayden White and Fredric Jameson', in *The Expansion of England*, ed. Bill Schwarz (New York: Routledge, 1996), 72.

18 Damrosch, *Meetings of the Mind*, 60.

19 Barthes's reliance on the French title 'The Great Family of Man' in criticizing Steichen's project in general also appears problematic in that the speeches by Abraham Lincoln, which provided Edward Steichen with the organizing motif for his exhibition, offered both versions. Lincoln uses both 'the family of man' and 'the great family of men' in his addresses. While Barthes cannot really be blamed for failing to research the specific source of Steichen's phrase for his short review, the choice of the plain Lincoln quote by Steichen nevertheless challenges the legitimation for Barthes's overall strategy. Cf. Sandeen, *Picturing an Exhibition*, 43, 177. Abraham Lincoln, 'Message to Congress in Special Session, July 4, 1861', in *The Collected Works of Abraham Lincoln*, 9 vols, ed. Roy Basler (New Brunswick, NJ: Rutgers University Press, 1953–55), vol. 4, 426.

20 Penelope Niven, *Steichen: A Biography* (New York: Clarkson Potter, 1997), 21, 697. In his catalogue introduction, Steichen deliberately explained that the photographs in *The Family of Man* were concerned with 'the religious rather than religions'. *The Family of Man*, ed. Jerry Mason (New York: Simon and Schuster, 1955), 5. All further references to the catalogue will be cited in the text.

21 Damrosch writes, 'He failed to see what was before his eyes, because he failed to look across the Atlantic and consider the American cultural politics within and for which the exhibit had been created.' *Meetings of the Mind*, 59.

22 On the complex and contrary relationship between Roland Barthes and feminist discourse in general, see Michael Moriarty, *Roland Barthes* (Stanford, CA: Stanford University Press, 1991), 166–7.

23 Edward Steichen, 'Photography: Witness and Recorder of Humanity', *Wisconsin Magazine of History* 41 (1958): 166. Eugenia Kaledin generally stresses the progressive stance and strong presence of women in Steichen's 1950s exhibition: 'The '50s' acceptance of "man" as a generic term that included women had kept many people from recognizing that women were often unconsciously excluded in the prose of human rights emerging after World War [II]. Fortunately the show itself – the images that defined the family – made no such gender distinction. And many women photographers contributed to the exhibition. The 503 picture selections put together by Joan and Wayne Miller demonstrated as much about the lives of women and children as they told about the lives of men. And the captions chosen by Dorothy Norman managed to include quotations from the works of women writers as well as published texts from different cultures. It could not have been accidental that all four photos describing the solemn excitement of voting were of women. Later feminists would build on the title to create a more exclusive volume of photographs produced by the Ridge Press at Grosset Dunlap as *The Family of Woman* (1979).' *Daily Life in the United States, 1940–1959: Shifting Worlds* (Westport, CT: Greenwood, 2000), 176–7. Solomon-Godeau also noted that an impressive number of female photographers were included in *The Family of Man*, more than one regularly finds 'nowadays in most large group exhibitions' (35).

24 Eric Sandeen noted early on the difficulty of defining the precise origins of the phrase 'the family of man'. For his discussion of possible origins, whether Steichen took the phrase directly from speeches by Abraham Lincoln or from a poem by his brother-in-law Carl Sandburg, see Sandeen, *Picturing an Exhibition*, 43, 177. However, Sandeen does not discuss the impact of Lilian Steichen, Edward Steichen's younger sister. Lilian Steichen was an active socialist campaigner whose public talks on Lincoln, the 'pioneer suffragist', will have had a considerable impact on both her husband Carl Sandburg and her brother Edward. Penelope Niven, *Carl Sandburg: A Biography* (New York: Charles Scribner's Sons, 1991), 215; Niven, *Steichen*, 271; Barry Schwartz, *Abraham Lincoln and the Forge of National Memory* (Chicago: University of Chicago Press, 2003), 133. Among the first critics to explore the Steichen family's socialist leanings was Melinda Boyd Parsons. She describes Lilian as a 'committed socialist' and lists a vast web of connections in Milwaukee: 'Among the socialist friends of the Steichens were Winfield Gaylord, a state senator on the Social-Democratic Party (S.D.P.) ticket; Elizabeth Thomas, the S.D.P. secretary in Milwaukee; Carl Thompson, the S.D.P. state organizer; Victor Berger, a leading S.D.P. member; Emil Seidel, Milwaukee's first socialist mayor; and Charles Whitnall, the city treasurer under Seidel.' '"Moonlight on Darkening Ways": Concepts of Nature and the Artist in Edward and Lilian Steichen's Socialism', *American Art* 11 (1997): 68–87, 69, 85.

25 The phrase also needs to be set in a larger, transnational feminist context: 'Nancy Hewitt has pointed out that the world of 1848, when the Seneca Falls Convention on Woman's Rights took place, was one profoundly shaped by revolutions in Europe, the Mexican-American war, immigration to the United States, and the abolitionist movement – shaped, in other words, by the kind of transnational imagination as well as transnational linkages among women that these events entailed. The "Declaration of Sentiments" that Elizabeth Cady Stanton presented, while it explicitly engages in a rewriting of the US Constitution, begins by speaking of the "family of man" in decidedly universal terms.' Maureen Moynagh and Nancy Forestell (eds), *Documenting First Wave Feminisms* (Toronto: University of Toronto Press, 2012), 19.

26 Elizabeth Cady Stanton, 'Speech at the Seneca Falls Convention, 1848', in *Man Cannot Speak for Her: A Critical Study of Early Feminist Rhetoric*, ed. Kathryn Kohrs Campbell (New York: Praeger, 1989), 43.

27 Brian Norman, *The American Protest Essay and National Belonging: Addressing Division* (Albany: State University of New York Press, 2007), 48.

28 Eleanor Roosevelt, *My Day: The Best of Eleanor Roosevelt's Acclaimed Newspaper Columns, 1936–1962*, ed. David Emblidge (New York: Da Capo Press, 2001), 219.

29 Douglas Tallack, rev., 'Sandeen, Eric J. *Picturing an Exhibition:* The Family of Man *and 1950s America*', *Journal of American Studies* 30 (1996): 466.

30 Niven, *Steichen*, 297.

31 Edward Steichen, *A Life in Photography* (New York: Doubleday, 1963), n.p. This decisive statement was long ignored in Steichen scholarship. Penelope Niven included it in her biography (14), then Monique Berlier mentioned it in her review of criticism (211). Louis Kaplan discussed it for the first time in detail in 2005 in the context of his revisionist reading of the exhibition. *American Exposures: Photography and Community in the Twentieth Century* (Minneapolis: University of Minnesota Press, 2005), 68. For a more extensive discussion, see my 'Barack Obama and Edward Steichen: A Luxembourgian Seed and the American Liberal Presidency', in *Obama and Transnational American Studies*, ed. Alfred Hornung (Heidelberg: Winter, 2016), 417–54.

32 On the Luxembourg background of the Steichen family, see Rosch Krieps, *Steichen-Story I/II* (Luxemburg: Selbstverlag, 2004) and Jean-Claude Muller, '"Ech sin e Lëtzebuerger Jong…" Edward Steichen und sein Herkunftsland Luxemburg / Edward Steichen and Luxembourg, His Native Land', in *Edward Steichen: Portraits d'artistes – Die Künstlerporträts*, ed. Thomas Elsen and Christof Trepesch (Berlin: Deutscher Kunstverlag, 2014), 27–47.

33 In Milwaukee, Lilian 'and her mother were actively involved in party politics, had many longtime friends who were socialists, and passionately supported the socialistic ideals of equality, humane living conditions, and economic parity. They were especially concerned about the plight of working women and children, and they believed indignantly that women should be allowed to vote.' Niven, *Steichen*, 271. Steichen's Stuttgart photographs of some of the leading socialists of the time were reproduced in Robert Hunter's 1908 volume *Socialists at Work*. See also Patricia A. Johnston, *Real Fantasies: Edward Steichen's Advertising Photography* (Berkeley: University of California Press, 1997), 10–11, 288.

34 Niven, *Carl Sandburg*, 215.

35 Niven, *Steichen*, 332.

36 Ibid., 332. Schwartz notes that Lincoln was perceived in the beginning of the twentieth century as a 'champion' for women's rights. *Abraham Lincoln*, 133.

37 The journalist Agnes Meyer, who was to cover the international congress of suffragettes in 1909 in London, held that 'Steichen was unusually enlightened in his opinions about women's rights.' She noted that he 'was vehement about the "woman question", convinced that women could attain their rights only when they could vote. He was outraged over the economic inequities women suffered, wanting for women the same economic independence that empowered men.' Niven, *Steichen*, 297–8.

38 Azoulay, '*The Family of Man*', 32.

39 Vicki Goldberg and Robert Silberman, *American Photography: A Century of Images* (San Francisco: Chronicle Books, 1999), 142.

40 The reasons why the bomb was not reproduced in the exhibition catalogue are discussed at length by Sandeen, *Picturing an Exhibition*, 73–4. It should be added that the deluxe edition by Simon and Schuster had as its final image one of the 'photographic footnotes' by Wayne Miller which depicted his wife Joan Miller with their children in front of the hydrogen bomb (195, 207).

41 Sandeen, *Picturing an Exhibition*, 74.

42 Lawrence S. Wittner, *The Struggle Against the Bomb* (Stanford, CA: Stanford University Press, 1993), 19.

43 Significantly, Russell's warning was also reproduced in pronounced fashion in the catalogue: it was one of the few quotations in the catalogue presented on a whole page by itself (179).

44 Edward Steichen quoted from Bertrand Russell, 'Man's Peril from the Hydrogen Bomb', *The Listener* 52 (30 December 1954): 1, 135–6.

45 Wittner, *The Struggle Against the Bomb*, 5–7.

46 Wayne Miller noted that 'Steichen resisted any effort to soften or dilute the images he believed might be exposed to the threat of attack by McCarthy. This threat was real. […] It was a real worry.' Miller quoted in Mary Anne Staniszewski, *The Power of Display: A History of Exhibition Installations at the Museum of Modern Art* (Cambridge, MA: MIT Press, 1998), 254.

47 For a complex reading of the diversity of quotations, see also Christoph Ribbat, *Blickkontakt: zur Beziehungsgeschichte amerikanischer Literatur und Fotografie 1945–2000* (München: Fink, 2003), 123–30, 135.

48 Smith was seen as one of the most progressive and outspoken Southern writers on racial injustice. On the complex issues surrounding the associations with the book and its title, see Kathy A. Perkins and Judith Louise Stephens, 'Lillian Smith', in *Strange Fruit: Plays on Lynching by American Women*, ed. Kathy A. Perkins and Judith Louise Stephens (Bloomington: Indiana University Press, 1998), 221–5.

49 Constante Gonzalez Groba, 'Illness as Metaphor in the South: Lillian Smith's Diagnosis of a Schizophrenic Culture and a Metastasized Social Body', in *The Scourges of the South?*, ed. Thomas Ærvold Bjerre and Beata Zawadka (Newcastle upon Tyne: Cambridge Scholars Publishing, 2014), 133–48, 145.

50 Eric Sandeen notes another mistake with regards to Emmett Till: '[…] the construction of the "parents" of Emmett Till reveals a slippage that warrants further attention. Mamie Till Bradley was heroically a single parent.' 'The International Reception of *The Family of Man*', *History of Photography* 29, no. 4 (2005): 349.

51 John Roberts, *The Art of Interruption: Realism, Photography, and the Everyday* (Manchester: Manchester University Press, 1998), 124.

52 Guittard, 'Impressions photographiques', 132.

53 James, *Common Ground*, 72.

54 Susie Linfield, *The Cruel Radiance* (Chicago: University of Chicago Press, 2010), 19–25.

55 Blake Stimson, *The Pivot of the World: Photography and its Nation* (Cambridge, MA: MIT Press, 2006).

56 Fred Turner, '*The Family of Man* and the Politics of Attention in Cold War America', *Public Culture* 24 (2012): 55–84, 57.

57 Ibid., 58. As Ariella Azoulay has argued, Barthes rhetorically reduced this crucial openness and pluralism of *The Family of Man* to an essential unity. '*The Family of Man*', 31.

58 For a more extensive discussion of this aspect, see my 'Between Faking and F.S.A.: Edward Steichen's Forgotten Contribution to the Debates about Realism, Naturalism, and Photography', in *Revisionist Approaches to American Realism and Naturalism*, ed. Jutta Ernst, Sabina Matter-Seibel and Klaus Schmidt (Heidelberg: Winter, 2018), forthcoming. Cf. also Malcom R. Daniel, *Stieglitz, Steichen, Strand: Masterworks from the Metropolitan Museum of Art* (New Haven, CT: Yale University Press, 2010), 12–20; Ralph L. Harley, 'Edward Steichen's Modernist Art-Space', *History of Photography* 14, no. 1 (1990): 1–22; Katharina Hoffman, 'Sowing the Seeds / Setting the Stage: Steichen, Stieglitz, and *The Family of Man*', *History of Photography* 29, no. 4 (Winter 2005): 320–30.

59 See A. D. Coleman, 'Steichen Then, Now, and Again: Legacies of an Icon', in *Edward Steichen: Lives in Photography*, ed. Todd Brandow and William A. Ewing (Minneapolis and Lausanne: Foundation for the Exhibition of Photography and the Musée de l'Elysée, 2007), 277, and Olivier Lugon, 'Edward Steichen as Exhibition Designer', in *Edward Steichen: Lives in Photography*, 267–73.

60 The Mexican avant-garde artist and gallery owner Marius de Zayas Enriquez y Calmet already criticized in 1960 that Edward Steichen was overlooked as 'the initiator of the introduction of modern art in America'. DeZayas quoted in Niven, *Steichen*, 265.

61 Stieglitz remarked in 1942, 'When Steichen arrived he had brought with him a collection of the evolution of a painter I had never heard of: Matisse [...] It was in those Photo-Secession rooms that the ice was broken for modern art in America.' Nathan Lyons (ed.), *Photographers on Photography: A Critical Anthology* (Englewood Cliffs, NJ: Prentice-Hall, 1966), 125.

62 For a detailed account and full documentation of Steichen's role as modernist scout and curator, see my essay 'Edward Steichen: The "Lëtzebuerger Jong" who Brought Modernism to the New World', in *Edward Steichen* (Luxembourg: Musée National d'Histoire et d'Art Luxembourg, forthcoming 2018). For a revisionist account of Steichen's early career, see my monograph *Edward Steichen* (Luxembourg: Editions Saint-Paul, forthcoming, 2018).

63 Sandeen, *Picturing an Exhibition*, 43. See also Cara A. Finnegan, *Picturing Poverty: Print Culture and FSA Photographs* (Washington, DC: Smithsonian Institution Press, 2003), 120–67.

64 Edward Steichen, 'The F.S.A. Photographers', in *U.S. Camera Annual 1939*, ed. Tom Maloney (New York: Morrow, 1938), 43–66.

65 John Raeburn noted, 'Steichen's most palpable contribution to affirming documentary's stature was an appreciation of the FSA project in the 1939 annual [...] his was the first synoptic assessment of the three-year-old FSA project [...] Roy Stryker, head of the FSA's Historical Section, jubilantly reported to Lange that Steichen's endorsement had "done no end of good here" and that he was "astounded [...] at the number of people who have been impressed by this job", including especially his superiors in the federal agency.' *A Staggering Revolution: A Cultural History of Thirties Photography* (Chicago: University of Illinois Press, 2006), 102–3.

66 Lili Bezner, *Photography and Politics in America: From the New Deal into the Cold War* (Baltimore, MD: Johns Hopkins University Press, 1999), 128.

67 Turner, *The Democratic Surround*, 104.

68 For a review of Steichen's work as an exhibition designer, see Lugon, 'Edward Steichen', 267–73.

69 Steichen, *A Life in Photography*, n.p.

70 See James, *Common Ground*, 47–84; Stimson, *The Pivot of the World*, 59–103. For a distinct assessment of the montage in the context of John Berger's work, see Jochen Krautz, *Vom Sinn des Sichtbaren. John Bergers Ästhetik und Ethik als Impuls für die Kunstpädagogik am Beispiel der Fotografie* (Hamburg: Verlag Dr. Kovač, 2004), 319–40. See also Evelyn Runge who stresses the gaps and the subversion of expectations: *Glamour des Elends. Ethik, Ästhetik und Sozialkritik bei Sebastião Salgado und Jeff Wall* (Köln: Böhlau Verlag, 2012), 51.

71 For a critique of Barthes's interpretation from the perspective of a relational anthropology, see Madeline Ferretti-Theilig and Jochen Krautz, 'Sprechende Bilder der Menschheit. Relationale Bildpraxis am Beispiel der Ausstellung *The Family of Man*', in *Sprechende Bilder – Besprochene Bilder. Bild, Begriff und Sprachhandeln in der deiktisch-imaginativen Verständigungspraxis*, ed. Alexander Glas et al. (Munich: kopaed, 2016), 303–26.

72 Azoulay, '*The Family of Man*', 32. Susan Sontag, for instance, claimed that *The Family of Man* ruled out 'a historical understanding of reality'. *On Photography*, 33.

73 Ben Highmore notes, 'Roland Barthes was fascinated by the Berliner Ensemble and wrote enthusiastically of their work [...] Nowhere is the Brechtianism of Barthes more seriously felt than in his essays in *Mythologies*.' 'Disdained Everyday Fields', in *Modernism and Theory: A Critical Debate*, ed. Stephen Ross (New York: Routledge, 2009), 84.

74 Felski addresses in this context in particular the work of Henri Lefebvre, a neighbour and friend of Roland Barthes. *Doing Time: Feminist Theory and Postmodern Culture* (New York: New York University Press, 2000), 77–98. She questions the Marxist view 'that the habitual, home-centred aspects of daily life are outside, and in some sense antithetical to, the experience of an authentic modernity'. Ibid., 81.

75 In Felski's terms, Steichen's focus on the 'emotions in the everydayness of life' (4) may be viewed to help 'safeguard a sense of personal autonomy and dignity'. Ibid., 84.

76 Ibid., 85.

77 For a more detailed discussion of this aspect, see my 'Rhetorik des Details', 326–30.

78 Janine Marchessault, 'Manufacturing Humanism: Steichen/Burtynsky', *Prefix Photo* 15 (2007): 56.

79 Horkheimer, '*The Family of Man*', 60–1.

80 Ibid., 58.

81 Damrosch, *Meetings of the Mind*, 58.

82 Ibid., 59.

2 '*The Family of Man* – All of Us' (1958) and 'Photography' (1960)

Max Horkheimer

Editors' note

We present here for the first time in English two short texts on photography by Max Horkheimer, who was, along with the likes of Theodor Adorno, Herbert Marcuse and Erich Fromm, one of the founding figures of Frankfurt School philosophy, and social and critical theory. The first is the text of Horkheimer's address on the occasion of the opening of *The Family of Man* in Frankfurt at the Haus des deutschen Kunstwerks (House of German Arts and Crafts) on 25 October 1958; the second is a reflection on the nature and importance of photography written two years later. The Frankfurt showing *of The Family of Man* was organized by Amerika-Haus in co-operation with the Board of Trustees of Culture (Kuratorium Kulturelles Frankfurt), of which Horkheimer was a member. The text is taken from Max Horkheimer, 'Eröffnung der Photo-Ausstellung *The Family of Man* – Wir alle', *Gesammelte Schriften*, vol. 13, edited by Alfred Schmidt (Frankfurt: S. Fischer, 1989), 30–7. When *The Family of Man* opened in Frankfurt, Horkheimer was in his sixty-ninth year. He was invited to open the exhibition by Peter-Kristian Ledig, the Chairman of the Kuratorium Kulturelles. Horkheimer wrote back on 5 October 1958 (see illustration 13) explaining that ill health had necessitated an extended leave of absence from the university for him. 'That,' Horkheimer explained, 'is the reason why I usually decline invitations to give lectures.' But Horkheimer accepted Ledig's invitation, despite his ill health. 'However,' he continues in his letter, 'considering the subject matter and my relationship to the city of Frankfurt, I will grant your request to give a short introduction for the Kuratorium Kulturelles Frankfurt on the occasion of the opening of the exhibition of photographs *The Family of Man*. It will be my pleasure to share some of my thoughts about this event in this circle [...] I am well acquainted with the exhibition.' (The editors would like to thank Werner Sollors for bringing this letter to our attention.)

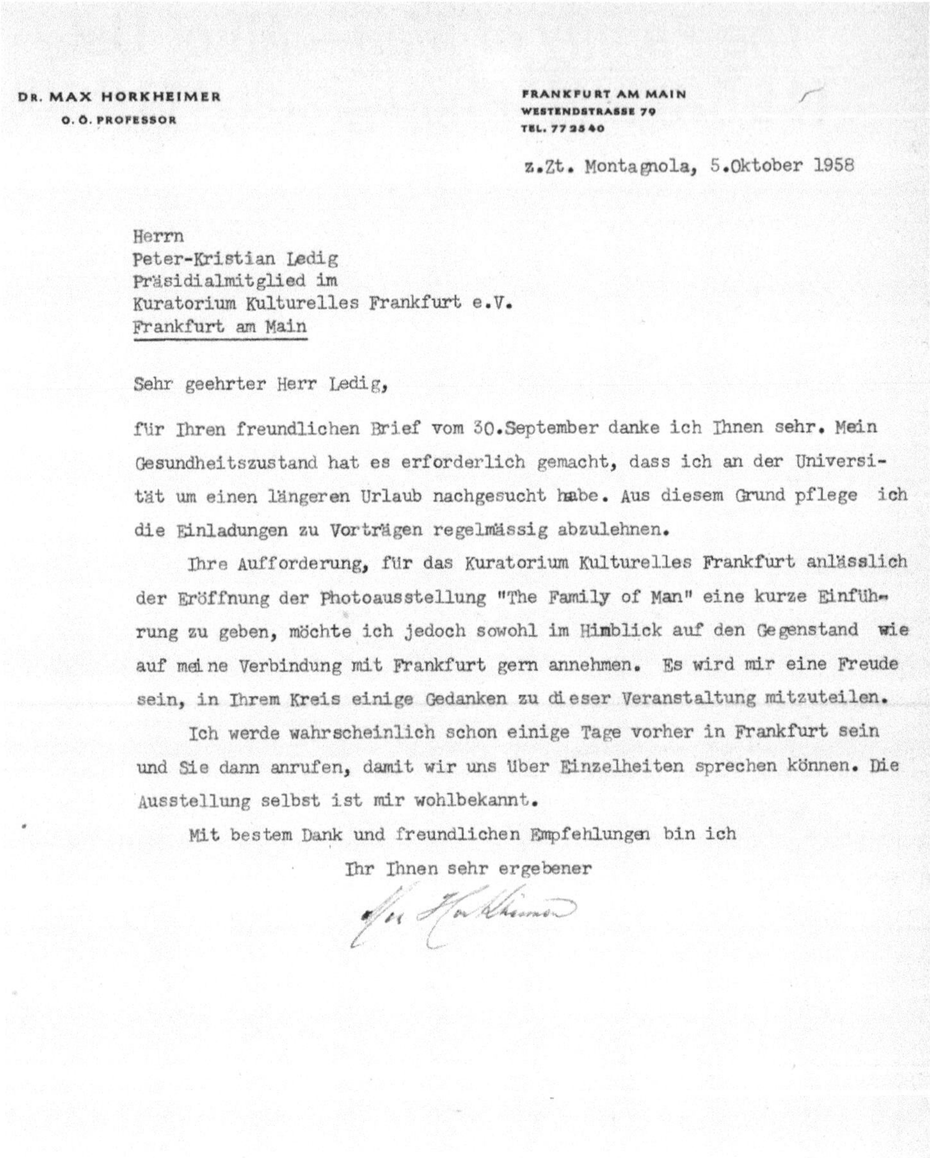

DR. MAX HORKHEIMER
O. Ö. PROFESSOR

FRANKFURT AM MAIN
WESTENDSTRASSE 79
TEL. 772540

z.Zt. Montagnola, 5.Oktober 1958

Herrn
Peter-Kristian Ledig
Präsidialmitglied im
Kuratorium Kulturelles Frankfurt e.V.
Frankfurt am Main

Sehr geehrter Herr Ledig,

für Ihren freundlichen Brief vom 30.September danke ich Ihnen sehr. Mein Gesundheitszustand hat es erforderlich gemacht, dass ich an der Universität um einen längeren Urlaub nachgesucht habe. Aus diesem Grund pflege ich die Einladungen zu Vorträgen regelmässig abzulehnen.

Ihre Aufforderung, für das Kuratorium Kulturelles Frankfurt anlässlich der Eröffnung der Photoausstellung "The Family of Man" eine kurze Einführung zu geben, möchte ich jedoch sowohl im Himblick auf den Gegenstand wie auf meine Verbindung mit Frankfurt gern annehmen. Es wird mir eine Freude sein, in Ihrem Kreis einige Gedanken zu dieser Veranstaltung mitzuteilen.

Ich werde wahrscheinlich schon einige Tage vorher in Frankfurt sein und Sie dann anrufen, damit wir uns über Einzelheiten sprechen können. Die Ausstellung selbst ist mir wohlbekannt.

Mit bestem Dank und freundlichen Empfehlungen bin ich

Ihr Ihnen sehr ergebener

13 Max Horkheimer's letter to Peter-Kristian Ledig, the Chairman of the Kuratorium Kulturelles Frankfurt e.V., 5 October 1958.

'Opening of the Photo-Exhibition *The Family of Man* – All of Us'

This exhibition that opens to the public in Frankfurt today has been seen by millions of people in many countries across the globe. As hardly any other aesthetic event of recent times, it has brought large numbers of people happiness and stimulation; it has created memories that will endure. It is a symbol of common bonds among human beings that are shared in spite of many political differences; it is a symbol of their essential identity despite differences in their individual and national character, or as we philosophers say, it is a symbol of the identity of human beings in their non-identity. The very great success the exhibition has had everywhere seems to me not least of all to be due to its particular philosophical outlook, a disposition that European – above all the great German philosophical tradition – and American philosophy have in common. And that is respect for the individual, no matter under what sun, in what latitude, into what social class or religious faith he may have been born. The core of Immanuel Kant's moral philosophy is that everything with a human countenance should never be solely a means, but should at the same time always also be an end. In spite of considerable theoretical differences, the fundamental tenor of the new American philosophy, from Ralph Emerson [sic] to William James and John Dewey, to Pluralism and the so-called New Individualism, is consistent with the practical aspect of Kant's idealism. If one wanted to name the difference, one could perhaps assert that due to the tradition of the early settlers – which is still very much alive – and to the feeling Americans have that they have a common background in that they come from many different countries and yet have the same home country, in America there has always been an awareness that there are close ties of kinship between all members of the human race, that there is a brotherhood of mankind. In the divided Europe of the last centuries on the other hand, the awareness of a shared identity was essentially only to be found among the educated elite. And only now, in the face of the serious threat from beyond our borders, has it become the common property of all individuals. A German professor who emigrated to America in the last century, Francis Lieber, formulated the idea that is expressed in this exhibition as follows: 'With the ancients everything was strictly national; religion, politics, knowledge, literature, art, acknowledgment of law, all were local; with us … there are wires of mental telegraphs which cross all those red and blue and yellow lines. And who can say that the time will not arrive when that broad sea of history … this commonweal of active and cultivated nations, shall extend over the face of our planet?' This exhibition illustrates this way of thinking; indeed it is representative of all the forces that are now counteracting the severe cultural shocks and regressive movements that have occurred in Europe in recent years. In this context it is eminently constructive.

Thanks to the progressive, humane moments that, inextricably entangled with the negative ones, are part of our technology-driven economy, the disparity, the delay in the consciousness of the fact that there is one human race is gradually being made up among the peoples on the globe. Nevertheless, a characteristic change has taken place as against the past centuries in the way the oneness of mankind is experienced. In the work of the German and American thinkers I have just mentioned, the idea that there exists a common bond between all people occupies an important theoretical position. Mankind is a decisive factor in their philosophy, an idea, a concept, that with the good will and consciousness of human actors will one day be realized. That one should contribute to this development is part of their philosophy. The title of Kant's 'Idea for a Universal History with a Cosmopolitan Purpose' expresses the intellectual nature of this conception, which was decisive in the Enlightenment and in Idealism. In order to grasp the *idea* of mankind, which had yet to become conscious of itself as mankind, an all-encompassing concept was needed. An effort to define the concept had to be made. These philosophers, who found themselves to be pioneers of this way of thinking, were unable to point to anything in the real world that corresponded to their ideas. Idea and perception, the present and the aim remained separate. Humanity for Kant was not an entity, a living instance of which had to be found, indeed, not even a form with a content, but a posit that, in connection with other philosophical ideas, underlies much of the historical work of individuals and peoples. The idea was abstract in the extreme.

With this exhibition things are different. The images show people of different races in a large number of different situations of everyday life: working, enjoying themselves, in peacetime, in wartime, dying, giving birth, individuals and crowds. They are shown the way cityscapes or stony deserts or animals would be shown, and pictures of these are interspersed among those of the people. Technology, photography, is not concerned with ideas. For photography there is only the real. For photography everything is an item, an object. And it is this, the actual reality, the orientation with regard to the way the camera is used and with regard to the many geographical and social locations, that undoubtedly accounts in part for the attraction this exhibition exerts on people today. Nevertheless, the tension between reality and idea, of which photographs as opposed to philosophy cannot speak, is constantly present here. And not simply through a title or explanations. It is a fact that because of our involvement with the many forms of motorized mobility, we are becoming more and more dependent on signs and images, and so consequently the mind tends to adapt to what can be experienced immediately, to pursue what is presented in an evocative manner and to get out of the habit of following longwinded intellectual processes. No one could possibly say how many people make the link from the pictures on show here to the idea of man or mankind, which, according to the philosophers, the individual should act in accordance with. But the curators who put this collection together, who, as they themselves explained, selected the images from millions of photographs from all corners of the earth, were obeying, possibly without being fully aware of it, an inner logic of the whole, of the way these pictures interact and address one another, which gives them in their entirety a meaningfulness that it is difficult to ignore. Their interrelatedness, which was not established consciously but which yet exists nevertheless, tells us that individual human beings within one group and one community of people in relation to another, should support rather than torment each other and work together to the best of their ability to bring about a mode of existence based on reason with which everyone can be satisfied. And which is certainly possible. The photos aim to encourage human beings to find happiness in the awareness that they can only be happy when individuals cease to suffer from misfortune or disaster that could have been averted through the efforts of all people. They aim to help bring about such a consciousness. So, in the final analysis, for both the pictures and the philosophers it is the idea that is important, and the exhibition seems to me to express the same thing as the thought, which cannot be put on show.

In addition to this, however, the picture achieves something that theory alone cannot: it allows the viewer to identify with it. Anyone who has been involved in education – and that is certainly not only those of us who are professors or teachers – has learnt in one way or another that young people's relationship with the world and ultimately their happiness later on in life depends on whether they are able to merge into and become one with things and people. Only in so far as someone not only loves himself, but is able to devote himself to – indeed lose himself in – the things and people he interacts with, can he regain a richer version of himself, can he develop his powers and lead a meaningful life. The meaning of a life depends on neither recognition nor success, however important a role they may play in the development of a particular individual, but on the ability to learn by actual experience, not simply to make calculations and take mental notes in order to learn more. What counts is the vital, generative interaction between the subject and the world. However, such interaction involves all the senses. It is incorrect to say that in a communion among individual people, even a purely intellectual one, only the mind is involved. There are both physiological and psychological effects. Between parents and children, husband and wife, between friends and between all people who like each other, voice, gestures, facial expression and appearance all play a part; not only what is said, but also the way it is said is crucial, because, as Goethe says, 'What is on the outside, that is on the inside,' and the two cannot be separated. And just as the inside sheds light on the outside, so the outside sheds light on the inside. Familiarity with both the inside *and* the outside of another human being are preconditions for being able to love them properly, and conversely, loving someone properly in turn leads to familiarity. Love, so Max Scheler once said, does not render us blind, it makes us able to see, and – we could add – only the person who can see, hear and feel is capable of love. Even Plato's Eros force, uplifting the spirit to eternal ideas, needed the knowledge of ephemeral things in order to achieve that infinite knowledge, which, for him, is the meaning of all human existence. That is why thought needs the image, that is why the image can lead us to people and things, that is why the image has the valuable and not infrequently also dangerous power that thought alone cannot exert – a power that the photograph possesses to a far greater degree than film.

In films, at least the popular ones, the important factor is suspense. In so far as the star is not the main attraction, it is all about excitement, about illusion, which grants us an hour of oblivion; and we are the last to place the responsibility for this behaviour on the individuals. Cinemas and sports stadia are responses to our rapidly changing social reality, which we have not yet come to terms with. With films, we cannot however linger on details, on the finer points, on which so much depends where understanding between human beings is concerned. This is only possible with the photograph, which is silent, which we can look at for as long as we want, and to which we can return. The origins of the kind of photography presented here are related to the literature which in its search of lost time aimed to discover aspects of things that are not perceived in the course of a life governed by obligations and routine. The photographers of those years before the First World War, to which the pictures in this exhibition refer back, aimed to name things and people with the very word which is not heard in the real world and yet which enables the spoken word to be recognized, by devoting themselves to one specific aspect which in practical life is unimportant, but which for the gaze of a child, of a yearning or lonely person is such an important aspect of a street, of an iron staircase, of a group of people or of a single person resting or walking past. The individual photographs claim to be not so much aesthetic objects as discoveries. They show what everyone sees without becoming aware of it. By directing the gaze at the familiar unfamiliar, they help those who look at them to gain a new, subtler relationship with things. For anyone who has once learned to see objects in this way, the senses are no longer simply functional; they are strangely altered and sharpened. In future he will see more vividly, and in a greater variety of ways than before. Indeed, this is what the exhibition has in common with true artists: it provides us with a new way of looking at things that we will never forget, of however little practical use it may be.

The experience we gain from the photographs is, as I said earlier, a feeling of identity. However manifold the objects and figures depicted may be, however different the ages, genders, nations, tribes, people and objects, it is precisely in this great variety and individuality, in which the smallest difference is crucial, that the viewer experiences his identity. He can even see himself in the native in the jungle. He senses, with a single exception perhaps, that if his fate had been different, he would have worn the same facial expression, the same smile, would have been superstitious, inhibited or desperate like all the people in these photographs. He senses this because the power of the images enables him to actually experience inwardly what he is seeing. Because if we perceive things properly, there is always an element of mimesis involved. Even the funny old magician from Bechuanaland, who has evoked so much laughter among the women and boys, has something about him that every one of us could have. No less than the Sicilian and Japanese peasants or the students in the lecture hall or the audience at the Paris Opera. It is not quite the same when what is being looked at is greater than the person looking: the genius. One can probably only comprehend and identify with something that one possesses oneself. However, what does seem to defy any identification at all is that which is completely and utterly evil, of which there are at least two instances here. This kind of evil arouses indignation. In this exhibition our mimetic powers seem to desert us when we have to identify with what is radically evil, although there is no doubt that it exists. While the viewer may develop an understanding for what is quite alien to him, certainly for the person in the dock, for the pariah or for a boisterous or frivolous individual, he simply cannot identify with the person whose aim is to cause fear and terror. And this only proves that, however great the suggestive powers of these pictures, however much they may stimulate feelings of identification, the exhibition nevertheless insists on the consciousness of the freedom and the responsibility of the individual. It sides with human beings yet at the same time does not absolve them of guilt; it inspires tolerance of weakness, but not of barbarism.

In conclusion, in the name of everyone here, I would like to thank the state of Hesse and the city of Frankfurt for making this exhibition possible and the American embassy for the assistance it has provided. This indeed is an event that in accordance with Frankfurt's tradition quite rightly and with special justification is taking place here. It was organized by the Board of Trustees of Culture in Frankfurt (Kuratorium Kulturelles Frankfurt) in co-operation with Amerika-Haus, and I am very happy to have the honor, as a member of and on behalf of the board, of declaring this exhibition open.

[Translated by Angela Oakeshott, with the assistance of Anna Maria Duplang, Hedwig Hinzmann, Gerd Hurm and Shamoon Zamir.]

***

Editors' note

Horkheimer gave the following talk on the occasion of the centennial celebrations of the Adox photochemical factory Dr. C. Schleussner GmbH at the 'Gesellschaftshaus im Zoo', Frankfurt am Main, 7 May 1960. Title and date were taken from the printed programme of the event, which is attached to the typescript in Horkheimer's estate. We include it here because it is, like the speech at the opening of *The Family of Man* in Frankfurt, a rare commentary on photography by Horkheimer, and because the two texts read together help us better understand Horkheimer's thinking about photography. The text is taken from Max Horkheimer, 'Die Bedeutung der Photographie für unsere Zeit', *Gesammelte Schriften*, vol. 13, edited by Alfred Schmidt (Frankfurt: S. Fischer, 1989), 38–43.

'The Importance of Photography for Our Time'

This beautiful exhibition at the Karmeliterkloster [Carmelite monastery], called *Hundert Jahre Photographie* [A Hundred Years of Photography], jointly organized by the City of Frankfurt and the Schleussnerwerke, whose opening we are celebrating today, shows images from a London collection dating from 1839 to 1939. Among these are portrait photographs by Étienne Carjat of Rossini, of Alexandre Dumas, and of Baudelaire. The viewer lingers and gazes in amazement at how differently Baudelaire presents himself compared with the other two. Baudelaire's appearance is a modern one, those of Rossini and Dumas belong to a different century. And yet they all died in the same decade. A young acquaintance with whom I talked about this, said: 'If they had been portrayed by a contemporary painter, it would not have been quite so obvious. He would have had his personal style and in his way of looking at things the difference would have probably disappeared.' This remark exposes a paradox. Photography, totally devoted to appearance, and which according to Baudelaire should not compete with painting, gave more of the essence than painting is thought capable of showing. 'If photography is to deputize for art,' he writes in his 'Salon of 1859', 'in some of art's activities, it will not be long before it has supplanted or corrupted art altogether ... Photography must, therefore, return to its true duty, which is that of handmaid of the arts and sciences, but their very humble handmaid, like printing and shorthand, which have neither created nor supplemented literature.' Presumably Baudelaire, like the Romantics, would not have called those portraitists artists; indeed, he may even have rejected the claim of portrait painting to be an art. Simply by looking at the three images we see that the relationship between photography and truth is not confined to a mere mimetic presentation of reality. Modernity is not a fact; here at least the photograph becomes an aesthetic comment.

Baudelaire hated facts, 'these horrible witnesses.' And who should understand him better than the present age, which (looking neither right nor left, its face turned to the standard of living) can hold on to an idea almost only in the form of slogans in election campaigns or in festive public oratory. Baudelaire belongs to that generation which for the first time on the European continent learned what it means to make the slogan 'Enrichissez vous!' its universal principle and everything else an accessory. Nineteenth-century France took over from eighteenth-century France the nominalistic doctrine that all knowledge is a knowledge of facts, that the only reality available is given in facts. Only with the one difference, that the eighteenth-century hypostasis of facts was deployed in the fight against injustice, against tyranny and superstition, and for liberty, while in the nineteenth century in the world of Louis Philippe and Napoleon, the adventurer nominalism remained and the passion for liberty passed. But fact by itself, without the will and the mind that determine it and provide with a form, make it a structure, a whole unit, without the interrelations established by the individual or society, is without meaning, an element of chaos. To depend on fact remains merely a phrase or is the expression of a lack of principles, if scientific, political or economic concepts have not already defined the place where the actual event will determine the direction. Baudelaire is correct not only with regard to art, which should express an idea, or, as he says, a dream, instead of throwing itself at the feet of external reality, but also with regard to science. In order to progress from one level of knowledge to a higher one, from obsolete concepts to new ones, indeed, even to be able to cope with existing concepts, requires the effort of thought, flexible and at the same time unshakeable decision, sensitivity, openness to circumstances and to their opposites, spontaneity of imagination, of fantasy. Only in such idea-driven relationships, in this penetration by the idea, does a fact become a fact and then again the idea-driven relationships once more become what they are, only now one with the wealth of experience provided by assimilated actual material.

What applies to fact also applies to photography as its double. On the one hand, it shares with everything that merely repeats a given reality the ability not only to gain meaning in a meaningful context but also to turn this process into what it is, and on the other hand, to serve a bad purpose and be branded by it without resistance. There is an infinite number of nuances of truth and fraud, stupid uniformity and productive genius, that exists between the surgeon, whose experienced hand is guided in an infinitely fine and precise movement by the x-ray, and the scheming copy writer who turns a picture into an infamous lie with his headline; between the person who takes the picture already with the intention of lying and the x-ray specialist in whose art lies the dedication and ingenuity of generations. Similar considerations apply to photography and to the human eye, of which photography is an extension. Whether someone looks around with hate or love, with inexperienced curiosity or loyalty or diligence, cannot be read simply by observing the eye alone. Likewise, what damage the camera in itself causes or what good work it accomplishes is not visible. In the course of its history, one stage of which we are celebrating here, the camera has improved only its technical capacity, just as the eye of a good observer eventually becomes more and better focused.

What is true for the single image, also applies to film, both on the big screen and on the television screen. Their aesthetic, moral and political potential is decided by the ability and responsibility of the individuals or groups who have unlimited options available to them. These unlimited options comprise contradiction. Its function is to communicate and develop an idea, to stimulate if not to generate wildness in a neurotic adolescent, just as it is its function to calm people and even to make them passive and suggestible. The whole technical world in which we live contributes to this state of affairs, and television and movies also have their share in it. In 1953 Americans owned 34 million television sets, which were on for five hours a day in the average household. We may well expect children who get to know the world through this medium to become accustomed to reacting to signs in ways different than Rousseau's Emile. They respond to predetermined, tested, stereotypical stimuli. On the other hand, rapid orientation in a thoroughly rationalized world, which this makes possible, creates unforeseen space, in a way free space, and not just leisure time in people's lives. Whether, confronted with a world in need (not only in need of economic aid from the developed countries), they fill this space with new promising activities, which the freedom created by technology opens up for them, or whether spontaneity and faith in the future are handed over to totalitarian masters depends on the substance and solidarity of society, the uses it makes of its achievements. It is always easy to describe the direct benefits and equally the dangers to civilization.

The path from silent to sound movies, from black and white to colour and finally to scented movies, which I have recently seen or rather smelled in New York, does not lead directly upward. Simply because the apparatus is always capable of doing more, does more, replaces more, it tends to exempt the imagination from the practice required for the creation of the image, which in a written text may lead to a decline in intellectual performance. The word, the well-formulated long sentence, the sophisticated idea are, as we know, going out of fashion, because the manifold sensations associated with them are for social reasons no longer appropriate. The replacement of the word by the image certainly plays a role in the mechanism underlying this development. But simplification may also bring about something new, something positive. The grinding down of language brought about by the rise of the middle class in Renaissance and Baroque England by no means led to the degeneration of thought, but to the control over things external and internal, which is of indispensable significance in the history of civilization. The flexibility of thought retained in all the linguistic simplification and rationalization was the prerequisite for the mission which was once fulfilled at that place in Europe. Maintaining and developing the forces that may emerge from the pragmatization of life today, both technical *and* intellectual – and here I am speaking pro domo – is necessary and at the same time a symptom. The development of the mind cannot be decreed. It can only be said that it has to do with faith in the future, with the conscious and unconscious faith which all peoples carry in their hearts.

[Translated by Hedwig Hinzmann, with the assistance of Anna Maria Duplang, Gerd Hurm, Angela Oakeshott and Shamoon Zamir.]

3 Max Horkheimer and *The Family of Man*

Martin Jay

> If only I knew a better term than humanity, that poor, provincial term of a half-educated European. But I don't.
>
> Max Horkheimer (1957–8)[1]

With no special fanfare or extended justification, the distinguished authors of the ambitious overview of twentieth-century art, *Art Since 1900*, all stalwarts of the influential journal *October*, refer in passing to Edward Steichen's 'blockbuster exhibition of post-war photographic ideology, *The Family of Man* at the Museum of Modern Art in 1955'.[2] The context for this casual dismissal is an argument about the transfiguration of pre-war avant-garde and social documentary photography into the advertising and fashion vehicle of consumer capitalism in the so-called New York School, which rose to prominence in the post-war era. Having absorbed the critiques of Steichen's show levelled by Roland Barthes, Susan Sontag, Allan Sekula, John Berger, Abigail Solomon-Godeau and a host of lesser commentators, they echo their scorn for *The Family of Man* as an ideological exercise in sentimental humanism in the service of Cold War propaganda and the middlebrow visual culture typified by *Life* magazine.[3]

Given the now widespread disdain for the triumphalist American culture of the 1950s, this offhand characterization of the show will not be surprising. But it has its cost, as the authors of *Art Since 1900* remain oblivious to the burgeoning resistance to the conventional wisdom, which seeks to restore at least some of the once glittering reputation enjoyed by the exhibition when it was first seen by millions around the world in the 1950s. Starting with Eric Sandeen's 1995 *Picturing an Exhibition* and gathering momentum in later essays by Blake Stimson, Fred Turner, Sarah E. James, Gerd Hurm and others, a more nuanced, forgiving, even positive estimation of the political intentions, aesthetic achievements and popular impact of *The Family of Man* has been advanced.[4] In this revisionist effort, unexpected ammunition has been supplied by the recent rediscovery of a forgotten text by the Frankfurt School's leading figure,

Max Horkheimer, which accompanied the show when it opened in that German city in 1958.[5]

What are the implications, I want to ask, of Horkheimer's delayed insertion in the debate? Can remembering his intervention help counter the still powerful grip of the negative characterization of the exhibition as little more than an exercise in 'photographic ideology'? Does his enthusiasm for the exhibition in the specific context of a post-war Germany still struggling to move beyond its recent Nazi past and deal with its divided present translate into a more general legitimation of its cultural import and political effect, one that can be effective today? Or does the more sceptical attitude of the Frankfurt School towards humanism – an attitude expressed in an essay by Horkheimer called 'The Concept of Man' written just a year before his Introduction to the exhibition – suggest a less comfortable fit between his position and that of those seeking to rescue *The Family of Man* from the charge of photographic ideology?[6]

The occasion for Horkheimer's talk, the exhibition's opening on 25 October 1958 at Frankfurt's Amerika-Haus, an institution funded by the American government, was hardly auspicious for the full display of his critical skills. Having recently returned to Germany to re-establish the Institut für Sozialforschung, with support enabled by his mutual trust with the enlightened US High Commissioner for Germany John H. McCloy, Horkheimer understood his public mission as a re-educator of Germans, especially youth, in the democratic values he had learned in exile.[7] Although in private, he maintained many of the darkly pessimistic sentiments and intransigent radicalism he and Theodor W. Adorno had expressed in *Dialectic of Enlightenment* – a work, it should be noted, that remained out of print and absent from public discussion until pirated editions began to be circulated in the 1960s – in public, he was determined to play a constructive role in weaning Germany from the pathologies that had led to the Third Reich.[8] In the context of the Cold War, where Horkheimer increasingly came to discern similarities between Stalinism and Nazism, it was clear that he had no hesitation about siding with the West, despite its many defects.[9] Horkheimer, in fact, sought to retain his naturalized American citizenship, even as he returned to Europe to live out the remainder of his life. For all his dismay with the Culture Industry he had witnessed first-hand in exile, he considered himself an ambassador of the liberal democratic values, however imperfect their actual implementation, he had also absorbed during his sojourn in America.

Horkheimer began his Introduction to the exhibition by stressing what he saw as its implicit philosophical *point d'appui*, which he argued tied together American and European, most notably German, Idealist thought. Here significantly his touchstone was not Hegel, and certainly not Marx, but rather Immanuel Kant, who shared with American philosophers like Ralph Waldo Emerson and John Dewey a strong belief that the individual human being should be treated only as an end, and never as a means. If there were a difference between the two traditions, it lay in the additional American assumption, derived from the immigration of people from many different backgrounds, 'that there are close ties of kinship between all members of the human race, that there is a brotherhood of mankind'. This was a lesson that only an elite of educated Europeans had learned, because of the poison of national enmities.

To make his point, Horkheimer cited the hopeful words of Francis Lieber, whom he identified simply as 'a German professor who emigrated to America in the last century',[10] to the effect that nationalism might someday be replaced by a single global community. *The Family of Man*, he then argued, 'illustrates this way of thinking; indeed it is representative of all the forces that are now counteracting the severe cultural shocks and regressive movements that have occurred in Europe in recent years. In this context it is eminently constructive.' Once again turning to Kant to spin out his argument, he evoked the philosopher's celebrated essay of 1784, 'Idea for a Universal History with a Cosmopolitan Purpose',[11] claiming it provided a model not of the world as it was, but as it might be: 'Humanity for Kant was not an entity, a living instance of which had to be found, indeed, not even a form with a content, but a posit that, in connection with other philosophical ideas, underlies much of the historical work of individuals and peoples.' An 'idea', we should understand, meant in Kant's special vocabulary a purely theoretical concept to which no corresponding object could be given in sense experience and for which no synthetic a priori judgement, no cognitive claim, might therefore apply. By invoking it, Horkheimer was making clear what he saw as the regulative, counter-factual, even utopian quality of the notion of a unified humankind. As had Kant, he hoped that it might serve as a telos of human practice, rather than a description of what was destined to occur.

But because it spoke in the vaguest terms about humanity, Horkheimer went on, Kant's model was far too abstract. Steichen's exhibition happily provided a corrective to the abstraction of Kant's notion of mankind. It did so by drawing on photography's power to represent concrete differences rather than generic identities, the real motley variety of the world rather than a single model of human essence. But because of the way in which the exhibition had been organized, he went on, it transcended the irreconcilability or incommensurability of those differences. On the level of everyday life, it seemed to suggest, people in all cultures faced the same challenges and sought the same solutions. Without intention, the curators 'were obeying, possibly without being fully aware of it, an inner logic of the whole, of the way these pictures interact and address one another, which gives them in their entirety a meaningfulness that is difficult to ignore'. By showing similarities and the interrelatedness of apparent opposites, the exhibition 'tells us that individual human beings within a group and one community of people in relation to another, should support rather than torment each other and work together to the best of their ability to bring about a mode of existence based on reason with which everyone can be satisfied'. Thus the philosophical and visual ideals are ultimately the same, even though the abstract idea of what Kant would have called 'perpetual peace' could not actually be shown as such.

That admirable desideratum was anticipated instead through the way in which the exhibition abetted emotional identification with people of different backgrounds. Mimetic empathy was a path, Horkheimer observed, to the love that binds people together. In that effort, photographs, in fact images in general, were needed to supplement the abstractions of theoretical concepts:

> Even Plato's Eros force, uplifting the spirit to eternal ideas, needed the knowledge of ephemeral things in order to achieve infinite knowledge, which, for him, is the meaning of all human existence. That is why thought needs the image, that is why the image can lead us to people and things, that is why the image has the valuable and not infrequently also dangerous power that thought alone cannot exert [...].

Unlike cinema, photographs allow the viewer to linger with details, discover the unexpected, and disclose the unfamiliar. 'Indeed, this is what the exhibition has in common with true artists: it provides us with a new way of looking at things that we will never forget, of however little practical use it may be.'

Horkheimer finished his Introduction to the exhibition by returning to the question of identification, noting that there was an important exception to the mimetic empathy aroused by Steichen's selection of photographs, which appear in those that depict what he called, once again following Kant, 'radical evil'.[12] Because the exhibition thwarts such identifications in at least two cases – he doesn't tell us which or spell out exactly how they do so – it 'insists on the consciousness of the freedom and the responsibility of the individual. It sides with human beings yet at the same time does not absolve them of guilt; it inspires tolerance of weakness, but not of barbarism.'

With these remarks Horkheimer was clearly identifying with those who shared the exhibition's goals and ratified its methods for achieving them. But for a student of his *oeuvre*, much in this Introduction will seem very surprising. Unlike other critics of a scientistic version of Marxism, such as his erstwhile colleague Erich Fromm, he had always resisted the lure of a humanist alternative suggested by Marx's 1844 Paris manuscripts.[13] His evocation of Kant rather than Hegel or Marx, endorsing what Michel Foucault came to call Kant's 'empirico-transcendental doublet' of the individual and mankind,[14] was in tension with what are normally taken to be the primary philosophical inspirations for Frankfurt School Critical Theory. Nor do we find any indication of his lifelong fascination with Schopenhauer, whose illusionless pessimism he could still call in 1961 'the philosophic thought that is a match for reality'.[15]

Perhaps because of its Kantian perspective, the Introduction underplays the persistent power of intermediate identifications, whether with class, gender, nation, religion or status group, which resist, for good or for ill, abstract homogenization on the level of the whole or the isolated singular. Rather than uncritically celebrating the American cult of individuality, as he seems to in his paean to the exhibition, Horkheimer had long harboured doubts about its darker side. In *Dialectic of Enlightenment*, he and Adorno had bitterly remarked that

> the decay of individuality today not only teaches us to regard that category as historical but also raises doubts concerning its positive nature [...] In the autonomy and uniqueness of the individual, the resistance to the blind, regressive power of the irrational whole was crystallized. But that resistance was made possible only by the blindness and irrationality of the autonomous and unique individual.[16]

In the chapter entitled 'The Rise and Decline of the Individual' in his 1947 *Eclipse of Reason*, Horkheimer bemoaned the survival of the ideology of individual self-preservation at a time when there was no longer a coherent self to preserve. 'The dwindling away of individual thinking and resistance, as it is brought about by the economic and cultural mechanisms of modern industrialism, will render evolution towards the humane increasingly difficult.'[17]

But none of this bleak assessment of the weaknesses of the bourgeois humanist notion of the individual remained in his Introduction to *The Family of Man*. In addition, Horkheimer passed over in silence one of the most fateful moves in Kant's own argument in 'The Idea for a Universal History with a Cosmopolitan Purpose', which would have been inconvenient to foreground in this context: the philosopher's unsentimental justification of social conflict, or what he called 'asocial sociability', as the hidden mechanism of progress towards the goal of a cosmopolitan order of federated states. Instead of stressing the functional value of social strife, even violence, as had Kant, Horkheimer short-circuited the indirect process by which the ultimate pacification of social existence might be achieved. Unlike Hegel with his stress on the role of dialectical negation expressing the 'cunning of reason', and Marx with his valorization of the class struggle, he moved quickly from the still imperfect present to a more utopian world based on reason.

But perhaps most unexpected of all is Horkheimer's valorization of the power of images, photographic or otherwise, to give concrete meaning to the abstract yearnings expressed in philosophical language.[18] In the years after his return from exile, when Horkheimer came increasingly to identify with his Jewish roots, he often invoked the taboo on graven images, the *Bilderverbot*, in Exodus 20.1–7, as a still potent reason for Critical Theory's distrust of positive utopian fantasies.[19] Adorno would also frequently cite the same source in his characterizations of a doggedly negative dialectics, refusing all higher affirmative sublations.[20] The *Bilderverbot* extended as well in the other direction, as they invoked it as explanation for their distrust of attempts to give realistic aesthetic form to the experience of the Holocaust.[21] Although often extolling the virtues of mimetic similarity rather than conceptual subsumption as a way to avoid the domination of otherness, they were deeply suspicious of the ways in which it could slide into denigrating mimicry, a pattern they had witnessed first-hand in the Nazi mockery of Jews.[22] In his Introduction, however, mimesis is firmly on the side of empathetic identification alone.

The anomalous character of this text in Horkheimer's thinking in this era is even more apparent if we compare it with another essay written at virtually the same time, his 1957 'The Concept of Man'.[23] Impatient with the incessant pious chatter about the 'crisis of man' in the post-war era – a phenomenon trenchantly probed by the American intellectual historian Mark Greif in his recent *The Age of the Crisis of Man*[24] – Horkheimer argued that 'the word "man" no longer expresses the power of the subject who can resist the status quo, however heavily it may weigh upon him. Quite differently than in the context of critical philosophy, to speak of man today is to engage in the endless quest for an image of man that will provide orientation and guidance.'[25] The abstract appeal to 'man', whether anthropological or existential, is a deception designed to distract attention from the contradictory social realities that still smoulder beneath in an alienated totality that remains irrational to the core.

Rather than upholding the virtue of empathetic identification with individuals, 'The Concept of Man' repeats the bleak characterization of the fate of individuality in the modern world that Horkheimer had lamented in earlier works written in the shadow of the Holocaust, such as *Dialectic of Enlightenment* or *Eclipse of Reason*:

> The factors in the contemporary situation – population growth, a technology that is becoming fully automated, the centralization of economic and therefore political power, the increased rationality of the individual as a result of his work in industry – are inflicting upon life a degree of organization and manipulation that leaves the individual only enough spontaneity to launch himself onto the path prescribed for him.[26]

Any appeal to personal 'authenticity' is thus ideological, an 'empty well from which those who cannot achieve their own private life, their own decisions and inner power, fill up their dreams'.[27]

Significantly, Horkheimer bemoaned the ineffectiveness of the contemporary nuclear family in resisting these tendencies, an argument that drew on the empirical work the Institute had done on the crisis of the bourgeois family in the 1930s.[28] Because children were becoming ever more directly socialized by society, in particular by the culture industry, they could not develop the interior strength they needed to reject its conformist blandishments. The family was no longer a 'haven in a heartless world', defended by a nurturing mother, where an experience of childhood happiness might serve as a spur to critical reflection about its denial in later life.[29] Instead, the family's integrity had been eroded, so that it now functioned only as a porous shield against the penetration of commodification and the modern media. Ironically, the seemingly progressive entry of women into the labour force, Horkheimer worried, had had its costs: 'the principle of equality is penetrating even into the family, and the contrast between private and social spheres is being blunted. The emancipation of woman means that she must be the equal of her husband: each partner in the marriage (the very word "partner" is significant) is evaluated even within the home according to criteria that prevail in society at large.'[30] Such equality was a sinister expression of the exchange principle in bourgeois society in which everything qualitatively different was rendered quantitatively fungible.

Mentioning the erosion of the traditional family lamented by Horkheimer in 'The Concept of Man' raises the larger question of the symbolic function of the family in Steichen's exhibition, which operated on two levels: the repetition of parallel images of happy nuclear families in different cultures and the metaphor in the title implying that humanity as such should be seen as one giant family. Many critics of *The Family of Man* excoriated it precisely for its tacit affirmation of the still patriarchal, heteronormative nuclear family of the 1950s as a model of the family *tout court*. From our own perspective, at a time when families come in so many different varieties and the appeal to 'family values' has turned into a coded way to decry those developments from a conservative perspective, it is easy to mock the homogenizing effect of the images in the exhibition.

Defenders of the exhibition, however, have contended that a tacit distinction was at work behind the depiction of the ideal family, which ironically mirrored an opposition made by Horkheimer's own colleagues at the time in their classic study of *The Authoritarian Personality*.[31] Mindful of the ways in which fascism had been welcomed by personalities trained to obey tyrannical fathers rather than absorb maternal love, the authors of *The Authoritarian Personality* had argued that such families produced a child who 'can apparently never quite establish his personal and masculine identity; he thus has to look for it in a collective system where there is opportunity both for submission to the powerful and for retaliation upon the powerless'.[32] Unprejudiced 'democratic' characters, in contrast, 'received more love and therefore have basically more security in their relationships to their parents. Disagreements with, and resentment against, the parents are openly worked out, resulting in a much greater degree of independence from them. This independence is carried over into the subject's attitude toward social institutions and authorities in general.'[33] It was this version of the family, so champions of the exhibition have argued, that Steichen tacitly hoped to foster.

Although Horkheimer too favoured this version of the family, he feared in 'The Concept of Man' and elsewhere that it was in danger of disappearing even in ostensibly democratic countries such as the United States. This anxiety was not, however, apparent in his Introduction to the exhibition. Instead, he contented himself with vague assurances that the images exhorted people to 'support each other rather than torment each other and work together to the best of their ability to bring about a mode of existence based on reason with which everyone can be satisfied. And which is certainly possible.' This was clearly not the occasion, he must have reasoned, for sour pronouncements about the ubiquitous threats to the type of non-authoritarian family he thought was necessary to make that utopian hope a reality.

What about the exhibition's more general evocation of 'man' as a kind of extended family? In his Introduction, Horkheimer turned to the American 'melting pot' experience of coming from many different national backgrounds as the source, to cite his words once again, of the healthy 'awareness that there are close ties of kinship between all members of the human race, that there is a brotherhood of mankind'. Unlike Roland Barthes with his bitter question 'but why not ask the parents of Emmet [sic] Till, the young Negro assassinated by the Whites what *they* think of *The Great Family of Man*?',[34] he didn't pause to ponder how pervasive that awareness actually might be in the racially divided America of his day. Instead, he optimistically asserted that through the magic of empathetic visual identification, the viewer, and here he is talking to the citizens of Frankfurt, 'can even see himself in the native in the jungle'. Whether or not the reverse was just as likely to be true is not a question he felt compelled to pose. Nor did he voice any concern about the gender implications of evoking universal 'brotherhood' as the model of familial solidarity or think twice before invoking the stereotype of non-Westerners as 'natives in jungles'.

In response to these absences, recent defenders of the exhibition's intentions have pointed to Steichen's acknowledgment that the title had, in fact, been suggested by his brother-in-law, the poet Carl Sandburg, who had traced it to various speeches by no less admirable a figure than Abraham Lincoln.[35] The distinguished pedigree of the phrase, they contend, points to its implications not only for racial equality but also women's suffrage, which Lincoln had explicitly championed. So by tacitly endorsing the rhetoric of the human family and not foregrounding his anxiety over the crisis of actual families, Horkheimer, the inference might be drawn, was actually supporting the inclusivist agenda pursued by Steichen.

There is, however, another pedigree for the metaphor, which Horkheimer himself had in fact noted elsewhere with alarm. In his study of 'Authoritarianism and the Family Today', which appeared in 1949, he had noted that the Nazis had employed the rhetoric of the nation as a collective family, which had meant not only the suppression of class and other social differences but also the creation of dangerous pseudo-biological kinship distinctions that served to stigmatize alleged outsiders as racial inferiors. Extending the boundaries of the putative family to the species was admittedly designed to avoid such in/out group distinctions, but it tacitly perpetuated them when it came to the domination of other animals who were treated as not part of the family of man. Horkheimer, indebted as he was to Schopenhauer, was, in fact, an earlier critic of the instrumental treatment of animals.[36] But none of this anxiety about the ambiguous implications of humanism and the family metaphor was evident in his Introduction to the exhibition.

Nor did Horkheimer ponder the limits of understanding more general human relations in familial terms. Not only have patriarchal analogies been easily abused in anti-democratic defences of monarchy – think, for example, of Robert Filmer's *Patriarcha*, famously the target of John Locke's ire – but paternalist rule in general was in tension with the right of an allegedly 'immature' subaltern to full autonomy. Battered spouses and abused children were, after all, lamentably widespread practices, rarely protested until recent times.[37] The metaphor of brotherhood as a model of ideal human interaction, even when extended to mean siblings in general, was also vulnerable to the charge that it forgot the ability of brothers, at least since Cain's assault on Abel, to become rivals, indeed deadly ones. If humankind were really a family, might it not just as well be a dysfunctional as a functional one? Think, for example, of the house of Atreus, or even the family of Antigone, that epitome of sibling love, who was, it must be remembered, the daughter/sister of Oedipus, not exactly a model of filial piety.

More fundamentally, the extension of kinship to embrace all of the species, while on some attenuated genetic level plausible, ignores the powerful distinctions between endogenous and exogenous groupings that underlay the incest taboo so fundamental to human civilization. Politics, it might be said, is the art of learning to live with exogenous others, who may be marriage material, but until the knot is tied, are anything but kin, loving or otherwise. At best they may be recognizable neighbours in a tightly knit community, but are more often anonymous strangers within the borders of a more capacious and impersonal society or *a fortiori* aliens outside its borders. If politics means anything, it means dealing impersonally with rivals and adversaries, as well as friends, both genuine and of convenience, who are not in any meaningful sense bound to us by the affective ties of family. A political community, as we know, is more imagined than real, the inclusivity of its members premised on the exclusion of those outside its boundaries. We may owe temporary hospitality to strangers should they come to our shores seeking succor – Kant thought it was the one binding law of a cosmopolitan world order[38] – but not permanent domicile in the way we might to family members. Toleration of otherness and respect for what makes us all human does not mean absorbing the stranger into our family, no matter how extended we might construe it. Moral duty does not rest on ties of affection, indeed might at times contradict them, and it is impossible to build a healthy polity on emotional grounds alone. Indeed, as Hannah Arendt once remarked, 'love, by its very nature, is unworldly, and it is for this very reason rather than its rarity that is it not only apolitical but antipolitical, perhaps the most powerful of all antipolitical human forces'.[39]

All of these considerations were absent from Horkheimer's Introduction and did not surface to derail his enthusiasm for the familial metaphor underlying Steichen's exhibition. But before we dismiss him too quickly as yet another Cold War apologist for 'photographic ideology', it would be wise to pause with his self-evident motivation, which helps explain the difference between his response and that of Roland Barthes to the exhibition. In a Germany still struggling to move beyond the insidious ideology of racial hierarchy and ethnic exclusion that had brought such a ruinous outcome, it was necessary to swallow whatever qualms one might have about the potential costs of overly abstract humanist universalism and the inclusive implications of extending the metaphor of a family from the nation or race to the species as a whole. At a time when Martin Heidegger's elevation of Being over humanity as the central focus of philosophy posed a danger to the hope of making a clean break with the Nazi past, it was important to remind Germans that Kant still remained relevant and that his thought might be compatible with liberal American intellectual traditions as well. Against the existentialist insistence that essentialism was an outmoded philosophical concept that transformed one contingent set of conditions into a dubious universality of reductive sameness, it was healthy to remember the critical work that the concept of essence can do when it is transformed from an eternal truth into a normative potential to be realized historically.[40]

In contrast, Roland Barthes could draw on the very different lessons a Frenchman might have learned from the negative effects of an overly abstract humanism, which had lost its appreciation of the value of cultural difference and historical variation in its zeal to carry out its allegedly 'civilizing mission'. These lessons, as Stefanos Geroulanos has recently shown, were shared as early as the 1930s by many in France who developed anti-foundational negative anthropologies as a result.[41] Although there had long been religious condemnations of humanism, the innovation of these thinkers was their explicit atheism, which resisted the assumption that all men were the same because they were allegedly created in God's image. Barthes, it should be noted, made precisely this connection in attacking the putative unity underlying depictions of difference in images chosen by Steichen: 'this means postulating a human essence, and here is God re-introduced into our Exhibition: the diversity of men proclaims his power, his richness; the unity of gestures demonstrates his will'.[42] From the vantage point of an atheistic historicism, in which any positive philosophical anthropology was a 'myth' grounded in the secularization of religious universalism, the exhibition could only be ideological, and Horkheimer's defence of it a mystifying exercise in false consciousness.

From Barthes's perspective, it is thus easy to see why the exhibition might warrant dismissal as ideological, as indeed it also might, as we have noted, from that adopted in many of Horkheimer's other writings. But before we then conclude that this dismissal is the last word and reject the recent attempts at rebuttal, we need to put a little pressure on the vexed concept of ideology itself. When casually used, 'ideology' is a term of opprobrium suggesting false consciousness and mystification, either deliberate or not, and is implicitly opposed to the nobler ideals of truth, scientific knowledge, or at the least critique. It is understood to reflect either the interests of a group that employs it for its own partial ends, masking and/or justifying its power, or the unconscious effects of collective psychological stress, which generates it as a dubious way of relieving that stress (for example, through scapegoating mechanisms). As such, it acts as a distorting mirror or refracting filter through which reality is prevented from revealing itself in its unmediated and naked form.

But in addition to the explicitly negative connotation of the word, which draws on a positive alternative that is more often implied than forcefully defended, there is also a more complex, perhaps we might say dialectical implication, which acknowledges the latent critical function of ideology as well. Take, for example, the classical example of Marx's characterization of religion as the opiate of masses. The paragraph in his 'Contribution to the Critique of Hegel's *Philosophy of Right*: An Introduction', where this famous formulation appears, begins with the acknowledgment that 'religious suffering is at the same time an expression of real suffering and a protest against real suffering. Religion is the sigh of the oppressed creature, the sentiment of a heartless world, and the soul of soulless conditions.' Marx then goes on to say that critique, which was the basis of what later would become the method of historical materialism, 'has plucked the imaginary flowers from the chain, not in order that man shall bear the chain without caprice or consolation but so that he shall cast off the chain and pluck the living flower'.[43]

It is worth recalling these familiar lines to remind us that ideology critique may well depend on acknowledging the discontent, albeit in mediated and distorted form, generated by intolerable and unjust conditions, and the desire to relieve those conditions that is harboured in even the most insidiously consolatory ideological formations. Or to return to our main concern, it lets us recognize that we need not reduce our response to a culturally complex phenomenon like *The Family of Man* to either a simple-minded dismissal or a defensive celebration. In other words, even if its detractors had a point in decrying its inadvertent ideological function, the exhibition can also be credited with possessing a critical potential – that 'protest against real suffering' that Marx saw in religion – that also demands recognition.

Thus, even if Barthes is right to see a religious source of the humanist faith in a shared human essence, it is possible to acknowledge that origin not merely to unmask and debunk it, but rather to recognize that critical protest against an unjust status quo often appears, as Marx himself conceded, in the garb of religion.[44] If we take Horkheimer's interpretation of the exhibition as less a celebration of the present than a challenge to make a different and better future, his endorsement of an essential human condition as normative rather than descriptive and his adoption of the telos of history as perpetual peace as a Kantian counter-factual, regulative ideal with practical intent, we can discern the utopian impulse lurking beneath the surface of what may appear as unabashed Cold War ideology. Even if Horkheimer's Introduction should be situated in the larger context of his work, which provides ample ammunition for those who lament *The Family of Man*'s complicity with a problematic status quo, we can still honour his intention to read the exhibition against that grain and inspire a still volatile post-Nazi Germany to work through the unresolved issues of its recent past. Insofar as many of these issues still, alas, remain exigent in the twenty-first century, new sets of eyes can still profit from the experience of viewing Steichen's 'blockbuster exhibition of post-war photographic ideology'.

Notes

1 Max Horkheimer, 'Humanity', in *Dawn and Decline: Notes, 1926–1931 and 1950–1969*, trans. Michael Shaw (New York: Seabury Press, 1978), 153.

2 Hal Foster, Rosalind Krauss, Yves-Alain Bois and Benjamin H.D. Buchloh, *Art Since 1900: Modernism, Antimodernism, Postmodernism* (New York: Thames and Hudson, 2004), 426.

3 For a general survey of the exhibition's reception with most of the relevant references, see Monique Berlier, '*The Family of Man*: Readings of an Exhibition', in *Picturing the Past: Media, History and Photography*, ed. Bonnie Brennan and Hanno Hardt (Champaign: University of Illinois Press, 1999).

4 Eric J. Sandeen, *Picturing an Exhibition: The Family of Man and 1950's America* (Albuquerque: University of New Mexico Press, 1995); Blake Stimson, *The Pivot of the World: Photography and its Nation* (Cambridge, MA: MIT Press, 2006); Fred Turner, '*The Family of Man* and the Politics of Attention in Cold War America', *Public Culture* 24, no. 1 (2012); Sarah E. James, 'A Post-Fascist Family of Man? Cold War Humanism, Democracy and Photography in Germany', *Oxford Art Journal* 35, no. 3 (2012); Gerd Hurm, 'Die Rhetorik des Details: Barthes, Brecht und die epochale Fotoausstellung *The Family of Man*', in *grenzen & gestaltung: Figuren der Unterscheidung und Überschreitung in Literatur und Sprache*, ed. Nikolas Immer, Stefani Kugler and Nikolaus Ruge (Trier: WVT, 2015).

5 Max Horkheimer, 'Eröffnung der Photo-Austellung *The Family of Man* – Wir alle', in *Gesammelte Schriften*, ed. Alfred Schmidt, vol. 13 (Frankfurt: S. Fischer, 1989). See the translation in the present volume.

6 Max Horkheimer, 'The Concept of Man', in *Critique of Instrumental Reason*, trans. Matthew J. O'Connell et al. (New York: Seabury Press, 1974). For a consideration of this essay in the context of ecological issues and the humanist domination of nature, see Timothy W. Luke, 'Toward a Critique of Post-Human Reason: Revisiting "Nature" and "Humanity" in Horkheimer's "The Concept of Man"', in *Critical Ecologies: The Frankfurt School and Contemporary Environmental Crises*, ed. Andrew Biro (Toronto: University of Toronto Press, 2011).

7 Clemens Albrecht, '"Das Allerwichtigste ist, daß man die Jugend für sich gewinnt": Die kultur-und bildungspolitischen Pläne des Horkheimer-Kreises bei der Remigration', in *Die intellektuelle Gründung der Bundesrepublik*, ed. Clemens Albrecht et al. (Frankfurt: Campus Verlag, 1999).

8 Horkheimer acknowledged the limitations of his prewar Marxism, but remained loyal to its critique of bourgeois society and capitalist economics, as demonstrated by his 1956 conversations with Adorno, which have been published as *Towards a New Manifesto*, trans. Rodney Livingstone (London: Verso, 2011).

9 'I believe,' Horkheimer said in conversation with Adorno, 'that Europe and America are probably the best civilizations that history has produced up to now as far as prosperity and justice are concerned. The key point now is to ensure the preservation of these gains.' But then he added, 'that can be achieved only if we remain ruthlessly critical of this civilization [...] We have nothing in common with the Russian bureaucrats. But they stand for a greater right as opposed to Western culture. It is the fault of the West that the Russian Revolution went the way it did.' Ibid., 35–6.

10 Lieber (1798?–1872), who was called Franz before emigrating to America in 1827, was best known as the author of a code of honourable military conduct during the Civil War, which has been seen as the forerunner of the Geneva Convention.

11 For the original text and a selection of insightful discussions of its significance, see Amélie Oksenberg Rorty and James Schmidt (eds), *Kant's Idea for a Universal History with a Cosmopolitan Aim* (Cambridge: Cambridge University Press, 2009). It should be noted that Kant's 'Absicht' is variously translated as 'purpose', 'aim' and 'point of view'.

12 For Kant's discussion of this term, see *Religion with the Limits of Reason Alone* (1793), where he claimed it was innate in human nature, not something historically variable. For a recent discussion of its implications, see Richard Bernstein, *Radical Evil: A Philosophical Investigation* (New York: Blackwell, 2002).

13 For a discussion, see Martin Jay, 'The Frankfurt School's Critique of Marxist Humanism', in *Permanent Exiles: Essays on the Intellectual Migration from Germany to America* (New York: Columbia University Press, 1985).

14 Michel Foucault, *The Order of Things: An Archaeology of the Human Sciences* (London: Routledge, 1994), 322. For a discussion, see Béatrice Han, *Foucault's Critical Project: Between the Transcendental and the Historical*, trans. Edward Pile (Stanford, CA: Stanford University Press, 2002).

15 Max Horkheimer, 'Schopenhauer Today', in *Critique of Instrumental Reason*, trans. Matthew J. O'Connell et al. (New York: Seabury Press, 1974), 83.

16 Max Horkheimer and Theodor W. Adorno, *Dialectic of Enlightenment*, trans. Edmund Jephcott (Stanford, CA: Stanford University Press, 2002), 200.

17 Max Horkheimer, *Eclipse of Reason* (New York: Oxford University Press, 1947), 156.

18 It might be thought that Horkheimer's enthusiasm for photographs shows that he was in conversation with another émigré, Siegfried Kracauer, who also positively invoked the exhibition and the authenticating power of photographs in *The Theory of Film: The Redemption of Physical Reality* (New York: Oxford University Press, 1960), 310. But in fact, they had been personally at odds from the Weimar years on, despite their common friendship with Theodor W. Adorno. Kracauer, moreover, remained in New York, while Horkheimer had returned to Frankfurt. For a discussion of their fundamental theoretical differences, see Martin Jay, 'Mass Culture and Aesthetic Redemption: The Debate between Max Horkheimer and Siegfried Kracauer', in *Fin-de-siècle Socialism and Other Essays* (New York: Routledge, 1988).

19 Perhaps the first mention of it comes in 1947 in *Dialectic of Enlightenment*, 17–18. The Jewish taboo on images was also extended to a refusal to utter God's name, which is more prominent in this early passage.

20 For discussions, see Elizabeth A. Pritchard, 'Bilderverbot Meets Body in Theodor W. Adorno's Inverse Theology', *Harvard Theological Review* 95, no. 3 (July 2002); and Michael A. Rosenthal, 'Art and Politics in the Desert; German Exiles in California and the Biblical "Bilderverbot"', *New German Critique* 118 (Winter, 2013).

21 Adorno's celebrated injunction against writing poetry after Auschwitz expresses this reluctance in linguistic terms, but it was evident as well in their ascetic attitude towards aesthetic realism in general.

22 For discussions of the importance of mimesis in Critical Theory, which begins with Walter Benjamin's early essays 'On the Mimetic Faculty' and 'Doctrine of the Similar' and becomes increasingly important for Adorno, see Karla A. Schultz, *Mimesis on the Move: Theodor W. Adorno's Concept of Imitation* (Berne: Herbert & Cie Lang AG, 1990); Martin Jay, 'Mimesis and Mimetology: Adorno and Lacoue-Labarthe', in *Cultural Semantics: Keywords of our Time* (Amherst: University of Massachusetts Press, 1998); and Artemy Magun, 'Negativity (Dis) embodied: Philippe Lacoue-Labarthe and Theodor W. Adorno on Mimesis', *New German Critique* 118 (Winter, 2013).

23 Max Horkheimer, 'The Concept of Man' (1957), in Horkheimer, *The Critique of Instrumental Reason* (London: Verso, 2012), 1–33.

24 Mark Greif, *The Age of the Crisis of Man: Thought and Fiction in America, 1933–1973* (Princeton, NJ: Princeton University Press, 2015). He includes a discussion of *The Family of Man* in his analysis.

25 Horkheimer, 'The Concept of Man', 4.

26 Ibid.

27 Ibid., 6. The critique of authenticity was a staple of the Frankfurt School's attack on existentialism. See Martin Jay, 'Taking on the Stigma of Inauthenticity: Adorno's Critique of Genuineness', in *Essays from the Edge: Parerga and Paralipomena* (Charlottesville: University of Virginia Press, 2011).

28 Max Horkheimer, Erich Fromm and Herbert Marcuse, *Studien über Autorität und Familie: Forschungsberichte aus dem Institut für Sozialforschung*, 2 vols (Paris: Librarie Felix Alcan, 1936).

29 For a critique of Horkheimer's view of maternal warmth, see Mechthild Rumpf, '"Mystical Aura": Imagination and Reality of the "Maternal" in Horkheimer's Writings', in *On Max Horkheimer: New Perspectives*, ed. Seyla Benhabib, Wolfgang Bonß and John McCole (Cambridge, MA: MIT Press, 1993). The phrase 'haven in a heartless world', which Horkheimer did not directly use, is sometimes attributed to Marx, but it wasn't until Christopher Lasch's *Haven in a Heartless World: The Family Besieged* (New York: W.W. Norton & Co., 1977) that it gained widespread currency.

30 Horkheimer, 'The Concept of Man', 24.

31 T. W. Adorno et al., *The Authoritarian Personality*, 2 vols (New York: Harper and Brothers, 1950). For its relevance to the exhibition, see Turner, '*The Family of Man* and the Politics of Attention in Cold War America', 72.

32 Adorno et al., *The Authoritarian Personality*, vol. 1, 370.

33 Ibid., 357–8.

34 Roland Barthes, 'The Great Family of Man', in *Mythologies*, trans. Annette Lavers (New York: Noonday Press, 1972), 101. The title of the exhibition in France was 'The Great Family of Man'.

35 See the contribution by Gerd Hurm in this volume.

36 Ryan Gunderson, 'The First-generation Frankfurt School on the Animal Question: Foundation for a Normative Sociological Animal Studies', *Sociological Studies* 57, no. 3 (2014).

37 Richard Bessel, *Violence: A Modern Obsession* (London: Simon & Schuster, 2015), chap. 6.

38 Immanuel Kant, 'On Perpetual Peace', in *The Philosophy of Kant: Immanuel Kant's Moral and Political Writings*, ed. Carl J. Friedrich (New York: Modern Library, 1993), 492.

39 Hannah Arendt, *The Human Condition* (Chicago: University of Chicago Press, 1958), 218.

40 In the Frankfurt School's history, the most explicit defence of the critical potential of the concept came in Herbert Marcuse, 'The Concept of Essence' (1936), in *Negations: Essays in Critical Theory*, trans. Jeremy J. Shapiro (Boston: Beacon Press, 1968).

41 Stefanos Geroulanos, *An Atheism that is not Humanist Emerges in French Thought* (Stanford, CA: Stanford University Press, 2010).

42 Barthes, 'The Great Family of Man', 100.

43 Karl Marx, 'Contribution to the Critique of *Hegel's Philosophy of Right*', in *Early Writings*, ed. and trans. T. B. Bottomore (New York: McGraw-Hill, 1964), 43–4.

44 For a consideration of the role that religion played in the post-war discussion of human rights, see Samuel Moyn, *Christian Human Rights* (Philadelphia: University of Pennsylvania Press, 2015).

4 'The Camera Will Not Miss Anything' (1955)

The Family of Man at the Städtische Galerie

Wolfgang Koeppen

The exhibition of 503 photographs from 68 countries, which, in the Federal Republic, can be seen only in Munich, selected from 10,000 images of masters and amateurs and compiled on behalf of the Museum of Modern Art in New York by an old man, the 73-year-old photographer Edward Steichen, who has, with this collection, created the most beautiful monument to himself and to his faith in mankind – this show is extraordinary. It is a *comédie humaine*, written by the photographic lens, a human comedy of our time and it is both drama and tragedy, exactly as it was with Balzac, and even *contes drolatiques* are not missing. Mankind, all of us in our world of vanquished distances and unconquered discord, we, all of us, whether white-, black- or yellow-skinned, are captured here by the camera, from birth to death, in our happiness and our suffering, our work, our joys and our crimes. In some of these images we are the crown of creation, in others we cover this earth as though with leprosy. Photography does not hide anything. It will not miss anything. It captures on film or plate the surface of our being, but at times, and that happens in the pictures in this exhibition, it x-rays us and magically captures our souls. It succeeds in doing what only a great artist has the gift to do, catching the moment and making it eternal. No image in this collection is posed, and thus we see real life here and not any wishful euphoria, no contented homunculus without fear, without hunger, without greed, the way progressive and reactionary governments alike love man as their subject.

The eye of the camera here resembles the poet's gaze, and the photographs in this exhibition also are irrefutable proof of the truthfulness and the correct direction of contemporary literature, because a lens that sees only what is there contradicts by what it captures the attacks against the modern novel, as they have recently been made by *Life* magazine and everywhere in Germany, the accusation that fiction represents the world too gloomily and thus is untrue. All images of the show, even the gayest, even the friendly flute-playing Peruvian shepherd boy on the cover of the catalogue, are faces of melancholy. They are that because they are true, because they have reached, through an originally technical process, the truth of all art. In any laugh there is mourning. Seeing that now is not saddening, as a widespread misconception has it; this truth of life and its representation in art only strengthen and elevate the senses. Only a laugh that lacked any grief would be depressing because it would be completely inhumane. There is a picture of a little boy. He is nice. He is charming. He looks at his dog, a young fox terrier on a rope. It is an idyll on a stone staircase. And yet it is the melancholy that makes the image lively, that makes it human, that touches us. The melancholy here is in the face of the dog. He is too serious, the little dog, but it is only this ounce of bitterness that turns this photograph into a document of existence and makes it unique. Conversely, it is only in the stern face of the judge who is leafing thoughtfully through the legal code, in his deep sad eyes that have looked into the abyss, that the surprising, but clearly perceptible possibility of joy creates the beauty of the picture.

There are also images of inhumanity. They are breathtaking. There is a woman sitting at the roulette table. But she is no longer a woman. She is a specter. She is a ghost of gambling and greed. There are the hands of a worker. She assembles bolts. She probably gets paid on a piece basis. Her hands have become inhuman in their agility, the gripping tools of a robot on whom the rudiment of human features seems particularly sinister. There are young people. Their passion is toward death. They happily race toward it in a car they deliberately ride without holding the steering wheel. Then there is the dark panel of a tragedy, the work of an unknown German photographer: Jews are being deported from the burning Warsaw Ghetto toward annihilation. The Jews, children among them, are the human beings in the picture. They preserve man's dignity, or else the sight that deeply shocks would be unbearable. For in the front of the photograph stands the monster. He likes to do what he does. He feels in his uniform. He holds his pistol at the ready. If there is a hell – he is its son.

Some images are indiscrete in what they observe. The image of birth, the child still connected by the umbilical cord with the mother; the intimacy of lovers, probably seen through a telephoto lens; the pain of relatives at the open cardboard coffin of a Spanish boy. But it is an indiscretion that previously only the poet permitted himself who created the image of man out of himself, and it is legitimate because it is true.

The exhibition has much to teach. It teaches pride. Pride in human beauty, wisdom, goodness, decency, and labour. It teaches humility. Humility at human limitations, human poverty and suffering. Above all, the photographs teach fraternity. The improbably spruced up socialite mother from *Vogue* is the sister of the Negro mom in blue jeans, stretched out with her child on the bare ground. Not only the world but also man is indivisible. In this photographic exhibition we are looking at a mirror. We recognize ourselves. We are not alone, and each one of us is there for, is responsible for, everyone else, just as the Bible already put it with the question: 'Cain, where is thy brother Abel?'

Süddeutsche Zeitung, 21 November 1955, p. 276
[Translated by Werner Sollors.]

5 Two Letters to Edward Steichen

August Sander

Editors' note

The following are two of the six letters from August Sander to Edward Steichen, written between 20 March 1954 and 3 July 1956, that are in the archives of the Museum of Modern Art in New York (Museum of Modern Art Exhibition Records 569.25. Reproduced with permission from The Museum of Modern Art, NY (MoMA) 2017). Sander and Steichen had met in 1952 when Steichen had toured Europe meeting photographers as a way of inviting submissions for *The Family of Man*. The existing correspondence begins with Sander informing Steichen that he is sending a portfolio of his images for Steichen's consideration. Sander was among the most distinguished German photographers of the first half of the twentieth century but the remarkable portraits that made up his monumental *People of the Twentieth Century* were rejected by the National Socialists, and Sander largely gave up photography and retreated into rural isolation during the early years of World War II. Steichen's attention to his work, and his admiration for it, came then as an unexpected and welcome recognition. Three of Sander's photographs were included in *The Family of Man*.

***

Kuchhausen, 19. 7. 1955

August Sander
Kuchhausen
Post Leuscheid
Siegkreis

Dear Mr. Steichen!

It is about time to express my gratitude for the book on the exhibition that you sent.

The artistic work is so great and so beautiful that it is unequalled. I am overwhelmed by the great drama, 'the human being', an immortal document for the present and for the future, as well as for coming generations.

I thank you with all of my heart. My wife, too, is fascinated by the great work that you have achieved and shocked by the frightful fates which people had and still have to endure.

Immortal documents for photography.

My daughter had told us about the great artistic success of the exhibition and that she was very impressed and excited and proud to have met you in person.

I would have already written you long ago, but I have not been in good health recently, hence the delay.

With best regards,
Yours as always,

August Sander (and wife)

NB. I learned from an acquaintance from Frankfurt that a lady had seen the exhibition in New York and was very excited to see my photographs among the works. We would be very happy if the exhibition comes to Germany as well.

August Sander
Lichtbildner
Kuchhausen / Post Leuscheid
Siegkreis
Germany

Kuchhausen, 3 July 1956

My dear Mr. Steichen,

The transfer of the amount of 75 dollars, which I hadn't expected in any way, came as a surprise; for I considered it an honor to have made a small contribution to the greatest work that photography has brought to light. An epic of all mankind of our planet, something like this is simply unique.

All the acquaintances to whom I have sent your work are enthusiastic about the magnificent work; one might even publish a volume on your great work in summary. I have also received the photos of the exhibition from different countries, which you sent me, and in which you have also included my works, and I sincerely thank you for having done so.

I hope and wish that you can continue to achieve great things for the benefit of mankind and the development of photography.

So far, I'm still doing fine and am able to work; because for me, work makes life worth living. We are now preparing for the visit of our daughter from Washington, whom you have already met. She will be with us from the end of July until the beginning of September.

There is still a lot more to report and to tell, but I will do this later. Today, however, I would like to thank you for all the beautiful and good things you have done for me and offer you, on behalf of my wife and I, the sincerest of greetings.

Sincerely yours,

August Sander

[Source: The Museum of Modern Art Exhibition Records, 569.25. The Museum of Modern Art Archives, New York. Reproduced with permission from the Museum of Modern Art, New York City, 2017. Translated by Özge Calafato and Hedwig Hinzmann.]

6 *The Family of Man* in Munich

Visitors' Reactions

Shamoon Zamir

The Family of Man was shown in Munich from 19 November to 18 December in 1955. The exhibition's first stop in Europe had been Berlin (17 September–9 October), where it had been an American contribution to the city's fifth cultural festival, and where it had also proved to be an 'unheard-of success': the Hochschule für bildende Künste (Academy for Creative Arts), where the exhibition was shown in Berlin, counted an art exhibition to be a success if it drew 5,000 visitors over a three-week period; *The Family of Man* brought in over 12,000 in its first eight days and a total of 42,000 by the end of its three-week run. And the exhibition enjoyed a similar success in Bavaria during its four-week run at Munich's Städtische Lenbach-Galerie (Municipal Gallery), co-sponsored by Amerika Haus, where it was seen by 32,500 visitors, roughly a thousand per day.[1] The same team was responsible for hanging the exhibition in both Berlin and Munich, but the Munich installation appears to have been more successful. According to Dorothea von Stetten, Manager in the Exhibition Section of the American Embassy, the exhibition in Munich was 'more dramatic and more accentuated, and much better lit', an impression that is borne out by the available installation photographs from the two venues.[2] *The Family of Man* returned to Germany in 1958 and was seen in Frankfurt, Hamburg and Hanover. When the attendance figures for 1955 and 1958 from all five cities are combined, the number of German visitors to the exhibition comes to a total of 161,000.[3]

The international tour of *The Family of Man* was sponsored by the United States Information Agency (USIA, known abroad as the United States Information Service or USIS). The USIS in Germany promoted Steichen's show with a great deal of energy, and this effort undoubtedly contributed significantly to the immense popularity of the exhibition. In Munich, a press preview was held for 45 representatives of newspapers, magazines, radio and television from the city and other parts of Bavaria. This resulted in at least 101 articles and picture stories in 95 separate publications, with a total circulation of 5,680,000. Local radio and television provided almost 90

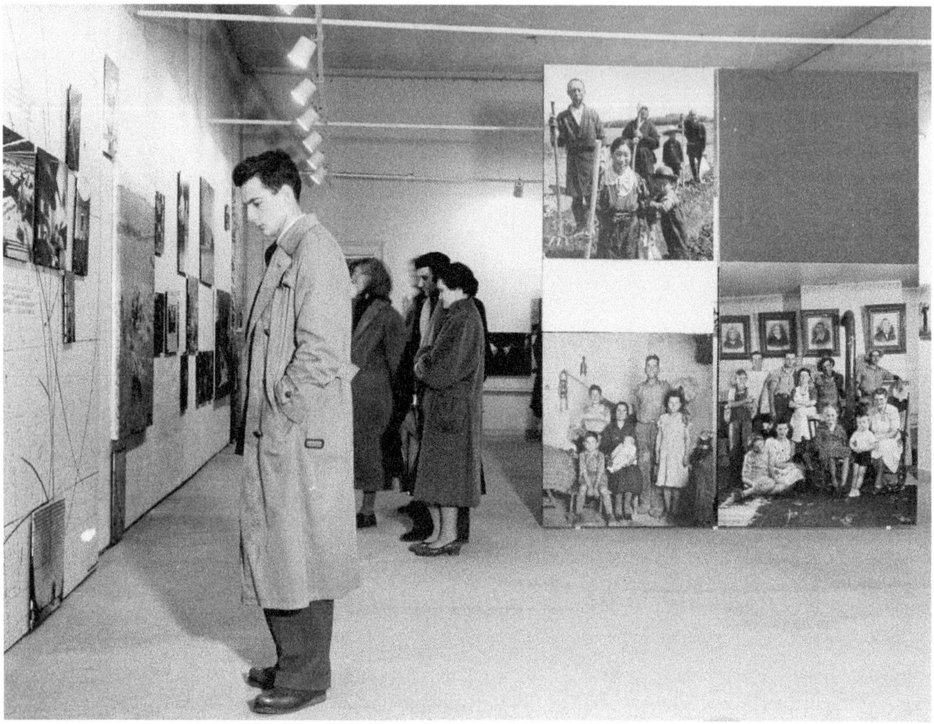

14 ***The Family of Man*** **at the Städtische Lenbach-Galerie, Munich, Germany, 19 November–18 December 1955.**

minutes of airtime and access to three million viewers and listeners.[4] Previously in Berlin similar previews for the media had been arranged, and in addition the USIS distributed several hundred copies of the book of the exhibition and organized 'extensive poster advertising'.[5] The enthusiastic endorsement of the respected critic Friedrich Luft seems to have been especially influential in Berlin. An actor, journalist and screenwriter, Luft was also 'a very influential Berlin cultural commentator'. He 'devoted one of his regular and widely listened-to broadcasts, usually reserved for film and theatre reviews, to a strongly favorable description of the exhibit, urging his listeners to go and see it'. According to the USIS report, 'for many Berliners this was the authoritative stamp of approval'.[6]

But neither the imprimatur of a cultural authority such as Luft, nor the efforts of the USIS, can fully explain the scale and enthusiasm of the public's response to Steichen's show. The USIS after all made similar efforts to promote other exhibitions it sponsored but without results to match – not in Germany, and not anywhere else in the world. We cannot properly account for the phenomenon that *The Family of Man* became without acknowledging the role that the public itself played in its promotion. As the USIS itself noted, 'the most successful instrument in promoting' attendance in the early stages of the exhibit in Berlin proved to be a 'sneak preview' organized for 'the day before the exhibit's official opening'. 'Personal letters were sent to some 500 photo dealers and camera club members' inviting them to a preview in the morning, and another 400 invitations were sent to another selected list for an afternoon preview the same day. Some 450 people came.[7] What is important about these sneak previews is that their success in bringing visitors to the exhibit was dependent not on further advertising and USIS-dictated publicity but on word of mouth, and on communicating a personal experience of Steichen's show.

The staggering number of people who went to see *The Family of Man* around the world is without question the most compelling fact about the exhibition, and yet this is also the aspect of the show that has received little or no critical attention. Although the attendance figures confirm a near uniform level of interest and appreciation across dozens of countries, we know nothing in detail of what visitors thought or felt, what in particular held their attention or did not, and why. This is hardly surprising since direct testimony about such matters appears not to have been collected while the exhibition was on tour, and is now, given the passing of the years, impossible to come by. Munich, however, provides us with a notable exception to this lacuna in our understanding of *The Family of Man*.

While *The Family of Man* (or *Wir Alle* – All of Us – as it was called in Germany) was in Munich, a city that had been under US occupation from 1945 to 1948, the research staff at the American Embassy's Office of Public Affairs commissioned DIVO, Gesellschaft für Markt- und Meinungsforschung m.b.h. from Frankfurt-Main, a respected German opinion survey organization, to prepare a report on visitors' reactions to the exhibit. This was one of a number of reports similarly commissioned in the decades following World War II to survey German responses to various exhibitions and cultural events organized by the US government authorities, as well as perceptions of American culture, society and politics.[8] A primary reason for why the American Embassy took such care to canvass public opinion in West Germany must have been because of the country's geopolitical importance in the Cold War in the aftermath of the war; it was a new ally for the US and an especially important partner in the struggle against the Soviet Union. No doubt this is why Berlin, the divided city at the very centre of Cold War confrontations, was picked as the first European venue for *The Family of Man*. It would be another six years before the wall dividing the east of the city from its western part would be built; this meant that at least a quarter, and perhaps as many as a third of the 42,000 visitors who came to see the show in Berlin (including Bertolt Brecht and a young Gerhard Richter) actually came from East Germany.[9]

We don't know what visitors from the 'Eastern Zone' made of Steichen's exhibition, but the survey from Munich does provide us with a remarkably detailed and wide-ranging summary of West German public opinion.[10] The survey is one of only two documents relating to *The Family of Man* that I am aware of that provide us with access to what several hundred visitors from a particular city and country, out of the final total of more than nine million from 48 countries, thought and felt about the exhibition (the other document, also an audience survey, is from Mexico City).[11] Inevitably, the recorded responses were mediated by the survey format and by at least some of the cultural and political imperatives that were behind the survey's commissioning. But it remains the case that these documents nevertheless provide us with a rare glimpse of some of the thoughts and feelings of *The Family of Man*'s international audience, a glimpse that is far more direct and more grounded in specifics than the broad celebrations in the media, or the undeniably forceful but also blunt facts of global attendance figures. This is especially true of the Munich report that is both methodologically more rigorous and self-aware than the Mexico City survey, and far more detailed and extensive in charting a wide variety of responses. The Munich survey, like the Mexico City one, has not previously been examined in the critical literature on *The Family of Man*; it is because of this, and because it makes a particularly invaluable contribution to the European dimensions of the present volume, that its findings are summarized here.

The Munich survey was based on interviews with 770 visitors conducted over the four weeks that the exhibition was in the city. A total of 298 of the visitors were interviewed as they left the exhibit, and 472 were interviewed at their homes by appointment, two or three days after their visit to the show: 'The purpose of this procedure was to locate possible differences between the immediate feelings and reactions of the audience and those judgments and views reported after some lapse of time during which discussions and exchange of impressions had most likely taken place' (i). The questionnaires used for the two sample groups were similar, though 'a greater number of questions, resulting from more detailed queries, were asked in the home interviews' (i). The findings of the survey were compiled along with comments and analysis by the research staff of the Office of Public Affairs at the American Embassy in a detailed and careful report, 87 pages in length, titled 'Visitors' Reactions to the "Family of Man" Exhibit', dated 23 January 1956. Though those interviewed at home would all have been Muenchners, at least some of those surveyed at the exhibition itself must have been from other parts of Bavaria: 'groups of university students, art students, factory workers, photo-clubs and other club groups came by bus, train and private car' to the show (without direct solicitation in fact) 'from all over South Germany'.[12]

The primary purpose of the survey for the United States Information Service (USIS) was to determine 'whether – and to what extent – the exhibit contributes to USIS objectives [...] in Germany'. Two questions were central to these determinations: '1) Do exhibit visitors recognize the theme of the show or is it simply considered an arty photographic exhibit and 2) Do visitors as a result of the exhibit credit the U.S. with sincere efforts to achieve peace and understanding among peoples of the world?' (i). The USIS research staff who compiled and analysed the findings of the survey were themselves quick to acknowledge that the survey only answered 'questions which arose among USIS policy officials in West Germany in considering the impact and effectiveness of [the] Steichen show in the light of USIS objectives'. This proves to be too limited a description; the survey in fact allows us to see much more than USIS preoccupations at work, whatever the original motivations behind its commissioning. But the authors of the report were especially perceptive when they noted a different limitation, one that all commentators on *The Family of Man* must acknowledge if they engage with the question of audience response and experience. 'In studying the effect of the show,' the report commented, 'we can only consider reactions which are verbal, hence surface expressions.' A proper understanding of the exhibit requires us to go below this verbal surface because 'a considerable part of the influence of the Steichen show is of such a subtle nature that the results are difficult to locate even with far-reaching probing techniques since these influences awaken purely emotional reactions' (6).

The exhibition had of course been devised by Steichen independently of the USIA and its programmatic objectives (which is not to say that consideration of cultural politics played no part at all in its early planning): the report itself reiterated at its very start Steichen's insistence that *The Family of Man* had been created 'with no propaganda intention of any kind whatsoever' (i). It is nevertheless the case that the international tour of the exhibition was very much under the USIS's control, with the organization in charge of all the publicity and having at least some control over adding and removing pictures to suit local contexts and sensitivities. The USIS had adopted the exhibition because its theme or message fitted well with the American government's international objectives. These objectives are articulated later in the report as explaining 'America and its ideals to the German public' and thereby creating 'more favorable attitudes towards the United States' (40). Steichen's humanist commitment to a sense of global collectivity was of course not as narrow as this, but it *was* telling that, while 'about half of the visitors had no opinion as to which country in the world does most to realize the ideals expressed in the exhibit', 40% of visitors named the United States and only 8% named European countries (with only 3% choosing Germany itself) (61). The authors of the report noted with understandable satisfaction that the 40% 'represents a very high score in a free answer situation' (62), and that almost three-quarters of both the exit and home interviewees 'received the impression through the exhibition that the United States is seriously trying to bring about understanding between the nations and races throughout the world' (66).

These figures are perhaps even more impressive when we consider that only just over 60% of the visitors appear to have been aware that the exhibition was US-sponsored (with 30% indicating 'America' or 'Americans' as the sponsors, another 30% naming MoMA, and 1% saying Amerika Haus, the co-sponsor, along with the Municipal Gallery, of the show in Munich) (62). The figure of 61% was clearly seen as too low by the USIS head office in Washington, and was raised as a matter of concern with the American Embassy staff in Germany. Milton Leavitt, Assistant Public Affairs Officer in Munich, and the person primarily responsible for the organization of the exhibition there, responded by saying that he had 'visited the exhibition each day' and that he was sure that in fact the percentage of people recognizing US sponsorship was higher. But Leavitt also argued astutely that it was 'more important to the [USIS] program to present a tremendously effective exhibit [...] than to present exhibits on which there is no doubt of their sponsorship but have them prove ineffectual (which has happened so often in the past)'.[13]

Leavitt had spent time with Steichen discussing the exhibition and listening to his lecture on photography and *The Family of Man*, when Steichen had first visited

Munich in September 1955 (while the exhibition was still in Berlin). He also delivered a lengthy speech outlining the major themes of the exhibition and the process by which the show had been put together by Steichen and his team at the Munich opening, and he may well have had a hand in the report on visitors' reactions in Munich.[14] Leavitt's comments on the effectiveness of the exhibition, and his implication that communicating the core philosophical message of the show was more important than ensuring awareness of its American sponsorship, would have been welcomed by Steichen for whom the USIS was first and foremost a vehicle for making *The Family of Man* accessible worldwide, and not a body in charge of the show's meanings. Steichen, who was certainly aware of the Munich report, must have been equally pleased that the survey focused above all on the broad scope as well as the particular iterations of this message, and on the ways in which these were understood by the visitors.

The report summarizes the findings of the survey as follows, and given the substantial evidence provided in support of it, the summary is accurate and credible:

> The 'Family of Man' exhibition in Munich attracted an audience of exceptionally high intellectual level and received an outstandingly favorable reception from almost all of its visitors. The ratings are the highest ever found for any exhibit including the 1954 'Atoms for Peace' exhibit in Berlin. There was frequent usage of such extremely favorable terms as 'superior', 'excellent', 'outstanding', 'without precedent' and 'magnificent' – terms which are rarely found in audience reactions studies. The emotionally-stirring and deeply moving effect of the Steichen show resulted in strong enthusiasm which was especially apparent in the exit interviews conducted immediately after the show.
>
> Although the differences between the two samples are only small, and, strictly speaking, statistically insignificant, two general tendencies are apparent. First, after a short time lapse, enthusiasm is slightly less and somewhat replaced by an appraisal which is still far above the ordinary. Second, clear understanding of the underlying idea *increases* with the passage of time.
>
> The ideals of the exhibit are clearly perceived. Its purposes and effects are described as stimulating thinking concerning the problems of the human community, and inspiring humanitarian feelings by presenting the unifying elements common to man and thus promoting friendship and peace among all nations and races. Therefore, one is justified in concluding that the pictorial approach of presenting the theme was highly successful. (1)

Perhaps the most important detail to note here is the 'exceptionally high intellectual level' of the audience: the measure here was not only in relation to the educational level of the public at large (one would expect visitors to a photographic exhibit at an art gallery to have above-average educational attainment); it was rather in comparison to the make-up of audiences for other exhibitions previously sponsored and organized by the USIS. According to the report, 84% of 'the rank and file people in West Germany have elementary schooling only'. By contrast, 89% of the visitors to the exhibition in

Munich were found to have gone beyond elementary school: 'In fact about twenty times as many persons with university training' were found in the audience 'as are to be found in the general population'. And the unusually high proportion of educated visitors was matched by 'a much greater proportion of men' than the USIS would have anticipated for one of its cultural or art shows.[15] It is not surprising then that there was also a disproportionately high representation of 'the prestige occupations and higher income groups': what the report refers to as 'upper middle class' and 'upper class' individuals made up 30% of the general population in Germany in 1955 but 84% of the audience surveyed; according to the survey, about 2% of the population had been to university, but the figure was 41% among the Munich visitors to the exhibit (1–2). These figures and breakdowns are important because they reveal an exceptionally high presence of the 'opinion-leading elements' (1). The report is right to conclude then that, 'considering the exceptionally high educational level of this particular audience, the findings [...] become even more important and gain in significance since members of the elite groups are usually found to be much more critical than other groups in the population' (6). One could add, in regard to the relatively high opinion of the United States expressed in the survey, that this educated and professional segment of the population is precisely the group one would expect to be most likely to be critical of American cultural propaganda and foreign policy.

Equally noteworthy is the near unanimity of opinion expressed between the 'less educated' (which was taken to mean those with an elementary school or secondary school education without Abitur (diploma)) and the 'more educated' (meaning university educated as well as those with the Abitur which was a necessary degree for studies at university): 52% of the former said they liked the exhibit 'extremely well', and 39% said they liked it 'very well'; the figures among the 'more educated' were 50% and 35% respectively (10).[16] In other words, right across the West German social and educational spectrum, from those with little more than an elementary education to university graduates, white collar professionals, and intellectuals such as Max Horkheimer, Wolfgang Koeppen and Siegfried Kracauer (as well as all newspapers and magazines), there is a near complete consensus about *The Family of Man*, and a remarkably positive assessment of its cultural achievement that stands apart from the many ideological critiques of the exhibition that were contemporary to it or have appeared regularly since the 1950s, and from accounts that have dismissed the exhibition as nothing more than American Cold War propaganda indistinguishable from the programmatic aims of the USIS. Only 2% of those interviewed saw the objectives of the exhibition as making 'propaganda for the United States' (1%), or 'to propagandize democracy' (1%) (41).

As the summary of the survey quoted above suggests, most visitors grasped the 'theme' or 'message' of the exhibition in more or less the terms in which Steichen had intended. And they responded with almost equal enthusiasm to Steichen's unusual presentation of the photographs. Roughly a quarter of the visitors who came to the Munich show had been to one or more photography exhibitions during the previous year, but the majority of them rated *The Family of Man* far more highly than any other photography show they had seen: 90% of the interviewees commented favourably on the 'composition and arrangement of the pictures' and on their 'shape and size' as aspects of the exhibition that had appealed to them (18), although the majority of those who did comment favourably on the aesthetics of the show did so while noting that Steichen's use of photography was only a vehicle for the message he wanted to convey (46–8). And almost every visitor who was interviewed said that they would recommend the exhibition to others, and agreed that the exhibition should be shown in other German cities (50). A significant number of the visitors (some 40%) pointed to the quality of the display and the revelation of the communicative potential of photography as one reason for making such a recommendation (16), but the overwhelming majority gave as a reason the importance of the underlying ideas of the exhibition, and emphasized 'its stimulating effect on thinking about problems of human life, promoting international understanding, inspiring humanitarian feelings, and explaining what is common to all men' (14). As one visitor put it, he or she would encourage others to come to the show 'because my relatives and friends would be led to see – as it happened to me – how absurd it is to believe that people of other races and nationalities, of another faith, or living under another governmental system would feel any differently from the way we feel' (15).

Only about a third of the visitors said that they had gained new insights or learned something new after visiting the exhibition. But this was hardly surprising given the educational level of the audience. Many would have 'very probably spent a considerable amount of their spiritual and intellectual life being concerned with the problems and philosophies expressed by the show', and would have already subscribed to Steichen's humanist message. 'Thus with most visitors the impact' of *The Family of Man* did not reside 'in the transmission of new ideas, but in the reactivation of old ones' (57). Given the prevalence of this shared belief in the common bonds that tie human beings together across cultures and times, the authors of the report were right to note that it was a 'tribute' to the achievement of *The Family of Man* 'that over two-thirds (68%) of those who basically felt that men are *too different* [which was 15% of those interviewed, 67] were impressed by the photos because they demonstrate the exact opposite (i.e. that races and nations fundamentally have more in common)' (56).

Broad assessments of the form and content of *The Family of Man* such as these are extremely valuable for anyone wanting to understand what 'ordinary people' or the 'general public' (as opposed to critics and academics) might have made of the exhibition in the 1950s, but perhaps the Munich survey contributes to this understanding even more by allowing us to drill down to more specific reactions and responses. In addition to assessments of the overall design and thematics of the exhibition, the survey maps audiences' responses to particular groups of photographs as well as to individual photographs, with many direct comments from visitors included as in all other sections of the survey.

The interviewees were first asked which group of pictures (defined by 'content categories') and which individual pictures produced 'the strongest impression' on them, and not which pictures they 'liked' or 'disliked' (32). The five categories of photographs which received the highest statistical responses were: children or children at play (40%); pictures of pregnancy and birth (26%); pictures of the creation of the world (22%); men at work (20%); and pictures of mothers with children (15%) (33). As far as individual photographs were concerned, the list was as follows: the hydrogen bomb explosion (13%); Ruth Orkin's six-picture sequence of children playing cards (11%); Wynn Bullock's large image of the light over water at the start of the exhibition (one of the 'creation of the world' images) (10%); the images of the Jews being rounded up by German soldiers in the Warsaw Ghetto (10%); the child with a soap bubble by Gjon Mili (8%); and Eugene Smith's image of his children walking into the garden that closed the exhibition (7%) (34).[17]

These rankings shift in interesting ways when visitors are asked to list which categories and photographs they most liked and disliked. The categories that made the 'strongest favorable impression' were: children at play (39%); pictures of the creations of the world (22%); men at work (18%); images of people playing, drinking and laughing (14%); and pictures of mothers with children (13%) (35).[18] The crucial difference between the list of categories that made the 'strongest impression' and those that made the 'strongest *favorable* impression' is that images of pregnancy and birth are missing from the second list. This category in fact comes top of those that made the 'strongest *unfavorable* impression' at 13%. The other categories in the disliked list are, in descending order: pictures of war, including the H-bomb explosion (8%); images of cruelty, inhumanity and brutality (7%); pictures of dances (3%); and photographs of hunger, misery and poverty (2%) (35).

A similar pattern of sentiment, political attitudes and sensitivities towards social mores and sexuality emerges in the lists of individual photographs that were liked and disliked. The photographs producing the 'strongest favorable impression' were: Orkin's children playing cards (11%); Bullock's light over the water (10%); Mili's child with the soap bubble (8%); Smith's children in the garden (7%); and Arthur Witman's American audience laughing at a show (also one of Steichen's favourite images and the first one he selected for the exhibition) (5%) (35).[19] It is worth mentioning that when 'the total number of responses mentioning pictures with favorable and unfavorable impressions' were compared, 'considerably more photos were named as producing favorable reactions than were named as creating adverse impressions': more than four times as many mentioned pictures producing favourable responses rather than those producing unfavourable impressions (36). Nevertheless, in the 'unfavorable' category, two images stood out from all others: the pictures of the hydrogen bomb explosion and of the Warsaw Ghetto were both disliked by 7% of the interviewees each, with all other disliked images receiving statistically negligible responses (36).

What is striking about the pattern that emerges from these responses is that the strongest disapproval and unease was attached to the realms of intimacy, rather than to politics. When asked if there were pictures that they thought should have been excluded from the exhibition, almost one fifth of those interviewed singled out 'pictures touching traditional taboos, such as childbirth, pregnancy, sex, and love'. Only 6% proposed the Warsaw Ghetto images (38). About a quarter of the respondents indicated that they were 'undecided' and the authors of the report rightly note that there were among these 'probably a number so inhibited as to be unable to express their resentment against pictures penetrating into taboo spheres'. Equally, 'it might also be that to some of these people the picture of the Warsaw Ghetto represents a taboo in the realm of national life' (37).

The staff of the American Embassy appear to have had some sense of the images that were likely to meet with disapproval or which were likely to cause unease before the exhibition actually opened in Berlin. At each international site where *The Family of Man* was shown, the senior Public Affairs Officer of the American Embassy was given final authority over the decision to exclude some pictures if it was thought that these would cause particular offence to local audiences. At many sites, some photos were also added to reflect local culture and society. In Berlin, 16 photographs in total were excluded from the show, and in Munich 12. There was an overlap of only four photographs between the two groups, a fact that supports the claim by the USIS office in Bonn that the reasons for the exclusions 'were quite definitely only technical ones', primarily to do with issues of size and space. The one exception to this was Bullock's large image of a young girl (the photographer's daughter in fact) seen lying naked and face down among foliage on a forest floor that was hung as part of the 'creation of the world' prologue to the exhibition. This particular image 'was not liked here' (meaning, one assumes, among the USIS staff in Bonn): otherwise, no 'psychological, political or ethical reasons existed' for the removal of the other images.[20] The Bullock image would certainly have offended those members of the audience who commented critically in Munich on the images that explored the taboo subjects of intimacy and sexuality. Seen in the company of a photograph of a galaxy from the Lick Observatory, Bullock's own 'light over water', as well as the caption from Genesis ('And God said, Let there be light ...'), the image was clearly meant to represent the birth of humankind embodied in the first woman (Steichen interestingly referred to the image as 'Lilith', Adam's rebellious first companion, rather than 'Eve'), but the USIS staff may have been right in thinking that the image, encountered so boldly at the very start of the exhibition, might prove too challenging for some of the German audience.[21]

There was also discussion among the USIS staff in Germany about whether or not to exclude the images from the Warsaw Ghetto but Joseph B. Phillips, the chief Public Affairs Officer, 'finally decided [...] to leave it [sic.] in'.[22] The decision to let the Warsaw pictures remain in the exhibition proved to be a good one because the visitors' reactions to these images, perhaps more so than with any other pictures in the show, let us see the traces of the kinds of debate and reflection that were generated by *The Family of Man*. For example, when visitors were asked which image had made the strongest impression on them, in almost every case the images identified in the exit interviews were less emphatically identified in the home interviews. The only exception to this were the Warsaw Ghetto images which had gained in the strength of impression they had made after visitors had had a few days to reflect on their experience of the exhibition. The photograph of the hydrogen bomb explosion was identified by 17% of those interviewed at the exit of the exhibition as having made the strongest impression on them, but this figure had gone down to 11% by the time of the home interviews. The Orkin photo sequence of the children playing cards also went down, from 13% to 8%. But the Warsaw Ghetto images went from 8% to 12% (34). When visitors were asked whether they detected any nationalist bias in the exhibition, about 10% of the home interviewees (the question was only asked of them) signalled a pro-American bias, and about the same number noted an anti-German one. The comments of the latter group appear to have been focused in particular on the inclusion of the Warsaw images. One visitor commented that 'the pictures showing the expulsion of the Jews and the photos of the Nuremberg trials were tendentious and placed Germany in a very unfavorable light'. (There were, in fact, no pictures from the trials: the Warsaw images were labelled in Munich, as elsewhere, as 'Nuremberg trial documents'.) Another said accurately that the pictures 'showed SS-men in Warsaw, but atrocities committed by other nations weren't published' (70). In this case the point was not that the images should not have been included (or that they were 'tendentious') but that representations of acts of inhumanity from other nations and cultures should also have been shown – something that *The Family of Man* in its first iteration at MoMA had done with dramatic effect, and without sparing the US. As Phillips noted in his report, 'remarks made by individuals as they walked through the display halls were particularly interesting and gave testimony to the emotional impact of this exhibit upon the observer'. He reports one remark in particular, made by a 'university professor who was with a small group of students' as they stood in front of the Warsaw Ghetto picture 'showing children and parents with arms raised at gunpoint': '[…] I don't know how much more I can impress upon you than that this is something we should never forget […] it is a thing which we must be ashamed of […] but what I want most to say is that some of you perhaps will soon be in uniform, and I want you to remember this: always keep in mind that the army that points guns at little children, that forces little children to raise their arms at gun point, has lost the fight before it ever began […]'[23] One of the photographs of the exhibition from Munich shows just such a group of young students as this professor may have been addressing standing before the Warsaw Ghetto images, and in the midst of a discussion (see illustration 15). And it is worth remembering that the notorious Nazi concentration camp at Dachau was not far from Munich.

Sarah E. James, in her study of the photographic cultures of Cold War Germany, East and West, has argued that the remarkable popularity of *The Family of Man* with West Germans can be put down to the exhibition's 'avowedly apolitical stance'.[24] James notes, as others have, that in West Germany after the war there was a retreat from politics and the unpalatable realities of the recent past into historical amnesia and the comforting security of the family. Steichen's celebration, then, of the family and of a universal humanism that supposedly put to one side the challenges of cultural and political difference settled easily into this collective escapism, and also helped to give it support. From this perspective, the injunction by the professor to his students in front of the photographs of the Warsaw Ghetto in the Munich Municipal Gallery not to forget history may seem too isolated and too unrepresentative an instance to serve as a sufficient corrective to this account of the fit between *The Family of Man* and post-war German culture. But we should remember that the professor and his students *were* representative of a very high percentage of the exhibition's audience. James's account of *The Family of Man* in Germany relies on a broad characterization of post-

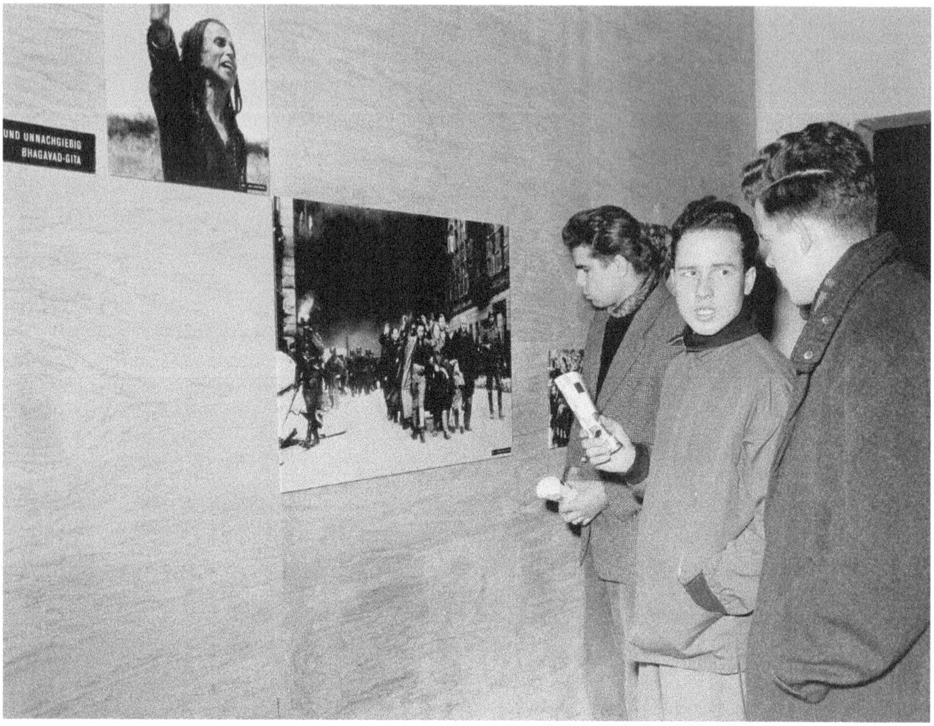

15 *The Family of Man* at the Städtische Lenbach-Galerie, Munich, Germany, 19 November–18 December 1955.

war German society as a whole but all segments of this society were not equally and proportionally represented in the audience that came to Steichen's exhibition. As the Munich survey indicates, the educational level of the visitors was considerably higher than both the average national level and the level of the audiences for other USIA-sponsored shows, and those with a university education made up a far greater proportion of the audience than in the general public at that time in Germany. We cannot then speak about the way *The Family of Man* would have enabled German citizens to negotiate issues of history and politics without being attentive specifically to the ways these issues would have been discussed and thought about by the more educated members of society. In this respect, the dialogue between the professor and his students about the Warsaw Ghetto images may in fact have been more representative of a larger part of *The Family of Man*'s German audience than is suggested by James's account.

It is true that the survey of the Munich visitors' reactions to the exhibition does not furnish us with comparable evidence of individual opinion or response because the interviews did not solicit extended comment on particular photographs. But the findings of the survey should nevertheless encourage us to pause and reconsider the broad cultural history James presents, and especially the way in which she formulates the work that *The Family of Man* did within this history. Only 6% of the interviewees suggested that the images from Warsaw should not have been included in the exhibition. As the survey itself notes, the Jewish genocide was for many Germans a taboo subject, and so some of the visitors may have been reluctant to speak about their reactions to the Warsaw Ghetto photographs. But if this means that the number of people who would have preferred for these images to be excluded from the exhibition was a little higher than 6%, then it must also be the case that the figure for those who indicated that these photographs were the ones that had the deepest impact on them must have been larger than that registered by the survey. Almost a quarter of those interviewed said that the two images from Warsaw and the image of the hydrogen bomb explosion, the most overtly political and historically specific photographs exhibited, were the photographs that made the strongest and most lasting impression on them, with the Warsaw images in fact generating increased reflection for many in the days following the visit to the gallery. It is less important for the present discussion to know *what* people thought about these images than to know that they *did* think about them. The photographs from the Warsaw Ghetto were only two images among the 500 or so that made up the exhibition, but Steichen was right to calculate that their startling effect would be disproportionate to their numerical marginalization, that they would force viewers to confront rather than evade history. This is not to say that historical amnesia was not a prevalent reality in post-war West German society; but it does not seem accurate or just to characterize *The Family of Man* as nothing more than a vehicle for this forgetting.

Equally problematic is James's claim that, on the one hand, 'the effort to democratize and Americanize West German culture in the 1950s might have made the exhibition's blatant American vision more palatable to a broad section of the West German public, or perhaps less glaringly obvious', and on the other, that Steichen's show would have been the target of 'an explicit animosity toward the darker side of American influences' which was 'increasingly felt by sections of the West German population, particularly the cultural elite, who decried the growing impact of American popular culture and the subsequent decline of a German *Hochkultur* (high culture)'.[25] The assessment of *The Family of Man* as an exhibition peddling an 'American vision' is widely shared, though almost always presented as a self-evident truth, rather than something that is demonstrated through the kind of discriminating analysis such a judgement requires. What concerns me here more immediately is the continued misfit between James's contextualization of *The Family of Man* within West German culture in the 1950s and the findings of the survey of the visitors' reactions to the exhibition in Munich. According to the survey, over 60% of those interviewed were fully aware that the exhibition was an American production. However, this did not result in either animosity towards the United States, or in the perception that the exhibition was propagating a particularly American vision of the world. On the contrary, the majority of the visitors articulated the view that the exhibition upheld what might be considered universal human values, and that the United States was then the nation disseminating these values more actively than any other.

It may be that such a view of both the exhibition and of America's international role was naïve, that Steichen's vision had indeed been made palatable by the very process of Americanization that should have been critically scrutinized. But if this is the case, then we need to both register and explain the fact that the very cultural elite James proposes as the opponents of American influence on West German culture, and as defenders of their own *Hochkultur*, formed a very large segment of *The Family of Man*'s audience in Munich, and appear to have given their enthusiastic assent to the exhibition. In this regard, the critical appraisals of the exhibition offered by Wolgang Koeppen and Max Horkheimer, both included for the first time in English in the present volume, provide forceful counterpoints to James's claims on behalf of the German cultural elite. In the years immediately preceding the first German tour of *The Family of Man*, Koeppen, who saw the exhibit in Munich, had published an accomplished trilogy of novels exploring Germany's recent past: *Pigeons on the Grass* (1951), *The Hothouse* (1953) and *Death in Rome* (1954) each tried in different ways to remember and to understand the continuing legacies of this past. And Horkheimer, in collaboration with his Frankfurt School colleague Theodor Adorno, had formulated stringent critiques of modern mass culture that rested on comparisons of fascist Germany and American popular culture.[26] The work of neither of these authors could be said to evade history and politics, nor to offer an unqualified or simple-minded endorsement of American culture. And yet both Koeppen and Horkheimer offer an equally enthusiastic affirmation of the humanistic vision of *The Family of Man*, not because it allows us to forget the challenge of difference, but because it brings us to a sense of human identity *through* difference.

Notes

1 The information on Berlin is from reports by Dorothea von Stetten, Manager, Exhibition Section, Office of Public Affairs, United States Embassy, Bonn, to Jackie Martin, United States Information Agency (USIA), Washington, DC, 29 September 1955 (Von Stetten to Martin, 29 September 1955); John E. McGowan, Deputy Public Affairs Officer, USIS Berlin, to USIA, Washington, DC, 23 September 1955 (McGowan to USIA, 23 September 1955); as well as an undated typed memo by an unidentified author in the files of the USIA. (The memo gives the attendance figure for Berlin as 44,000.) The details of dates, attendance figures, the opening ceremony and media coverage in Munich, are from a report by Joseph B. Phillips, the United States Information Service (USIS) Public Affairs Office, United States Embassy, Bonn, to the USIS office in Washington, DC, 6 February 1956 (Phillips to USIA Washington, 6 February 1956). For the von Stetten and McGowan reports and the undated memo, Box 1, and for the Phillips report, Box 3, Photographs and Clippings Relating to *The Family of Man* Exhibition, 1955–1956 (Photographs and Clippings, 1955–1956), Records of the US Information Agency, Record Group 306-FM (RG 306-FM), National Archives at College Park, College Park, MD (NACP). A copy of Phillips's report can also be found at International Council and International Programs Records, folder I.B.140, Museum of Modern Art (MoMA) Archives. Both Phillips and von Stetten note the impressive sales of the book of the exhibition as an indicator of the success of the exhibition.

2 Dorothea von Stetten to Edward Steichen, 28 November 1955, Museum of Modern Art Exhibition Records (MoMA Exhs.) 569.101, Museum of Modern Art Archives, New York (MoMA Archives). Stetten also notes that the press coverage was even more positive in Munich than in Berlin. Professor Guenther Gottwald, Head of the Architecture Department at the Berlin Academy of Creative Arts, and his assistants were responsible for hanging the exhibition in Berlin and Munich. For photographs of the installations of the exhibition in Berlin and Munich, consult Boxes 1 and 3 respectively, Photographs and Clippings Relating to *The Family of Man* Exhibition, 1955–1956, Records of the US Information Agency, Record Group 306-FM, National Archives at College Park, College Park, MD.

3 This figure is taken from an exhibition itinerary dated 1 May 1960, in the Edward Steichen Archive (ESA), VB.i.46, MoMA Archives. The Frankfurt, Hamburg and Hanover showings were in 1958 when the exhibition returned to Germany after having been shown in other countries. An itinerary prepared by *The Family of Man* museum in Clervaux, Luxembourg, confirms the Hamburg date and proposes 1958 as also the year for the Frankfurt and Hanover stops. The Frankfurt date is confirmed by Werner Sollors's contribution to this volume. There were recommendations that the exhibition be shown in other German cities, including a request as late as September 1960 from the newly founded photography museum in Dresden, then in the 'Eastern Zone' where the US had no 'official cultural exchange agreement' (Note from Porter A. McCray, Director of Circulating Exhibitions at MoMA, dated 12 September 1960, in the International Council and International Programs Records [IC/IP], VII.SP-ICE-55-10.3, MoMA Archives).

4 Phillips to USIS, 6 February 1956, Box 3, Photographs and Clippings, 1955–1956, RG306-FM, NACP.

5 Foreign Service Dispatch from John E. McGowan, Deputy Public Affairs Officer, USIS Berlin, to USIA, Washington, DC, 23 September 1955, Box 1, Photographs and Clippings Relating to *The Family of Man* Exhibition, 1955–1956, Records of the US Information Agency, Record Group 306-FM, National Archives at College Park, College Park, MD.

6 Phillips to USIS, 6 February 1956, Box 3, Photographs and Clippings, 1955–1956, RG306-FM, NACP. Dorothea von Stetten also argued that 'the most important promotion came from Radio critic Friedrich Luft (RIAS) who is regarded as the pope of the Berlin journalists. What he says is accepted by the Berliners' (Von Stetten to Martin, 29 September 1955, Photographs and Clippings, 1955–1956, RG306-FM, NACP).

7 McGowan to USIA, Washington, DC, 23 September 1955, Box I, Photographs and Clippings, 1955–1956, RG306-FM, NACP.

8 The report on 'Visitors' Reactions to *The Family of Man* Exhibit' is dated 23 January 1956 and, along with a number of other reports from Germany compiled by the USIS, can be accessed via the University of Illinois at Urbana-Champaign's library website. *The Family of Man* report can be found at http://libsysdigi.library.uiuc.edu/OCA/Books2009-10/visitorsreaction225unit/ (accessed 18 July 2016). All page references to the survey will be given in the text. Other reports, such as those on the 'Space Unlimited' exhibition, or 'West German Perspectives on US Culture and Politics', can be found by searching for 'U.S.I.S.'

9 One reason for the high attendance was that 'because of circumstances peculiar to Berlin, no entrance fee was charged'. It was also estimated that on 7 October, which was an official holiday, half of all visitors were from the GDR (Foreign Service Dispatch from John E. McGowan, Deputy Public Affairs Officer, USIS Berlin, to USIA, Washington, DC, 20 October 1955). According to an 'Operations Memorandum' sent by USIS Bonn to the Washington head office (10 January 1956), Brecht, 'famous East-zone pro-communist playwright', was photographed by a 'Berlin student' while visiting the show. For the dispatch and memorandum, and also the photograph of Brecht, Box 1, Photographs and Clippings relating to *The Family of Man* exhibition, 1955–1956, Records of the US Information Agency, Record Group 306-FM, National Archives at College Park, College Park, MD. For Richter, see the video and transcription of his conversation with Nicolas Serota (dated 11 October 2011) at: www.tate.org.uk/context-comment/video/gerhard-richter-panorama (accessed 18 July 2016). Speaking of how 'terrible' life was in the East, and how restricted personal freedom was, he also recalls that there was 'the possibility to go every year at least twice to West Berlin' to see 'movies and exhibitions'. It was on one such trip that he saw *The Family of Man*: 'This was a real shock for me, this show [...] to see these pictures, because I knew only paintings [...] they showed so much and they told so much these pictures, these photographs, told so much about modern life, my life.' Richter dates his own interest in photography from this moment when he encountered Steichen's exhibition because it showed him the 'power' of photography and 'what photography can do'.

10 On East German responses to *The Family of Man*, see Sarah E. James, *Common Ground: German Photographic Cultures Across the Iron Curtain* (New Haven, CT: Yale University Press, 2013), 61–3. James notes that though the exhibition was viewed critically by some sections of the East German authorities, in general the reception in the media and by the public was positive.

11 The Mexico City survey is a report on visitor reactions similar to the Munich report, though much shorter and less detailed. It was commissioned by the US Embassy, and is based on 636 oral and written interviews conducted during October and November 1955. '*The Family of Man*: A Study of Audience Reactions', Box 16, International Survey Research Reports, 1953–1964, Records of the US Information Agency, Record Group 306, National Archives at College Park, College Park, MD. My thanks to Anke Reitz for sharing this document with me. The findings of this document are, in some ways, very similar to those from Munich; they will be examined in a longer discussion of audience reactions elsewhere.

12 Phillips to USIA, Washington, DC, 6 February 1956, Box 3, Photographs and Clippings, 1955–1956, RG306-FM, NACP.

13 Milton Leavitt, Assistant Public Affairs Office, US Embassy, Munich, to Jackie Martin, USIA Washington, DC,15 February 1956, Box 3, Photographs and Clippings relating to *The Family of Man* exhibition, 1955–1956, Records of the US Information Agency, Record Group 306-FM, National Archives at College Park, College Park, MD.

14 Steichen was in Munich on 20–21 September. For details of the visit, see report from Leavitt in the Foreign Service Dispatch, 18 October 1955, from USIS Bonn to the Department of State, Washington, DC, Box 3, Photographs and Clippings relating to *The Family of Man* exhibition, 1955–1956, Records of the US Information Agency, Record Group 306-FM, National Archives at College Park, College Park, MD. The text of

Leavitt's speech from the Munich opening can also be found here.

15 Some 61% of those interviewed were men, whereas men only made up 45.6% of the general population. Some 39% of the interviewees were women whereas women made up 54.4% of the general population. It is also interesting to note that while unmarried individuals made up just under 24% of the population, they accounted for 54% of the interviewees, and although 63.5% of Germans were married, this group accounted for only 37% of those interviewed. Of the interviewees, 38% were aged between 20 and 29, and 55% were 30 and above (2).

16 There was a slightly greater differentiation among men and women: 48% of men said they liked the show 'extremely well' and 38% said 'very well'; among women the numbers were 55% and 36% (10).

17 For these photographs, see Edward Steichen, *The Family of Man* (New York: Museum of Modern Art, 1955), title page (Bullock's 'light over water'); 40 (Orkin); 165–6 (Warsaw Ghetto, though the book of the exhibition only includes one of the two images from Warsaw in the exhibition); 189 (Mili); and 192 (Smith).

18 One reason why the images of children at play made a particularly strong impression may have been because the exhibition in Munich was, as von Stetten claimed, better hung and more dramatically and effectively lit than in Berlin. In her letter to Steichen she noted in particular the 'great impact' of the 'contrast between the serious sections' dealing with topics such as 'Atomic Energy' or the 'United Nations on the one hand, and the playing children on the other. The latter has such an exuberant gaiety and brightness which I feel was lost in the somewhat subdued Berlin room' (28 November 1955, MoMA Exhs., 569.101, MoMA Archives).

19 For the Witman image, see Steichen, *The Family of Man*, 109.

20 Operations Memorandum, 20 December 1955, from USIS Bonn, to Jackie Martin, USIA Washington, DC, Box 3, Photographs and Clippings relating to *The Family of Man* exhibition, 1955–1956, Records of the US Information Agency, Record Group 306-FM, National Archives at College Park, College Park, MD. The memorandum lists all the images excluded by number. I have not found lists of any images that were added in Berlin or Munich. For Bullock's image of the naked girl, see Steichen, *The Family of Man*, 5.

21 On Steichen's referring to the image as 'Lilith', see his letter to Wynn Bullock, 28 December 1954, MoMA Exhs., 569.5, MoMA Archives. Steichen acknowledged receipt of the image negative and wrote, 'The child will be used as leading into the prologue of the creation. I am inclined to label the picture of the child as Lilith.'

22 Von Stetten to Martin, 29 September 1955, Photographs and Clippings, 1955–1956, RG306-FM, NACP. It is clear from the installation photographs that there were *two* photographs from the Warsaw Ghetto in Munich, but this note, like some of the other documents relating to the exhibition in Germany, refers to a single image. One of the Warsaw images, of the little boy with his arms raised, was also not included in the book of the exhibition. In a reply to von Stetten, Martin says she has 'the interesting story concerning the use of the Warsaw Ghetto photo in the Berlin showing' from Steichen but she gives no further details (Jackie Martin to Dorothea von Stetten, 22 November 1955, Box 1, Photographs and Clippings relating to *The Family of Man* exhibition, 1955–1956, Records of the US Information Agency, Record Group 306-FM, National Archives at College Park, MD).

23 Phillips to USIA Washington, DC, 6 February 1956, Box 3, Photographs and Clippings, 1955–1956, RG 306-FM, NACP.

24 James, *Common Ground*, 62.

25 Ibid.

26 See in particular the chapter on 'The Culture Industry: Enlightenment as Mass Deception', in Theodor Adorno and Max Horkheimer, *Dialectics of Enlightenment* (New York: Social Studies Association, 1944).

7 *The Family of Man*

Looking at the Photographs Now and and Remembering a Visit in the 1950s[1]

Werner Sollors

On 26 January 1955, after much anticipatory news coverage, an unusual exhibition opened at the Museum of Modern Art (MoMA) in New York. Widely debated, Edward Steichen's *The Family of Man* became extraordinarily popular, and its close to 500 photographs have been seen by around 10 million visitors at 100 or so sites worldwide. In his multi-year selection and planning process, Steichen had the help of photographer Wayne Miller; photographer, editor and advocate for social causes Dorothy Norman, who was close to Alfred Stieglitz but had never worked with Steichen before; poet Carl Sandburg, who was Steichen's brother-in-law; Walter-Gropius-trained architect Paul Rudolph; and Dutch avant-gardist painter Leo Lionni, who, some months after the opening, created an adaptation of the exhibition that served as catalogue and sold 5 million copies.

The fact that the show was offered free of admission at some places cannot account for its popularity, nor can support from the United States Information Agency (which was not even two years old at the time of the opening at the MoMA) explain the successes at Paris, Amsterdam, Berlin, Munich, Torino, Guatemala City, Mexico City, Johannesburg, Moscow, Seoul and Tokyo. I saw the exhibition as a teenager in 1958 in Frankfurt, where, in cooperation with the Amerika-Haus, it was held in the Haus des Deutschen Kunsthandwerks, the building where art publishers exhibited during the Frankfurt Book Fair (see illustration 68). I shall include memories of that visit and review a few photographs and features of *The Family of Man* more closely (both exhibition and book) against the background of reactions these images have received, while also thinking a bit more generally about the exhibition. I do not retread the familiar debates generated by Roland Barthes, Jacques Barzun, Hilton Kramer, Dwight MacDonald and Susan Sontag, debates that led to dismissals of *The Family of Man* as Cold War American middlebrow popular culture.

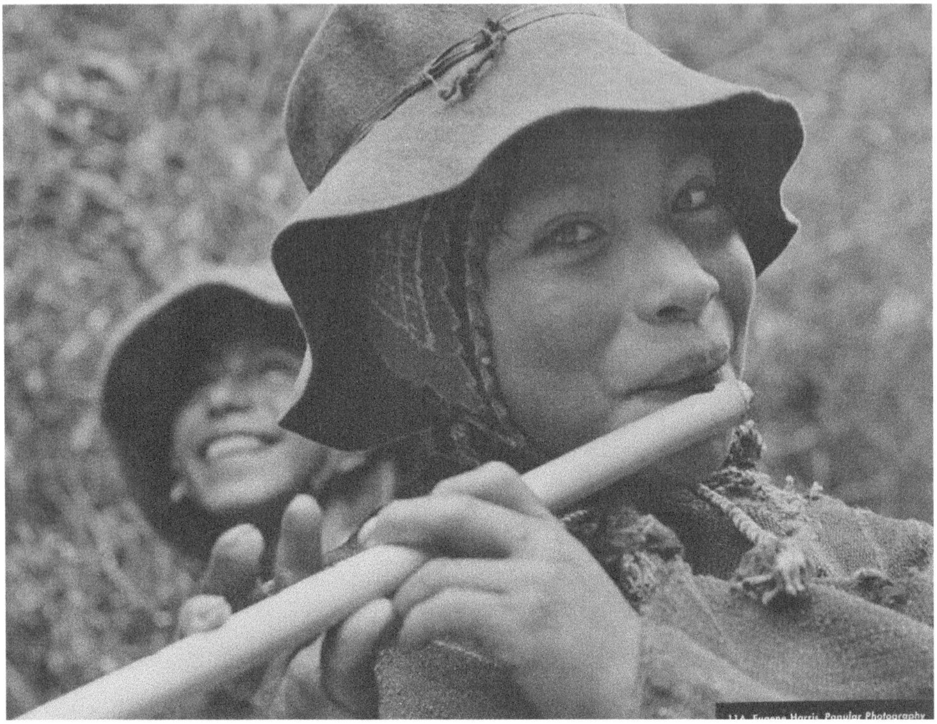

16 Eugene Harris, *Popular Photography.*

An abridged leaflet-sized excerpt from the book of the exhibition with the original cover image seemed cool and jazzy to me, with its bold strokes of colours, clear design and the striking photograph of the flute player at the centre, whose eyes seemed to follow you (see illustration 16). Latin American flute players having not yet flooded European cities, the cover image suggested freshness, and I kept this mini-catalogue in modernist company in a party basement, with jazz posters, a Matisse print, a wind-up gramophone with a 78 record of Dizzy Gillespie's *Thermodynamics* and a few complimentary early issues of the photo journal *Magnum*. I was thus surprised that a recent critic saw in 'Lionni's abstract design' a 'programmatic adherence to earthly and racial boundaries [...] as if the world were one continuous continental landmass, and each race its own nation, stepping forth into the global marketplace of neocolonialism'.[2] This critic did not comment on the photograph that ultimately was to appear and remain at the centre of the colourful abstract design, Eugene V. Harris's figure of the Peruvian piper and his companion that had first appeared in *Popular Photography*.

According to Steichen's own explanation, 'the gay Pan-like Peruvian boy playing the flute' expressed 'a little trace of mischief, but much sweetness – that's the song of life'.[34] The *New York Times* called the figure 'a cheerful young piper', and for Monique Berlier the 'photograph of a merry Peruvian flutist' conveyed an 'optimistic mood'.[5] The Berlin *Tagesspiegel* criticized the show with its 'photo of a Peruvian shepherd's boy playing the flute', for it 'represents something that lacks truth, namely that life consisted only of sweetness, of eternal youth, and of lovely and friendly melodies'.[6] When Peru's ambassador Fernando Berckemeyer visited the exhibition in Washington he admired 'the photograph of a Peruvian Indian tootling a primitive flute'.[7] The German modernist novelist Wolfgang Koeppen, whose novels *Pigeon in the Grass*, *The Hothouse* and *Death in Rome* and travelogue *Journey to America* have been translated into English and whose first post-war book was an account of a Jewish survivor that he edited, saw something else altogether when he visited the show in Munich in 1955:

> All images of the show, even the gayest, even the friendly flute-playing Peruvian shepherd boy on the cover of the catalogue, are faces of melancholy. They are that because they are true, because they have reached, through an originally technical process, the truth of all art. In any laugh there is mourning. Seeing that now is not saddening, as a widespread misconception has it; this truth of life and its representation in art only strengthen and elevate the senses. Only a laugh that lacked any grief would be depressing because it would be completely inhumane.[8]

The African American science fiction writer Samuel Delaney offered a different, more detailed reading:

> The exhibit's colophonic image was a closeup photographic portrait of a young Peruvian Indian – under the slouch hat and the embroidered cap beneath it, boy or girl, it's unclear to most Americans – playing a flute and looking slyly at the viewer, while a more distant, similarly dressed youngster in the background gazes joyously at the sky, as if apprehending the answering music of the Universe.[9]

Looking closely at the photograph, Delaney called attention to the sexual ambiguity of the flute player, as if addressing criticism of the show for what is now called heteronormativity.

The flutist's face appeared on exhibition posters, publicity materials and catalogue covers. In a 1955 USIA documentary, Steichen starts his tour in front of the flute player. The image also was displayed 'about 25' different times in the original exhibition and reappeared five times in the book of the exhibition.[10] Though it is present only once in the permanent Family of Man installation at Schlass Klierf (or château de Clervaux), a UNESCO Memory of the World site, it is reproduced by the roadside as one approaches Clervaux. Viewers thus kept encountering, and readers soon viewed, this portrait as 'a familiar face' among so many new faces.

It was furthermore an image placed next to several different aphorisms. When appearing, in the exhibition book, between photographs of a Japanese wedding ceremony (by Werner Bischof) and of a Czech marriage procession (by Robert Capa), accompanied by the Pueblo Indian saying, 'We shall be one person', the flute player may appear like a Cupid figure who brings lovers together (all the time looking enigmatically or whimsically at us) (FoM 14–15). The Czech wedding procession includes musicians, and the Peruvian enhances the presence of music here and throughout, functioning, as Katherine Hoffman wrote, like 'a musical leitmotif, helping to hold the exhibit together, and pointing to the role of music as a significant expressive universal language'.[11] Tellingly, the flute player does not appear in sequences on labour, suffering, or war.

Steichen wished *The Family of Man* to be understood in musical terms. He explained that 'This was not constructed as an exhibition. This was constructed like a piece of music, a sequence of movements – soft, violent – then ending up with joyousness.'[12] In his unsurpassed study, Eric Sandeen examined the musical–visual connection in the planning of the exhibition:

> This photograph of a Peruvian flute player was to be displayed at several stations in the exhibition. Miller placed [...] prints [...] wherever they seemed to fit. A caption from the exhibition, attributed to Plato, expressed the proper sentiment: 'Music and rhythm find their way into the secret places of the soul.' [...] As Miller remembers, some discussion had been made about wiring the exhibition space for recorded music, but the idea had been abandoned as distracting. Nevertheless, including another celebratory art form had appealed to the organizers.[13]

The photography show thus drew on 'another universal, nonverbal language' and found in the image of the flute player 'the missing accompaniment for the exhibition'.[14]

The placement of the photograph next to Bischof's shot of a Japanese wedding may carry additional significance, for Eugene Harris had brought Miller and Steichen the news of Bischof's death. Bischof and Harris 'had been photographing in Peru when Bischof died in an automobile accident. Harris brought with him some of his own work from South America, including the photograph of the flute player.'[15] Bischof's death could also add an undertone of mourning to the image, providing a reason for the melancholy Koeppen sensed in the Peruvian photograph.

Delaney, after outlining various themes of *The Family of Man*, similarly stated that 'the arrangement was musical, rather than directly didactic – which surely contributed to the exhibit's popularity'.[16] This distinguished the show from Weimar political exhibitions and didactic installations of the interwar period. Rob Kroes extended further the visual–musical link: 'If Steichen's hopes for the universal language and appeal of photographs resembled the appeal of music, the two media were merged in the image of a Peruvian flute player [...] his inviting eyes leading viewers along like a pied piper.'[17]

Pan-like, cheery, a pied piper with a little trace of mischief, but much sweetness, an embodiment of eternal youth, of the spirit of music, of lovely and friendly melodies, substituting for the missing musical accompaniment, yet also androgynous, looking slyly, or with inviting eyes, or seeming melancholy and perhaps serving as a reminder of Bischof's death – the key image of the Peruvian flute player is a close-up portrait of a subject who is also looking *at us* and seems to make us wonder about its contexts. None is given, for withholding contexts is programmatic in *The Family of Man.* Thus different moods can be read into the face, the other figure in the back, or the image as a whole. Since repetition creates familiarity, the feeling that we may still not really 'know' this face, yet begin to find it familiar, may also create some uneasiness, and perhaps that is why, in a well-researched survey of visitors to the Munich show, there was some grumbling that 'some pictures, the flute player, for instance, appear too often'.[18]

Installation

The repetition of the same image may create the effect of a musical leitmotif, but it also underlines Walter Benjamin's notion of the photograph's technological reproducibility and suggests the loss of the aura of an individual work of art. It was as if Steichen wilfully wanted to separate *The Family of Man*'s version of photography from any competition with painting or with art photography by stressing its pliability to be multiplied (ten versions of the entire exhibit were ultimately in existence) as well as by letting the photographs be enlarged, cropped and even spliced into each other, printed without borders on cheap paper and mounted, unmatted, without frames and unprotected by glass, on Lucite boards suspended from ceilings, giving Paul Rudolph at MoMA and designers at all subsequent shows, including Natalie Jacoby's installation at Clervaux, 'a real engineering task'.[19] Wayne Miller explained their procedure:

> [W]e were dealing with concepts of communication that depended upon size, juxtapositions, and sequences. Some of the photographs were quite large – ceiling to floor. The largest one was of Mt. Williamson by Ansel Adams. It was about 10 feet high and 12 feet wide. We used an English paper that came in 40-inch-wide rolls. We had to make it in four panels, and it was quite a trick to match the quality of each panel.[20]

I remember being surprised by the unusually suspended, different-sized prints at the exhibition I saw in Frankfurt and, researching that exhibition's background now, I learned that, even though it reused materials from an earlier Miró show, the installation costs were significant.[21]

That only photographs were shown must have shocked those visitors who expected a MoMA show to include paintings. This is illustrated by an episode Hilton Kramer reports of a 'stubborn lady' who 'demanded her admission refunded on the grounds that no paintings were on view'.[22] Aline Saarinen, reviewing *The*

Family of Man in a piece tellingly entitled 'The Camera versus the Artist', drew a sharp distinction between painting and photography: 'But photography is the marvelous, anonymous folk-art of our time.'[23] She may have echoed Steichen, who had encouraged amateur submissions and included some of their photography and who was quoted as saying at the Washington, DC, opening, 'If you photograph the things around you – the things you know and understand – you will open the door for a universal folk art, the greatest the world has seen, where everyone becomes an artist.'[24] Saarinen's attempt to separate painting from photography went further:

> A painting, however realistic, is always an abstraction. A photograph, no matter how abstract, is always basically actual. The painter starts with an empty canvas and creates an image seen or imagined. The photographer starts with the finished image and creates by selectivity.[25]

This drew the ire of Ben Shahn, a socially engaged painter who had also worked as Farm Security Administration photographer alongside Dorothea Lange and Walker Evans (one of Shahn's FSA photographs was included in *The Family of Man*). Responding to Saarinen in the *New York Times*, Shahn wrote, 'On behalf of the photographer I would take issue with the term "folk-art." Photography is a very highly developed art and keenly sophisticated. Both qualities are just the opposite of the earnest awkwardness and simplicity of folk-art.' Shahn proposed that 'painting is able to call much more out of the artist himself, and is able to contain a fuller expression of the artist's own capacities than is photography'. However, as if to stress that he was not criticizing Steichen through Saarinen, Shahn mentioned 'the magnificent photographic exhibition arranged by Edward Steichen at the Museum of Modern Art and called *The Family of Man*'.[26]

Steichen's collaborator and aphorism-co-provider Norman was clear about what distinguished Steichen's approach from painting as well as from art photography in the Stieglitz tradition:

> Stieglitz [...] consistently opposed the practice of permitting anyone else to make one's prints for one [...] [H]e objected increasingly to the use of artificial light, as to any and all enlargements – especially to 'insensitive' enlarging paper. He believed in contact printing, as in attempting to obtain the most supreme print quality possible [...] He rebelled against exhibitions, as against photographs themselves, based on literary ideas; against what he called 'sporadic' undertakings of any kind [...] He disapproved of reproductions not created with the utmost consideration for the 'sense of touch' of the originals from which they were made [...] And, as for the practice of making one's prints for reproduction only, this was virtually inconceivable to him.[27]

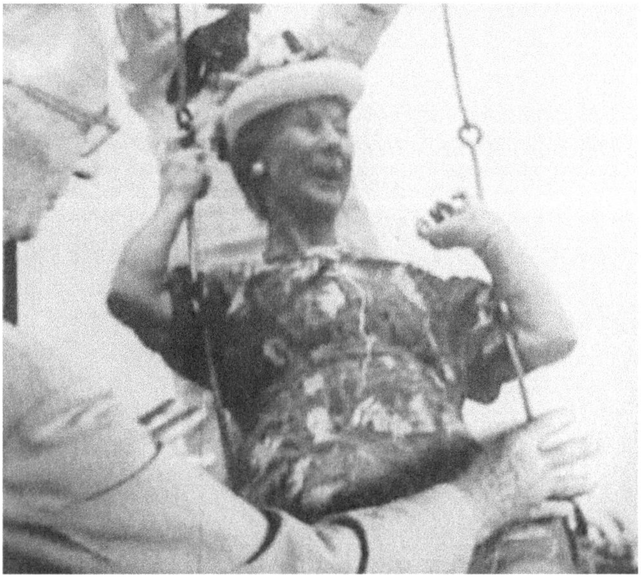

17 Film still from *La Grande Famille des Hommes*, film by USIS, 1956.

Norman summarized that 'almost everything to which Stieglitz most objected was done in one form or another in connection with the *Family of Man* exhibit'. Indeed, Steichen went so far as to mount two life-sized photographs, Kosti Ruohomoa's older couple on a swing (see illustration 17) and Brassaï's young couple kissing while on a swing boat, on two sides of a panel that, swing-like, could be moved back and forth. In a USIA film, Steichen himself sets the panel in motion.[28] The sequence of children from around the world playing ring-around-the-rosy was itself mounted on a carousel. The pregnancy-and-childbirth unit was placed in an installation reminiscent of an obstetrics ward. Steichen and Miller also included a mirror in a series of close-ups on faces, thus literalizing the metaphor they had offered for the show, conceived, as Steichen wrote, 'as a mirror of the universal elements and emotions in the everydayness of life – as a mirror of the essential oneness of mankind throughout the world'.[29] They removed the mirror after two weeks, because it seemed 'corny and wrong'.[30]

Captionlessness and Crowds

Except for the general aphorisms, photographs were presented without captions, dates or names of the artists; the book of the exhibition identified images by name of country, photographer and venue in which the photograph had previously appeared, but also gave no titles, dates or other details. In the exit interviews of the Munich audience, 7% complained about 'inappropriate captions and too meager text' and asked for names of photographers and even for cameras used, lens openings and exposures.[31] Ironically, by violating the rules of art photography, Steichen made museums and the broader public more receptive to it. In 1959, when the *Family of Man* was still circulating, MoMA opened a room devoted to photography. The article reporting it referred back to Steichen's show.[32]

Withholding contextual information intensifies the concentrated gaze at each image itself (rather than at identifying signage). The cover image of the flutist gave us a first sense that 'cold' readings of a single image may diverge from each other, perhaps more than those of fully identified photographs. Uncertainty also makes the viewer search for substitute contexts elsewhere – and in *The Family of Man*, that elsewhere is in other images and their arrangement in 'sequences'.

Entering the exhibition or opening the book of the exhibition, the first image after the Peruvian musician is Pat English's monumental photograph of a crowd in England (see illustration 35). English transforms the huge image of the crowd effectively into wallpaper-like material that Steichen had pasted on the portal through which one entered the exhibition, the 'entrance arch'. It also appears as backdrop to D. A. Pennebaker's 1959 documentary of the Moscow show, *Opening an Exhibition*.[33] It is in front of this image that Steichen signed a copy of the exhibition book for then Vice President Richard Nixon; a publicity photograph outlined the Peruvian ambassador against English's British crowd.[34] Lionni adapted English's photograph as decorative end papers of the book, a sea of faces looking toward the left of the viewer and forming a rug-like design when one squints or steps back.[35] Were they looking for Queen Elizabeth at her 1953 coronation? Even though one can make out some people who appear to be looking at us when we zoom in on the photograph, its primary function seems to be to highlight the difference between photographic portraits and photographic backdrops. This is neatly captured in the co-presence of flute player and English crowd. By the way, I did not remember the English crowd photograph at all, even though it was so prominently displayed at the exhibition.

However, I do remember another crowd photograph very vividly, Andreas Feininger's telephoto view of Fifth Avenue, which was blown up to such a large format that one could easily see the numbered street signs, the flattened cars, partly obscured in the side streets, and the faces of a whole number of pedestrians on the upside-down V-shaped, 15-people-wide sidewalk (FoM 142 and 204) (see illustration 18). Its original caption in *Life* magazine was 'Anonymity in a Fifth Avenue Crowd', yet I remember this image as holding a kind of cosmopolitan promise of the intensity of a really crowded metropolis, and the one-way arrows, even the parking prohibitions, seemed attractively exotic from the point of view of Frankfurt, where traffic was still light. Had I seen the photograph's original caption, I might have been prompted to perceive it differently – or to forget it. (I thus experienced the advantage of captionlessness.) Leafing through the book of the exhibition now, I noticed the rhythmic recurrence of crowd photographs, with the Paris opera by Walter Sanders, Edmund Bert Gerard's American indoor meeting and Maria Bordy's UN General Assembly (FoM 100, 175, and 184–5). Framed by the endpapers (or the exhibition's entrance arch), crowd scenes surround all other images.

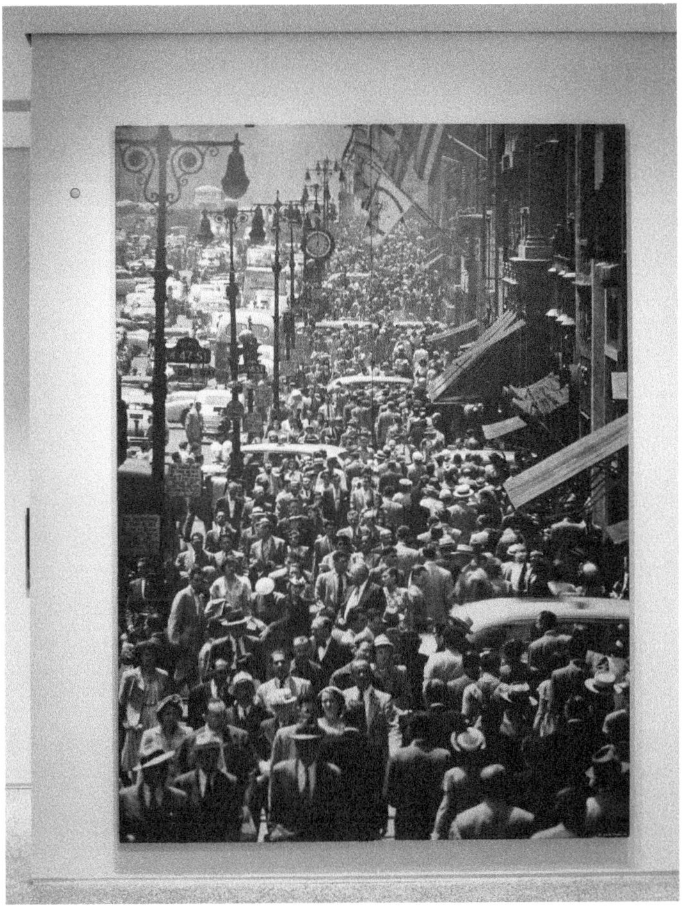

18 ***The Family of Man*** **installation at Clervaux Castle. Theme 'Relationships': Andreas Feininger.**

Montage?

The close-up and the crowd scene are also features of film language, according to Siegfried Kracauer, for they are among the truly 'cinematic' qualities that distinguish film from what he dismissively calls 'canned theatre'.[36] Norman noted that *The Family of Man* was 'more related to the motion picture tradition than to that of Stieglitz – Steichen having functioned as a kind of director'.[37] Is the sequence of images for the visitor of *The Family of Man* like that for the viewer of film montage? Lev Kuleshov undertook the famous experiment of cutting a close-up of a man's face, first against a bowl of soup, then against a dead girl in a coffin, and finally, against a woman reclining on a divan: and in the first case, viewers perceived the man's face expressing hunger, in the second, mourning, and in the third, happiness.[38] Has the form of *The Family of Man* followed a filmic grammar and forced viewers, by withholding historical and authorial information and guiding them through a montage of images, to read pictures in sequence, as in a film? There is a storyline that takes the viewer from natural grandeur, sexual love, marriage, birth, motherhood, childhood, family peace, family struggle, fatherhood, family as institution, work, play, music, dance, scholarship, science, old age, death, loneliness, mourning, suffering, art, law, group communication and politics to violence, then back to young love and ending with children.[39] The path through the exhibition could thus mark the viewer's passive reception of that narrative line, with a big arrow propelling them through the 'thematic tunnel' of the show.[40]

Perhaps on the most crowded days – Washington's Birthday 1955 at the MoMA, or pretty much any day at the Moscow showing – visitor flow was regulated this way. But as Fred Turner has stressed, using the floor plan published in *Popular Photography* in 1955, viewers had many different options of traversing the exhibition once they had passed the birth room and before they reached the eight-foot-tall colour transparency of the atomic explosion, the 'single image that every viewer had to confront before moving on'.[41] The fear of atomic annihilation was a sensation Steichen did want to convey, even heavy-handedly, but otherwise, as Turner writes, 'each image offered a viewer a potential moment of identification' and the ensemble of images by which the viewers were surrounded on all sides encouraged them

> [...] to rearrange [them] within their own psyches. In the process of aggregating and organizing these images, visitors could, at least in theory, engage in a degree of self-formation not open to citizens of authoritarian regimes. Most important, they could emerge from this process as psychologically whole and self-directing.[42]

It was as if Steichen left Kuleshov's different montage options available to viewers who could arrange them in many different sequences, and Bayer's notion of the surround view strengthened this feature.[43]

Some reviewers indicate how they recombined and respliced images against each other, and imagined other changes to the arrangement. Rolf Seeliger, for example, wanted more didacticism: he found that the show tells viewers, 'All of you [...] this is what you are like!' But Seeliger would have found it better if the admonition had been, 'All of you [...] you must change so that things will be different!'[44] In order to achieve that, Seeliger proposed that there should be more contrastive groupings, for example the Chinese boy with the bowl and the Diane Arbus photograph of father and son reading the newspaper; or the dead soldier next to the UN plenary meeting; or the shocking photograph of the Warsaw Ghetto next to the carnival party; and Anne Frank's belief in human goodness should be complemented by the information that she died after suffering terribly in the Bergen-Belsen concentration camp. Turner is right in suggesting that viewers had many choices of looking at single photographs in isolation, of following the offer of the groupings Steichen made, or of making altogether new combinations and contrasts.

The Bomb

All black-and-white photographs were ultimately spliced against the vast colour slide representing the threat of total destruction. (This may be one source for Koeppen's melancholy readings.) Fred Turner concludes that revisiting this varied, free and anti-authoritarian exhibition with its hope for tolerance and peace, permits viewers today 'to glimpse a holistic, individualistic, utopian vision that would animate the countercultural outbursts to come'.[45] I remember leaving the exhibition and talking with my parents about the threat of nuclear war, and I want to remember that I saw the photograph of an atomic explosion. When I now look at the book of the exhibition, which contains the image of the atomic explosion only in one of Wayne Miller's 'photographic footnotes' (an imaginative new genre!), I am no longer sure whether the conversation about the bomb had supplied a cover memory.

Melancholy

One image rarely commented on is Clemens Kalischer's photograph of a young boy with a dog on a stoop. Koeppen found that in this 'idyll on a stone staircase' it is 'the face of the dog' that makes it melancholy. 'He is too serious, the little dog, but it is only this ounce of bitterness that turns this photograph into a document of existence and makes it unique.' Koeppen's view of Dan Wiener's portrait of a judge is similarly melancholy: 'it is only in the stern face of the judge who is leafing thoughtfully through the legal code, in his deep sad eyes that have looked into the abyss, that the surprising, but clearly perceptible possibility of joy creates the beauty of the picture'. By contrast, the Polish poet Witold Wirpsza strikes a formalist note, his protest against reading photographs in thematic sequences rather than as single works, and he focuses on the V and W shapes he notices in the judge's face, hands, and law book.

> The majority of furrows on his face; symmetrically; they're arranged
> In an inverted V; from the eyes, from the nose, from the mouth. The
> hands, too; symmetrically; in the letter
> V, uninverted (on open volumes of codices, i.e., on
> Very broadly stretched V's). Attorney? Prosecutor?
> Judge? Toga: lawyer. A concerned (exhausted?) actor. Acting,
> In the old parlance: comedia (intending no
> Offence) is recorded in the little black flecks
> In the horizontal furrows of his forehead (from heavy lifting;
> symmetrically;
> The eyebrows). But in comedia (how else to save mankind from
> Evil? The punishment ennobles the society, does it not? Everything
> Depends upon the crumpled little aluminum idol of interpretation,
> right,

Friend?), and so, in comedia (several times repeating
The word: comedia), so in comedia he fades, he melts away;
Without symmetry; concern; then only an exhausting (formerly
In parentheses) remains: this gerund is not spelled
With a 'V.'
                At his neck the photograph shows a very
Busy tie.[46]

In another brief reading of the photograph of the factory woman's hands, taken by the Albanian American Gjon Mili, Koeppen comments, 'There are the hands of a worker. She assembles bolts. She probably gets paid on a piece basis. Her hands have become inhuman in their agility, the gripping tools of a robot on whom the rudiment of human features seems particularly sinister' (FoM 78). Mili was represented with several photographs and was among the more experimental artists in the exhibition, working early on with an electronic flash that he could set off in rapid repetition, thus creating single- and multiple-exposure 'stroboscopic' photographs (FoM C 101, 104, 189).[47]

Childbirth and Family

When Koeppen looked at Miller's 'image of birth, the child still connected by the umbilical cord with the mother', he praised it for being 'indiscreet' in what it observes: 'But it is an indiscretion that previously only the poet permitted himself who created the image of man out of himself, and it is legitimate because it is true.'[48]

It is another photograph that I vividly remember. In 1958, pregnancies were secretive affairs and seeing a child being born was simply a cultural impossibility. I had seen fetuses in formaldehyde jars in Frankfurt's natural history museum, but Miller's photograph was an unveiling for me as a teenager. The newborn being lifted up diagonally, reflecting the photographer's flashlight, the enormous umbilical cord, the doctor's shiny rubber gloves and the mother's (or nurse's?) gloved hands reaching out for the child – the fabric of bed sheet and doctor's coat, mask and head covering forming the background for most of the photograph – made me share a private, perhaps tabooed, world in a dramatic, fleeting moment. (I am wondering now, whether apart from my idiosyncratic reaction to Feininger's Fifth Avenue, my memory apparatus follows Steichen's script in that I think I recall best the flute player, childbirth and nuclear explosion photographs.) Learning that Wayne Miller, the father of David, the child being born, photographed his own wife, and that the child's grandfather oversaw the delivery, gave the image new familial contexts.[49] Miller (who was like an adopted son to Steichen) included his family lavishly, for example in that photographic footnote in front of the atomic mushroom cloud: Family of – the artists' own families? This sense of family is strengthened by a photograph of Steichen's own mother – probably the only one that is dated – spliced, in the exhibition book, into a decorative image of a wheat field.

Surround View

At the centre of the exhibition were the 'Family of Man central theme pictures', globally conceived sequences on labour, eating, singing, dancing, drinking, playing, learning, thinking and teaching. Here was perhaps the heart of intuitively sensing human sameness despite all the differences. And here viewers had many choices, as Turner stressed, in facing the many images that surrounded them in a carefully constructed three-dimensional environment:

> In a single glance, viewers could take in a Japanese farm family in traditional dress, a polygamous African family outside their hut, two images of rural Italian farm families, and a multigenerational, white American family, posed around a woodstove, with portraits of nineteenth-century ancestors on the wall behind them. Seen individually, these images could be read as stereotypical depictions of 'primitive' Africans, 'tradition-bound' Japanese and Italians, and 'hillbilly' Americans. But seen together, as they were meant to be, the images *challenged* stereotypes. Far from privileging either whites or Americans, the photographs in fact equated them with two groups suffering extraordinary prejudice in America at that moment – Africans (and, implicitly, African Americans) and our former enemies, the Japanese – and with our other former enemies, the Italians [...]
>
> Moreover, viewers encountered those images at eye level, overhead, and well below the waist. They were in fact surrounded by the families of the globe.[50]

Unlike in film, they could linger at some images and hurry by others. And readers and reviewers have taken both routes.

Let us follow Turner then, linger a bit at the 'learning' sequence and examine a photographic pair in the exhibition's book, Alfred Eisenstaedt's photograph of the Czech auditorium and the neighbouring image from Bechuanaland by (Pat English's husband) Nat Farbman (see illustration 19). (The exhibit's arrangement was different: the photographs were not right next to each other and displayed in different sizes (FoM 120–1).) Samuel Delaney literally moved into these two pages with a lecture-long exegesis, questioning the implicit claim that, like their format, 'on some level, the contents of the two pictures are *also* identical', as they represent education. His reading takes him to a series of binary opposites (night–day, naked–clothed, listening–taking notes, camera looking down–looking up, etc.). These opposites suggest a development from left to right, but then Delaney also reads it from right to left, and concludes that *The Family of Man*

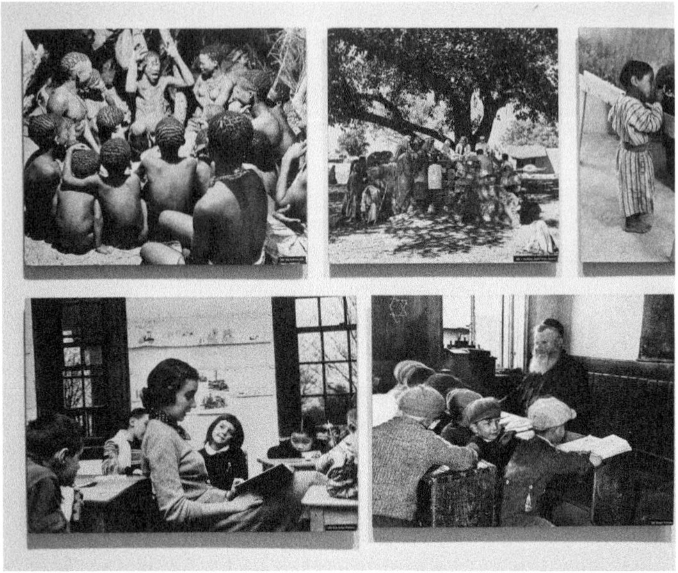

19 *The Family of Man* installation at Clervaux Castle. Theme 'Learning, thinking and teaching': (from left to right) Nat Farbman, J. De Pietro (John Philips), Ruth Orkin and Roman Vishniac.

is 'not a reproduction of the world' but 'a work of art'.[51] Here is an extract from Delaney's iconographic approach to Eisenstaedt:

> The right-hand photograph [...] shows a deeply raked, stadium-style lecture hall, suggesting a European university, in which we see, from slightly off center, ten rows of alert, university-aged young people (with another row of standees crowded at the back, bulging down into the single aisle visible at the far right of the photo). A high, undraped window, even further to the right, lets in the daylight that suffuses the faces of the fifteen-to-twenty odd students nearest. But these are only a fraction of the hundred or more we see in their barely curved rows throughout the well-lit lecture hall. All give their attention – or busily take notes, textbooks and notebooks open before them – to an unseen speaker, somewhere in the lecture well, outside the frame, somewhere off to the lower right [...] All the students appear to be white. The young men wear jackets and ties. The young women are, for the most part, neatly attired. Four of them, by my count, wear hats. Several overcoats hang forward over the lowest curved row of desks, as if the young folks have hurried to the lecture on a winter's day. The lowest figure in the right-hand corner, a woman, leans back, somewhat uncharacteristically. She wears a man's white shirt over a dark T-shirt and a wristwatch. Her arms too are folded beneath her breasts, putting her in pointed dialogue with the

> young African woman in the other picture – sophisticated Western bohemian skepticism (today most American students would read it as 'dykey') vs. smiling, if joking, native approval (in her innocent nudity, surely the young African woman is heterosexual, or at least innocently polymorphous; as are the two male adolescents).[52]

Reading this image (as he read the flute player) in terms of disturbing the charge of heteronormativity, Delaney misreads the girls' outerwear (which looks like a raincoat over a dark pullover to me) and misses the politics of a medical school classroom in Czechoslovakia recently turned Communist, with so many female students.

Holocaust

The Warsaw Ghetto photograph hit a particularly raw nerve in Germany in the 1950s[53] (see illustrations 16, 33). (I have seen it so many times in the meantime that I am not sure now whether I remember it from *The Family of Man*.) It gets mentioned by all German reviews I found and provoked adverse reactions in the survey for its 'presentation of Germans in an unfavorable light'. One respondent wrote, 'There was one feature of the exhibition which I didn't like. That is, that they showed a picture of Warsaw, of Jewish inhabitants and of armed members of the SS, while refraining from showing atrocities committed by other nations.'[54] This photograph and that of the 'a-bomb explosion' were the two images least liked by 7 to 8% of the people surveyed.

Max Horkheimer, who gave the opening remarks at the Frankfurt exhibition, only *hints* at the Warsaw photograph when he states that 'what does seem to defy any identification at all is that which is completely and utterly evil, of which there are at least two instances in the exhibition. This kind of evil arouses indignation.' (May one assume that the other instance was the photograph of the hydrogen bomb?) Wolfgang Koeppen accounts for this image more fully as the embodiment of the lowest rung of hell, as part of what he calls 'images of inhumanity':

> [T]here is the dark panel of a tragedy, the work of an unknown German photographer: Jews are being deported from the burning Warsaw ghetto toward annihilation. The Jews, children among them, are the human beings in the picture. They preserve man's dignity, or else the view that deeply shocks would be unbearable. For in the front of the photograph stands the monster. He likes to do what he does. He feels in his uniform. He holds his pistol at the ready. If there is a hell – he is its son.

Yet the inclusion of this photograph, which inspired this reading and upset some viewers in Germany, seemed hypocritical to some critics who deplored the absences of true atrocity photographs from the Time-Life archives.[55] The Warsaw photograph, which spoke to many without contextualization, is actually one about which quite a bit of context is known – though the German photographer who took it remains unknown. It comes from the Stroop Report, a grim parody of the family photo album. The United States Holocaust Memorial Museum Photo Archives identified some of the subjects, Yehudit Neyer (born Tolub), her mother-in-law, her daughter and her father, Avraham Neyer (the only one to survive).[56] The SS man on the right, whom Koeppen saw as the inhabitant of hell, has not been identified, though the SD trooper pictured in the more famous Stroop Report photograph that shows a little boy with his hands up was SS-Rottenführer Josef Bloesche. Polish authorities identified and found him, using this photograph; he was tried by a Polish court in 1969, sentenced to death and executed in July of that year.[57] Does this context change what we see in the photograph?

Conclusion

As Monica Bravo put it, 'If nothing else, Steichen won for [...] photography a mass audience.'[58] Since *The Family of Man* was most likely also the first photographic exhibition I visited, I can say that I was, and am, among that mass – though I don't remember any crowds at the exhibit. In fact, despite a vast and costly advertising campaign that included all Frankfurt movie theatres, the show I saw, running from 25 October to 29 November 1958, attracted a far lower than expected number of visitors, forcing the Kuratorium Kulturelles Frankfurt to cover a substantial deficit.[59]

The progressive aspects of *The Family of Man* are impressive. It has long been known that its intellectual ancestry goes back to Bauhaus displays and political exhibitions of the interwar period whose didactic approach Steichen modified; that it drew on, and included, FSA photography; that Wayne Miller began his career with a project on the Negro in Chicago that connected him with sociologist Horace Cayton and that he worked for *Ebony* magazine; that black photographers Gordon Parks and Roy DeCarava were included; and that Native American texts and images were also much in evidence. Gerd Hurm has traced the feminist origins of Steichen's project back to the Declaration of Sentiments. Katharina Fackler, arguing against John Szarkowski, has shown that *The Family of Man* influenced the photography for the 'War on Poverty' of the Johnson administration.[60] Though the report that Walter Ulbricht was intrigued by *The Family of Man* does nothing for its progressive credentials, it does suggest that the exhibition transcended Cold War East–West boundaries.[61] The fact that Bertolt Brecht visited the show at the Hochschule für Bildende Künste in West Berlin on 7 October 1955 is more noteworthy (see illustration 4).[62] Part of a progressive and multi-ethnic American tradition, then, *The Family of Man* popularized photography as a social medium. I felt encouraged by the show in my teenage pacifist modernist leanings and in my wish for global understanding and greater social equality.

Reviewing *The Family of Man*'s reception more broadly for this chapter, I found it encouraging to read Ben Shahn calling the exhibition 'magnificent' and found myself in agreement with Max Horkheimer's assessment that *The Family of Man* 'sides with human beings yet at the same time does not absolve them of guilt; it inspires tolerance of weakness, but not of barbarism'.[63] Horkheimer was happy to be invited to give the opening remarks in Frankfurt to the show that he already knew well at the time.[64] I particularly liked Horkheimer's term '*Selbigkeit*' in his remarks, referring to the discovery of 'identity' in the sense of sameness across social divides:

> However manifold the objects and figures depicted may be, however different the ages, genders, nations, tribes, people and objects, it is precisely in this great variety and individuality, in which the smallest difference is crucial, that the viewer experiences his identity [*Selbigkeit*].[65]

Seeing the photographs, like perceiving all things properly, has its mimetic elements. But that has its limits – not for reasons of cultural relativism but of ethics – Horkheimer writes:

> In this exhibition our mimetic powers seem to desert us when we have to identify with what is radically evil, although there is no doubt that it exists. While the viewer may develop an understanding for what is quite alien to him, certainly for the person in the dock, for the pariah or for a boisterous or frivolous individual, he simply cannot identify with the person whose aim is to cause fear and terror. And this only proves that, however great the suggestive powers of these pictures, however much they may stimulate feelings of identification, the exhibition nevertheless insists on the consciousness of the freedom and the responsibility of the individual.[66]

Kracauer, near the end of his *Theory of Film,* also invokes *Mimesis*, Erich Auerbach's in his case, who observed that the random moments of life represented by the modern novel concern 'the elementary things which men in general have in common' and suggested that 'the differences between men's ways of life and forms of thought have already lessened [...] It is still a long way to a common life of mankind on earth, but the goal begins to be visible.' And here Kracauer thinks of photography as the ideal medium for this task:

> Auerbach might have added that the task of rendering visible mankind on its way toward this goal is reserved for the photographic media; they alone are in a position to record the material aspects of common daily life in many places. It is not by coincidence that the idea of *The Family of Man* was conceived by a born photographer. And one reason for the world-wide response to Edward Steichen's exhibition must be laid precisely to the fact that it consists of photographs – images bound to authenticate the reality of the vision they feature.[67]

The contemporary German philosopher Wolfgang Welsch recognized the utopianism of the show when he expressed his belief that the transcultural age might, with its mixing of patterns of culture, bring along a reduction of cultural differences: 'Perhaps we will, in the age of transculturality,' Welsch wrote, 'truly come closer to the old dream of a "Family of Man."'[68] Wolfgang Koeppen's summary view may serve as conclusion:

> The exhibition has much to teach. It teaches pride. Pride in human beauty, wisdom, goodness, decency, and labor. It teaches humility. Humility at human limitations, human poverty, and suffering. Above all, the photographs teach fraternity. The improbably spruced up socialite mother from *Vogue* is the sister of the Negro mom in blue jeans, stretched out with her child on the bare ground. Not only the world but also man is indivisible. In this photography exhibition we look at a mirror. We recognize ourselves. We are not alone, and each one of us is there for, is responsible for, everyone else, just as the Bible already put it with the question: 'Cain, where is thy brother Abel?'[69]

The Family of Man may be as much needed today as it was in the 1950s.

Notes

1 I thank Gerd Hurm and Shamoon Zamir for inviting me, and Anke Reitz, Jean Back, Bob Krieps, and Odile Simon, Universität Trier, NYUAD, and the Centre national de l'audiovisuel for their support of this project. Helpful archivists include Claudia Schüßler at the Institut für Stadtgeschichte Frankfurt, Dr Ursula Keitz at the Städtische Galerie im Lenbachhaus München, Philip Koch at the Wolfgang-Koeppen-Archiv Greifswald, and Judith Cohen, Director of Photographic Services at the United States Holocaust Memorial Museum.

2 Allan Sekula, 'The Traffic in Photographs', *Art Journal* 41, no. 1 (1981): 23.

3 Judith Crist, 'Modern Museum to Show "Family of Man" Photos', *New York Herald Tribune*, 23 January 1955, 24.

4 A journalist in *Photo-Presse* described the photograph's effect: 'Zwischen all dem Ernsten und Heiteren tönt unaufhörlich die Ewige Melodie des Lebens. Der Strom des Lebens fließt weiter, unbekümmert um Einzelschicksale.' H. Starke, 'Das Menschenleben in 503 Photos', *Photo-Presse* 10, no. 43 (1955): 4, quoted in Schmidt-Linsenhoff, 'Verleugnete Bilder, *The Family of Man* und die Shoa', in *The Family of Man 1955–2001*, ed. Jean Back and Schmidt-Linsenhoff (Marburg: Jona-Verlag, 2004), 92.

5 Jacob Deschin, '"Family of Man": Panoramic Show Opens at Modern Museum', *New York Times*, 30 January 1955, X17; Monique Berlier, '*The Family of Man:* Readings of an Exhibition', in *Picturing the Past: Media, History, and Photography*, ed. Bonnie Brennen and Hanno Hardt (Urbana: University of Illinois Press, 1999), 215.

6 Cited in 'Visitors' Reactions to the "Family of Man" Exhibit', Report No. 225, Series 2 ([Bonn]: Research Staff, Office of Public Affairs, American Embassy, 23 January 1956): 82. Institut für Stadtgeschichte Frankfurt.

7 Ruth Shumaker, 'It's a Wonderful One World, Steichen and Guests Agree at Exhibit', *Washington Post*, 1 July 1955, 59.

8 Wolfgang Koeppen, 'Der Kamera entgeht nichts', clipping from *Süddeutsche Zeitung*, 21 November 1955, 276, Wolfgang Koeppen Archiv Greifswald M56 (my translation).

9 Samuel R. Delaney and Matthew Cheney, *The Jewel-Hinged Jaw: Notes on the Language of Science Fiction* (Middletown, CT: Wesleyan University Press, 2009), 'Appendix A: Midcentury', 204.

10 Judith Crist, *New York Herald Tribune*, 23 January 1955, 24; Edward Steichen, *The Family of Man* (New York: Maco Publishing and the Museum of Modern Art, 1955), 8, 15, 37, 97, 187. Hereafter the book of the exhibition is cited in the text as 'FoM'.

11 Katherine Hoffman, 'Sowing the Seeds / Setting the Stage: Steichen, Stieglitz, and *The Family of Man*', *History of Photography* 29, no. 4 (Winter 2005): 321.

12 'Modern Museum', *New York Herald Tribune*, 23 January 1955, 24.

13 Eric J. Sandeen, *Picturing an Exhibition: The Family of Man and 1950s America* (Albuquerque: University of New Mexico Press, 1995), 45. The Plato quotation may have been made up, perhaps by Dorothy Norman.

14 Sandeen, *Picturing an Exhibition*, 45.

15 Ibid., 45.

16 Delaney, 'Appendix A', 204.

17 Rob Kroes, *Photographic Memories: Private Pictures, Public Images, and American History* (Hanover, NH: Dartmouth College Press, 2007), 118–19. See also Hoffman, 'Sowing the Seeds', 321: 'Steichen's *Family of Man* exhibition may be viewed as a *Gesamtkunstwerk* as it incorporated literary and poetic elements, drama, visual arts and dance motifs. For example, the Peruvian flute player, a photograph taken by Eugene Harris and published in *Popular Photography*, was repeated several times in the exhibition and was the cover image for the catalogue [...] It may be viewed as a musical leitmotif, helping to hold the exhibit together, and pointing to the role of music as a significant expressive universal language. The accompanying caption for one of the piper images, from St.-John Perse, stated: "Music and rhythm find their swing, sweetness, to the last palpitation of the evening and the breeze"! Four pages later, music is evoked again, in a quotation from Plato: "Music and rhythm find their way into the secret places of the soul."'

18 Some 4% of visitors, according to 'Visitors' Reactions', 25.

19 'Assembly of Steichen Art Exhibit Provides Real Engineering Task', *Washington Post*, 17 June 1955, 22.

20 Wayne Miller, 'World War II and the Family of Man', in *Witness in Our Time: Working Lives of Documentary Photographers*, 2nd edn, ed. Ken Light (Washington, DC: Smithsonian Books, 2010), 51.

21 Kuratorium Kulturelles Frankfurt (KKF) V 96 / 54: letter to Fa. Peter & Schauss, 8 October 1958. Interestingly, in a memorandum of a 18 September 1958 meeting, architect Rolf Volhard summarized that this already quite pathos-laden and sentimental show should not be intensified with additional effects in presentation. Institut für Stadtgeschichte Frankfurt.

22 Hilton Kramer, 'Exhibiting the Family of Man: "The World's Most Talked about Photographs"', *Commentary* 20, no. 4 (October 1955): 364.

23 Aline B. Saarinen, 'The Camera versus the Artist', *New York Times*, 6 February 1955, X10; also reprinted in 'The Controversial Family of Man', *Aperture* 3, no. 1 (1955): 7.

24 'It's a Wonderful One World', *Washington Post*, 1 July 1955, 59.

25 Saarinen, 'Camera', X10.

26 Ben Shahn, 'Art versus the Camera' (Letter), *New York Times*, 13 February 1955, 123.

27 Dorothy Norman, in 'The Controversial Family of Man', special section of *Aperture* 3, no. 1 (1955): 12.

28 At http://www.ina.fr/video/VDD11021509 9:05–9:24 (accessed 10 January 2016). The respective images appear in C114 and 115.

29 Steichen, *The Family of Man*, Introduction, 4.

30 Fred Turner, '*The Family of Man* and the Politics of Attention in Cold War America', *Public Culture* 24, no. 1 (2012): 80.

31 'Visitors' Reactions', 25.

32 'Museum Plans a Gallery for Photography', *New York Times*, 22 November 1959, X19.

33 Online at http://vdownload.eu/watch/14038295-opening-in-moscow-1959-d-a-pennebaker.html (accessed 15 May 2015).

34 'Portfolio', 357; Eric J. Sandeen, 'The International Reception of *The Family of Man*', *History of Photography* 29, no. 4 (2005): 348, shows that Berckemeyer was also somewhat awkwardly placed right in front of Nina Leen's large picture of a multigenerational American family. This was part of Steichen's strategy of assembling photographs of people looking at *Family of Man* images, or as Steichen put it, 'people in the audience looked at the pictures, and the people in the pictures looked back at them. They recognized each other.' Quoted in Kevin Salemme, 'Chasing Shadows: Steichen's Dream of the Universal', *History of Photography* 29, no. 4 (2005): 377.

35 Asking Google Images to search for the endpaper photograph, one gets back images of ornamental structures. Only when feeding Google Images an enlarged detail, does it return us to photography – in fact, to *The Family of Man*.

36 *Theory of Film: The Redemption of Physical Reality* (Princeton, NJ: Princeton University Press, 1997), 154–5.

37 Norman, 'Controversial', 16.

38 See Pudovkin's account and https://www.youtube.com/watch?v=_gGI3LJ7vHc (accessed 10 January 2016).

39 I am here following Delaney's neat enumeration of the contents of the exhibition.

40 Turner, '*The Family of Man*', 76.

41 Ibid., 80. The image has been identified as that of the detonation of test *Mike*, Operation Ivy, Enewetak Atoll, 31 October 1952. See John O'Brian, 'The Nuclear Family of Man', *Asia Pacific Journal: Japan Focus*, http://japanfocus.org/-John-O_Brian/2816/article.html (accessed 10 January 2016).

42 Turner, '*The Family of Man*', 84.

43 Koeppen, 'Kamera'.

44 Rolf Seeliger, 'Testament der Photolinse', unidentified newspaper clipping in 'Pressespiegel', Städtische Galerie München.

45 Turner, '*The Family of Man*', 84.

46 Witold Wirpsza, '4. Prawo', in *Komentarze do fotografii The Family of Man* (Kraków: Wydawnictwo Literackie, 1962), 14. Translation by Benjamin Paloff in this volume.

47 Mili also directed the visually and sonically excellent jazz film *Jammin' the Blues*, https://www.youtube.com/watch?v=E4Or9ospJrU (accessed 10 January 2016).

48 Koeppen, 'Kamera'.

49 Miller, 45. He also refers to the exhibit's photographs as 'family', 51.

50 Turner, '*The Family of Man*', 78, 79.

51 Delaney, 'Appendix A', 216.

52 Ibid., 212. Compare Max Horkheimer's brief comment: 'Even the funny old magician from Bechuanaland, who has evoked so much laughter among the women and boys, has something about him that every one of us could have. No less than the Sicilian and Japanese peasants or the students in the lecture hall or the audience at the Paris Opera.'

53 The photographer Gabriele Nothelfer suggested that the 1955 Berlin visitors were grateful for the absence of atrocity photographs, cited in Schmidt-Linsenhoff, 'Verleugnete Bilder', 90.

54 'Visitors' Reactions'.

55 See Schmidt-Linsenhoff, 'Verleugnete Bilder'.

56 Desig #481.902 W/S #26536 CD # 0230, United States Holocaust Memorial Museum, Washington, DC.

57 Information provided by Judith Cohen. This second photograph is now the subject of monograph-length studies. See, for example, Dan Porat, *The Boy: A Holocaust Story* (New York: Hill & Wang, 2010).

58 Monica Bravo, 'Aesthetics of Reception? A Jaussian Reading of *The Family of Man*', *Art Criticism* 14, no. 1 (2009): 26.

59 KKF V 96 / 54: see LUMINA-Propaganda-Liste, 1 August 1958, and letters of 4 November 1958 and 19 January and 8 February 1959. The Munich show had more than 30,000 visitors, which director of the Galerie Arthur Rümann found 'regrettable', except that the surplus permitted him to buy more work by Munich artists. See 'Ankäufe der städtischen Galerie München 1946/1956', 44.

60 Katharina Fackler, 'Picturing the Poor: Poverty, Photography, and Politics in the 1960s', ms. 2015; John Szarkowski, *The Family of Man*, in *The Museum of Modern Art at Mid-Century: At Home and Abroad*, ed. John Elderfield (New York: MoMA, 1994), 12–37.

61 Karl Gernot Kuehn, *Caught: The Art of Photography in the German Democratic Republic* (Berkeley: University of California Press, 1997), 56–7.

62 Sandeen, 'International Reception', 352, mentions the photograph demonstrating Brecht's presence, and Gerd Hurm and Shamoon Zamir refer to Brecht's visit in the context of Brecht's *Kriegsfibel* and *Aus der Friedensfibel*. See their contributions to this volume.

63 Max Horkheimer, 'Opening of the Photo-Exhibition *The Family of Man* – All of Us', 62.

64 KKF V 96 / 54: Horkheimer letter to Peter-Kristian Ledig, 5 October 1958, in response to Ledig's letter of invitation, 30 September 1958. Horkheimer was a member of the Kuratorium Kulturelles Frankfurt.

65 Horkheimer, 'Opening', 61.

66 Ibid., 61–2.

67 Kracauer, *Theory of Film*, 310.

68 Wolfgang Welsch, 'Was ist eigentlich Transkulturalität?' (2010), http://www2.uni-jena.de/welsch/papers/W_Welsch_Was_ist_Transkulturalit%C3%A4t.pdf (accessed 11 January 2016).

69 Koeppen, 'Kamera'.

8 Picture and Image

Another Look at *The Family of Man*

Winfried Fluck

One of my starting points in this chapter is the hermeneutical claim that, no matter how hard we try to be historically accurate and specific, we cannot arrive at something like the true facts that speak for themselves, because facts and data have to be interpreted in order to make sense. Inevitably, interpretations will be shaped by underlying assumptions that are not always openly acknowledged and thematized, although they play an important part in guiding our selection and analysis of the data. Thus, instead of focusing on omissions in an interpretation, it seems more productive to look at its underlying assumptions and to see how productive and convincing they are.

And there is a second starting point: no matter how many single observations we make and how free we are in making them, these single observations will have to be integrated into a narrative at one point if they are to make any sense. Thus, interpretations usually come in the form of narratives. In the case of *The Family of Man*, I basically see two narratives at work: a common-humanity narrative that praises the exhibition for its propagation of universal values, and a lack-of-difference narrative that criticizes the exhibition for erasing difference, inequality and injustice in its propagation of universal values. These two narratives have dominated the discussions of *The Family of Man* in the past decades. They are represented in exemplary fashion in texts by Max Horkheimer and Roland Barthes which I will discuss and compare in the first part of this chapter, focusing on their underlying assumptions, their 'prejudices', if you wish. In the second part of the chapter, I want to take up the challenge of this volume to have another look at the *The Family of Man* exhibition in order to consider the possibility of an alternative narrative. In this section, I take my point of departure from some basic reflections on the act of viewing pictures and then look more closely at some of the pictures themselves. Indeed, in trying to save *The Family of Man* from the Barthes verdict, some scholars seem to have given in to the temptation to run away from the pictures themselves.

***

But let me start with a look at, and comparison of, the texts by Horkheimer and Barthes, both of them responses to the exhibition of *The Family of Man,* shown in the case of Barthes in Paris and in the case of Horkheimer in Frankfurt. One point that provides a comparison between the two texts with special interest is that their comments on the exhibition are based on very different assumptions about the function of images and of spectatorship, assumptions that reflect a major shift in post-World War II intellectual history. This shift sets in in the 1960s and is one from a liberal consensus to what has been called a new cultural radicalism which is already anticipated in Barthes's review.

The liberal consensus view is basically reform-minded, relying on visions of democratization, democratic institutions and democratic change to which art, including pictures and images, may make transformative contributions. As Horkheimer hopes, if viewers of *The Family of Man* exhibition are touched by images of our common humanity, they may change their attitudes and their behaviour, and violent conflicts may become less likely in the future. In order to have a positive impact on viewers, however, and to transform them, the picture has to have a certain aesthetic quality. For liberal or social democratic theories of social change, aesthetics is a key category. Exhibitions have a particular function in this liberal world: not primarily to document something, but to provide the possibility of a transformative experience. Or, to put it more precisely in the case of photography: to document something in such a way – in such an artful way, to be more precise – that it can lead to a transformative experience. In the liberal consensus view, mass culture is a threat, a betrayal of the potential of art. Thus it is important to support cultural events that are based on certain aesthetic visions. One may assume that this was one of the reasons for Horkheimer's strong support of the Frankfurt exhibition of *The Family of Man.*[1]

Cultural radicalism emerged as a theoretical position in the wake of the Paris May of 1968 that took on a programmatic dimension in approaches like poststructuralism or structural Marxism, and gained its strongest appeal in the work of Barthes, Lacan, Althusser, Derrida and Foucault. For cultural radicalism, the common-humanity narrative is based on liberal illusions that merely help to cement a perpetuation of the status quo in power relations. What liberals, including left liberals and orthodox Marxists, do not want to recognize is that the source of power does not lie in political institutions with their assumption that individuals possess agency and can put up resistance. For cultural radicalism, the true source of power lies in culture as the realm where subjects are constituted, not by their own self-consciousness, but through linguistic or semiotic structures, discursive fields or – in the field of vision – by technological apparatuses like the filmic apparatus. This means that before individuals can begin to make choices, culture has already constituted them as subjects. And the dominant theory for this form of subject constitution is that of interpellation, the discursive positioning of an individual into a particular subject position.

This is where images become crucial in cultural radicalism. For how can an individual be convinced to take on a particular subject position? The answer is: especially by images, and the exemplary situation in which this takes place is Lacan's mirror stage in which the child sees itself as another in the mirror – as another, because the mirror creates the illusion of a full person which the child is not – and begins to form an identity on the basis of this mirror image. However, since the image is an illusion, this identity is built on a misrecognition. For poststructuralists, recognition – for example through pictures – is thus the imposition of a false identity, and although Barthes does not yet use the Lacanian-Althusserian terminology, his critique already points in that direction. By providing images, that is, illusions, of a common humanity, *The Family of Man* exhibition creates a basic misrecognition, namely that of a communality in which difference is erased. And because this misrecognition is a basic constituent of identity, Barthes does not have to look at aesthetic details. I think I am exaggerating only a little bit when I claim that for Barthes, although he uses a different terminology, *The Family of Man* re-enacts the mirror stage.

What is interesting about this claim in the context of our discussion is its tacit assumption about the viewer and the viewing process. How do pictures reach the viewer? Explicitly or implicitly, consciously or unconsciously, every interpretation of pictures needs a theory of effect – that is, a theory of how a picture reaches and affects the viewer. The theory of interpellation is built on the idea of identification, although the concept is now shorn of all psychological and emotional dimensions. The cultural object achieves its effect not by appealing to any social or psychological dispositions, but simply by the act of spectator positioning through the technological apparatus and its product, the image; like the child who does not become aware of what is going on in the mirror stage, the viewer most likely will not even be aware of how spectator positioning leads to the creation of a subject position into which he is subjected. In liberal scenarios, the viewer stands in front of a picture and makes a decision on whether to become involved or opt for other forms of reception; in cultural radicalism, the viewer is most likely not even aware that a choice has already been made on his behalf. And precisely because images have the power of interpellation, their critique must be radical, as it is in the case of Barthes. Where difference has been erased, the critic has to come to the rescue, because the aesthetic object itself can no longer do the work. It is a mere surface phenomenon and the critic has to unmask photography's claims of merely representing what is there.

Debates about theories of effect have not really been an issue in cultural radicalism (and, unfortunately also not in discussions of *The Family of Man*). In cultural radicalism, terms like spectator positioning or subject positioning have by and large replaced the term identification, but although this shift seems to imply that the determining force is no longer the viewer who actively identifies with a character or object, but the technical apparatus that does the positioning, the underlying theory of effect still is – in fact, even more so than before – that of identification. Thus, ironically enough, in the case of *The Family of Man*, both narratives – the common-humanity narrative and the difference narrative – are based on a theory of reception that can be characterized as a form of identification. What, however, if we decide that this is an insufficient way of describing the act of viewing, not only in the case of *The Family of Man*, but in principle?

One reason why theories of effect based on assumptions of identification can appear plausible or even self-evident may lie in the fact that the term identification can refer to two different aspects of the act of viewing that are often conflated in interpretations. Rita Felski provides an excellent description of this conflation when she writes:

> Identification can denote a formal *alignment* with a character, as encouraged by techniques of focalization, point of view, or narrative structure [or, one might add to Felski's list: spectator positioning] while also referencing an experiential allegiance with a character, as manifested in a felt sense of affinity or attachment. Critiques of identification tend to conflate these issues, assuming that readers formerly aligned with a fictional persona cannot help but swallow the ideologies represented by that persona wholesale.[2]

Indeed, the difference between the two conflicting narratives about *The Family of Man* can be traced back to these two different ideas of identification. When Horkheimer praises *The Family of Man* – and photographs more generally – for their power to invite identification with our common humanity (he actually uses the term identification), he clearly has an experiential allegiance in mind that can be created by well-crafted pictures.[3] Photography is more effective in achieving such an allegiance than philosophy or even film; however, because of photography's power to stimulate identification, Horkheimer in the end also has to draw a line, for otherwise photography might be used to manipulate us. For once, Horkheimer claims, we cannot identify with the completely and utterly evil, so that our humanity protects us, so to speak, from the wrong kind of identification, and secondly, it is one of the special achievements of *The Family of Man* exhibition that, in Horkheimer's view, it continues to insist on the freedom and the responsibility of the individual.[4] For Barthes, on the other hand, such moral qualifications are irrelevant. Because of its apparently unmediated facticity, photography induces us to accept it as a truthful representation of reality, thereby covering up – as in the case of Emmett Till he mentions – not only the true nature of reality, but also photography's potential to function as a medium of misrecognition.

From the point of view of cultural radicalism, Horkheimer's view of photography must appear touchingly naïve. What he praises about photography – its power to create a convincing reality effect – is the source of all evil for Barthes, because it seduces us to mistake the picture's surface depiction for reality and thus to overlook and ignore difference, for example the difference created by inequality. And there is another interesting contrast: Horkheimer praises photography as a medium, because, in contrast for example to film, it does not overwhelm the viewer:

> With films, we cannot [...] linger on details, on the finer points, on which so much depends where understanding between human beings is concerned. This is only possible with the photograph, which is silent, which we can look at for as long as we want, and to which we can return.

For Barthes, on the other hand, it is precisely these finer points that are the source of a fundamental misrecognition, because they create the illusionary reality effect of verisimilitude that makes us trust the picture as a truthful representation of reality.[5]

***

The conflicting views of the function of pictures that we have been tracing raise the interesting question of how the sense-making activities of the viewer can be described. As reception aesthetics has argued, literary texts cannot but have dimensions of indeterminacy, blanks and suspended connectivities that leave space for the reader's imagination in the act of reading. Reception can thus never be mere mimesis or identification. But in contrast to literature, photographs do not seem to have these indeterminate spaces; on the contrary, as Barthes argues, they can do their ideological work precisely because they create a complete illusion of reality. Does the viewer have no imaginary space left, then, in photography? The controversy about *The Family of Man* suggests the opposite, because, obviously, by looking at the same pictures, viewers have nevertheless come up with entirely different narratives about them. This reminds us of an important point, namely the ontological non-identity between reality and its representation, no matter how hard realism or photography may try to overcome it. Because of this non-identity we can never truly know reality or a person depicted in a picture, which means that although we see them directly in front of us as part of a picture, we nevertheless have to imagine them in order to bring them to life.

What kind of person is this man shown in the picture (see illustration 20)? What kind of person is this woman? The picture does not tell us, except for suggesting a certain self-assured dignity. But all appeals to a common humanity that we are supposed to share with these persons will be moot if we do not give them some attributes by means of our own imagination (such as, for example, dignity, endurance or vulnerability). Since we have never met any of the characters that are depicted in *The Family of Man*, we have to bring them to life by drawing on our own imaginary associations, feelings and bodily sensations, for otherwise the pictures would remain meaningless to us. This does *not* mean that we merely project our own imaginary onto the picture. We cannot ignore the facticity of the picture. But it means that the picture and our image of it are not identical.[6] The picture guides and limits our perception, but the depicted world can only become meaningful and provide an aesthetic experience if it is imagined and brought to life by the viewer. This means that in the act of reception the picture comes to represent two things at the same time: the world depicted in the picture and the cognitive, imaginary,

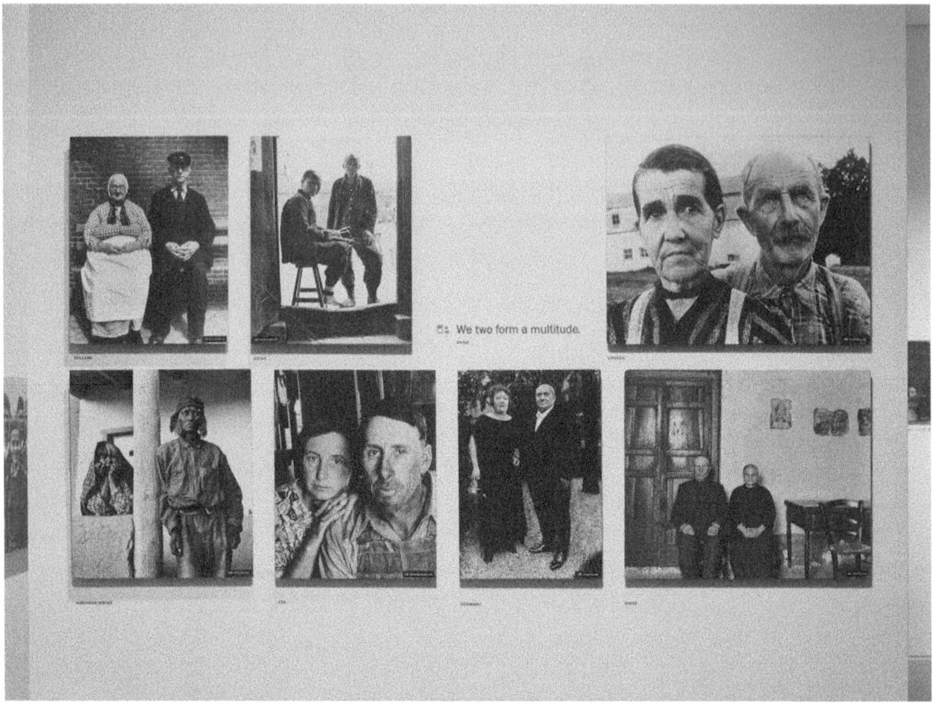

20 *The Family of Man* installation at Clervaux Castle. Theme 'UN': (from right to left) Emmy Andriesse, Dmitri Kessel, John Philips, Alma Lavenson, Alfred Eisenstaedt, August Sander and Vito Fiorenza.

emotional and affective dimensions added to it by the viewer in order to give the picture meaning and significance. To be sure, the picture always remains the same, but the image we have of the picture is always different and explains why critics, just as in the case of literature, can rarely agree on the interpretation of a picture and can never exhaust its full meaning. It is also the explanation why the *Family of Man* exhibition could work globally in different cultural contexts, because although these audiences saw the same pictures, they came up with their own different images of them. In this respect, looking at photography is not categorically different from reading. Both produce a state 'in between' in which we are, in the words of Wolfgang Iser, 'both ourselves and somebody else at the same time'.[7]

The Family of Man takes this theory of reception, that is, the fact that pictures are transformed into images in the act of viewing, as its starting point. One of the promises of *The Family of Man* is that of a documentation of a wide variety of human experiences that are nevertheless common to us all and thus enhance our possibilities for an imaginary transfer.

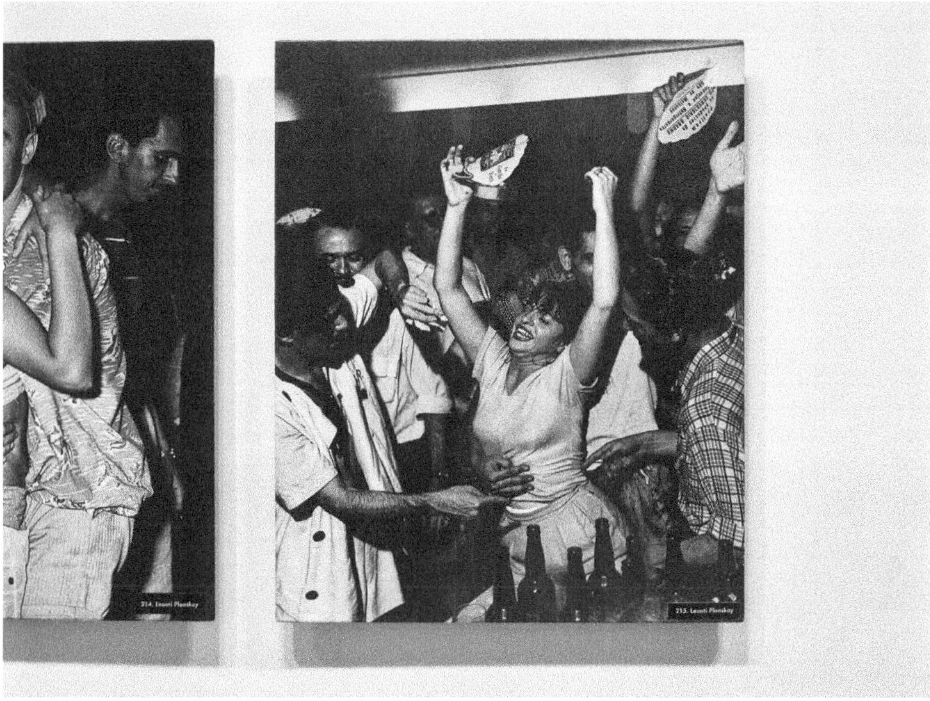

21 *The Family of Man* installation at Clervaux Castle. Theme 'Drinking': Leonti Planskoy.

When we look at the picture of the dancing woman (see illustration 21), for example, we do not simply take away from it information about other cultures or see people engage in a common activity. We look at somebody who is at the same time acting out something that we may find interesting or desirable. We may not identify with the woman but our imagination may be engaged because of the exuberant movement in which she is pictured. The picture is thus not merely a documentation but a simulation of reality; the pictorial documentation is at the same time a performance, the whole picture the strong, effective stimulation of an image – strong because it evokes associations of vitality, excess, a willingness to suspend control temporarily. In other words, the picture evokes a state of being in which the viewer usually does not find him- or herself but that may for that very reason stimulate his or her imaginary. And precisely because the photograph only claims to document reality, it can be so effective in stimulating an imaginary dimension that goes beyond mere documentation.

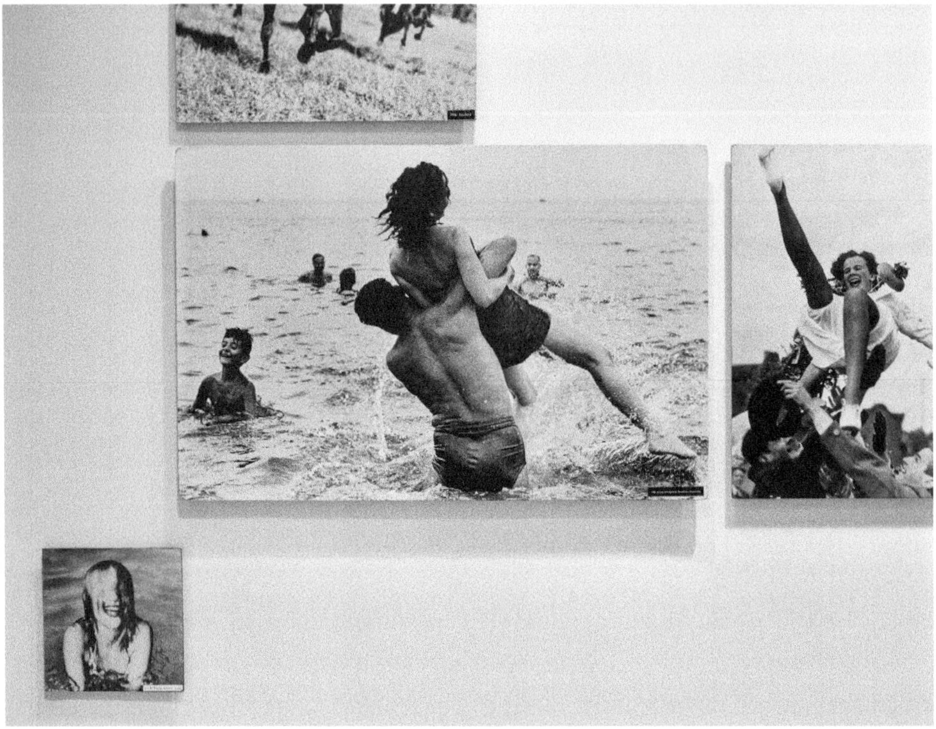

22 ***The Family of Man* installation at Clervaux Castle. Theme 'Playing': (centre) Garry Winogrand.**

In fact, the exuberant moment is one of the key motifs in *The Family of Man* (see illustration 22). These pictures show us persons that go beyond the routine of everyday life and hence challenge us in our own identity either in appearance, behaviour or emotional state. They evoke situations in which we may consider alternatives that may extend our own identity – however, not in the mode of an identification, but as a very selective transfer of certain qualities. We may take the mood of exuberance from the picture of a dancing woman, without identifying with her appearance or particular form of bodily self-expression.[8] From that point of view, photographs can function as imaginary self-extensions in a playful, experimental mode that, for the time being, enable us to acquire traits of somebody else, but only on the condition that we can also remain ourselves. Children, by the way, are especially useful for this: they are ourselves in a playful mood. We all want to be Huckleberry Finns (see illustration 23).

If we approach *The Family of Man* from that perspective, our focus of interpretation must shift. In this context, the organization of the exhibition in sections is significant. The image of the dancing woman is included in a section in which we

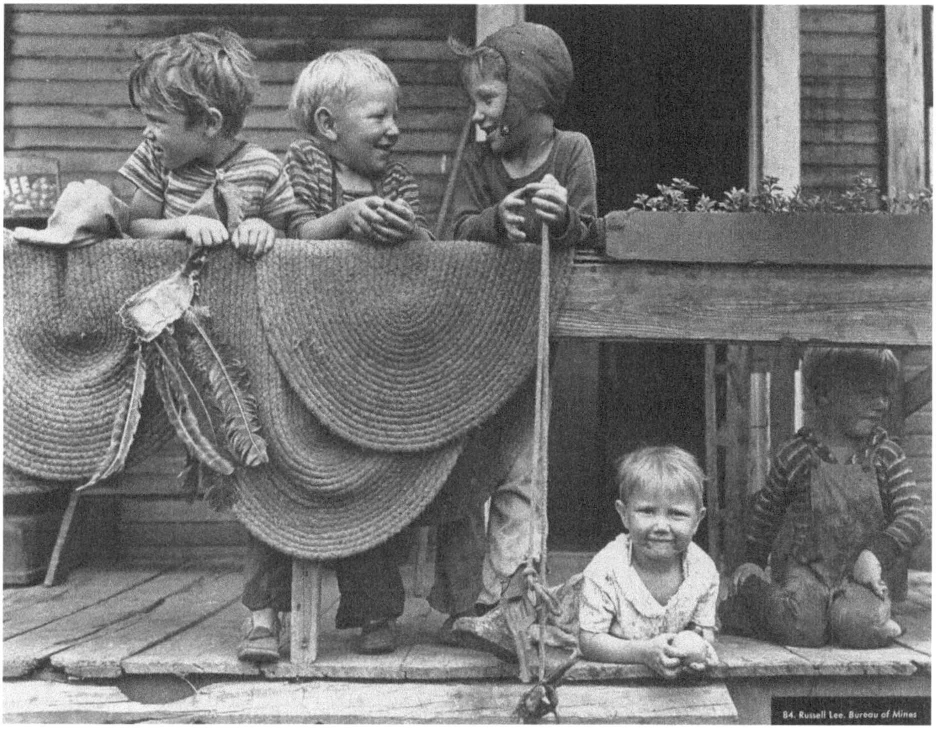

23 Russell Lee, Department of the Interior. Solid Fuels Administration for War 19 April 1943–30 June 1947.

find pictures of various lively social occasions, including several different versions of dancing, ranging from boogie-woogie to ballroom dancing and folk dancing. These are not merely documentations of different styles, however. They capture special moments. Our attitude therefore is no longer, look, people all over the world like to dance, but see what kind of imaginary possibilities dancing opens up: sensuous excess but also controlled body movement, status provocation or status affirmation, national or regional self-recognition, but also its hilarious deconstruction when a region is represented by a pair of panties. In other words, these pictures do not simply tell us that people all over the world like to dance; rather they use that fact in order to stage a range of new and alternative possibilities of the self. In that sense, *The Family of Man* is not simply a documentation of universal humanity, but of post-war cultural history and, more specifically, of possibilities of the self that dominated the imaginary of the times.

Now, to argue that the gap between picture and image is the basis for our reception of photography and its special appeal draws attention to an important aspect but does not yet explain the special popular appeal of *The Family of Man.*

For this we have to look more closely at the exhibition, and not just in terms of its good intentions and its at the time progressive liberal politics but in terms of its qualities as photographs. The strong impact of the exhibition is produced by its pictures after all, so that audiences can be affected by them although they may not know anything about what Steichen or others said about them. Clearly, the photographs have particular features in terms of their themes, their photographic styles and their compositional features – features that from the point of view of a transfer theory should be especially effective in making use of the gap between picture and image by stimulating our imaginary activities.

***

The exhibition achieves this by three basic aesthetic strategies: the first, in terms of theme, is the everydayness of the experiences that are shown. People work hard and, throughout, there is something like a heroism of daily life, of people accepting life as it is and trying to make the best of it. In order to create special moments and experiences, people have to fall back on time-tested traditions and family events, because they can provide special occasions in an otherwise plain and unspectacular world. Life is taken down to the level of a common denominator; what is striking is an absence of the importance of status. In pictures of crowd scenes we usually see no leader, only a dehierarchized audience. This common denominator opens up the space for imaginary activities which are not yet narrowed down by particular status concerns.

Where dress, social milieu and conspicuous consumption are not supposed to provide distinction, we have to go back to the one feature that always distinguishes human beings: their faces. This explains the high quantity of portraits in the exhibition and their populist thirties-style (see illustration 24).[9]

These portraits show plain people – the everyday theme – but all of them as people who deserve our respect. Again, such portraits are especially effective in stimulating imaginary activities, because, just as in life, we see faces as expressive of a person and its character which we cannot see or be sure of – in other words, which we have to make up.

This is also the point where the aesthetic dimension of the photographs comes in which is, of course, an important part of the appeal of the exhibition – although reading the secondary literature on the exhibition one may not always think so. I am not referring to a particular aesthetic programme but to what may be called the common aesthetic denominator of all the different photographic styles and approaches in the exhibition, their attempt to capture a particular poetic moment – which is something photographs can do especially well. For example, the exhibition does not simply show that people all over the world engage in courtship; the photographs try to capture the special moment where that pursuit produces a poetic, if only fleeting transformation of everyday life (see illustration 25).

For me the message of *The Family of Man* is not that we all share a common humanity, but that, although everyday life may be hard and unglamorous, it

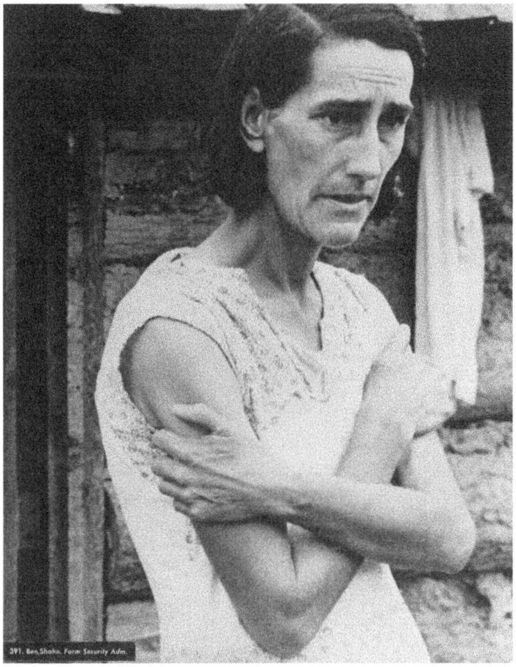

24 Ben Shahn, FSA.

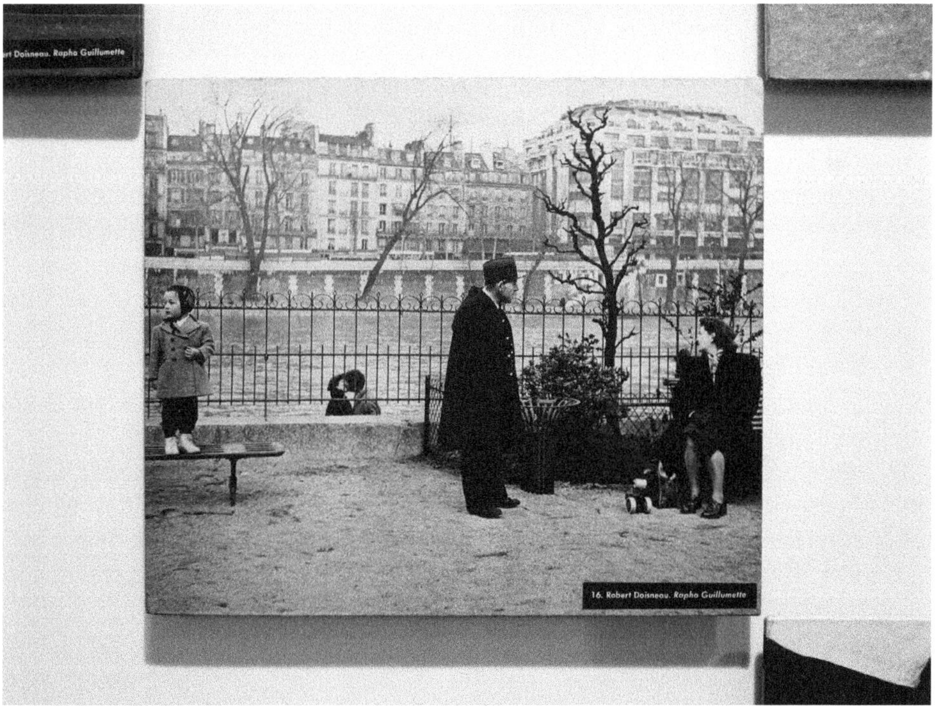

25 *The Family of Man* installation at Clervaux Castle. Theme 'Lovers': Robert Doisneau.

nevertheless still produces those special, poetic moments that photography wants to make us aware of and that we should cherish as special possibilities of the self. In fact, one may even go one step further and claim that photography has a special potential for transforming everyday life into a special moment. In real life, the fleeting moment will go by without our becoming aware of its poetic potential. Photography can arrest that moment and can help us to take another look at it, becoming aware for the first time of how special that fleeting moment may be. As Horkheimer puts it, 'The individual photographs claim to be not so much aesthetic objects as discoveries. They show what everyone sees without becoming aware of it.'

The traces of this aestheticization are everywhere to be found in the exhibition once one begins to look. The pictures of genesis, for example, offer a poetic picture in black and white and draw our attention to the fact that black-and-white photography has a special potential for aestheticization by producing stark contrasts, unexpected patterns and high drama. And although this may run against the grain of majority opinion on the exhibition, even the picture of the hydrogen bomb produces a stark aesthetic moment in which the apocalypse, almost in the fashion of the landscape painter Frederic Church, is turning into a sublime landscape. I think that in the context of the exhibition, the picture fits very well aesthetically, but it does not work in terms of message – in other words, it works as an image, not as a narrative – because it is far too poetic in its sublimity. But more generally speaking, it is notable that almost every picture in the exhibition is carefully composed, often has unusual perspectives or overwhelming wide angles, shows all kinds of sometimes unexpected patterns, and thus manages to capture our attention. This is not an ethnographic exhibition of the family of man; it is an exhibition that tries to define and exhibit the poetic potential of photography and that uses the family of man as a subject matter because this opens up an entirely new range of poetic possibilities. The exhibition does not merely depict birth or death, love or work; it provides unexpected angles on these facts of life in a way that pulls us into an imaginary engagement. If something is lacking in research about *The Family of Man*, it is not historical specificity, but close readings and appreciations of the pictures in terms of their composition and aesthetic power.

This focus on the poetic moment is significant in the larger context of my argument, because the aesthetic power that gets us engaged also opens up the gap between picture and image. In his chapter in this book, Werner Sollors provides some illustrations by speaking of his own associations of Fifth Avenue, or quoting Wolfgang Koeppen's description of the picture with the little dog – both examples of how a picture is transformed into an image in the act of reception. And there is yet another very effective source of fuelling and stimulating the imaginary and that is a strategy of decontextualization. Often, as for example in FSA photography, we see single pictures in the context of a narrative. In most cases, *The Family of Man* eliminates context, because the poetic moment, being fleeting and rare, must interrupt and cut off the narrative; only as long as it remains isolated can it remain distinct. Again, this strategy can be effective in stimulating our own imaginary activities: since the picture refuses to provide a narrative, we will have to come up with a narrative of our own; that is, we are driven by the decontextualization to turn picture into image.

Finally, an aesthetic of the poetic moment – and this leads us to a third strong source of the exhibition's appeal – transforms (moments of) everyday life into something special. By doing so, it provides distinction, and distinction is a supreme source of recognition. The pictures show an everyday activity or a common person or a traditional event in a new light and thus elevate them above everydayness. By doing so, these pictures make the event or the persons special, if only for a moment. They elevate the moment to deserve recognition. And since we know now that this would not work without a transfer on our side, the moment of recognition is also a moment of self-recognition in which we get a renewed sense of the possibilities of life.

***

It is certainly true, as the difference-narrative argues, that these possibilities are not fully representative of human diversity, that there is a gender bias at work (also in images of the poetic moment) and that there still prevails an exotic image of otherness. I do not want to deny these critical points, but I want to argue that focusing on them prevents us from clarifying what the exhibition achieves as an aesthetic project. It is not simply a naïve liberal confirmation of a universal humanity narrative, but an inventory of imaginary possibilities of the self at a particular time. To criticize this display for what it is not doing poses the risk of failing to notice what it does.

I have therefore proposed to replace the two dominant narratives in the discussion of *The Family of Man* – the common-humanity narrative and the difference narrative – by a third one that may be called a narrative of poetic self-recognition. The difference can be easily described: while the other two narratives remain tied to a theory of effect based, in the final analysis, on ideas of identification, the self-recognition narrative reconceptualizes the act of viewing as a transfer in which picture and viewer interact. As we have seen, this has several consequences. One is a necessary differentiation in interpretation between picture and image. Although a photographic picture may depict reality as it is, the picture is transformed into an image in the act of viewing by adding imaginary and affective dimensions, for otherwise the viewer could not provide the picture with meaning and significance. This means, however, that the image is no longer identical with the picture and that an interpretation merely in terms of its representational value, and not in terms of the aesthetic experience the exhibition aims to provide, must remain incomplete.

A difference narrative, I said at the beginning, is based on the assumption of an identification that leads to what was later called interpellation. A transfer theory undermines that claim, because it provides reception with a dimension of unpredictability. We can never be entirely sure what the viewer finds useful. But useful for what? Why do people look at photographs in the first place? In Horkheimer's opening remarks it is the wish to see how others live; one might call this some kind of intercultural recognition, and if we are willing to engage in this intercultural recognition, the world will be a better place. In Barthes's review, it is the desire to be confirmed in one's own illusion of misrecognition. However, if we stress the interactive nature of the act of viewing, then an imaginary dimension is added that exceeds our identity and offers this imaginary and aesthetic surplus as another possibility of the self. I would therefore like to call this process self-recognition and have already argued in other contexts that fictional texts can be especially useful in providing self-recognition.[10] But pictures, and more specifically, photographs may be able to do the same and perhaps even more effectively. If we ignore the role the imaginary plays in the act of viewing, we may be missing that potential. And if we ignore this dimension, we are in danger of missing the significance of the important event in cultural history that *The Family of Man* is.

Notes

1 As one of the best-known proponents of Frankfurt School critical theory, Horkheimer would not be considered a typical liberal. But for whatever reason, his opening remarks at *The Family of Man* exhibition follow a strictly liberal line of argumentation. The term 'liberal consensus', now established as a term for the dominant intellectual position in the 1950s, comprises not only liberalism, but also the reform-minded Left and a critical theory softened somewhat by the challenge of establishing a functioning democracy in post-war Germany.

2 Rita Felski, *Uses of Literature* (Oxford: Blackwell, 2008), 34.

3 Cf. Horkheimer: 'In addition to this, however, the picture achieves something that theory alone cannot: it allows the viewer to identify with it.' For Horkheimer, identification is a potentially productive form of mimesis, whereas for Barthes it is the source of a fundamental misrecognition.

4 Cf. Horkheimer: 'And this only proves that, however great the suggestive powers of these pictures, however much they may stimulate feelings of identification, the exhibition nevertheless insists on the consciousness of the freedom and the responsibility of the individual.'

5 This line of argumentation explains poststructuralism's sweeping critique of classical realism. For many critics arguing on the basis of a liberal consensus, classical realism was the most promising form of social criticism in literature. Cultural radicalism turns this view on its head: the literature that was considered the most critical before, is now the politically most pernicious, because it creates an effective illusion of reality.

6 For a more detailed presentation of this transfer theory of viewing, see my essay 'Aesthetic Theory of the Image', in Fluck, *Romance with America? Essays on Culture, Literature, and American Studies*, ed. Laura Bieger and Johannes Voelz (Heidelberg: Winter, 2009), 409–31.

7 Wolfgang Iser, 'Representation: A Performative Act', in *Prospecting: From Reader Response to Literary Anthropology*, ed. Wolfgang Iser (Baltimore, MD: Johns Hopkins University Press, 1989), 244.

8 In this sense, the picture also provides a good illustration for the fact that the imaginary engagement and transfer of the viewer does not necessarily have to take place along gender lines. Both male and female viewers may engage with the performance of exuberance.

9 For an analysis of the role of faces in the documentary photography of the Farm Security Administration, see my essay 'Poor Like Us: Poverty and Recognition in American Photography', *Amerikastudien / American Studies* 55, no. 1 (2010): 63–93.

10 See my essay on 'Reading for Recognition', *New Literary History* 44, no. 1 (2013): 45–67.

9 Structures of Rhyme, Forms of Participation

The Family of Man as Exhibition

Shamoon Zamir

> In the cinema and television, the image is revealed at a pace set by the director. In the exhibition gallery, the visitor sets his own pace. He can go forward and then retreat or hurry along according to his own impulse and mood as these are stimulated by the exhibition. In the creation of such an exhibition [as *The Family of Man*], resources are brought into play that are not available elsewhere. The contrast in scale of images, the shifting of focal points, the intriguing perspective of long- and short-range visibility with the images to come being glimpsed beyond the images at hand – all these permit the spectator an active participation that no other form of visual communication can give.
>
> Edward Steichen (1963)[1]

Many accounts of *The Family of Man* restrict descriptions of the exhibition to how it guided visitors through the stages of the human life cycle, how representations of birth, childhood, teenage life, adulthood and death were intertwined with scenes of family intimacy and nurturing, play, education, work, leisure activities, and how the physical design of the exhibition embodied the idea of human commonality by immersing visitors in a spectacular and overwhelming visual articulation of its grand theme. Some accounts additionally acknowledge the inclusion of images of social protest, war and the pursuit of justice through law, suffrage and collective governance, and reframe Steichen's project as a progressive, liberal plea for an incorporative cosmopolitanism. But no matter how these accounts interpret the exhibition's particular brand of humanism, whether they are sympathetic to or critical of its social and ethical impulses, they have one thing in common: they do not engage in close readings of *The Family of Man*, no sustained consideration, that is, of how exactly a particular image sequence or room constructed its meanings, of how one room was in dialogue with another, or how certain visual motifs travelled and changed through the exhibition and why. This is because in reducing the exhibition to a grand theme, and by focusing on how this theme is carried by a supposedly propulsive curatorial design, they present Steichen's installation as a structure that seeks to resolve all contradictions and difficulties within a unified message. Such an approach projects onto the exhibition design an aesthetic and conceptual logic that renders close examination irrelevant; the broad truth or meaning is what matters, not its particular iteration. The crafted architecture of *The Family of Man* in fact activated meanings and experiences far more varied than those made visible by either the persistent focus on a singular thematics or on Steichen's curatorial achievement as a machine for compelling attention into what effectively amounts to distraction. In what follows, I do no more than begin to look at what I take to be neglected aspects of *The Family of Man*'s exhibition design as it was installed at the Museum of Modern Art (MoMA) in 1955, and to suggest some of the ways in which this may also begin to reshape our understanding of the show.[2]

Olivier Lugon offers a representative statement of the approach to the exhibition that combines the thematic and formal emphases from which I suggest it is necessary to move away in order to take a fresh look at *The Family of Man*:

> Everything [...] hinged on the continual displacement of the beholder, whose every movement interiorized the theme of the endless flow of time and life [...] According to this logic, nothing should interrupt the flow of visitors, no image should so arrest the eye that the movement of the masses comes to a halt [...] The ideal some fifty years earlier [when Steichen curated exhibitions at Stieglitz's 291 gallery] of prolonged attention when viewing a photograph here was taken as a sign of failure. A steady flow of visitors was favored over focused reflection. Spectators were being invited, in a way, to look without looking, especially when faced with the most problematic images. Social and political disorders were displayed only to be immediately forgotten, to be appreciated in passing as generic images of 'man's inhumanity to man'.[3]

Steichen's own description of his MoMA installation, the first part of which is quoted as the epigraph to this chapter, contradicts Lugon's account at almost every point. Steichen suggests that the purpose of the design of *The Family of Man* was in fact to make available a variety of speeds by encouraging the viewer's freedom, and not, as accounts such as Lugon's would suggest, to impose a relentless forward flow that herded the viewer through. The viewer can 'hurry along', as Steichen says, but he or she can also 'go forward and then retreat'. This forward and backward movement is the movement of reflection through comparison invited by the shifting perspectives and juxtapositions of the exhibition; and as the readings that follow demonstrate, it should be understood not only as a physical movement, a bodily manifestation of the mind negotiating the range of meanings and effects immediately before it, but also as a mental movement back and forth across rooms and sequences that occurs even as the viewer progresses through the exhibition, and that uses the memory of what has already been seen to construct patterns of connection between these rooms and sequences that cut across the flow of the exhibition. Steichen's viewer is not passive; nor is the viewer's exercise of freedom a wilful resistance to the restrictive manipulations of the exhibition design. Steichen's description proposes instead that *The Family of Man* becomes active in its meanings when the agency of the viewer and that of the exhibition itself work in dialogue, when 'impulse and mood [...] are stimulated by the exhibition'.

On one level *The Family of Man* certainly invited the viewer to experience it most immediately as a flow. However, this one-directional flow carried within it many eddies and countercurrents. If the sweeping flow unfolded through a progressive succession of images and themes, the countermovements were shaped above all by a series of visual associations which accumulated as the viewer moved through the exhibition, a detail or a motif from one image being picked up by another, often several rooms apart, the recollection of the earlier image creating the backward pull and pause of memory even as the narrative and the architecture of the exhibition moved the viewer forwards in both space and time. I have called these visual associations rhymes because they construct the mental and affective experiences of the viewer as an ever-shifting configuration that is first and foremost musical in its operations, and that cannot always be put into words and explained easily.

Visitors were not invited to 'look without looking' at 'the most problematic images', and 'social and political disorders' were not displayed only so that they could 'immediately be forgotten'. Steichen's design integrated, or tried to integrate, difficult and unpalatable truths as necessary conditions for accepting the exhibition's concluding resolutions. *The Family of Man* was a comedy: it was governed by the mythos of spring and the spirit of union and reconciliation; its final image showed a boy and a girl walking together out of deep shadows into the bright sunlight of a leafy garden, and the images of children in the last room were crowned by a quotation from *As You Like It*.[4] But just as in a Shakespearean comedy or a novel by Jane Austen the troubling notes continue to reverberate through the final reassuring resolution, so too in *The Family of Man* our grasp of the ending is poorer if we have already erased the memory of the drama that has brought us to it.

The representations of the life cycle and the celebrations of everyday life in *The Family of Man* should be understood as only chapters in a larger narrative. The exhibition moves from the private to the public realm, from the enclosure of family life, from necessity and labour, from the distractions and pleasures of leisure, to education and thought, and to social and political engagement. The narrative of the human life cycle actually came to an end roughly halfway through the exhibition. At the end of the fifth room were two convex panels hung with images of death and mourning (FoM 142). As visitors passed between these panels, they faced a floor-to-ceiling photograph (by Andreas Feininger) of a crowded Fifth Avenue at mid-afternoon. The architecture of the exhibition created, in other words, a ritual passage from death into the living community of the contemporary world.[5] From this point on, the thematic emphasis of the exhibition shifted to a focus on social inequality, protest, public debate, suffrage, law and government. To the extent that images of private and family life continued to appear, such as images of young adults at play, they did so now as a point of contrast to the public world and its imperatives unfolding before them. In the final room, the family was in fact absorbed into the United Nations (see illustration 1).[6]

The Family of Man structures this larger narrative with a formal intricacy that has not been acknowledged before. This is a claim that has significant implications for our understanding of the meanings of the exhibition; it is also a claim that requires a renewed examination of what Fred Turner, in what is perhaps the most compelling reading of Steichen's exhibition design to date, has referred to as 'modes of attention' and the 'politics of attention'.[7] Where Eric Sandeen, in his foundational study, devoted most of his discussion to the cultural and political contexts of *The Family of Man*, Turner shifts his focus to an analysis of the formal aspects of the exhibition and offers a highly persuasive framing of the role played by the architectural and display dynamics of the MoMA installation in furthering the humanist ambitions of Steichen's project within the liberal cultural and social imperatives of 1950s America. Turner proposes that 'a deeply democratic, even utopian, impulse [...] drove the show and much of the early audience response to it' because there was an 'antiauthoritarian politics behind its design and the modes of attention it solicited from visitors'.[8] Turner carefully unfolds this assessment within an account of the post-war debates about the natures of authoritarian and democratic personalities, and about the cultural modes needed for fostering and developing the latter. This contextualization provides a strong foundation for the claim that '*The Family of Man* thus became less a vehicle for a single message than a three-dimensional arena in which visitors could practice acts of mutual recognition, choice, and empathy – the core perceptual and affective skills on which democracy depended.'[9]

But when Turner moves from his conceptualization of the overall structure of the MoMA installation to an actual reading of it, he reverts to a walk-through description that is much the same as Sandeen's earlier and equally general one.[10] Turner pauses only once to comment at any length on a particular image group: the photographs of American, Japanese, Italian and Bechuanaland (today Botswana) families that form the thematic and physical pivot of the whole exhibition (see illustration 2). As Turner notes, 'seen individually, these images could be read as stereotypical depictions of "primitive" Africans, "tradition-bound" Japanese and Italians, and "hillbilly" Americans. But seen together, as they were meant to be, the images *challenged* stereotypes.' They did not privilege 'whites or Americans', but in fact 'equated' them with groups that were at that time the objects of prejudice or hostility, because of their race or because they were former enemies from the recent war. 'To stand among these images,' then, 'was not to perceive the Africans or Japanese as somehow lesser people but, instead, to recognize a *likeness* between them and more dominant groups. Though the images certainly echoed stereotypes, they also solicited empathy – and that at a time when such fellow feeling was rare in the United States.'[11]

On the one hand, this is a largely accurate distillation of the liberal project of *The Family of Man* – and the reading of form and content I develop works to an extent within the critical framework established by Turner, and in sympathy with his political assessment. On the other hand, Turner's account, like so many less compelling accounts of the exhibition, distorts in significant ways the political, ethical and affective complexities of Steichen's design by bypassing altogether the numerous problems with which the show confronts, and the questions it poses to, its own globally incorporative cultural ambitions, and to its celebratory view of the family. Most surprisingly perhaps, despite the fact that Turner draws attention to the democratic potential of *The Family of Man*, he does not engage at all with the actual representation of democratic and global citizenship throughout the second half of the exhibition. One way to signal what is at stake here is to say that, in the example of the family photographs presented by Turner as illustrative of the cultural meanings and formal processes of the exhibition, empathy is both solicited and given too easily for it to be a true test for the politics of participatory democracy in mid-century America.

There were other passages in the MoMA version of *The Family of Man* that were, in their aesthetic strategies and their cultural meanings, more difficult than the one Turner chooses as exemplary. In these passages, there was a more acute sense that empathy, and so too 'mutual recognition' and 'choice', involve a *labour*, that they are ends to be *achieved*, because in order to get to them the viewer must first confront the challenge posed by the many varieties of cultural and social displacements of the self the exhibition invited. The process of negotiating the mental and affective experiences generated by the network of associations I have called the structures of rhyme did not, properly speaking, present viewers with a set of choices between a range of identifications that were driven by the impulses of empathy and mutual recognition, though these impulses were, in their own right, active throughout the exhibition. Rather, the rhymes and associations entangled the viewers in the vying claims of multiple cultural and social realities, claims that choice must assess if it is to become the *informed* choice that is a necessity for participatory democracy. One of the most frequently repeated assertions about *The Family of Man* is that it ignores the claims of difference and history in its insistent celebration of a common humanity or human nature. At least some of the images and layouts I examine in fact insist on cultural and social difference as the reality that must be faced if choosing commonality is to have any real meaning – these images measure the viewers' understanding and acceptance of the common ground proposed by the exhibition by the degree of their critical reflection on their own social location and cultural selves in relation to others.

I examine the second and seventh rooms or sections of the exhibition as it was installed at MoMA (see illustration 26). The second room contained images of mothers with children and of fathers with sons and so can be read easily as only a continuation of the first long room that presented viewers with images of lovers,

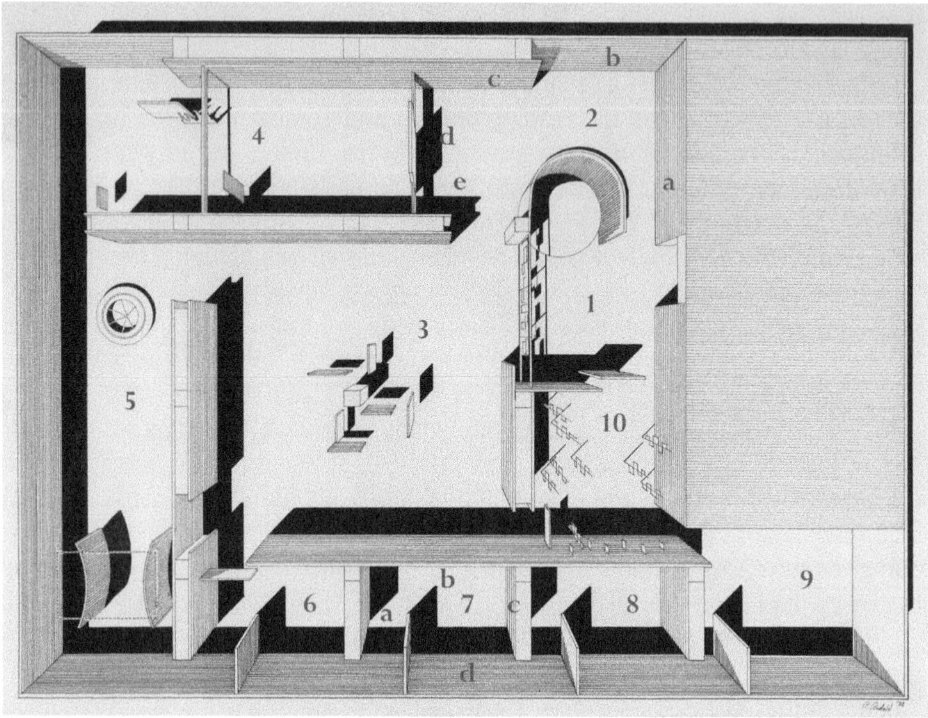

26 Floor plan, *The Family of Man*, on view 24 January–8 May 1955 at the Museum of Modern Art, New York City.

marriage, pregnancy, childbirth and motherly nurture of babies. At the very end of the first room were photographs of children at play, and as the viewers turned left from these into the second room, the theme of play was continued on the right-hand wall, thus further connecting the two rooms. But the second room also displayed images that marked striking departures from the reassuring narrative of affection and joy established by the images (or at least by most of the images) in the previous room. There were images of abandoned and lonely children and shocking images of children committing acts of violence against other children and against adults. Equally significant was the introduction into the continued theme of motherhood and nurturing of differences of race and class. The second room was, then, an interruption in the exhibition's flowing celebration of family life. This is important because all viewers had to move through this room before reaching the large space of the third room with the group of American, Bechuanaland, Japanese and Italian family pictures at its centre; in other words, the disjunctive experience of the second room helped frame an approach to the pivotal statement of the exhibition's core theme. It is clear from the rest of Steichen's exhibition design that the experience of the second room was not intended merely as a momentary disturbance that was to be absorbed by the cosmopolitan empathy and fellowship of the family group portraits. The second room introduced notes into the exhibition that continued to sound throughout its later movements. The visual motifs and layouts of the second room were most notably picked up in remarkably subtle and unexpected ways in the seventh room that dealt with hard times and famine, man's inhumanity to man, and social protest and revolt. If the family group portraits were the most obvious axis around which the exhibition revolved, the dialogue between rooms two and seven signalled another structuring axis that ran in parallel throughout the installation. The reading of the second room is, then, also an entrance into a reading of this larger structure and dynamic.

***

At the threshold of what we can take as the second room or section, visitors found themselves at a distance of about 27 feet from the back wall, and this is more or less the point from which Ezra Stoller took his installation shot of the room (see illustration 27).[12] The central panel of the back wall was a floor-to-ceiling image of a leafless tree, and on this panel had been fixed a series of small prints (wall 2d). From

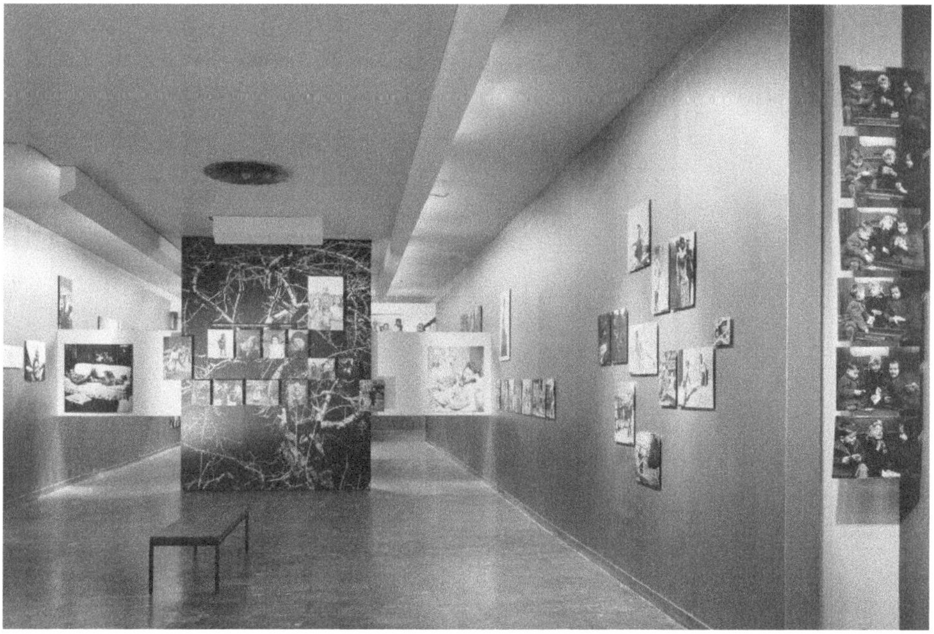

27 ***The Family of Man*** **at the Museum of Modern Art, New York City.**

the threshold, one could have seen that these images were also of children, but it would not have been clear what exactly the children were doing. By contrast, on the two white panels that extended to the left and right of the central panel, there were two large photographs whose contents would have been quite clear. To the left was a picture (38" x 38", by Diane and Allan Arbus, FoM53) of a father and son lying on a couch together, reading. On the right was the image (38" x 33¼", by Wayne Miller, FoM 33) that would have been clearest of all: a mother lying down, with her young daughter sitting on the bed beside her holding a baby. This picture more than any other would have immediately suggested a continuity between the first and the second rooms: the woman was in fact Joan Miller, Wayne Miller's wife, the same woman visitors had seen giving birth in the childbirth section of the first room. And the baby we see being held by the girl is the same child seen being born in the first.

Once visitors moved further into the second part of section two, they would have seen more clearly the row of seven photographs along the right wall (wall 2c), all of them identical in their vertical dimension (16') (see illustration 28). Six of these

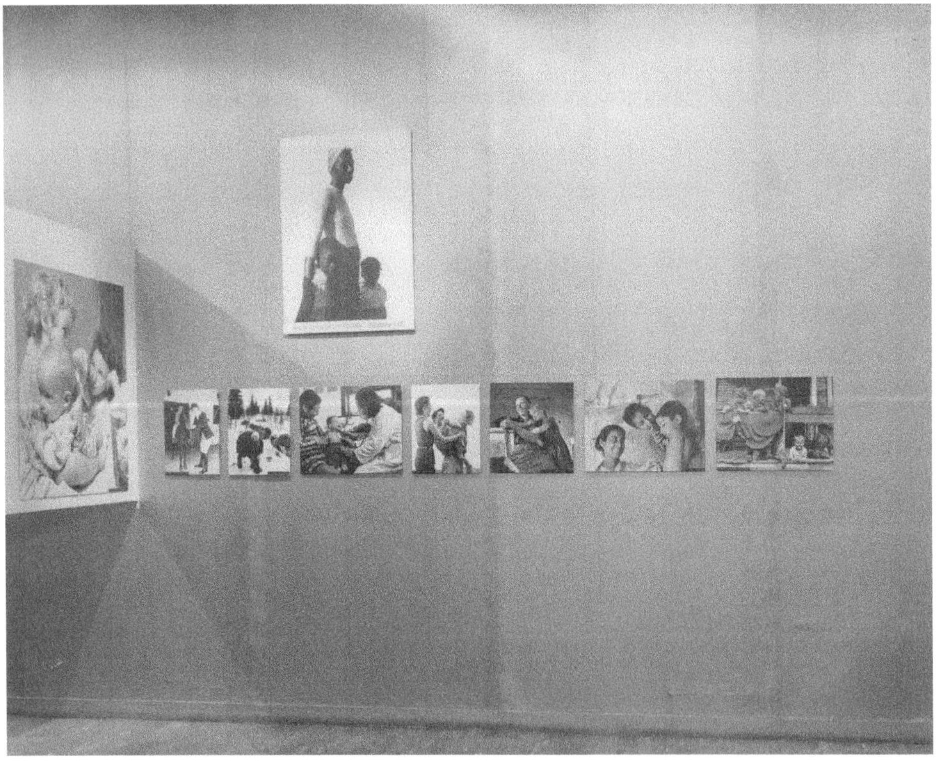

28 Rolf Petersen, installation view of *The Family of Man* at the Museum of Modern Art, New York City, 1955.

showed mothers with young children – the exception was the first image in the sequence. This showed a group of shabbily dressed boys on a back porch, clearly at a pause in the midst of play. This image linked back then to the previous two clusters of images of children at play. This strategy of using an image as a sort of stitch to connect sequences, to create continuity between them, was one that was used repeatedly throughout the exhibition. This line of photographs guided visitors to the large photograph of the young Miller family, the image that most loudly declared this continuity. But the second room presented the viewer with much more than a mere repetition of the themes from the opening section of the exhibition: it staged a continuity only to invite the viewer to reflect critically on the familial forms so far introduced.

The image of the Miller family, along with the matching image of the father and son on the couch to its left, together appear to encapsulate what has so often been claimed, and criticized, as the core ideology of *The Family of Man*: the white, bourgeois American family lifted from the pages of *Life* magazine, and constructed by the exhibition as the universal familial norm for the MoMA visitors who imagined themselves reflected in the images before them. But it was precisely at this point, and this early on in the exhibition, that Steichen's layout invited the audience to hold back from projecting its own cultural assumptions and social values as normative and universal.

The photos of mothers and children along the right wall of the second room conducted visitors not only to the Miller family but also to the large photograph of an African American woman with two children by Consuelo Kanaga (34" x 25¾", FoM 32) placed towards the farthest corner of the right wall, at a 90-degree angle to the Miller photograph. The uniform line of pictures of mothers and children along the wall pointed to the Miller photograph as a climactic and emphatic statement of the themes of motherhood and family. The Kanaga image was placed literally above and outside the directional and thematic flow of this photographic sequence. The physical dynamics of Steichen's display, the way that it proposed a movement for the body of the viewer, is important here. The smaller pictures were placed a little below eye level and would have required the viewer wanting to see them properly to approach them and to bend down or to tilt the head slightly. As viewers came to the end of this row of images, they would have turned to face the Miller image which was hung so that the eye level was at the centre of the image, and the size of the image produced an immersive experience of familial intimacy quite distinct from the experience of looking at such a photograph in the family album of a relative, friend or stranger. The Kanaga image, on the other hand, was hung above eye level. Given the contrast in size between it and the photographs below it, and its pronounced verticality, both in format and content, it would have required viewers to step back and look up. What they would have faced as they did so was a dramatic shift in mood and meaning.

The Kanaga image served as an interlocutor and inquisitor of both the Miller photograph and of the MoMA visitors themselves. There is as much love in the Kanaga photograph as there is in any of the other images of mothers and children.

But the sense of joy that marks all the other images has been drained from it. In its place there is a sense of a stony yet precarious fortitude born of adversity. The intense glare of the afternoon light that flattens the woman and her two children against the harsh white of the breeze block wall contrasts sharply with the comforting domestic interior in Miller's image, and the differences of race and class between white and black families would have been as immediately apparent to the visitors to *The Family of Man* at MoMA as they are to us today. And of course these same differences would have marked an equal distance between most of the visitors themselves and the family in Kanaga's photograph.

What is perhaps most remarkable about Kanaga's image is the way in which the eyes of the mother and the two children transform the mere appearance of difference into an active question about the place of difference within the exhibition's quest for commonality. Steichen's layout and his choice of photographs for this section of the second room both signal an awareness of this potential in the image. Out of all the mothers-and-children images in this room, Kanaga's is the only one in which any of the subjects directly look at the photographer-viewer, and Steichen's placing of the image above eye level, a tactic that accentuates the effect of Kanaga's low shooting angle, means that the image would have looked down at the viewer, not in judgement but as cautiously interrogative. Is this family the 'same' as the Miller family? Can this family be incorporated into 'the family of man' *without* an acknowledgement of what separates it from the Miller family? Is it really the case that Steichen is oblivious to the differences his own exhibition design foregrounds? Does this design invite an inattentive immersion in the broad spectacle of image constellations or does it make possible a more reflective engagement? The eyes of the little girl in the shadow of her mother are just visible; they are hard to read but the way the girl holds her left arm behind her and clings to her mother with her right betokens a sense of apprehension and unease. The boy's engagement with the photographer is less reserved and cautious, and his eyes are not yet marked by the wariness, hardship and fatigue that are evident in his mother's eyes. The photographer is a stranger and the holding back of trust is palpable in the sense of awkwardness in the image, and in the sense of both affection and vulnerability in the way the mother's right arm pulls her son to her side. The Miller photograph is very much a family photograph made public; the mother, daughter and son are enclosed in their own world; the viewer who is a stranger is not a shaping presence in the scene because the photographer is the husband and the father, and so part of the private world pictured, rather than an intruder in it. In the Kanaga image it seems as if the family has been stopped as it walked down the street and been asked to exhibit in a public space the bonds that hold it together, and at the same time to expose the marks of the social and cultural forces that make such cohesion a perpetual travail. Kanaga's achievement as a photographer, in this image at least, hovers on the border of predictable social documentary, but Steichen's placing of the image high up on the wall structures, in the context of the other images in the sequence around it, a relationship with the MoMA visitor that forestalls the potential objectification of subjects in social documentary and brings to the fore the sense of dignity and agency also available in the image.

Roland Barthes articulated what has been widely repeated as the standard critique of *The Family of Man* when he argued that the exhibition erased the differences of time, place, culture and social experience, or in other words, history itself; that instead of pursuing a 'progressive humanism' fully engaged with these differences, it proposed a 'myth of the human "condition"' sustained by an appeal to a human commonality grounded in nature. Barthes drives home his point most sharply by deploying rhetorically the facts of racial violence and inequality to pose the question of 'History' to *The Family of Man*: 'why not ask the parents of Emmet [sic] Till, the young Negro assassinated by the Whites what *they* think of *The Great Family of Man*?'; 'let us also ask the North African workers of the Goutte d'Or district in Paris what they think of *The Great Family of Man*'.[13]

The Kanaga photograph of the African American mother and her two children, I would argue, already asks the question about history and difference that Barthes wants to address to the exhibition. It is in fact an early formulation of a series of such questions that emerge as the exhibition unfolds. Later sections of the exhibition included images precisely of the racial violence and the legacies of colonialism Barthes invoked as challenges to the exhibition: room seven included, at least in the first iteration of *The Family of Man*, a graphic image of the lynching of an African American man, and one of a South African black man protesting against the rule of apartheid. The photograph of the lynching had been removed by the time the exhibition reached Paris, but the South African image was still in the show.

I have used Barthes's articulation of the claims of history to describe what I see as the work done by the Kanaga image within *The Family of Man*, and so to try and turn this articulation, and the assessment it supports, against themselves. But a mere reversal of the terms by which Barthes structures his assessment is not sufficient for opening up a richer reading of Steichen's exhibition. An 'eternal lyricism' does exercise a strong pull throughout the exhibition but the true and most meaningful opposite of history in Steichen's design is not nature, but private life and its resistance to history, a resistance to what John Berger has called history's 'monopoly of time'.[14] In the Miller photograph, the family is enclosed not only in its own space but also in its own time. For the Miller photograph to act as a true interlocutor of the Kanaga image it had to offer something more than mere bourgeois self-regard, to be more than a weak foil for the challenge of difference. Barthes's sense of the deficiencies of *The Family of Man* must have been shaped, at least partly, by the recent experience of war. The war made certain political and ethical concerns imperatives, and Steichen's response to these seemed inadequate to Barthes. But Steichen's deployment of the Miller photograph, whatever its original context, in relation to difference and as counterpoint to what Barthes calls history, must be understood as having its own historicity. The people who came to see the exhibition at MoMA, and the majority of the millions who saw it around the world, had lived through several years of a war unprecedented in its global scale and violence, years when it must have seemed as if life consisted of *nothing but* history. In the years that followed the close of the war, the claims of private life must have been felt especially keenly, and in ways that it may be difficult to grasp for those of us, at least within the relative security and stability of Western Europe and North America, who continue to grapple with *The Family of Man*. The affective intensity of this appeal was, I suspect, a significant factor contributing to the worldwide success of the exhibition.

In order, then, to recover a true sense of dialogue in the juxtaposition of the Miller and Kanaga photographs, we need to reimagine the lines of force that might have structured the visual experience generated for the MoMA audience by this juxtaposition, and others like it, in 1955. We need, for one thing, to imagine what it must have been like for a largely white and middle-class audience at MoMA to be looking at the Kanaga photograph in tandem with Miller's only months after the Supreme Court's (17 May 1954) decision in the case of *Brown vs. Board of Education* had abolished segregation in American schools. *The Family of Man* in fact offers a sustained engagement with race, inequality and injustice that is remarkable given the fact that it predates the dramatic developments of the Civil Rights movement in the second half of the decade.

Looking back from the twenty-first century, after the Civil Rights movement, feminism, multiculturalism, anti-colonial movements and post-colonial studies and the many theorizations of difference have all reshaped our perceptual and cultural frameworks, it is perhaps easier to accord immediate sympathy to Kanaga's African American family than it is do so with Miller's white family. An awareness of issues of class, gender, ethnicity and cultural and patriarchal hegemony that have in many ways overdetermined our understanding of the post-war United States, and given us the cliché of 'the conformist fifties', may help us better understand the relationship between these two photographs, but it may also get in the way of this understanding. For the vast majority of MoMA visitors, Miller's photograph would have been less mediated, and the Kanaga photograph would have posed a more radical challenge than it does today, a challenge that Steichen's layout did its best to ensure that the visitors faced. The identification of the mother and two children in the Kanaga image as Americans in the small caption attached to the photograph, and the contemporaneity signalled by their clothing were, it would seem, calculated to add emphasis to this address to the audience: the Kanaga image was 'sandwiched' between two large photographs of black individuals, a picture by Lennart Nilsson of a mother cradling an infant in a forest in the Belgian Congo, and one by Nat Farbman from Bechuanaland of a father teaching his son to hunt (wall 2e, FoM 28, 51); the Nilsson image brought the sequence of images of mothers and children in the first room to a climax and the Farbman image concluded the fathers and son sequence in the second room that followed the Kanaga and Miller images; in both the Nilsson and Farbman photographs, the figures were near naked, in a forest or hunting on the savannah, and could easily have been read as 'primitive' and so as distant 'others'; the same could not be said of the mother and children in the Kanaga image, and Steichen's layout seemed designed to bring home to the MoMA visitors the proximity of their African American compatriots.[15]

The Kanaga photograph was not the only image to introduce a dissonant note into the second room, and not the only one to articulate the challenge of prejudice in the midst of cosmopolitan diversity. As mentioned earlier, there was a cluster of

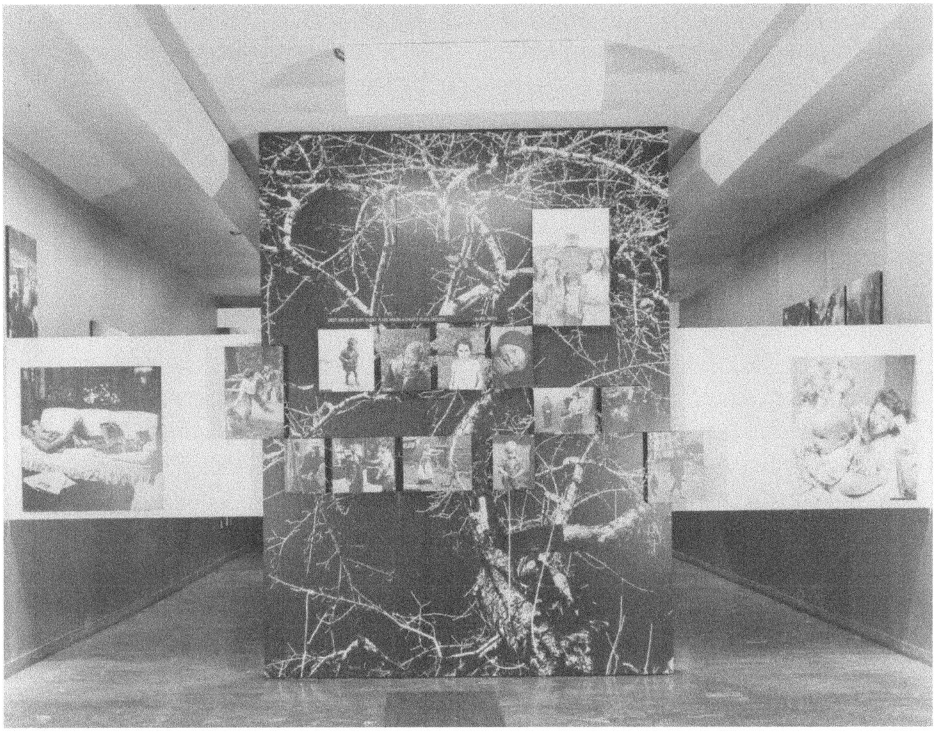

29 Rolf Petersen, installation view of *The Family of Man* at the Museum of Modern Art, New York City, 1955.

images considerably smaller than the Miller and Kanaga photographs placed on the central panel of the back wall, to the left of the Miller family. These images fell, broadly, into two groups: images that recast childhood nurture as forms of abandonment and isolation, and those that recast play as forms of violence (see illustration 29). If the size and location of the Kanaga photograph constructed for it had a declarative impact and the ability to subordinate the viewers to its own gaze, making them step back and look up, the smaller pictures on the back wall relied on a perceptual intimacy for their affect on viewers. They only revealed their contents fully as visitors approached them, and the fact that almost all of them were placed either just above or just below the average eye line meant that the viewer was encouraged to lean in a little if he or she wanted to take a better look. These images were pasted onto the floor-to-ceiling image of gnarled and leafless branches and twigs (the image was by Steichen himself though he was not identified as the photographer), and the faces of the children in them seemed to emerge out of the dark interior of the woody entanglements that Steichen's display used as a metaphor for what the textual caption (from Lillian Smith) across the top of these images referred to as 'that silent place where a child's fears crouch'.

Nothing in the exhibition so far had prepared visitors for these images. The photographs of childhood aggression in particular were visually and emotionally eruptive, and especially unsettling: the clenched fist of the boy about to hit another; the little boy about to bring down a plank of wood on a woman who has raised her hands to protect herself; almost the same gestures caught in a fight between a girl and a boy over what appears to be a soft toy; and perhaps the most unnerving image of all, a young girl tied to a tree, 'caught', in film critic Vernon Young's apt description, 'in a twist of fear that she may be the victim in a game that has gone too far' (FoM 46–7).[16]

The pictures of isolated children to the left of those of childhood violence were moving but the majority of them could more easily be assimilated into the conventions of social documentary – they were very much the kinds of images that had become familiar in the United States thanks to the many documentary projects undertaken by the Farm Security Administration during the 1930s. Six of the nine appeared to be images drawn from the rural and urban poor, but three clearly registered abandonment within the context of the middle-class world: a mother sits on a comfortable chair, preoccupied with the contents of a box on her lap, while a young and apprehensive boy stands pressed against the wall behind her, his hands clasped in a gesture of patient waiting and fear (FoM 134); in the midst of a busy party with musicians where all is in motion, a young girl is caught standing alone, ignored by the adults in the room (FoM 132); and a well dressed mother strides down a city street, her young son following behind, his head bowed (FoM 47).[17]

These images, and the images of aggression in which markers of class were either unclear or not emphatically underlined, did not allow the MoMA audience to easily distance itself from the social experiences shown. Both to the left and to the right an image from this cluster extended beyond the central panel and encroached onto the image of the father and son by Diane and Allan Arbus and the Miller photograph, as if to indicate that the realities made visible on the central panel could not simply be cordoned off from the more comfortable securities of the larger family photographs. And it was the photograph of the striding mother, clearly middle class, that overlapped with the panel with the Miller family photograph, as if this woman was walking straight into the family's space.

The connection between the back panel and the images of maternal and paternal nurture to either side of it was made equally, though with more varied affect, by Steichen's metaphorical use of the tree in his layout. The leafless branches of the tree in the large back panel photograph, which stood for a blighted childhood, referred the visitors back to the Kanaga image and to the text placed immediately beneath it: 'She is a tree of life to them … (Proverbs 3:18).'[18] The sharp ironies of this contrast would have added another layer to the way visitors saw the African American mother. The text from Proverbs only reinforces what is already evident in the photograph itself: that the mother is a figure of shelter, strength and sustenance. But the contrast with the lifeless tree of the back panel pushes to the fore her sameness with the mothers in the other images around her rather than her difference. They are all, equally, trees of life to their children.

This does not contradict or undermine my own earlier reading that the function of the Kanaga family portrait was to help introduce the claims of difference into the exhibition. It is in fact one of the effects consistently achieved by Steichen's exhibition design that a shift in perspective can reconfigure the meanings of a particular image or group of images, and in some instances this happened several times over as visitors moved through the rooms. The Kanaga image is a good example of this because it functioned within this structure of multiplicity in ways other than those already noted for it.

More often than not in *The Family of Man* the quotations from world literature and folk traditions, chosen by Dorothy Norman, were placed among, above or below image groups. This created the sense that the images were collectively constellated around the theme signalled by the text. In the case of the Kanaga photograph (and there are other examples of this in the exhibition) the text from Proverbs is attached directly to the bottom edge of the image, as if, even as it applied to all the images of motherhood around it, it somehow applied more specifically or more emphatically to the African American mother. The exhibition design used the metaphor of the tree to construct this individualized link, I believe, because what connected Kanaga's family portrait and the images of childhood violence and abandonment was not just a contrastive view of parental care and its failure, but also the problem of race and racism. This thematic engagement was only obliquely present in the images on the back panel but it is something that becomes visible as we reflect further on the design of this section of the exhibition, and then on its relationship with later sections.

The back panel photographs of children departed from the expectations established by the exhibition so far in another important respect: all 13 images were of white children (and three white adult women), whereas all the previous sequences, like all the ones that were to follow, displayed cultural and ethnic diversity. And nine were from the United States, the other four being from Canada, Poland, Italy and Sweden. So the focus was entirely on North America and Western Europe. It was as if Steichen wanted to hold a mirror up to an audience he knew would, at least in the United States, be largely white and predominantly middle class. This group of images would seem then to shift attention away from familial nurture to something like childhood fractures in the 'white psyche', broadly understood beyond the causal explanations of a particular class or environment. One could argue that to the extent that these images focused implicitly on 'whiteness', they could be read as addressing, though extremely obliquely, the issue of race; the caption that accompanied these images made such a reading more plausible.

As noted earlier, the quotation that accompanies this set of photographs is taken from the work of Lillian Smith: 'deep inside in that silent place where a child's fears crouch'. There is nothing in the quotation itself to indicate that issues of race are of concern. But Smith, herself white and Southern, was known almost exclusively for her outspoken and controversial critiques of the culture of segregation and prejudice in the American South. Her novel *Strange Fruit* (1944) dramatized both an interracial romance and lynching. Even though the book was banned in Boston and

Detroit, and briefly banned also from being mailed through the US Postal Service, until Eleanor Roosevelt intervened and had her husband remove the prohibition, it proved to be an enormous commercial success nationwide. The essays in *Killers of a Dream* (1949) explored the psychological damage done to children, white and black, by the culture of segregation, and the ways in which the seeds of racism and racial violence are sown at this early stage. The 'lessons' learned in childhood were, Smith declared, 'the white man's burden'.[19] The quotation used in the exhibition was from *The Journey* (1954), published just months before the exhibition opened; it was extracted from an account of childhood fears of death in the face of high levels of illness and mortality in the South, rather than from a discussion of racism.[20] But the recognition of Lillian Smith's name would have been far more important than identifying the source of the quotation. The association of Smith with issues of racism would have been available to any visitor with a basic familiarity with contemporary literary culture and social debate, and the exhibition's layout ensured that visitors would have read Smith's name under the gaze of the African American woman in Kanaga's photograph.

To read the Smith quotation as something more than a comment on universal childhood psychology, to read it additionally as an indirect comment on racism, and so as a sort of response to the Kanaga photograph and the 'tree of life' text attached to it, may with justification appear as an *over*-reading, at least at this stage of the discussion. But when we turn from the second room to the seventh, we will see that photographs that dealt with racial inequality and violence in the later room created some of the strongest links back to the earlier section of the exhibition, not only to the Kanaga image but also to the images of childhood isolation and aggression. Once these connections are seen, it becomes more difficult to put aside the larger range of meanings Smith's words would have made available in 1950s America.[21]

***

Roughly 15 feet in width and 22 feet in length, with an entrance at one end and an exit at the opposite end, the seventh room, like the room before it and the one after, was more conventional in its structure than some of the other spaces in the exhibition. As Sandeen has noted, the 'traffic flow was much more constricted' in the later sections of the MoMA installation. These rooms were 'the most traditionally arranged', and required 'the contemplation and introspection of a more confined space'.[22] My own reading suggests that the demands of contemplation and introspection were in fact always present in *The Family of Man*, albeit in a variety of forms, but Sandeen does register accurately a certain shift in pace and attention in the exhibition brought about by the changes in spatial design.

Along the right wall (wall 7d) were photographs of young adults, engaged largely in leisure activities: fooling around on the beach, racing along in an open-top car, jammed together on a crowded dance floor (see illustration 30). While most of these images included both young men and women, five portraits of young women

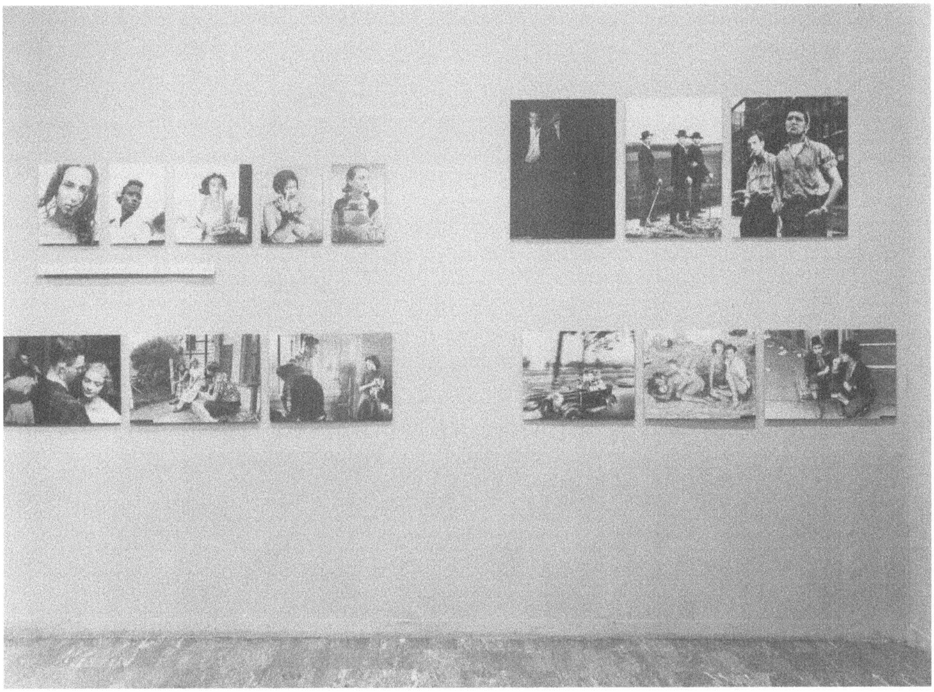

30 Rolf Petersen, installation view of *The Family of Man* at the Museum of Modern Art, New York City, 1955.

were placed along the top edge of the display. Each showed a closely cropped, individual face, and in each case the eyes were turned away to the right. Three of the portraits seemed to be concerned with appearance: the woman from South Africa was applying make-up; the white American woman was holding a hair brush in her hand; and the African American woman was smartly dressed, with a large flower prominently placed in her hair. The portrait to the far left was less fashionably turned out but no less an example of introverted beauty. The remaining portrait, a white American and the youngest of the five women, signalled studiousness rather than vanity: she held a clipboard, book and pen. There were no equivalent portraits of young men, though there were three images to the right of men in groups of twos and threes, and in each case, in contrast to the portraits of women, the men stared out at the viewer. These gendered visual dynamics, as I hope to demonstrate, played a significant part in how visitors were invited to understand the images on the opposite wall in this room, and also the connections between the images in the seventh room and those encountered earlier in the second.

The wall opposite the pictures of young adults, and the two shorter side walls of the room, all to the left of the entrance, presented visitors with very different

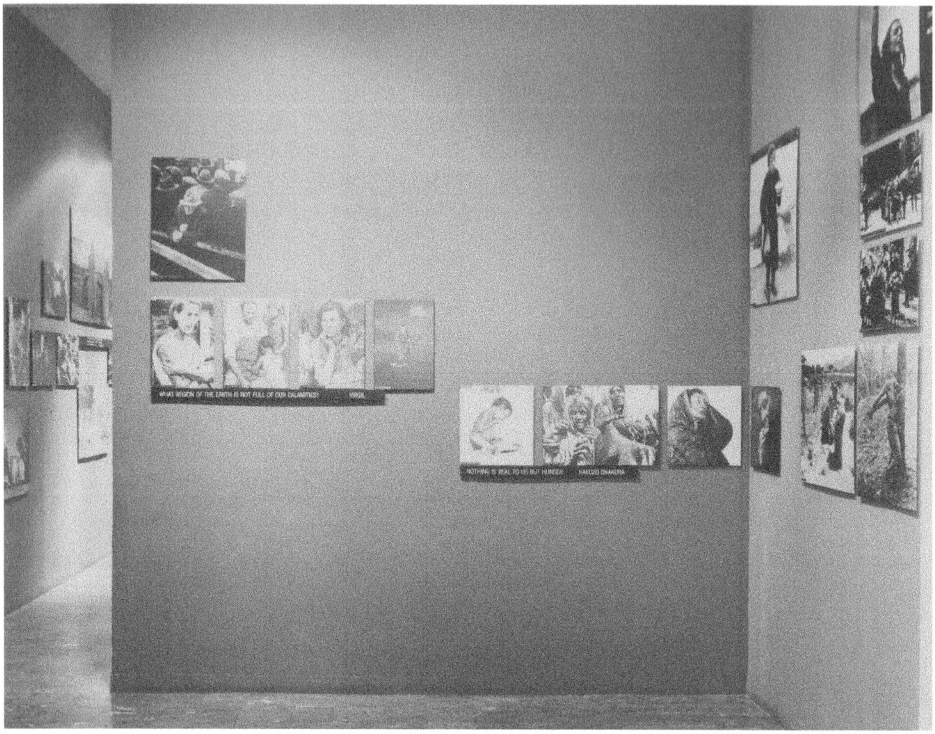

31 Rolf Petersen, installation view of *The Family of Man* at the Museum of Modern Art, New York City, 1955.

realities. Immediately to the left of the entrance, on the short sidewall and extending a little onto the long wall (walls 7a and b), were images of hunger, famine and hard times (see illustration 31). Apart from the spill over from this sequence, the long one was divided into two sections of unequal length. The first and shorter one dealt with man's inhumanity to man (see illustration 32). The second, which extended across the remainder of the wall and along the short wall at the farthest end of the room (wall 7c), displayed pictures mostly of social protest and revolt (see illustrations 33 and 34). It was these photographs along the left side of the room that presented visitors with a series of visual motifs that most consistently invited them to recognize, and so to reflect on, associations between the images in this room and those they had seen in the second, though these were not the only images in the seventh room to propose such connections.

Among the photographs of hunger was Dorothea Lange's 'Migrant Mother' (1936) (FoM 151), the most widely reproduced photograph from the 1930s documentary archive of the Farm Security Administration. The composition of Lange's photograph, with the two children pressed close against the mother and

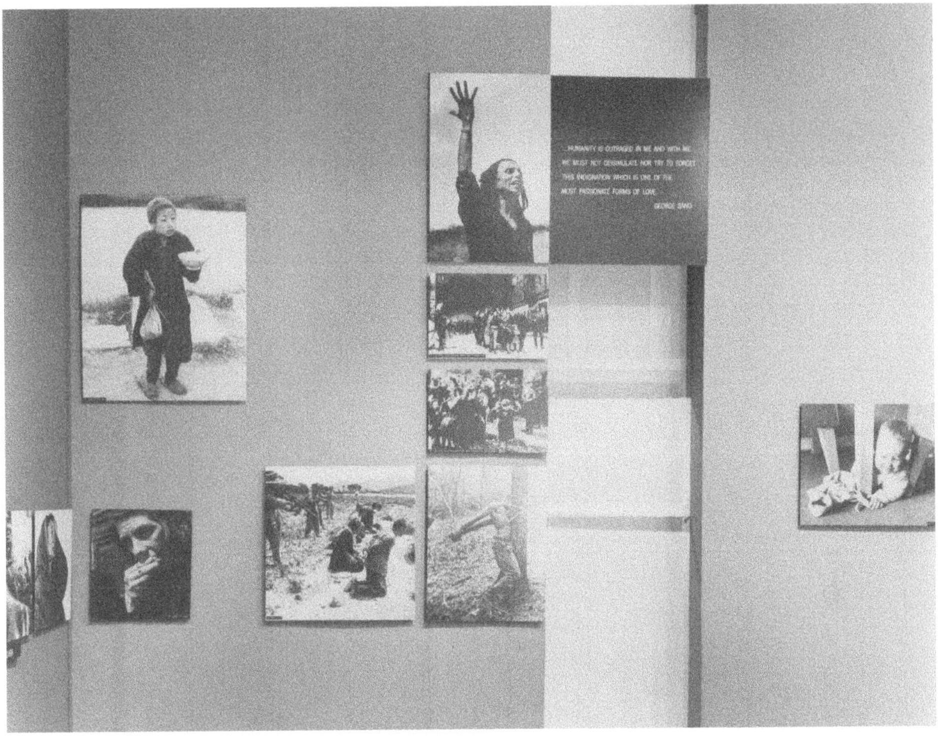

32 Rolf Petersen, installation view of *The Family of Man* at the Museum of Modern Art, New York City, 1955.

the baby in her arms, recalled the portrait of Joan Miller and her daughter and son, though the social reality captured by Lange was closer to the world of Kanaga's African American family than to Miller's, and the care-worn distraction of Lange's mother separated her from the motherly attentiveness and solicitude of the women in both Miller's and Kanaga's images. The photograph of the animated and vocal Korean women behind a wooden barrier and a barbed wire fence could equally be read as a transfiguration of the three silent and still Canadian girls, slightly bemused, behind a wire fence on the central tree panel in the second room, the largest of the images there (FoM 169, 48).

Steichen made explicit the associations between the seventh room and the second by placing to the immediate left of the picture of the Korean demonstrators two images that otherwise seem entirely out of place: one was of a crawling and crying baby caught between the legs of two chairs and a table, as if in a cage; the other showed a young child behind the slats of a wooden gate (FoM 168). These photographs were positioned in between the images of inhumane acts and those of social protest but appeared to make little sense as a segue between

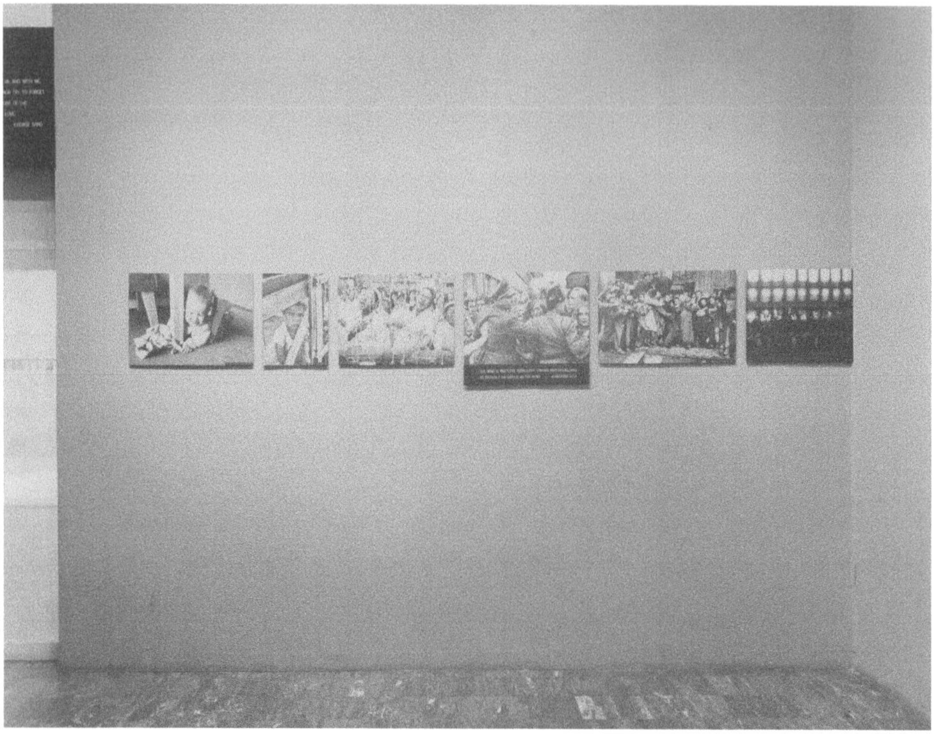

33 Rolf Petersen, installation view of *The Family of Man* at the Museum of Modern Art, New York City, 1955.

these two sections. Their purpose, in fact, was to recall the images of the isolated and abandoned children from the second room. As if to underline this purpose, the picture of the trapped baby was by Wayne Miller and showed the very son held by Miller's daughter in the family portrait in the second room, and the same child visitors had seen being born in the birth section of the first. And on the wall opposite, among the portraits of single women, were two photographs that further consolidated the structure of the seventh room as a transformed version of the second. The beautiful white woman with the hairbrush looked quite like Joan Miller; she was at least recognizably of the same type. And the young black woman to her left, though more elegantly dressed than the African American mother in the second room, was nevertheless the subject of a portrait by none other than Consuelo Kanaga. These two women were younger than the mothers seen earlier; they seemed preoccupied with themselves and their appearance and not turned outward towards the needs of others. There was then both an actual and a symbolic gulf between them and the two isolated children on the wall opposite. But the women also looked onto the images of social protest, and

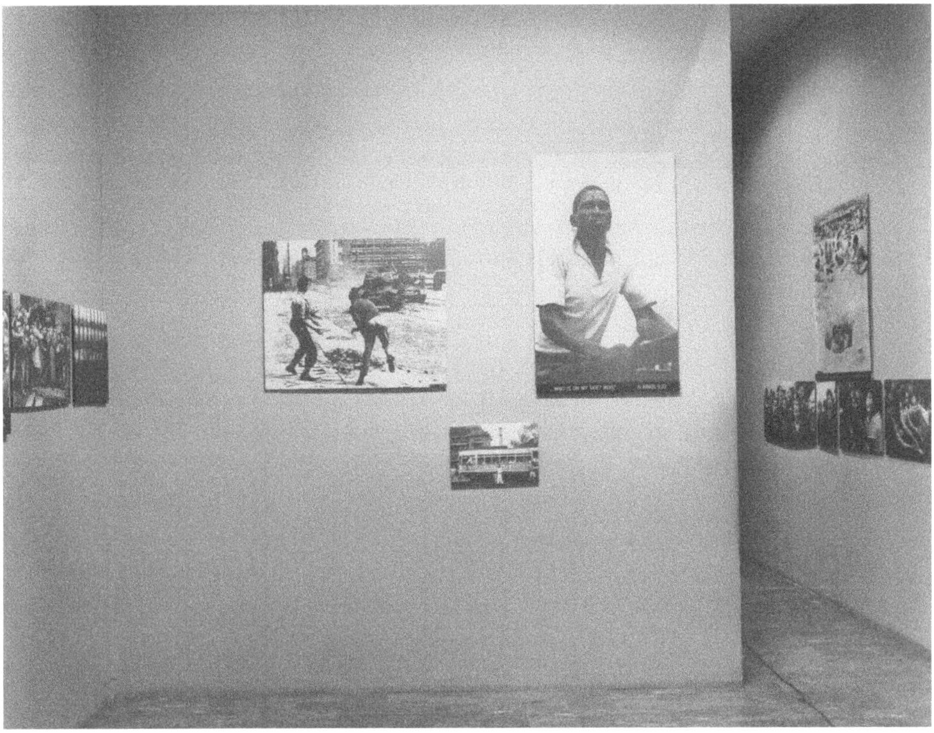

34 Rolf Petersen, installation view of *The Family of Man* at the Museum of Modern Art, New York City, 1955.

these photographs announced a move into an active participation in the public realm that was different to both the self-enclosure of individual identity and the activities that define the private realm of family life.

One function of the rhymes constructed by Steichen between the second and the seventh rooms was then to signal an evolution of agency. In the transformation of the Canadian children into the Korean protestors, it is as if the younger North American girls had pushed out of their childhood passivity and perplexity into social activism. A similar shift in agency is suggested by Homer Page's striking photograph of a black South African man with a marching bass drum mallet in his hand that Steichen placed at the end of the sequence of social protest photographs (FoM 171). The physical dimensions of this print (46" x 29.5"), its placement (above the eye line and above the other images in the sequence) and its low shooting angle and the consequent verticality of its composition all recall Kanaga's photograph of the African American mother and her two children. Here too, as with the transformation of the Canadian girls into the Korean female protesters, hesitation and a familial protectiveness are transformed into purposive, socially engaged action. The inquisitorial gaze of the black woman that subjects the viewer to its scrutiny in Kanaga's image becomes aspirational in the photograph of the South African man. If the viewer experiences empathetic identification when looking at Page's photograph, he or she shares also the hope that is implied by the drummer's eyes that seem turned towards the sky. And as with the Kanaga family portrait, the portrait of the South African Man was accompanied by a Biblical quotation, and here too the text was attached directly to the bottom edge of the image: 'Who is on my side? Who?' (2 Kings 9.32). The implicitly interrogative gaze of the African American mother is here turned explicitly into an active question that asks the viewer to define his or her own commitments. There is nothing in Page's portrait of the South African man to indicate that the man is engaged in political activity, but Steichen's placing of the image as the climactic statement in a sequence of protest images clearly invited such a reading. The drum makes the protest audible, gives it a 'voice', just as the open mouths of the Korean demonstrators suggest speech. And it also signals a pointed transformation of the symbolism of the photograph of the Peruvian flute player which was repeated as a figure of harmony at several points throughout the exhibition. The movement from Kanaga's photograph to Page's can be described, then, as a movement from interiority to exteriority, from the enclosing familial embrace shaped by conditions of social and racial inequality to an active struggle against these forms of division and prejudice.

But racial prejudice was addressed most directly and forcefully by what was without question the most startling and most shocking visual rhyme between the seventh and the second rooms: this was the rhyme between the graphic image of the slumped body of a dead African American man tied to a tree, his hands bound behind his back, the visual record of a lynching, and the photograph seen earlier in the exhibition of the young girl also tied to a tree, her hands also bound tightly behind her, her turning body and blurred face captured in what looks like a moment of panic. It may be that the placing of the quotation from Lillian Smith above the picture of this girl, and above all the pictures of childhood violence and isolation, was merely fortuitous. If so, it proved to be a remarkable accident of design that nevertheless helped bring into view a configuration of unexpected meanings within a visual network that stretched across the exhibition.

In dwelling on Smith as a point of reference I am not suggesting that her inclusion in the exhibition was intended as a 'key' to meanings and connections otherwise invisible. Knowing who Smith was and what her writings were about added a focusing perspective on what tied the second and the seventh rooms together, but it was not a necessary condition for understanding or affectively experiencing the workings of these ties. The comparative readings of the images I have pursued should make it clear that the structures of rhyme and association that configured *The Family of Man* were equally available to any visitor attentive to the complexity and subtlety of Steichen's visual orchestration independently of its textual accompaniments. If these connections set in motion critical reflection, they did so because they were first experienced, and perhaps more powerfully so, as a kind of disturbing consonance at the edge of consciousness, like a refrain from an earlier moment that haunts the unfolding of the later stages of a musical composition and stirs memory into activity.

The connections built up within the seventh room itself were experienced altogether more directly. The association made by Steichen's layout between American racial prejudice and violence and South African apartheid was potentially explosive. The daring and power of Steichen's challenge to the self-comforting clichés of American exceptionalism become clearer still when we register that not only did he place the photograph of the lynching in dialogue with the photograph of the South African man, but also placed it below two photographs of Jews being rounded up by Nazi soldiers in the Warsaw Ghetto in 1943, and next to an image of blindfolded prisoners kneeling by a roadside and about to be executed by Chinese soldiers (FoM 166–7).[23]

The photograph of the Chinese execution was added to the exhibition several weeks after the opening at MoMA. Both it and the lynching photograph were then removed from the show some time later. The claim, often repeated, that the lynching image was removed after only two weeks is erroneous. The picture appears to have remained in the show up to the first week of April at least, so into the eleventh week of the exhibition's fifteen-week run at MoMA, and it may have remained in the show even longer. This means that roughly two-thirds of the 270,000 visitors to MoMA, and maybe more, would have seen the image, and so also the iteration of *The Family of Man* that I have been examining. It is no doubt true, as Wayne Miller claimed, that one reason why Steichen decided to remove the image was because he came to see it as 'dissonant to the composition' and 'to the theme', its graphic quality too much of an interruptive 'focal point', distracting visitors from the exhibition as a whole.[24] But a discussion among leading cultural figures in New York and Washington, not only about the impact of the photograph on the exhibition but above all about how the image would be received abroad, equally influenced Steichen's decision, as did the publicity given to the photograph by *Life* in a multi-page photo-spread on the exhibition published in the 14 February edition of the magazine.[25]

The eventual removal of the lynching photograph from *The Family of Man* evidenced a regrettable failure of nerve on Steichen's part, and it blunted the edge of the exhibition's politics. But it is not the case that the removal simply negated the exhibition's many social and political engagements and challenges. As John Roberts has argued, 'in a period when the representation of black peoples in the [American] illustrated magazines as other than victims and "primitives" was politically non-existent' and when there was 'violent anti-leftism and racism in the USA', Steichen's inclusion of 'a number of non-stereotypical images of black Americans' was 'actually progressive'.[26] Roberts's description, a welcome corrective though it is to many accounts of the exhibition, is perhaps too anodyne in its generality to capture precisely the energies that animate Steichen's exhibition design. The African American women in Kanaga's portraits and the South African man in Page's can certainly be characterized as 'non-stereotypical' but what makes them truly ‘progressive’ is not their mere inclusion in the show but the way Steichen’s command of design implies (one could also say wishes for and encourages) a movement from the inequalities of the status quo to social protest, and does so by framing this movement not with a common ‘blackness’ or human nature, but within a racism that is common to the United States and South Africa. This linkage would have been made with less force once the lynching photograph was removed, but it would have remained available to visitors nonetheless. The problems of race and the struggle against inequality were very much in the air. The anti-segregation decision in the case of *Brown vs. Board of Education* inevitably framed the representations of race and racism in the exhibition, but 1955 was also the year that would conclude, only seven months after the close of Steichen’s show at MoMA but while it was still touring the US, with Rosa Parks’s refusal, on 1 December 1955, to give up her seat on a bus to a white man in Montgomery, Alabama, an act which not only sparked the Montgomery bus boycott but also inaugurated the Civil Rights movement. One has only to imagine what it might have been like to encounter the dialogue between the African American mother and her children, and the South African drummer at this juncture to understand how Steichen’s exhibition design proposed a series of challenging social and political engagements to the visitors to *The Family of Man*.

Notes

1 New York: Bonanza Books, 1984, chap. 13 (no page numbers).

2 This chapter is an extract from a more detailed examination of the exhibition design, itself part of what will be a book-length study.

3 Olivier Lugon, 'Edward Steichen as Exhibition Designer', in *Edward Steichen: Lives in Photography*, ed. Todd Brandow and William E. Ewing (Minneapolis and Lausanne: Foundation for the Exhibition of Photography and the Musée de l'Elysée, 2007), 271.

4 This is W. Eugene Smith's famous 'The Walk to Paradise Garden' (1946). See Edward Steichen, *The Family of Man* (New York: Museum of Modern Art, 1955), 192. All further citations will be given in the text as 'FoM'.

5 Eric Sandeen, *Picturing an Exhibition: The Family of Man and 1950s America* (Albuquerque: University of New Mexico Press, 1995), 48, reads this passage quite differently as indicating that 'individual suffering was transcended by mankind's endurance'.

6 My framing of the narrative of *The Family of Man* as a movement from the private to the public realm is of course indebted to Hannah Arendt's *The Human Condition* (1958), which appeared only three years after the opening of Steichen's exhibit at MoMA, and to Arendt's discussion of the relation of thought and action in the *vita activa*. Ariella Azoulay's '*The Family of Man*: A Visual Universal Declaration of Human Rights', in *The Human Snapshot*, ed. Thomas Keenan and Tirdad Zolghadar (Feldmeilen; Anandale-on-Hudson, Berlin: LUMA Foundation, Center for Curatorial Studies, Bard College; Sternberg Press, 2013), 19–48, is the only other account I know that significantly reframes the humanism of the exhibition through a new assessment of its politics. Azoulay reads the exhibition 'as an archive containing the visual proxy of the United Nations' 1948 Universal Declaration of Human Rights' (20). While the reading presented here shares some of the political and ethical emphases of Azoulay's reassessment, it pursues a very different analysis of the formal properties of the MoMA installation, and of the way these shaped the meanings of the exhibition.

7 Fred Turner, '*The Family of Man* and the Politics of Attention in Cold War America', *Public Culture* 24, no. 1 (2012): 55–84. The article appeared in a revised form in Turner's *The Democratic Surround: Multimedia and American Liberalism from World War II to the Psychedelic Sixties* (Chicago: University of Chicago Press, 2013), chap. 6, 'The Museum of Modern Art makes the World a Family', 181–212.

8 Turner, '*The Family of Man* and the Politics of Attention', 57.

9 Turner, '*The Family of Man* and the Politics of Attention', 58.

10 Ibid., 76–81; Sandeen, *Picturing an Exhibition*, 46–9.

11 Ibid., 78. Emphasis in the original.

12 The measurement is from the detailed architectural floor plan (Museum of Modern Art, New York, Edward Steichen Archive V.B.i.24*).

13 Roland Barthes, *Mythologies*, trans. Annette Lavers (orig. 1957; London: Vintage, 2009), 122, 123–4. The exhibition was titled 'La *Grande* Famille des Hommes' when exhibited in France, hence Barthes's use of 'Great'. The Goutte d'Or is a neighbourhood in the 18th arrondissement of Paris with a large North African population.

14 John Berger, 'Appearances', in Berger and Jean Mohr, *Another Way of Telling* (New York: Random House, 1982), 104. See also Shamoon Zamir, *The Gift of the Face: Portraiture and Time in Edward S. Curtis's The North American Indian* (Chapel Hill: University of North Carolina Press, 2014), chap. 4, 'Against History's Monopoly of Time', 55–102.

15 For a more conventional ideological reading of these two images, see Marianne Hirsch, *Family Frames: Photography, Narrative* *and Postmemory* (Cambridge, MA: Harvard University Press, 1997), 58–65.

16 Young, 'Fugue of Faces', in Young, *On Film: Unpopular Essays on a Popular Art* (Chicago: Quadrangle Books, 1972), 49.

17 The first two of these images were moved in the book to a much later section: 132, 134.

18 Ellipsis in the original. The King James version gives the full verse as follows: 'She *is* a tree of life to them that lay hold upon her: and happy *is every one* that retaineth her.' In the English Standard version it is, 'She is a tree of life to those who lay hold of her; those who hold her fast are called blessed.'

19 'The Lessons' is the title of the fifth chapter of the book and 'The White Man's Burden' of the second part of the book. The Supreme Court had declared that 'segregation of white and colored children in public schools has a detrimental effect upon the colored children'.

20 Lillian Smith, *The Journey* (1954; New York: W.W. Norton, 1965), 43.

21 Gerd Hurm, in his contribution to the present volume, also suggests that the Smith quotation was meant to signal a concern with racism.

22 Sandeen, *Picturing an Exhibition*, 48.

23 Only one of the Warsaw Ghetto images is reproduced in the book of the exhibition.

24 Miller interviewed by Sandeen, November 1984. In Sandeen, *Picturing an Exhibition*, 50.

25 This account of the photographs of the lynching and the execution is based on a series of letters, written between late February and mid-March, between Neill Phillips, a retired Rear Admiral from the US Navy who was an important figure in the cultural world of Washington, DC; John Walker, Chief Curator at the National Gallery of Art in DC; Philip Graham, President and Chief Executive Officer of the *Washington Post*; and William Burden, President of MoMA (Museum of Modern Art, New York, Museum of Modern Art Exhibition Records 569.85). It also draws on the transcript of a discussion between Steichen and staff at the United States Information Agency in Washington, DC, from 27 April 1955 (MoMA Exhibition Records 569.87). Before removing the lynching photograph, Steichen revised the label for the image and added a date: 1937. This would have been in March. The image of the Chinese execution appears to have been added at the same time. After the images were removed, Steichen must also have resized and rearranged the images from the Warsaw Ghetto in order to recalibrate the display; this is how they appeared subsequently in all the travelling versions of the exhibition in both the United States and abroad. As far as I am aware, the inclusion and removal of the photograph of the execution, and the changes made to the lynching and Warsaw Ghetto photographs have not been discussed before. I hope to provide a more detailed account of all these revisions elsewhere. The *Life* magazine spread (132–43) not only reproduced the lynching photograph, but actually combined images from the second and seventh rooms across two pages, as if the editors had also registered some of the associations I have noted: the picture of the girl tied to the tree was placed directly opposite the photograph of the lynched man (140–1).

26 John Roberts, *The Art of Interruption: Realism, Photography and the Everyday* (Manchester: Manchester University Press, 1998), 122.

10 A Humanism of Relation

Aesthetics and Philosophy of Place in *The Family of Man*

Kerstin Schmidt

Introduction: New Ways of Looking at *The Family of Man*

In contrast to the harsh criticism that Steichen's *The Family of Man* has been subjected to, media theorist Fred Turner comes to a rather surprising conclusion in his recent article on the exhibit. He claims that '*The Family of Man* [...] sought to make visible a new, more diverse, and more tolerant vision of both the United States and the globe and to do it in such a way as to enhance viewers' intellectual and emotional independence.'[1] To say that *The Family of Man* helped create a diverse and tolerant society consisting of independent human beings had not been the gist of the argument that characterized much of the abundant *Family of Man* criticism until then.[2] In his article, Turner focuses on a contextualization of the perennial exhibit in the Cold War climate, arguing that Steichen's exhibition fostered a more democratic type of personality and in the end even prefigured, at least to some degree, the protest and civil liberty developments associated with the 1960s. This astounding conclusion takes issue with the standard evaluations of *The Family of Man* as an exhibition that followed the model of a conservative, propagandistic photojournalist picture book. This negative evaluation was accentuated by Roland Barthes's slanting review in which he called the exhibit 'sentimentalized', arguing that it failed to express a 'progressive humanism'.[3]

Turner's argument is based on the concept of personality types that gained relevance after World War II. According to this theory, the authoritarian type was considered as supportive of totalitarian regimes, with Germany or Japan prefiguring as prime examples of this type. The so-called democratic character, by comparison, supported the development of a diverse, tolerant society that America came to epitomize. Based on the conviction that totalitarianism was not a only a political but also a psychological condition, Theodor Adorno and others then conducted studies of the so-called authoritarian mind. According to them, a typical German family set-up, with a cruel unforgiving father demanding absolute obedience, were among the factors leading to the spread of the authoritarian type.[4] The success of this type is predicated on a system of evaluation based on 'likeness', that is, the nation is conceptualized in terms of a family whose coherence is based on being *alike* while sharp distinctions ward off everything and everyone seen as different and outside of the nation/family structure. The role of mass media was crucial in the propagation and spread of this pattern among an increasing number of individuals who would then imitate it. So, for Edward Steichen's Museum of Modern Art (MoMA) exhibit, the question was how one could conceptualize an exhibition that strengthened a democratic and liberal spirit.

The role of the mass media for the creation and support of the authoritarian mind was hotly debated at the time. Scholars wondered if mass media could also be used towards the creation of a democratic, tolerant and plural personality which brought the question whether there was something intrinsic to a given mass medium, such as the radio, that catered to a deindividualized totalitarian mindset. How could mass media be used to promote a democratic character? This question applied to countries such as Germany with a recent history of totalitarianism, but it also concerned the US as a society riven by the severe problems of racism and class inequality. In this context, Turner points out, the Museum of Modern Art took on the role of a forum for democratic initiative and debate. Steichen's *The Road to Victory* (1942) was a first successful exhibition using the Bauhaus installation technique that came to characterize *The Family of Man*, and Turner can demonstrate how this show's particular make-up compels viewers to perform a high degree of agency during their visit to the show.[5] The stress on individual agency, the argument ran, foils tendencies towards a totalitarian personality, enhancing instead an individualized and largely self-determined viewing and evaluating process. Even when viewers see photographs of people *unlike* themselves, such as the African family, they can identify a more structural *likeness* because of the basic similarity in family structure. Thus, Turner concludes, the show 'solicited empathy', making it impossible to develop strict differentiations based on 'unlikeness' that easily leads to an authoritarian mindset, especially when supported by mass mediated totalitarian propaganda.[6]

Turner's striking analysis repeatedly turns to the eminent role of the installation design without providing an in-depth discussion of the design itself. Turner even identifies the particular design of the exhibition space as a desideratum in scholarly criticism when he points out that the 'manner of their [the photographs'] installation at MoMA goes largely unanalyzed'.[7] He includes the design scheme into his article to some degree but his discussion is geared towards a different goal, namely the analysis of a Cold War politics of attention. Mary Anne Staniszewski provides an excellent and detailed description of the original installation design, but seems less interested in theorizing the role of space and place for the design.[8] But the spatial and platial aesthetics of the exhibition are, as I will argue, of paramount importance for its continuing success, and in the following I shall propose a theoretical framework to read the significance of place and space for this particular exhibit.

Turner's more positive reading of *The Family of Man* seems to strike a chord in more general terms as it echoes a recently regained popularity and appreciation of Steichen's exhibit after decades of critical if not dismissive evaluations. This criticism was often harsh, capitalizing for the most part on the show's purportedly reactionary presentation of a triumphant, Western, heteronormative narrative that posited a universal human condition. This let the exhibit seem dated and rather biased to many viewers and scholars alike. In contrast to this vein of criticism, my investigation will focus on the particular arrangement, the 'placement' of the exhibit's photographs, arguing especially that the highly innovative and daring aesthetic design of the exhibition space let *The Family of Man* appear as an example of the progressive humanism that Barthes had seen so critically in his evaluation of the exhibit. I will demonstrate how the installation design of the 1955 show in MoMA, on which my chapter concentrates, as well as the present installation at Clervaux, engage the viewer in active, dynamic and relational modes of perception, experience and thought that thwart challenges of monolithic sentimentality. In order to substantiate my claim, the construction and arrangement of the exhibition space, the single and group placements of the photographic material as well as the design of the place as a whole, will be discussed in light of recent theories of the philosophy of place. Drawing on the work of philosophers Jeff Malpas, Edward Casey and Donald Davidson, I will develop a conceptual framework for a critical reading of the exhibition's aesthetics of place and use this framework for an analytical walk through *The Family of Man*. Finally, my chapter will propose ways in which Steichen's show responds to, and actively enhances, a renewed and more general interest in the old idea of humanism that is, by Steichen's platial design, presented as related, dynamic and progressive.

Seen from a historical perspective, Steichen's exhibit draws on a variety of precursors in American literary and cultural practice who have attempted to collect the world and gather the human family: Walt Whitman's *Leaves of Grass*, for example, with its endless catalogues listing as many different people, occupations, places, emotions as possible. Like the single leaves of grass that make up a lawn or meadow, Whitman saw the human family as an egalitarian entity consisting of individuals that nevertheless form a nation, or human family.[9] Despite Whitman's rather blatant focus on the individual leaf of grass, that is, the 'I', and despite his exuberant praise of America as the greatest country, he programmatically makes an effort of drawing the whole world into his major work. As is true for Whitman, *The Family of Man* seems to speak to the same fundamental human concern, that is, to collect, embrace, the family of humankind, and, as I argue, this remains of great relevance to this day. The huge body of scholarly analysis that has been devoted to this singular exhibition, the unimaginable number of catalogues sold and the millions of viewers who have seen the show all testify to *The Family of Man*'s continuing importance.[10] The editors of the present volume identify one of their major goals as the exploration of new ways in which the epochal exhibition can remain relevant for twenty-first-century challenges. So rather than being a mere addition to an already exhaustive body of secondary studies, this collection asks for a new assessment and exploration into the possible meanings that this highly contested, but also incredibly popular photographic project could have in store for contemporary artistic and social practices. During a trip to Clervaux with graduate students, I noticed that this younger audience was neither appalled by a supposedly reactionary sentimentalism nor put off by the unrestrained Cold War propaganda; what mattered to them was the show's overall objective: to assemble and present humanity. What was true for the small group of students seems to express a larger trend as well: a renewed interest in *The Family of Man* arguably echoes a revitalization of the idea of humanism that has ostensibly gained momentum in the recent past. This may come as a surprise in times that have, more often than not, been labelled as 'posthuman'.

Granted that *The Family of Man* is an example of Cold War propaganda, selling the American dream, some have even called it 'hard-core propaganda'.[11] Its blatant political agenda is clear, as is the intention to persuade. It had a clear-cut religious message as there were hardly any references to non-Christian sacred writing, with the exception of the Bhagavad Gita, as has been frequently pointed out. Other non-Western sources were either secular, or borrowed from folk knowledge or mythic traditions. This 'camera testament', as Sandburg had famously called *The Family of Man*, hardly left any doubts that humanity was basically patriarchal, heterosexual and informed by values and ideas that we would today identify with typical 1950s middle-class American life.[12] But the show can also be seen from a different vantage point, as Turner's emphasis on a contextual reading leads him to conclude:

> But at one of the most gender-conservative, race-sensitive and hyper militarized moments in American history, *The Family of Man* presented a three-dimensional environment in which Americans were asked to accept practitioners of alternative sexuality (polygamy) and members of routinely demonized groups (Africans, Japanese, and Communist Russians and Chinese) as people like themselves. And they were asked to reject warfare as a crime against the species.[13]

The perspective that the show is far less conservative when seen against the background of a fairly conservative decade in American culture has probably been neglected in recent scholarship and criticism. After all, the show's immense and unbroken popularity testifies to the fact that it must have struck a chord in its 1955 audience and in audiences all over the world ever since.[14] As a colleague pointed out the other day, the book catalogue of *The Family of Man* was at a time more widely circulated than the phone book.

The Philosophy of Place and Steichen's Installation Design

My chapter has very little to do with the catalogue of the exhibition, but it has all to do with the original design of the place, of the exhibition space, in light of more recent theories developed by the so-called philosophy of place. In other words, what makes *The Family of Man* interesting for a contemporary audience, and for contemporary artistic practice, is its installation design.[15] The current exhibit in Luxemburg emulates the original design to a high degree, and the exhibit's success seems to underline that this was a correct curatorial decision. The exhibition tells the story of 'the family of man', of humankind, in terms of a linear tale, a 'folktale',[16] but the tale is a three-dimensional walk-through with a strong emphasis on the integration of the spectator. The spectator is compelled by the story's formal design to actively integrate and participate in that story. *The Family of Man* is a picture sequence modified as an environment. It has often been pointed out that the installation strategy was taken from advertising, as the exhibition's co-designer Paul Rudolph (Steichen and Rudolph worked on the design together) was greatly influenced by Herbert Bayer who, like Steichen, had worked in advertising and had created advertisements for corporate clients. Both were trained in methods to capture and persuade a mass audience. Bayer especially is known for believing that installation methods could be adjusted to achieve any goal, be it 'enlightenment, advertising, education'.[17] The gallery was seen as a dynamic physical space that was determined, in form and structure, by the idea to activate and engage the human beings moving through it. Some 40 years after the first show, the *Family*'s designer, Paul Rudolph, reflects the idea of the exhibition design:

> *The Family of Man* was a very important thing for me because I had never really considered the idea of heightening the experience that one has in an exhibition in relation to what the exhibition is intended to say and tell [...] Exhibition design can deal very much with storytelling, unlike architecture. I was fascinated with the idea of the psychology of space and what could be manipulated in purely architectural terms, by this I mean space and light, vistas, space, color, and sequence.[18]

The notion of the 'psychology of space' implies a sense of activation, meaning that space can be designed to actively work towards a particular intention. An exhibition can function as a space for an intense, 'heightened' experience that the designer was well aware of. The particular design of an exhibition space, the platial arrangement of the photographs, is hence of considerable importance for the show's effect. For me, it is especially the treatment of place that is of paramount importance in order to make this exhibition relevant for a twenty-first-century audience. So I would like to offer a more detailed reading of the place, or, to be precise, the conceptualization of place, the place of the photos in relation to their viewers. For this purpose, I propose to read the exhibit in light of the concept of philosophical topography as developed by the eminent philosopher of place Jeff Malpas, who has, together with Edward S. Casey and a few other scholars, produced a rich body of theoretical ruminations on the philosophical idea and significance of place as a key category of human experience. Without going into too much philosophical detail, allow me a brief sketch of the basic mode and elements of topographic philosophy according to Malpas.

In much scholarship on the notions of space and place, there is a tendency towards a rather careless use of the terms, treating one as inclusive of the other and vice versa. Some theorists have produced more nuanced distinctions between both terms (e.g. Casey), while yet other theorists, such as Doreen Massey, reject the difference altogether in quite considered argumentation. The differentiation between space and place has perhaps never been entirely clear, as both concepts are intricately related to one another, and neither has it been unchanging. Malpas's clarification as put forth in his essay 'Thinking Topographically: Place, Space, and Geography' will serve as a basis for my discussion of the role of space and place in *The Family of Man*. For Malpas, space implies 'openness, expansiveness, and "room"'.[19] Seen this way, space is closely tied to the void, to nothingness and expanse. Space veers toward regularity, homogeneity and uniformity, and as it has an underlying structure, Malpas thinks it can be measured and is quantifiable. He resorts to the term's etymology, reminding us that via the Latin *spatium* or the Greek *stadium*, the term carries a sense of the 'measurable distance or interval'. Place, by comparison, is specified as being bound and related to a sense of limit and surface (seen as a limit): '*topos*', Malpas writes, 'is a boundary or bounding surface'. As in the Greek *chora*, place appears in terms of contemporary ideas of place as a 'locus of meaning, memory, identity' (Malpas). In this sense, place can be seen as having character and content and is thus defined, in contrast to space, by qualitative aspects. As a consequence of the qualitative aspect of place, places are heterogeneous, they contain differences and can on these grounds be differentiated from other places.

This differentiation brings the notion of 'relationality' into the picture, as places necessarily related to one another: 'No place exists except in relation to other places! And every place contains other places that are related within it' (Malpas). What is characteristic of a given place is an aspect that emerged as a consequence of the relation, and not the separation, between different places. The activity of 'mapping' exemplifies this relationship. In order to explain the condition, Malpas describes the work of a traditional cartographer before the times of aerial surveying. What was important for the work of traditional cartography was the bodily engagement of the cartographer with the landscape, as the body had to move in and relate to the environment in order to perform the task of surveying it.

Malpas acknowledges that space and place are related, not exclusively because of the linguistic and historical bonds between both concepts. Place, he points out, implies the sense of openness, expansiveness and room that is constitutive of space and that he had earlier identified as being central to space. Place hence becomes a 'sort of opened space', but one that does have a limit. The 'bounded space of a place' is intricately connected to time and is not static but 'essentially dynamic', as boundaries in general are dynamic constructs. So, according to Malpas, the sense of place is characterized by the three following features: 'First, place as bound and ground; second, place as open and dynamic; third, place as relational and superficial. These elements of place are the basis for the idea of a philosophical topography' (Malpas).

Malpas's conclusion is that place is central to understanding human being; he sees it as providing the frame for all human appearance that we can then study. Human being is determined by and, according to Malpas, even 'founded in place'; in other words, it is 'placed' (Malpas). But this placedness retains an important and notable openness, dynamics and indeterminacy in which the human can appear and act. Taking the relationality back into the picture, human identity is related to the 'identity of places in which human lives are embedded' (Malpas). The topographic is thus a key element in the form of the human, and as it is dynamic it shapes and keeps shaping the individual and connective subjectivities in a given bounded space. This way of thinking puts the processual and the productive at the centre of attention, which Malpas underscores when he resorts to Heidegger who wrote that 'a boundary is not that at which something stops but [...] that from which something begins its presencing' (Malpas). This productivity encompasses the notion of place itself, not just the boundary. But importantly, boundaries are established as dynamic, and as connecting rather than separating. Thus, a given place always admits the other, the different, the new.

The sense of interrelation was theorized by Donald Davidson in his work on triangulation, where he conceived of the idea that the topographical field is formed by the relatedness of the single elements within it, and can only be understood by the 'mapping' of this relatedness (Malpas). In Donaldson, this mutual relation figures as the relatedness between self, other and thing. So, any place can only be understood if one understands the relations between the elements in a processual, dynamic way.[20]

In this sense, we can only gain access to a certain place, area or region by being at a certain place within it. Only our own 'being placed' opens up a region, a world. So, the visitor to *The Family of Man* enters the bounded space, seen as open and relational, and by the particular design of the exhibition that I will describe below, I argue, what is strengthened is precisely the relational function within the place between viewer, viewed and the world in between.

The spatial design of the exhibit can be seen as a pronounced engagement with issues of space and place. Upon entering the exhibit, the viewer was initially faced with a prologue of images that each expressed a sense of timelessness and eternal conditions. Among them was a telescope photograph of Orion, then a naked child lying on the ground of what looks like an ancient forest, followed by a picture of a tribeswoman coupled with a mask from the Ice Age. Opposite the entrance was a photomural showing a river flowing into the ocean shown together with a picture of a pregnant woman's torso (see illustration 35). One of the captions read 'And God said, let there be light, Genesis 1.3'. The flow of water served as a metaphor for the flow of human life, but also as a sense of the stream of visitors passing through the exhibition space and, by analogy, through a vision of humanity – a narrative flow as well.

Passing through the entrance way, the visitor was framed by photos of masses of people as if humanity was assembled as a crowd of people whose individual faces were almost unidentifiable in the picture (see illustration 36). The large-scale photo was presented at the beginning of the exhibit as if the viewer were invited to join in the crowd and place herself among the multitude of people on earth. At the entrance, next to the landscape in China, was the tiny photo of a Peruvian flute player by Eugene V. Harris that featured in much of the publicity materials of the exhibit.

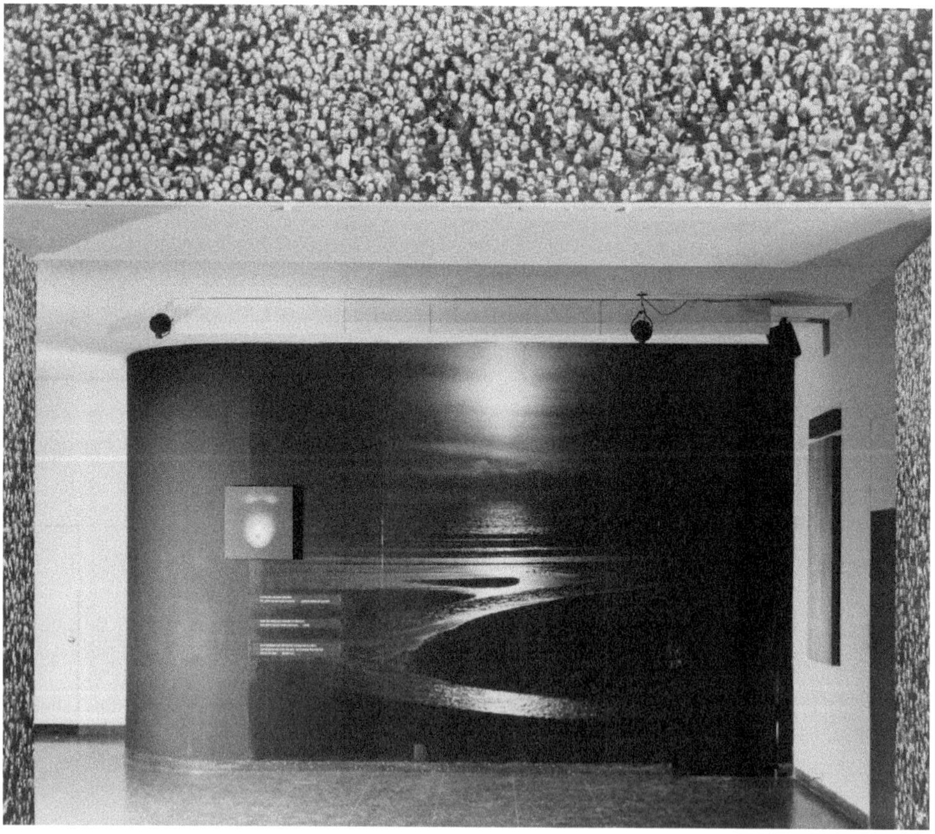

35 ***The Family of Man*** **at the Museum of Modern Art, New York City.**

To the right of the Chinese landscape was a transparent wall structure letting the viewer see a panorama of the exhibition as a whole. On the transparent wall were pictures of lovers, of weddings, and the like. So, a viewer was confronted with a plane of pictures, in front of a deep-space view of the rest of the exhibition and, if you will, the 'rest' of humankind. Behind every scene of marriage were deep histories of the people in their relations to yet other people, this particular order seemed to say. This mixture of solids and voids on a surface, in addition to doublings of picture surfaces that can be viewed simultaneously, comes close to a multilayered investigation into the stories and experiences of humankind, by compelling the viewer to investigate the relations between single scenes and moments presented on individual photographs in relation to herself and other viewers that she would see.

Steichen, with the help of Rudolph, used a wide variety of forms in his concept of exhibition design. He seemed to play with forms, choosing circles, squares, rectangles or hemispheres as formal structures, according to which he arranged the exhibit. The formal structure of the display also affected the viewer as she walked through the space. If the items on display were arranged as a circle, the visitor, too, was inclined to see the pictures in a given sequence in space that could be meaningful for the reception of the photos. In addition to the use of different geometrical shapes, Steichen and Rudolph notably made use of transparent or semi-transparent background structures. Some pictures at the start of the exhibition were hung on a wall made of transparent lucite, thus allowing the viewer a peek to the larger exhibition space. Other photographs, such as the panel showing an older and a younger couple on each side, were hung from the ceiling. In the original installation, this panel could even be swung by the viewer like the swing that was presented.[21] This hanging technique hence encouraged active viewer participation. Walking through the exhibit, one would also have noticed the particular lighting design, carefully developed to highlight certain pictures or perspectives while leaving others in darker areas. The lighting acted as a further guide through the exhibit, enforcing some views while discouraging others. The installation design was a path through the exhibit, a path that left, however, room for individual detours. These detours were shapes that let the viewer wander around exhibits, turn about to look at the other side of a panel, bowing down to look at a photograph on the lower side of a wall, or looking way up, coming closer to a picture of smaller size. The picture arrangement hence encouraged, even demanded, a range of bodily movements from the attentive spectator, hence involving the spectator in a most active intellectual and bodily sense. The entire body had to respond to the exhibit, and it was not principally, or exclusively, an intellectual stimulation. Even though the exhibit basically laid out a prescribed path for the viewer, the play with forms and the occasional detours described above lent the exhibit a little bit of an air of a maze through which the viewer had to wander.

The centrepiece of *The Family of Man*, the photographs of families from Sicily, Japan, Bechuanaland and the United States (see illustration 2), is a good case in point. The photos were enlarged, double-sided and duplicated in a particular arrangement that in fact resembled a sculpture rather than a traditional two-dimensional photography exhibit. The viewer was encouraged to look at the pictures from a variety of perspectives: one would walk around them and turn around to see the other side of the photograph. The photographs were arranged as if one would walk around the families, see them from all sides and eventually project oneself as well as other viewers of the exhibition into the family arrangements. In the manner of a detective, the viewer could look for doubles of the families within the arrangement, trying to study the structural principle and find out more about its design. In her description of this particular installation, Staniszewski perceptively notes that the design lets the viewers 'virtually embrace' the families.[22] That the floor in the original design was made of pebbles added a very distinct bodily sensation to it. In other words, the viewer was fully immersed in the families from different parts of the globe.

The viewer entered into a triangular relation and the resulting sense of immersion triggered the feeling of empathy with the families. This emotional power was noted in a 1955 review of *The Family of Man* by photographer Barbara Morgan who described the mechanism thus:

> In comprehending the show the individual himself is also enlarged, for these photographs are not photographs only – they are also phantom images of our co-citizens; this woman into whose photographic eyes I now look is perhaps today weeding her family's rice paddy, or boiling a fish in coconut milk. Can you look at the polygamist family group and imagine the different norms that make them live happily in their society which is so unlike – yet like – our own? Empathy with these hundreds of human being truly expands our sense of values.[23]

The space of the exhibition as a relational, dynamic and processual place supports identification with the people in the pictures, Morgan's 'phantom images of our co-citizens'. The viewer looks at the people in the pictures, who are at the same time *like* herself as well as *unlike* herself, and can still see them as enlargements of her own self.

A similar full immersion was likely to occur in the ring-around-the-rosy arrangement of pictures of children at play (see illustration 38). The visitors walked around the pictures of children, then also looking at other visitors looking at the display vis-à-vis one's own position in the circle. The particular platial arrangement almost threw the viewer into a situation of actually playing 'ring around the rosy' with the other viewers who are put into the same position by the formal display of the pictures. Form, once again, was key in expressing what the photos are about.

Photographs were hence installed in myriad platial arrangements, ranging from a more traditional placement on a solid wall structure at eye level through placement above the visitor's head or towards the bottom of the wall, to dynamic layouts that involved the spectator's whole body. A further important effect of this layout was

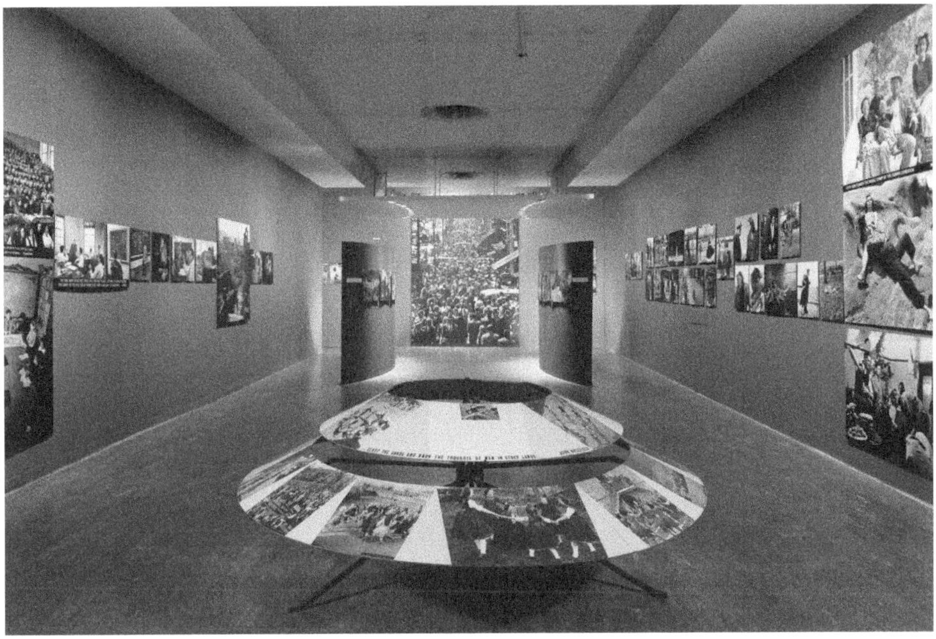

36 *The Family of Man* at the Museum of Modern Art, New York City.

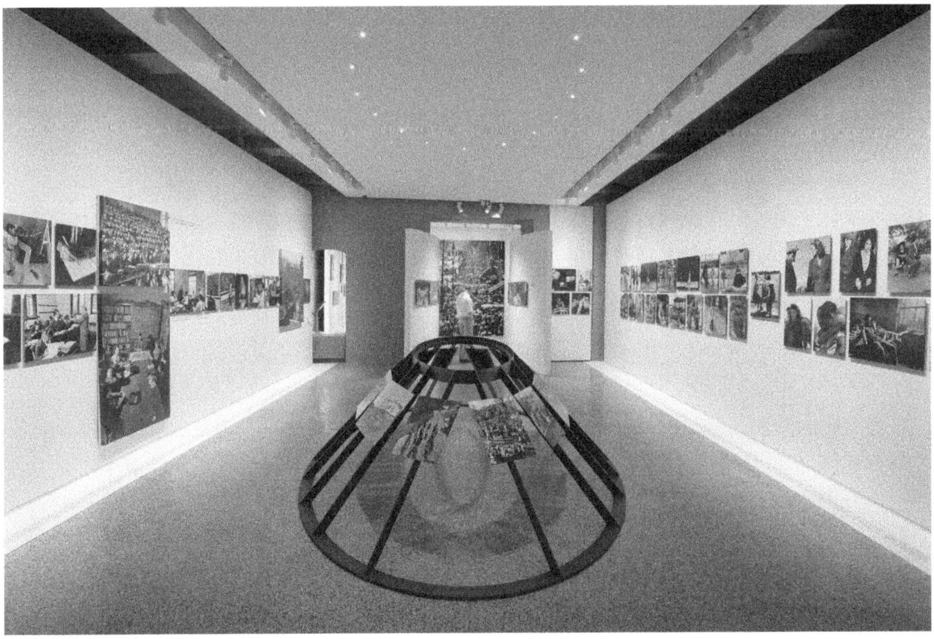

37 *The Family of Man* installation at Clervaux Castle. Theme 'Learning, thinking, teaching, ring-around-the-rosy-stand, human relations and death'.

a certain pace that it encouraged: as the viewer was put into different viewing situations, forcing particular bodily connections with the items on display, the show would speed up the viewing process, throw the viewer into ring-around-the-rosy chases, and thus had a certain tempo at different sections of the show. The rate of viewing a certain number of pictures per time unit was largely determined by the spatial positioning of the pictures, whether one dominated a whole room or whether several were positioned in a helter-skelter arrangement in one and the same spot.

The importance of the show's spatial arrangement is highlighted in the death section of the exhibit as well. Here, the spectator passed through a narrow alley-like space in which both sides showed pictures of funerals, graveyards and people in sorrow and mourning. At the far end of the passage was a large-size photomural of a busy Fifth Avenue crowd. Walking toward the picture of the crowd, the viewer would turn left and see, once again at the very end of the passage, a photo of the altar room of a church suffused with light on the crucifix as centrepiece. The show would repeatedly open up such vistas, offering views of different scenes, often thematically suggestive ones, and hence encouraging the viewer to make respective connections by entering into the relational, dynamic place.

In stark contrast to the printed catalogue of *The Family of Man*, the exhibition showed the photos of middle-aged and older couples, each accompanied by the caption 'We two form a multitude', as mounted on the photomural of UN delegates (see Frontispiece). In the original installation, the picture of the couples were attached at right angles to the picture of the assembly as a whole, thus adding depth and perspective to the exhibit. By comparison, the catalogue of *The Family of Man*, as Sandeen notes, 'flattened the presentation to two dimensions' as the picture of the couples are simply printed on a different page.[24] The explicit triangular layout forces the viewer to relate to the presentation of the multitude of political representatives as well as the examples of 'twos' forming that multitude. A dynamic relationship between viewer, representatives and couples as well as other viewers in the room is hence enforced, encouraging the reader to reflect on the lives of the couples on display as well as her own and that of others while also focusing on the mechanisms of political organizations that abstractly express and direct those lives. The juxtaposition between single viewer, abstract political entity and other individuals living lives around the globe as does the viewer of the exhibit puts the viewer in the same position as the many couples that make up the people on earth that the UN, in turn, represents.

The final section of *The Family of Man* shows numerous pictures of happy children (see illustration 38). That may, in itself, be considered a rather flat ending for an exhibition that catered to easily palatable mass tastes anyway. But what is interesting is, once again, the innovative and persuasive layout of this section. The photographs were mounted on poles in a seemingly pell-mell, disorganized arrangement, and the walls of this section were originally painted in tones of pink. *The Family of Man* designer Rudolph was well aware of the trouble with ending an exhibit such as this one: 'How to end the show was a difficult thing. You couldn't end with the atom bomb. It was about the idea of childhood and was about rebirth.

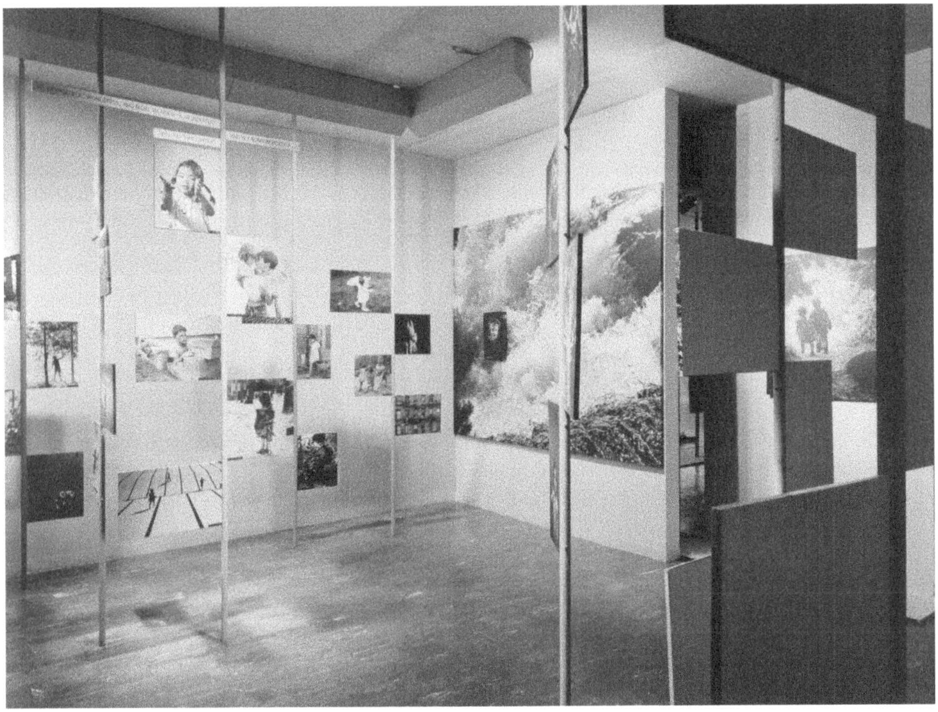

38 ***The Family of Man* at the Museum of Modern Art, New York City.**

It was done in pink, warm color. It was light.'[25] It is plain to see that such choices let the exhibit appear as naive, if not outright conservative, and as given to nostalgia as critical judgement. But regardless of differences in personal taste, the design of the place and its explicit multi-directionality make *The Family of Man* a daring and intellectually stimulating enterprise. Especially in this last section, photos were displayed in the manner of street signs pointing in different, also opposing directions, thus paying homages to all corners of the world and all the turns that lives could take. Some point towards the viewer, addressing him or her directly; for others, again, one needs to move around in order to see. The viewer, and hence history at any given moment of viewing, is actively called upon. And, as Rudolph rightly says, it was light that was speaking directly to people's sensory system – a design of immersion.

One could easily imagine other ways of addressing and immersing the spectator, for instance by choosing other, more problematic topics. As is general knowledge by now, the photograph of a lynched African American man was taken down after the opening of the show,[26] hence sparing the spectator the overt racism rampant in contemporary US society. Repeatedly, mirror-like arrangements have been pointed out as a central design pattern in *The Family of Man*,[27] but I would argue that the installation design is not about the simple reflection in terms of a one-on-one correspondence; rather, the show enhances a multi-directional dialogical structure in complex triangular relationships that induce the participatory, or connective, character of the thus designed place.

Such interconnective aspects have been pointed out, in slightly different terms, by Siegfried Kracauer, who argues in his *Theory of Film* (1960) that *The Family of Man* foregrounded an 'emancipatory intercultural communication'.[28] Even the smallest similarities that are made visible and the shared experience of visiting the exhibit produce a social fabric that enhances communication and that has elsewhere been called a virtual 'iconography of emotion'.[29] This design primarily serves as an enabler for connection, both between viewer and photograph as well as in between single viewers. Steichen's everyday archive enforces triangulation between viewer, exhibit and other viewers, and even if what is on display is basically lifeless objects, these assume a 'life of their own' in the connective environment and thus work as active promoters of relations that each viewer is continuously asked to make by the exhibition design. In a recent interview, Bruno Latour connects the human and the non-human world, stressing the abundance of relations that each item, each 'object', brings up in terms similar to those created by *The Family of Man*'s design:

> Things are not objects. In fact, they are precisely the opposite of objects. When we are focused on things, we are actually also focused on ourselves. When I am focusing on the attachment of this coffee cup, I am actually getting back to myself quite fast, as well as to the entire history of Italian coffee-making, the people who are harvesting the coffee, etc. This cup of coffee is an assembly.[30]

Conclusion: A Humanism of Relation in Place

A focus on place has often been associated with a rather conservative, if not reactionary ideology, suggesting a sense of 'Heimat' that has unfortunately been key to Nazi or, more generally, totalitarian politics. In stark contrast, the focus on place in recent and contemporary theory in the wake of the spatial turn treats place as productive, dynamic and processual. The platial design of *The Family of Man* is, as I have tried to show, key to a more democratic reading of this millennial exhibit and to a more positive evaluation of the show in terms of a progressive humanism. In his famous critique, Roland Barthes presented *The Family of Man* as a rather deplorable, reactionary piece of sentimental humanism.[31] Barthes explicitly brings up the well-known case of Emmett Till, the young African American who was lynched in Mississippi at the age of 14, and he asks the provocative question of why not ask Till's parents what they thought of '*The Great Family of Man*'?[32] When mentioning Emmett Till, Barthes correctly reminds us of the severe problems that the show ostensibly left out. The insistence of the similarity of supposedly universal human categories of experience, such as, for example, birth, love, marriage, death and so on, paper over the more diverse and historically contingent experiences of humankind. He calls for a 'progressive humanism' that, as I have proposed, lies precisely in the reading of *The Family of Man*'s design in terms of the philosophy of place. The platial design of the exhibit lays bare a dynamic and inherently relational sense of place that supports a progressive kind of humanism. Put differently, the dynamic, bodily involvement of the viewer, the powerful integration of viewer into triangular relationships of perception and recognition, continually changes 'the family of man', making room for history as each viewer interacts with the photographs presented and thus truly may constitute a dynamic, critical and relational family of humankind. This exhibition, perhaps more than any other, is a participatory archive; it encourages, by design, the continual creation and recreation of a three-dimensional map of the world, a cartographic space, dependent on each viewer entering the bounded space of the place. Thus, this may well be seen as a humanism of a most progressive kind, as each viewer changes the place with the relations that she/he brings along, creates, enforces or colours in a different light. This chimes with Horkheimer's observation of the high degree of 'interrelatedness' that this show triggers, as he wonders how many people have made the 'link from the pictures on show here to the idea of man or mankind'.

Notes

1 Fred Turner, '*The Family of Man* and the Politics of Attention in Cold War America', *Public Culture* 24, no. 1 (2012): 81.

2 For critiques of *The Family of Man* from a variety of perspectives and vantage points, see, for example, Roland Barthes, 'La grande famille des hommes', in *Mythologies* (Paris: Seuil, 1957), 173–6; Christopher Phillips, 'The Judgment Seat of Photography', *October* 22 (1982): 27–63; John Berger, 'Uses of Photography: For Susan Sontag', in Berger, *Understanding a Photograph* (London: Penguin Books, 2013), 49–60; Allan Sekula, 'The Traffic in Photographs', *Art Journal* 41, no. 1 (1981): 15–21; and Abigail Solomon-Godeau, *Photography at the Dock: Essays on Photographic History, Institutions and Practices* (Minneapolis: University of Minnesota Press, 1994). For a summary of critical responses, see Turner, '*The Family of Man*', 56, and Monique Berlier, '*The Family of Man*: Readings of an Exhibition', in *Picturing the Past: Media, History, and Photography*, ed. Bonnie Brennan and Hanno Hardt (Urbana: University of Illinois Press, 1999), 206–41.

3 Barthes, 'The Great Family of Man', 100, 101.

4 Cf. Turner, '*The Family of Man*', 57, 62–4.

5 Cf. Gerd Hurm's chapter in this collection for the section on Steichen's early exhibition designs. As Hurm shows, Steichen's efforts as a modernist curator preceded Bauhaus installations, thus he corrects the misleading impression in secondary studies that the modernist design of *The Family of Man* was superimposed on Steichen's rather naive understanding of photographic montage.

6 Turner, '*The Family of Man*', 78.

7 Ibid., 61.

8 See Mary Anne Staniszewski, *The Power of Display: A History of Exhibition Installation Design at the Museum of Modern Art* (Cambridge, MA: MIT Press, 1998), chap. 4.

9 One of the possible sources for the title, *The Family of Man*, was Sandburg's Whitmanesque 1936 poem 'The People, Yes'. See Eric J. Sandeen, *Picturing an Exhibition: The Family of Man and 1950s America* (Albuquerque: University of New Mexico Press, 1995), 43–4.

10 For a detailed overview of numbers and data relevant to the exhibition, see, e.g., John Szarkowski, '*The Family of Man.*' *The Museum of Modern Art at Mid-Century: At Home and Abroad*, ed. John Elderfield (New York: Museum of Modern Art, 1994), 12–37, and Sandeen, *Picturing an Exhibition*, esp. ch. 2.

11 Staniszewski, *The Power of Display*, 221.

12 The Sandburg quote is from his 'Prologue' to Edward Steichen, *The Family of Man* (New York: Maco Publishing and the Museum of Modern Art, 1955), 5.

13 Turner, '*The Family of Man*', 83.

14 See Sandeen, *Picturing an Exhibition*, esp. chs 4 and 5.

15 In terms of the original installation design of *The Family of Man*, I rely on Mary Anne Staniszewski's description of it in *The Power of Display*, on Eric Sandeen's presentation in *Picturing an Exhibition* as well as on personal conversations with Eric Sandeen for which I am very grateful.

16 Staniszewski, *The Power of Display*, 210.

17 Quoted in Staniszewski, *The Power of Display*, 220.

18 Ibid., 238.

19 Jeff Malpas, 'Thinking Topographically: Place, Space, and Geography', http://jeffmalpas.

com/wp-content/uploads/2013/02/Thinking-Topographically-Place-Space-and-Geography.pdf (accessed 2 December 2016). All further references are given in the text as 'Malpas'.

20 Jeff Malpas, 'Triangulation and Philosophy: A Davidsonian Landscape', in *Triangulation from an Epistemological Point of View*, ed. Maria Cristina Amoretti and Gerhard Preyer (Frankfurt et al.: Ontos Verlag, 2011), 257–79; J. E. Malpas, *Donald Davidson and the Mirror of Meaning: Holism, Truth, Interpretation* (Cambridge: Cambridge University Press, 1992), esp. chs 3, 4.

21 Staniszewski, *The Power of Display*, 241.

22 Ibid.

23 Quoted in Turner, '*The Family of Man*', 82.

24 Sandeen, *Picturing an Exhibition*, 86.

25 Staniszewski, *The Power of Display*, 249.

26 E.g., Staniszewski, *The Power of Display*, 251.

27 Notably, a mirror was part of the original show. It was taken away by Steichen and Miller two weeks after the show's opening because they believed it was 'corny and wrong'. See Turner, '*The Family of Man*', 80; Staniszewski, *The Power of Display*, 244, and others.

28 Siegfried Kracauer, *Theory of Film: The Redemption of Physical Reality* (1960; Princeton, NJ: Princeton University Press, 1997), 310.

29 Janine Marchessault, 'Manufacturing Humanism: Steichen/Burtynsky', *Prefix Photo* 15 (2007): 57.

30 Quoted in Marchessault, 'Manufacturing Humanism', 66–7.

31 See Gerd Hurm's encompassing discussion of Barthes's reading of the show in this volume.

32 Barthes, '*The Great Family of Man*', 101. Italics in the original.

11 Re-exhibiting *The Family of Man*

Luxembourg 2013

Anke Reitz

As a travelling exhibition in the 1950s and 1960s, *The Family of Man*, in line with the vision of its creator Edward Steichen, transcended national, cultural and political barriers, based on the confidence in the communicative powers of photography as a universal language. The exhibition was adapted to changing contexts and concepts over time; the last complete set of the travelling version arrived in Luxembourg at the end of its European tour in 1964, after a first presentation had been declined by the Luxembourg authorities in the 1950s. As a final step of the exhibition's itinerancy, and upon Steichen's request, *The Family of Man* was bequeathed to his native country in the hope of securing a permanent display for what he considered to be the most important work of his career, a work that epitomized his modernist and humanist ideas about what photography should be and what it could achieve in a global context.

This chapter will reflect from an institutional point of view on *The Family of Man* and its re-exhibition as a form of curatorial practice, and within the context of a history of exhibition design. This text will thus look at the process of reinstalling *The Family of Man* as a permanent collection at Clervaux Castle, Luxembourg; and it will examine the continuing connection between visitors' reactions today and the ideas expressed in the opening address for the exhibition's showing in Frankfurt by Max Horkheimer. To close, I will refer to Barthes's notes on photography for some reflections on the identificational strategies and processes at work when we look at photographs, especially those of *The Family of Man*.

***

The Family of Man came to Luxembourg as an exhibition and made its way through the years to become a heritage collection. It was exhibited at various stages and with various backdrops throughout the Grand Duchy: from an initial presentation at the former State Museum (today the Musée National d'Histoire et d'Art (MNHA), the National Museum of History and Art), it travelled the country and was displayed in its entirety or in part on several occasions before being incorporated into the archives of the incipient Centre national de l'audiovisuel (CNA), Luxembourg's national institute for audiovisual arts, in 1989. With its institutionalization, the transformation process from exhibition to archive collection and from temporary show to permanent display of a heritage began. The original photographic panels were reassembled and underwent photographic restoration, and the exhibition went on permanent display in 1994 at Clervaux Castle (a twelfth-century building largely reconstructed after World War II) in the north of Luxembourg.[1] The collection prints and the exhibition rooms then underwent further restoration almost two decades later and the exhibition was re-presented in a revised installation in 2013. This second renovation and restoration project addressed issues of long-term conservation and creating a suitable environment for the collection on the level of contemporary museology, including the institutional approach to heritage as well as creating new ways of access for different publics. I will concentrate on this second reinstallation of the collection under the auspices of the CNA, and on the considerations that guided the curatorial decisions.[2]

Both the 1994 and 2013 presentations were governed by the concept of a complete restitution of the collection in accordance with its original historical precepts. Also the decision was taken to exhibit the restored original prints and keep the historical traces they bear as part of the heritage instead of displaying reproductions.[3] Fidelity to the narrative and the spatial presentation of the exhibition themes was paramount. The frame for the spatial reinstallation was set by the 'installation instructions' compiled by the Museum of Modern Art (MoMA), which accompanied every travelling version of the show to ensure the homogeneity of the presentations and the compliance with the overall ideas and design by Steichen. Further sources for studying the historical design concept included floor plans and black-and-white installation photographs of the MoMA presentation. In addition, photographs of *The Family of Man* at various exhibition venues also helped shape the ideas and concept for adapting the collection to its permanent galleries and guided its interpretation within the space design.

Taking into account the complex visual and spatial strategies employed by *The Family of Man* and their physical and psychological impact on the viewer, the adaptation to a permanent gallery was not only guided by matters of design and historical coherence, but also had to consider issues regarding the changing context and status of the exhibition over the years. The reinstallation of the collection and the redesign of the exhibition space in Clervaux were governed by a twofold set of questions of interpretation and conservation alike. The re-exhibiting of an exhibition decades after the original showing necessarily involves a reinterpretation determined by changing historical and cultural contexts. One of the challenges we faced was how to render this visible via the redesign of the exhibition. This effort involved revisiting not only the original montaged installation and layouts, but also the early evolution of the idea of the exhibition during the planning stage, the exhibition's world tour, the political and ideological issues it raised and also the varied history of its reception. In addition, the photographs' materiality had to be considered within an approach of preventive conservation from the perspective of a commitment to long-term presentation, which at some stages had an impact on the design of the collection's reinstallation. All this is today part of the legacy of *The Family of Man* and forms a rich fabric of multiple and layered temporalities and histories.

The final exhibition model decided on at Clervaux translated on a surface level the exhibition's narrative from the large square space that occupied the whole of MoMA's second floor in 1955 to the rectangular exhibition galleries in the castle spread across two floors (see illustrations 39 and 7). From a display and overall scenography perspective, this interpretation involved altering *The Family of Man*'s original appearance and creating a new setting, in which the exhibition's narrative could unfold in suitably contemporary ways without violating its historical intentions and imperatives. A clear imaginary line was drawn between historical fidelity to the original MoMA show and its narrative, when it came to following its chronological unfolding and presentation of its thematic chapters, and the contemporary spatial interpretation. This meant taking into account what makes it a piece of heritage today and, in doing so, insinuating into the reinstallation the shift from then to now, and from the travelling exhibition to a permanent presentation of a heritage collection as an object of study. This was done, for example, by disregarding certain facts that could not be confidently reconstituted, such as the exact original wall colour or lighting. Other elements, such as distances between photographs and spatial perspectives also had to be altered in order to accommodate the show in its new setting (see illustration 37). Although an integral and important part of the exhibition design and of the visitor experience at MoMA (not necessarily in the various international venues), the additional dramatic effect conveyed by the deployment of these scenographic elements went against the contemporary aspiration and concept of creating a present and 'scientific' distance within the reinstallation in order to reflect the amount of time separating it from the original. Presenting *The Family of Man* in a space in which care has been taken to employ a 'neutral' design language in keeping with contemporary museology and the conception of the 'white cube' helps to anchor the reconceptualization of the collection into an object of study within the scenography. The creation of distance in the exhibition design inserts a break and generates an opportunity for a contemporary interpretation for the visitor: the distance from the original allows for a critical analysis of the exhibition's visual strategies and the deconstruction of their emotional impact. As a side note, the issue of lighting also takes into account conservational observations and norms regarding the exhibition of historical photographs, which call for a maximum light intensity of 50 lux on the picture surface. With regard to other aspects of the installation, today's exhibition design retains the form and function of the original display without replicating the original materials and feel, as seen for instance in the adaptation of the lovers and birth sections at the beginning of the reinstallation: at MoMA, the visitor entering the

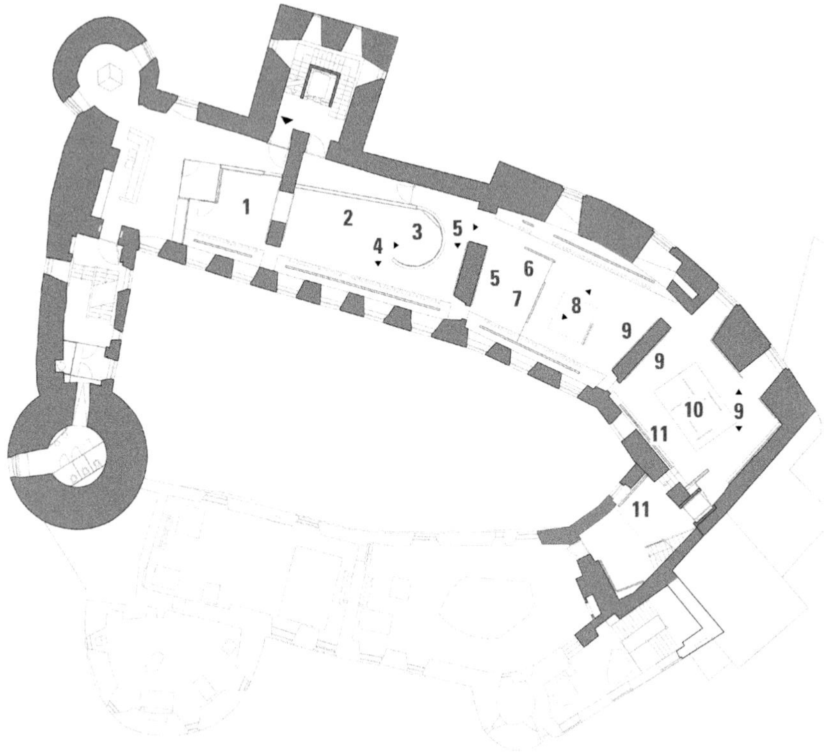
1
2
3
4
5
5
6
7
8
9
9
10
9
11
11

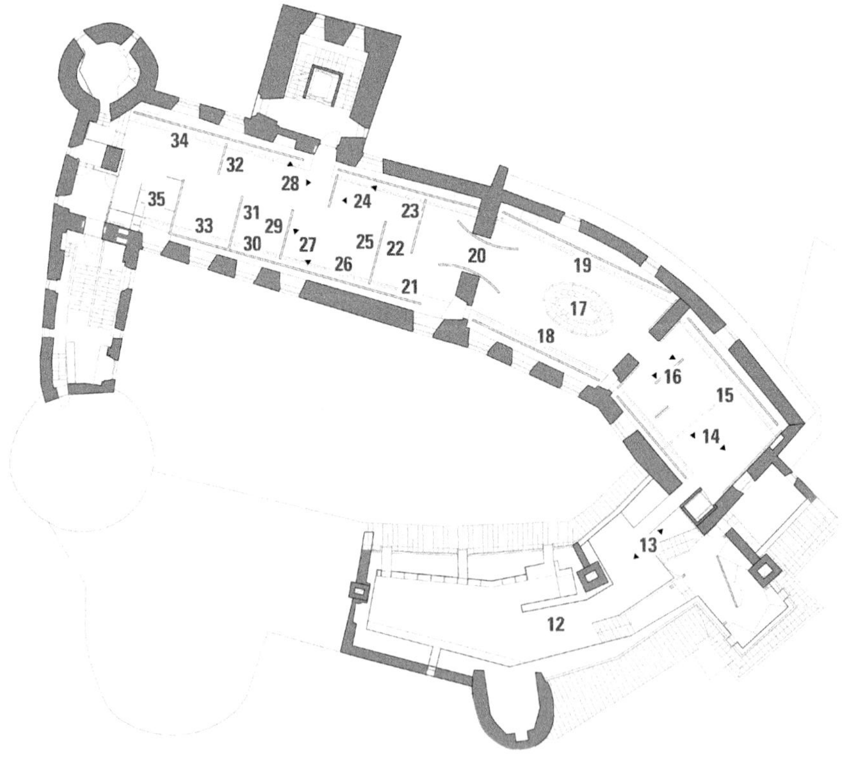
34
32
28
24
23
35
31
29
33
27
25
22
30
26
21
20
19
17
18
16
15
14
13
12

exhibition was faced with a simultaneous spectacle of pictures of lovers displayed on a transparent background that allowed a view through to later rooms, revealing how the narrative would develop and a preview of the core theme of the family pictures. From the lovers' theme the visitor was carried on to the pictures of birth, mounted on a white transparent curtain forming a half-circle, with the sense of the circle reinforced by a focused ceiling light, the two together creating a separate space and atmosphere for these photographs. For the theme's transposition to Clervaux, the architecture of the castle prevented an opening of the perspectives behind the lovers' theme; a straightforwardly chronological approach was therefore adopted. The curtain of the birth theme has been replaced with a metal grid, retaining something of the original form (the half circle) and function (transparency), without recreating the medical atmosphere of the original presentation.[4] Also the lighting was adapted here to the 'neutrality' of the general presentation without singular treatment for specific pictures or themes (a decision also guided by conservation precepts) (see illustrations 40, 41).

39 *(facing page)* Installation of *The Family of Man* at Clervaux Castle (2013). Themes: 1. Prologue: Creation of universe – Creation of man, 2. Lovers, 3. Childbirth, 4. Mothers and children, 5. Children playing, 6. Fathers and sons, 7. Disturbed children, 8. Agriculture, 9. Labour, 10. 'Family of man' central theme pictures, 11. Household and office work, 12. Eating, 13. Folk-singing, 14. Drinking, playing, 15. Dancing, 16. Music, 17. Ring-around-the-rosy-stand, 18. Learning, thinking and teaching, 19. Human relations, 20. Death, 21. Grief, pity, 22. Dreamers, 23. Loneliness, 24. Religion, 25. Hard times and famine, 26. Man's inhumanity to man, 27. Rebels, 28. Youth, 29. Justice, 30. Public debate, 31. Faces of war, 32. Dead soldier, 33. H-bomb explosion, 34. United Nations, 35. Children.

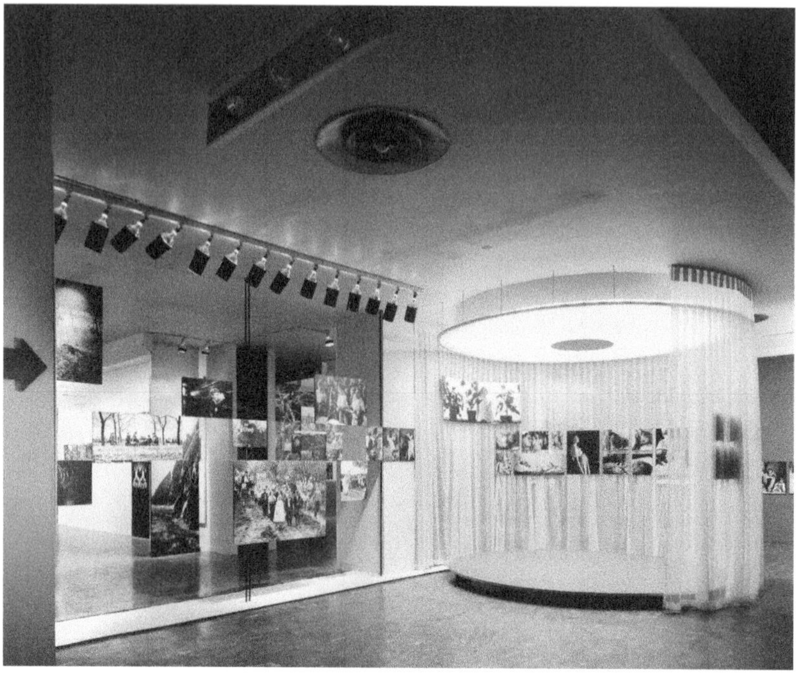

40 *The Family of Man* at the Museum of Modern Art, New York City.

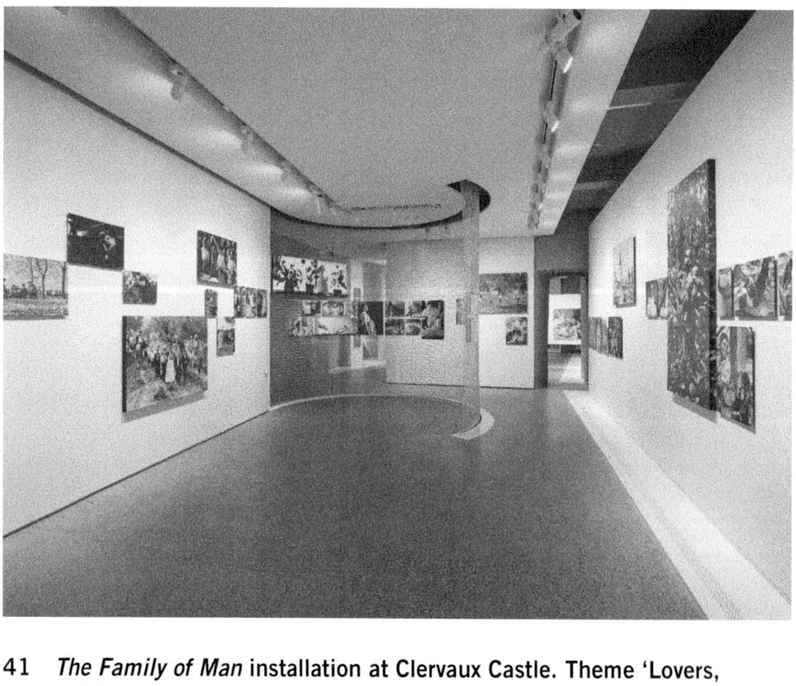

41 *The Family of Man* installation at Clervaux Castle. Theme 'Lovers, childbirth, mothers and children'.

Another example of deviating design and consequent different exhibition experience that reflect the shift in time from 1955 to 2013 can be seen in the presentation of the H-bomb picture. The MoMA visitor, wandering through the second part of the exhibition and its increasingly dramatic tone, arrives at the culminating point in a darkened room in front of the back-lit colour transparency of an H-bomb explosion, filling the entire room and reminding the visitor of the imminent concerns and threats of the time, before discovering the closing pictures of the UN Assembly and children. In accordance with the general approach of dedramatizing the exhibition through the abstraction of additional scenographic effects, the H-bomb picture is displayed in Clervaux on the background of a white wall, without a compulsory stop in the flow of the visit, something that would not have been possible architecturally at Clervaux (see illustration 43).[5] Following the scheme of the exhibition's travelling versions, the original black-and-white print of the photograph has also been retained. The decision about its position within the 2013 presentation takes account of its original 1955 location at MoMA, but also of the quite different dialogues of the picture with its surrounding photographs during the travelling exhibitions. A more direct and open dialogue has thus been constructed between the bomb and its neighbouring pictures, especially the photograph of the United Nations Assembly: the two now face each other, a difference in the display that hints at a shift in interpretation as dependent on changing historical contexts. The distance in time from the nuclear threat during the Cold War and thus from the direct connection between the exhibition and the visitor's present frame of reference is followed today by a shift in the public reception of this theme not anymore as nucleus of the exhibition itself, but rather as an abstract and symbolic danger.

The presentation of the collection in Clervaux on the one hand involves a double conception of the exhibition as a historical artefact and an object of study, while on the other hand it functions as a prolongation of *The Family of Man*'s world tour. In 'Remembering Exhibitions' Reesa Greenberg refers to the reassembling and re-presenting of past exhibitions as replica: 'In most replica exhibitions,' she writes, 'there is some deviation from the original, and the art is often supplemented by archival documentation ranging from exhibition photographs to documents relating to the show's reception. Usually, these exhibitions are large-scale homage or anniversary exhibitions, designed to isolate an important moment in art history, to promote research, and to underscore the singularity of a given exhibition.'[6] This description concurs with the threefold intention of the reinstallation at Clervaux: rendering the experience of the exhibition to make it as close as possible to the original for a contemporary audience; encouraging reflection on a special moment in the history of exhibition design and photography; and in addition, promoting the conservation of an international but also national photographic heritage. The prolongation of the exhibition's history as a travelling show in Clervaux avoids the obtrusive inclusion of interpretative texts or other media within the exhibition space itself, what Reesa Greenberg refers to as 'archival documentation'. It was deemed important to ensure for the viewer at Clervaux as far as possible an 'unmediated' access to the exhibition free from other sources and interpretations, to approximate the original impact of Steichen's photoessay even if the contemporary design of the space brings (and is intended to bring) its influence to bear on the viewer's experience. This practice carries, of course, the risk of objectifying and museifying the exhibition by removing its historical contexts, suggesting for it an aesthetic autonomy and asserting new elements of 'truth'. This is a difficulty built into our approach to the heritage that is intentioned to be balanced with a new mediation concept. As observed in a study of visitor reactions and experiences during the exhibition's installation at Clervaux Castle during the 1994–2010 period, visitors reacted mostly emotionally to *The Family of Man*, in a way that was disengaged from the exhibition's historical origins. By being disconnected from part of its history, the exhibition's humanist statement was simultaneously rendered more powerful and timeless, but also naïve. The display of the collection without interpretative media in the exhibition rooms favoured a more immutable aesthetic statement, suppressing the distance in time from the original. Conceptualizing the exhibition as a re-exhibition opens up the possibility of considering it as a form of expression and as a medium in itself, 'rather than a seemingly neutral, nodal medium for presenting individual art works'.[7]

To facilitate and ensure the awareness of the historical layers in the 2013 presentation, 'archival documentation' was incorporated into the redesign of the exhibition in different forms, separate from the original narrative and as unobtrusively as possible. An application for a mini iPad has been designed to accompany visitors on their journey through Steichen's narrative, unfolding a parallel path of access, understanding and interpretation. The mediation approach trusts the visitors' ability to create sense out of what they see and concentrates on what they may not deduce. Besides a basic historical and interpretative line, the application gives access for example to information on the exhibition's history and circulation, restoration insights and interviews, building the context for a new historical narrative: it maps the evolution and status shift from exhibition to heritage collection, and it contextualizes Steichen's voice as a curator, creating various paths of access and enabling different forms of engagement – emotional, historical, critical. The integration of installation photographs of various venues where *The Family of Man* was shown illustrates the shifts in time and space and acquaints the viewer with the comings and goings between past and present to the 'benefit of an actualised interpretation of the past through the present moment'.[8] This documentation is extended with a museum library halfway through the exhibition, collecting primary and secondary documents, photographer's monographs, critical and theoretical publications, as well as the books of other photographic projects inspired by *The Family of Man*.

This alternative access to the collection through historical contextualization forms an additional layer in the fabric of display at Clervaux. Within the emerging and widening interest in exhibitions as subjects of repetition and of study and as part of art history, the reinstallation of *The Family of Man* had to be placed into a historical and self-reflexive framework, reflecting on photography and history, the exhibition as a medium within its history and particular curatorial and archival practices.

***

In the sequence of exhibitions starting in the 1920s that used modernist design ideas and spatial strategies and the photograph as a document and instrument for visual persuasion, *The Family of Man* occupies the end of an era marked by the belief in photography as a universal language and a 'last gasp of humanity-as-family'.[9] The centrality of vision in the Western epistemological paradigm, combined with architectural artifice in exhibition design, turns the viewer into an active agent in the production of meaning within a field of dynamic vision. In the post-war years, when photography was also developing as a means of communication in illustrated magazines, *The Family of Man* was seen as 'the culmination of the principles of the exhibition based on expanded vision',[10] as theorized by Herbert Bayer, the Bauhaus designer who collaborated with Steichen at MoMA in the years just before *The Family of Man*; it 'represented the end of the historical moment in which photography was key to visual paradigms and techniques'.[11] This place in history may help explain the different critical approaches to the exhibition's humanist claims lodged between antagonist scholarly currents.[12]

Although the universalist claims for the medium and language of photography have been widely criticized within academic literature since *The Family of Man*, and photography has been increasingly theorized within historically and culturally specific frameworks, the exhibition's popular reception history is to the present day characterized by the embracing of the humanist message, along with the acceptance of photography as a collective tool of communication and its endorsement as a 'natural' language. For the general public, I would claim that the belief in photography's indexical relation to reality contributes to the exhibition still being seen today within its initial frame of reference in terms of connecting people, and it positions photomontage as an effectual visual tool and psychological strategy. *The Family of Man* is a product of its time and for its time, but interestingly the recent reception of the exhibition seems to hint at some 'universal' aspect to the humanist ideas depicted by Steichen – at least at a comprehension of those values over time. The viewing experience of the exhibition remains for a large part of the public connected to an emotional journey, activating personal memories and associated feelings, and functions as a captivating narrative with some abstract points of connection to the world of today. By no means can the positive reception of the exhibit be equated with the ignorance of the discourse's construction (formerly and today), but parallels can be drawn with film reception, where the momentary adherence for the time of the fiction to a story does not imply a belief in its factual reality. From today's viewpoint on the reinstallation, this makes it all the more important to accurately contextualize the exhibition within its time and to discuss or render transparent its visual communicative strategies.

At this point, I would like to introduce Max Horkheimer into the argument and his notion of identification with regard to the exhibition in the context of his opening address for the Frankfurt stop of *The Family of Man* in 1958. The German version of the exhibition featured the subtitle 'wir alle' ('all of us'), and so induced the idea of a communal representation and experience from the outset. The use of 'us' presupposed a communal entity and a shared feeling of belonging. In his opening talk, Horkheimer stressed the constructive effect of the show in a post-war world and the implication of the viewer in the process of constructing meaning: *The Family of Man* is more than the sum of its parts, the single photographs, made possible by a productive tension between the general idea or thought and the picture reality. According to Ariella Azoulay, this productive tension is made possible and emphasized by the juxtaposition of pictures without captions – Steichen's much criticized practice of decontextualization – and opens up the possibilities for the production of meaning.[13] The latter involves the imagination of the viewer, which in turn is activated via identification and empathy. For Horkheimer, the exhibition allows the viewer to experience identity within difference helped by the representation of the everyday and the experience of familiarity as an emotional connection with some depictions in spite of others. And it is precisely this emotional connection via identification that continues to involve viewers to the present day and that makes a difference to critical approaches to the exhibition based solely on the catalogue. In the catalogue, the visual argument is not experienced physically and psychologically in the same way. In my experience in welcoming researchers, critics and journalists, I have come across several individuals who, despite being critically well informed and educated about *The Family of Man*, visiting the exhibition experienced emotional involvement against their intellectual critical will. Love it or hate it, indifference is not an option.[14]

Approaching *The Family of Man* through the lens of identification makes the exhibition contingent and personal via the viewer's appropriation. It opens up new possibilities of difference and for subjectifying the exhibition, its derived ideas and its reception rather than objectifying it as Steichen's immutable statement.[15] Through the viewer as an active element in the production of meaning, 'the exhibition can be seen as constituting a frontier or space of encounter whose meaning was potentially remade by its viewers and receivers across the globe, who were by no means passive recipients of its stated aims but active agents in the ways they chose to apprehend and make use of it'.[16] The production of meaning is thus understood as context-determined, shifting and personally negotiated. In this sense, a global detailed research of the exhibition's reception history would make a valuable addition to the field of study.

Against this background, the studies by Margaret Olin of the photograph as a relational art may be invoked: 'photography gains power as a relational art, its meaning determined not only by what it looks like but also by the relationship we are invited to have with it'.[17] Photography facilitates relations, and as Olin puts it, 'photography [...] makes connections with people'.[18] The visual and emotional connections seem more direct and obvious than the physical ones, when applied to

The Family of Man as a museum object. Observing visitors in the museum's galleries confirms that one of the exhibition's achievements is the creation of dialogue – not only between pictures, but also between viewers. This is often accompanied by physical gestures that involve showing and touching – the exhibited photographs included. From the perspective of a conservator, this of course constitutes an act of transgression of the museological 'rules of conduct' with regard to works of art, placing the latter at risk of deterioration. From the perspective of a historian reflecting on *The Family of Man*, its identificatory strategies and patterns of spectator involvement, this act is a gift, testifying by its very nature to the performative and relational aspects of the exhibition and to its haptic qualities. Returning briefly to the curatorial decisions within the context of the reinstallation, it must be noted that a conscious curatorial choice was made not to add a physical barrier between artwork and viewer as a measure of protection, in order to allow the relational and communicative strategies of the exhibition to unfold as originally intended. The gesture of touch within the context of the exhibition today furthermore suggests that the *material* status of photography as an artwork (at least concerning the unframed works of the exhibited heritage) and as a historical trace is still being contested by the wider public – and this because of its potential of mechanical reproduction.

To conclude the reflections on identification as a possibility of approaching the viewing of the exhibit, I will call upon Roland Barthes. But rather than discuss his most cited review of the exhibition in his article '*The Great Family of Man*', I will focus on one of his later texts, *Camera Lucida*, and endeavour to relate his theorization of his personal approach to photography to Horkheimer's notion of identification as applied to *The Family of Man*. In *Camera Lucida*, Barthes approaches photography from a subjective point of view, using the observation of his personal reactions to a photograph as a starting point. On the basis of an indexical understanding of photography's relation to reality and over the course of his analysis, he identifies the *studium* as related to a culture, a referent to a kind of knowledge, through which emotion passes and is mediated. Here we can already observe that the decontextualized photographs of *The Family of Man* sometimes oppose this kind of analysis or cultural reference beyond a certain point, because of the absence of captions (and this factual reference is what today's typical museumgoers miss). The *punctum*, in Barthes's essay, is what permits a personal relation to what is represented; this is what allows a relational and emotional transfer between photograph and viewer. Something personal is activated and added to the photograph in the process through an element that 'touches' the viewer. The *punctum* converts the connection to the picture to a personal and subjective involvement and allows the photograph to always be actualized anew through the activation of personal memories and emotions. Time is condensed and fictionalized within this connection and the comings and goings between the represented reality and the viewer's present. So can we claim the *punctum* to be just another facet of the process of identification? Photography and the belief in its indexicality facilitate identification, but the latter is (in *The Family of Man*) not necessarily based on the representation's supposed congruence with reality or the identification of a particular scene, but rather on its recognizable effects of familiarity. In this sense, the photographs of the exhibition exert an effect – tied to the *punctum* – and, in the words of Olin, 'act rather than represent'.[19] Olin goes on to say, 'a reading of *Camera Lucida* suggests that the most significant indexical power of the photograph may consequently lie not in the relation between the photograph and its subject but in the relation between the photograph and its beholder, or user, in what I would like to call a "performative index" or an "index of identification"'.[20] This interpretation of Barthes's analysis may be seen as an attempt to reconcile him with *The Family of Man*, not as a statement understood through history, but via the actualization of its photographs within the realm of subjectivity. Here, *The Family of Man* is not understood solely as the constructed whole and its emanating, overarching idea as a myth of humanity's essence, but the analysis goes back to the constitutive parts, permitting a dialogue, subjective and shifting, within various frames contingent upon time and space.

***

The Family of Man is a piece of heritage and a phenomenon which has kept some of its mystery over time. By outlining the considerations that guided the contemporary curatorial practice of the re-exhibition and by placing the viewer's approach to the collection within the interpretative context of access via identification, I am not arguing against a historical understanding of the exhibition. On the contrary, all the formulated critiques on and approaches to *The Family of Man* over time and the problematization of its strategies of representation are all 'true', precious and necessary steps within the historical understanding of the exhibition and its shifting frames of reference. Exploring the issue of identification with regard to the exhibit allows insights to be gained and possibly explains some of the power and appeal the exhibition still holds for visitors today, via an actualization of its narrative through the activation of a personal connection. This contribution intends to pave the way for questions and to encourage discussions and this volume will hopefully lead to a proliferation of approaches within research, by advocating not just *one* interpretative approach for or against Steichen's legacy, but rather allowing it to fluctuate with and over time. Today, the exhibition is seen as a piece of heritage and an archive undergoing gradual change; it is always fragmentary, as is memory. The contemporary museological approach to the object of study is thus defined by these multiple directions and attitudes within research, which is seen as an ongoing process and dialogue with its object in different and evolving contexts. Finally, besides generating the phenomenon of uniting and connecting so many people worldwide to the photographic representation of humanity as a concept, the real ingenuity of Steichen and his collaborators possibly lies in their ability to keep the discussions going after all this time.

Notes

1 During his last visit to the Grand Duchy in 1966, Edward Steichen seems to have expressed the wish to see *The Family of Man* permanently displayed at Clervaux Castle. A first showing in 1975 presented about 200 prints of the original exhibition without considering Steichen's design, before being rediscovered and restored by the CNA at the beginning of the 1990s.

2 The restoration and conservation processes were documented over time. For an overview of the first restoration campaign in the 1990s, see Jean Back and Gabriel Bauret (eds), *The Family of Man: Témoignages et Documents* (Luxembourg: Art Events, CNA and Ministère des Affaires Culturelles, 1994); the second restoration campaign preceding the reinstallation in 2013 is documented in a film entitled *The Family of Man & The Bitter Years: A Heritage Restoration Project* (CNA, 2013), included in the publication *Steichen's Castle and Tower: The Family of Man/Clervaux – The Bitter Years/ Dudelange* (Dudelange: CNA, 2013).

3 At this point it should be mentioned that the contextual preservation and conservation as heritage at Clervaux stand in contrast to what Steichen initially intended. His concept was bound to the medium of photography, and its ability of mechanical reproduction, but not to the materiality or the authenticity of the original as conceived by the art market or the museum. This can be seen for example in the material decisions he made to produce and reproduce several exhibition sets for widespread circulation and communication – not for the preservation of a permanent heritage. Over time, the collection's changing status also drew attention to the material production as part of the documentation of the heritage, its processes of creation and finally its circulation, which left a lasting impact on the object.

4 From the designer's point of view the range of materials used was reduced. Only a few are employed throughout the exhibition design and these had to conform to the conservation needs of the photographs. (So, for example, materials that easily accumulate dust particles, or plain wood that releases acid over time were avoided.)

5 In accordance with the historical approach to the exhibition and its (re)installation, access is given to the original picture of the bomb as displayed at MoMA in the iPad application and in the presentation of a three-dimensional reconstitution of the New York showing of the exhibition at the museum library.

6 Reesa Greenberg, 'Remembering Exhibitions: From Point to Line to Web' (Tate Papers, Autumn 2009), 3, http://www.tate.org.uk/research/publications/tate-papers/12 (accessed 25 April 2016).

7 Greenberg, 'Remembering Exhibitions', 3.

8 Elitza Dulguerova, 'L'expérience et son double: notes sur la reconstruction d'expositions et la photographie', *Intermédialités: histoire et théorie des arts, des lettres et des techniques* [Intermediality: History and Theory of the Arts, Literature and Technologies] 15 (2010), http://id.erudit.org/iderudit/044674ar (accessed 30 March 2016): 59.

9 Tirdad Zolghadr, introduction in Thomas Keenan and Tirdad Zolghadr (eds), *The Human Snapshot* (Feldmeilen, New York and Berlin: LUMA, Centre for Curatorial Studies, Bard College and Sternberg Press, 2003), 16.

10 Jorge Ribalta, *Public Photographic Spaces: Exhibitions of Propaganda, from* Pressa *to The Family of Man, 1928–1955* (Barcelona: MACBA, 2008), 24.

11 Ibid., 26.

12 See Winfried Fluck's contribution to this volume which resituates the exhibition within this intellectual debate.

13 Ariella Azoulay, '*The Family of Man*: A Visual Universal Declaration of Human Rights', in Thomas Keenan and Tirdad Zolghadr (eds), *The Human Snapshot* (Feldmeilen, New York and Berlin: LUMA, Centre for Curatorial Studies, Bard College and Sternberg Press, 2003), 19–49.

14 For further readings and interpretation of the exhibition as connected to the active process of identification, see Blake Stimson, *The Pivot of the World: Photography and its Nation* (Cambridge, MA: MIT Press, 2006), and Fred Turner's article '*The Family of Man* and the Politics of Attention in Cold War America', *Public Culture* 24, no. 1 (2012): 55–84.

15 See also the theorization of the space between picture and image by Winfried Fluck in this volume.

16 Tamar Garb, 'Rethinking Sekula from the Global South: Humanist Photography Revisited', *Grey Room* 55 (Spring 2014): 41.

17 Margaret Olin, *Touching Photographs* (Chicago: University of Chicago Press, 2012), 3.

18 Ibid., ix.

19 Ibid., 17.

20 Ibid., 69.

12 *Et in Arcadia Ego*

The Family of Man as Cold War Pastoral

Miles Orvell

The underlying conception of *The Family of Man* has been criticized almost from its first days and is often repeated: in emphasizing sameness across cultures, Edward Steichen erased cultural difference, creating a sentimental ethnography of universal harmony. Roland Barthes was one of the first to articulate this critique:

> Everything here, the content and appeal of the pictures, the discourse which justifies them, aims to suppress the determining weight of History: we are held back at the surface of an identity, prevented precisely by sentimentality from penetrating into this ulterior zone of human behavior where historical alienation introduces some 'differences' which we shall here quite simply call 'injustice.'[1]

Steichen does invite Barthes's response to some degree, especially if we take him at his word in introducing the printed version. The exhibition, he says, 'was conceived as a mirror of the universal elements and emotions in the everydayness of life – as a mirror of the essential oneness of mankind throughout the world'.[2] But on the next page Steichen complicates things by affirming that the 'mirror', if that's what it is, shows us not simply harmony and beauty but also 'the stupid and destructive things' people have done to the environment.[3] In any case, the *content* of the exhibition makes an argument that goes far beyond Steichen's ingratiating introduction, establishing a normative discourse that attempts to persuade us of how we must act in the world and providing the premise for a vision of global amity. Perhaps, as Barthes alleges, Steichen suppresses the 'weight of History' that has created cultural difference; but from another perspective, the entire concept of *The Family of Man* is historical: its rationale is the new historical fact of the hydrogen bomb, and it is arguing that the 'differences' we assume to exist can explode us and our world.

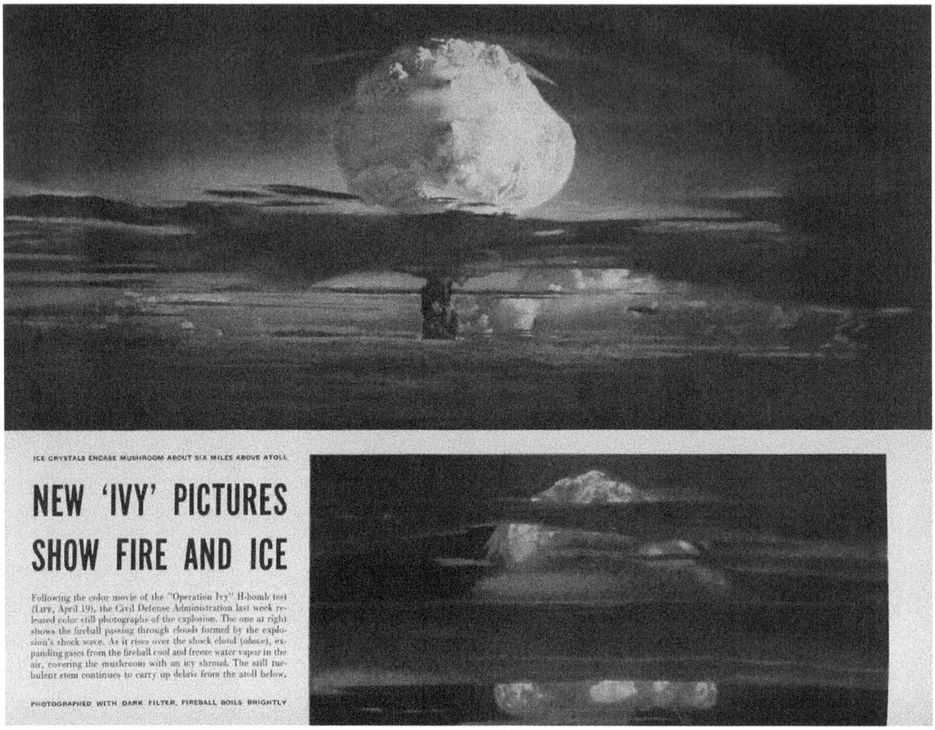

ICE CRYSTALS ENCASE MUSHROOM ABOUT SIX MILES ABOVE ATOLL

NEW 'IVY' PICTURES SHOW FIRE AND ICE

Following the color movie of the "Operation Ivy" H-bomb test (LIFE, April 19), the Civil Defense Administration last week released color still photographs of the explosion. The one at right shows the fireball passing through clouds formed by the explosion's shock wave. As it rises over the shock cloud (*above*), expanding gases from the fireball cool and freeze water vapor in the air, covering the mushroom with an icy shroud. The still turbulent stem continues to carry up debris from the atoll below.

PHOTOGRAPHED WITH DARK FILTER, FIREBALL BOILS BRIGHTLY

42 From the pages of *Life Magazine*, 3 May 1954, pp. 54–5. It was the smaller of the two images seen here that was used in the exhibition at MoMA.

Steichen's argument, we might say, is addressed to the 'common man' and rests on the utopian premise, articulated by Rousseau, that the general will informs and legitimizes the power of the state. That is the argument that Max Horkheimer implicitly adopts when he reads the exhibition as an experience that draws us into the shared lives of our fellow human beings, allowing us to identify with the persons in the images that we see – except for the very few images of barbarism, from which Horkheimer assumes we must recoil.[4] For Horkheimer, the logic of the exhibition supports the argument that to the extent that goodwill is shared and promoted and barbarism rejected, mankind will secure a more peaceful future.

Horkheimer makes no mention in his response to the exhibition in Germany of the hydrogen bomb image, which in the original Museum of Modern Art (MoMA) show was a back-lit colour transparency, mural-sized, occupying its own niche (see illustration 42). (In travelling versions, which I'll discuss later, a large black-and-white image was used (see illustration 43).) The bomb, I would argue, is the central image in the exhibition, the lynchpin of Steichen's argument. Steichen is saying not simply, we must love good and reject evil. He is saying, we must love good and reject evil – or else. 'Or else' means in this case that we risk another war, which would be, given our atomic weapons, the final war, the war of total destruction. Of course one might read the giant luminous bomb image as a Cold War threat as well, a warning to the rest of the world, a warning to our 'enemies', that we've got the power to kill you. But that power to kill is also suicidal, for the bomb is a threat to all mankind, not just the enemy. (By the 1950s, nuclear weapons were already proliferating beyond the United States.) If the bomb is used, then the perceived differences represented in *The Family of Man* – between rich and poor, first world and developing world, city and farm, scientist and hunter – will be erased, not by love but by death. And that of course is a possibility that has crossed the mind of more than one dystopian novelist.

But leaving aside the 'real world' of politics and war and considering *The Family of Man* on its own terms, as a work of popular art that is at the same time didactic, I want to propose that we consider the exhibition as a Cold War pastoral, a photographic narrative that represents an idyllic – albeit cyclical – view of human experience, leading us to the climax of the exhibition: the hydrogen bomb. The bomb intrudes upon the idyll, threatening to destroy the cycles of life and death: in that sense, the logic and structure of the exhibition call to mind one variant of the pastoral genre, in which the fact of death – often in the form of a death's head or a tomb discovered in the wilderness – is intruded upon the otherwise bucolic scene of shepherds and shepherdesses. In fact, looking at the colour image of the bomb used by Steichen, one might indeed think of it as a death's head: the skull-like form, the curved glowing dome of a head, the line of glowing 'teeth'. Whether or not we perceive the bomb blast as a skull, it functions metaphorically like a death's head, an emblem of destruction. In effect, the MoMA exhibition is a walk-through pastoral, which we can subtitle *Et in Arcadia Ego,* and we the viewers are the shepherds who are strolling through this world that we think we understand, until we encounter a sight that stops us dead.

The iconography of the Arcadian skull goes back at least to Guercino's painting, *Et in Arcadia Ego* (1618–22), in which the shepherds come across a death's head in a wooded area and stare at it pensively. The skull is perched on a stone pedestal with the inscription *Et in Arcadia Ego*, and we take it that the rustics are being reminded that even in the rural paradise of forest and glen, there is death, as if the skull might be saying, 'I too am in Arcadia.' The implication is usually taken as a moralistic one – along the lines of the Vanitas theme, warning the shepherds of the vanity of earthly pleasures. Poussin painted the theme twice – in 1627 and in 1637 – and it is the earlier version that sustains the Guercino notion of the speaking death's head. (A later version, showing shepherds contemplating a tomb with the same inscription, but no skull, is often taken as the 'voice' of the dead person in the sarcophagus, who is saying, 'I too have lived in Arcady', a more elegiac tone perhaps but still a warning that death comes to all.)[5]

But importantly, Steichen's purpose is not to reproduce the familiar sentiments of Arcadian iconography; he doesn't want to say merely, let's not forget death. In fact, a good deal of the imagery in *The Family of Man* already incorporates death and suffering: calling the exhibition an Arcadian idyll interrupted by the hydrogen bomb does not do justice to the fulness of life and death (hunger, war, violence, not to mention natural causes) that is a part of the story Steichen is telling. The bomb/skull is not warning us away from earthly pleasures, nor is it enjoining us to seek them while there is still time. And if there is a place for religion and spiritual belief in *The Family of Man*, the point is not to offer God as the 'answer' to the human dilemma we have created for ourselves. Rather, it is warning us that we may be so colossally stupid as to bring death on ourselves, as opposed to suffering the inevitable and universal fate: we may destroy the world entirely, through the force of our great hydrogen bomb. And that is a different message from the seventeenth-century pastoral, a more political message surely and also a more existential message, saying in effect that the future (life or death) is in our collective hands. We have only to make sure our governments don't pull the trigger.

I have been discussing *The Family of Man* until now, as if it is one thing. But that is not the case: in addition to the MoMA exhibition, the ur-version, we also have the many versions of the show that travelled the world, with slightly varied content. What the travelling exhibits shared, however, is the absence of the colour hydrogen bomb image that is the central and climactic point in the MoMA show. Instead, at best, they used a black-and-white version of the bomb cloud, an image that is not as pictorially shocking as the colour image in MoMA (see illustration 43). Incidentally, the travelling show bomb is not a black-and-white version of the colour image; rather it is an image taken at a different moment in the November 1952 detonation of 'Ivy Mike' over Enewetak, and probably a more dramatic photograph – in the medium of black and white – than the colour image would have been if it had been printed in black and white. But if the exhibition versions of *The Family of Man* have their differences, we need to put them all collectively against the book version of the show. In the book version, we actually have no image of the hydrogen bomb at all – a point I will return to. The one exception to that statement is the special edition published in 1955 with an appendix portfolio of Ezra Stoller's installation photos. In that portfolio – offered as a footnote photograph – is an image not by Stoller but by Wayne Miller, a black-and-white snapshot that does contain the original H-bomb photo from MoMA.

My argument in what follows has two parts. First, I want to read *The Family of Man* through the lens of the new consciousness that was born in the post-war era – the possible total destruction of human life that was emblematized in the H-bomb. In the second part of my discussion, I argue that the original show at the Museum of Modern Art and the book version of the exhibition that followed it are significantly different: the absence of the hydrogen bomb photograph, even a black-and-white version, produces an argument that is muted, almost to the point of vanishing.

If, as I am arguing, the hydrogen bomb photograph chosen by Steichen for the original exhibition is the key to understanding what *The Family of Man* was about, we must observe that it was even more significant by virtue of what it was not: the H-bomb explosion was not the familiar mushroom cloud but was instead a more

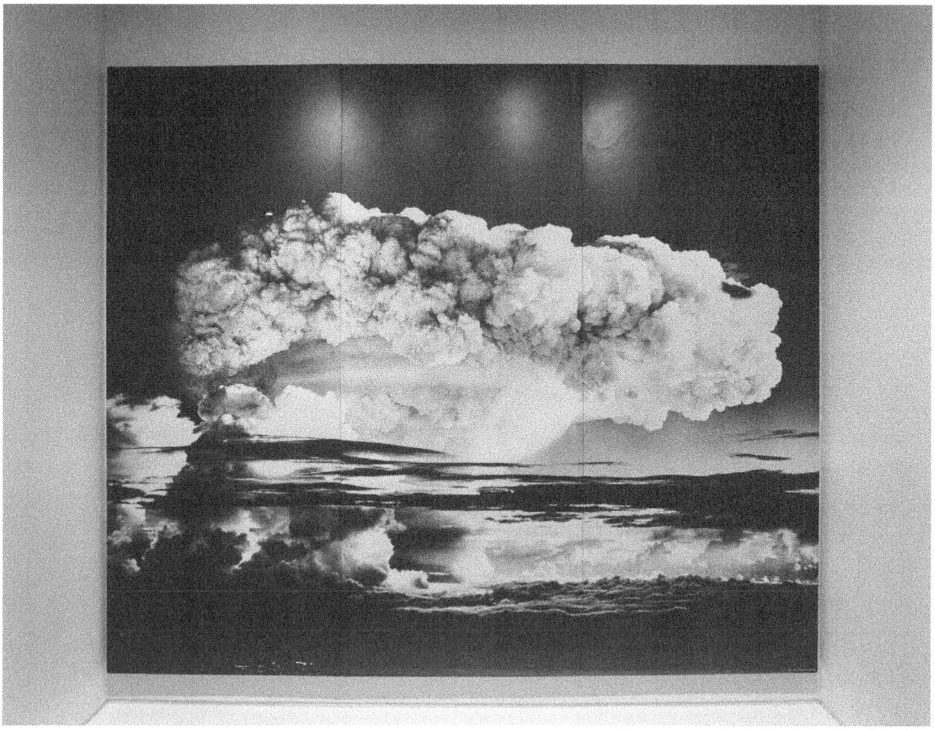

43 ***The Family of Man*** **installation at Clervaux Castle. Theme 'H-bomb explosion'. Atomic Energy Commission.**

threatening form, a mountainous cloud – red, yellow and orange – with darker horizontal bands across the central form, set against a black sky. I have called it a skull/bomb. To understand Steichen's choice and to understand the impact the bomb photo was intended to have in the exhibition, we must first step back and explore the way nuclear weapons were understood by the general public in the ten years between the destruction of Japan's two cities and the mounting of *The Family of Man* at the Museum of Modern Art.

***

Although the hydrogen bomb had been exploded experimentally in 1952, it was not seen by the public as a visual event until 1954. Up to 1954, when people thought of nuclear weapons, they were thinking of the old atomic bomb, which they had already absorbed into their experience of the exotic, so that the old mushroom cloud was almost a familiar friend. (Bikini, the site of nuclear tests beginning in 1946, gave us the name of our abbreviated bathing suits.) We can see the way the image of the bomb explosion over Nagasaki was cocooned within an aesthetic of the sublime, including its contradictions of terror and beauty, in the writings of journalist William Laurence, who was the first to describe it. For Laurence, the sight is monstrous and frightening, but also sublime, a shifting cloud of organic forms – mushrooms and flowers. Laurence was commissioned by the US Army to accompany the aeroplane crews observing the drop and to report on what he saw – the only journalist to have official permission to do so. In a piece published by *Life* magazine, Laurence described the unfolding clouds 'struggling in an elemental fury, like a creature in the act of breaking the bonds that held it down. In a few seconds it had freed itself from its gigantic stem and floated upward with tremendous speed [...] But no sooner did this happen when another mushroom, smaller in size than the first one, began emerging out of the pillar. It was as though the decapitated monster was growing a new head.'[6] Despite the menacing forms of the mushroom cloud, Laurence saw it finally as a visual wonder – a flower, a rose even: 'As the first mushroom floated off into the blue, it changed its shape into a flowerlike form, its giant petal curving downward, creamy-white outside, rose-colored inside. It still retained that shape when we last gazed at it from a distance of about 200 miles.'[7]

There were other forms of aesthetic appreciation besides the sublime, especially as imagery of nuclear testing began to appear in the mass media. For example, in addition to the abstract kinetic beauty of the mushroom cloud, the desert testing grounds near Alamogordo, New Mexico, were yielding aerial images whose beauty seemed paradoxically to cancel out the explosive horror of the blast: 'The first atomic bomb's crater is a great green blossom in the desert near Alamogordo. The lighter splash around the dark center, which was made when the explosion's heat melted the desert sand, is a layer of glass 2,400 feet across'.[8] In the same article, a close-up photograph of the crater's surface reveals abstract biomorphic patterns that look like they would have attracted Edward Weston's eye; *Life*'s caption combines both the scientific and the aesthetic response: 'close-up of crater's surface shows how the heat of the atomic explosion destroyed a desert plant and melted sand into weird shapes of crude glass'.[9] Meanwhile, in another image, the radiation from the crater fragments produces a black-and-white film exposure that looks like one of Man Ray's rayographs.[10] It was as if the modernist aesthetic was the editorial lens through which the bomb was seen.

In other ways as well during the early 1950s the bomb was being assimilated into American culture as almost a 'natural' force, more particularly a force that Americans could deal with, almost with aplomb, assuming the US might ever become a target. The US Army Field Forces Chief declared, troops 'have no particular reason to fear the atomic bomb more than any other weapon'.[11] But if troops are used to danger, what about the civilian population? For it was clear, within a few short years of the atom bomb's explosion, that other countries, and especially the USSR, had the power to destroy American cities, just as the US had the power to destroy theirs. Given this possibility, US citizens had to be 'prepared', and nuclear proliferation brought with it the proliferation of nuclear fallout shelters in urban centres of the United States, marked by a special black-and-orange sign, and the construction of personal shelters underground – stocked with canned foods, detective novels and checkered tablecloths – across the rural areas of the United States.

Yet another way the bomb was domesticated was through the plausible fiction of scientific rhetoric, with its measurements of bodily and material damage following a blast. Seven months after Hiroshima and Nagasaki, the effects of the bomb were described in *Life* magazine (11 March 1946) in the form of a chilling summary by the US Commission sent to Japan to study the effects of the bomb on buildings and on people. The language was graphic: 'internal organs were ruptured [...] Practically everybody within a radius of 6,500 feet was killed or seriously injured and all buildings crushed or disemboweled'.[12] In the subsequent pages, *Life* reported on the effects of heat on the skin (clothing imprinted on the body), of gamma rays (internal bleeding), of shock waves (inner organs rupturing) and on the material damage: frame buildings were smashed to pieces, while steel frame buildings were stripped of their masonry. Yet as gruesome as these details were, they were sanitized by the use of simple drawings that schematized and neutralized the descriptions, turning the horror of reality into something one might see in a high school science textbook.

Talking about the science of the bomb and of nuclear reactors helped distance the average citizen from the horror, and the mass media regularly carried stories dealing with the force of explosions, along with the stop-motion depiction of blasts using high-speed camera techniques. Images like these were spectacular as science and as art and contributed to the American public's pride in the nation's technological prowess.[13]

***

In asking why in 1952 Steichen may have decided to begin the work of creating an exhibition devoted to world peace, we can point to two events in that year: one is the publication of photographs revealing the total destruction of Hiroshima and Nagasaki in 1945; the second is the testing of the hydrogen bomb on Enewetak, an atoll in the Pacific. Only in 1952, following the withdrawal of the US occupying forces and the lifting of the press ban, did images of the destruction of the two original Japanese targets – Hiroshima and Nagasaki – finally reach the general public in the pages of *Life*.[14] We are talking, just to be clear, about the atomic bomb, not the later hydrogen bomb. In the 29 September issue, *Life*'s readers were shown the five ghastly photographs taken by Yoshito Matsushige immediately after the bombing of Hiroshima, the only images taken on that day. Matsushige captured the survivors, their clothes shredded, as they huddle together; and in one image a police officer is sitting at a desk issuing certificates – though what purpose they served, except to comfort the survivors through the fiction of a still extant bureaucracy, is hard to imagine. In one image, a dark shadow drapes concrete steps, the putative remains of a pulverized victim.

Life also printed Yosuke Yamahata's photos of Nagasaki, originally commissioned by the Japanese government immediately after the bomb so that they could be used to reinvigorate the war effort; resisting that intention, the photographer had withheld the inflammatory images, and in the confusion after the atomic bombs and in the weeks before Japan's surrender, they were forgotten.[15] Taken in the immediate aftermath of the bomb, the photographs show the physical ruins of the blasts – twisted rails, the smoking ruins of buildings, an occasional structure or tree standing here and there – and the suffering of those who survived, usually for a short time only, with torn limbs and severe burns. These previously suppressed images were now visible to both Japanese and American audiences. The Japanese had known the horrifying statistics – 260,000 dead, 160,000 wounded – but the photographs had a stronger impact than any numbers when they were published seven years after the war's end in Japan: *Life* tells us they elicited not so much anger against the United States as a strong sentiment against any future wars. The American response to the photographs, to judge from the letters printed by *Life*, expressed shock and sorrow at the images, but also a sense that the bomb was a necessary evil, in having saved the lives of American soldiers who were about to invade Japan.[16]

The second major event of 1952 was the testing of the hydrogen bomb on the Enewetak atoll in the Pacific, and we can assume that Captain Steichen – given his recent service as head of naval photography during the war – was informed of the event. For despite the warnings and premonitions of *Time* and *Life* immediately after the bombings of Japan in 1945, not to mention admonitions by many atomic scientists, along with the creation of anti-nuclear war organizations, the years following the end of World War II were marked by the continuing expansion of nuclear testing, above and below ground. It is most important to note the difference in public consciousness that resulted from the advent of the hydrogen bomb, as opposed to the earlier atomic bombs. The destructive power of the atomic bomb was horrifying. But the hydrogen or fusion bomb was in another category altogether, ten times more powerful than the A-bomb, and its destructive power dwarfed the earlier atomic bomb.

Two years after the initial testing of the H-bomb, *Life* magazine showed the range of its destructive power and the possibility – or rather the impossibility – of evacuating urban population centres in the event of attack. For it was simply impossible to imagine an urban centre surviving, as *Life* made clear in an article jauntily titled, '5–4–3–2–1 and the Hydrogen Age is Upon Us'. With photographs from the 1952 bomb test, released by the US government in 1954, the article makes clear that the hydrogen bomb changes everything, and especially the question of survival: 'The device which vaporized Elugelab also obliterated all previous plans for US civil defense, which were based on estimates of A-bomb damage.'[17] Instead of total destruction within a radius of one mile (atom bomb), the new weapon destroyed everything within four to five miles, with extensive damage beyond that.

Life describes the various plans of major US cities with a straight face, but it's painfully clear that survival is an impossible dream. Major cities bombed with the H-bomb will be obliterated.

If the advent of the hydrogen bomb in 1952 was the catalyst for Steichen to imagine an exhibition that would address the urgent problem of world peace, *The Family of Man* did not spring from Steichen's brow without prior inspiration, antecedent and ancestry. We know that when he saw the 1938 Grand Central Station exhibition of the Farm Security Administration photographs, which pictured the ravages of the Great Depression, the former aesthete and modernist was inspired with a new sense of what photography could do as a public medium. A few years later, while serving as commander of naval photography in World War II, Steichen had mounted an exhibition at the Museum of Modern Art, *The Road to Victory* (1942), that was designed to inspire a vibrant patriotic response; tracing the American character from the westward expansion into 'virgin land' (the text was by Carl Sandburg), the exhibition portrayed a nation whose determination and strength were unassailable. A subsequent Steichen exhibition, *Power in the Pacific* (1945), celebrated the naval might of the United States in the Pacific, where Steichen himself had directed photographic operations.[18] Both of these exhibitions were developing new techniques of pictorial narrative, with Steichen experimenting with picture size, thematic grouping, dramatic sequencing and visual direction; Bauhaus designer Herbert Bayer, working in the US since the late 1930s, was a key contributor to the exhibition designs (he had left MoMA by the time of *The Family of Man* but his influence is still apparent in the exhibition design); *The Family of Man* was devised by architect Paul Rudolph, whose designs typically inflected modernist simplicity with a complexity that is visible in the floor plan of the MoMA exhibition.[19]

By the time he conceived *The Family of Man*, Steichen had perfected the art of exhibition design as a pictorial narrative that would exploit photography as a vehicle for political communication.[20] Also, by the early 1950s, Steichen had moved far beyond the rousing patriotism of his earlier exhibitions and far beyond any celebration of military power (though he still liked to be called 'Captain'): his message now, in the face of the horrifying nuclear arms race and in the chilled and threatening political climate of the Cold War, was the necessity of global cooperation and peace. Steichen was not alone in making this argument: yet another likely inspiration was a magazine feature that ran in the *Ladies Home Journal* from March 1948 to March 1949, called *People are People the World Over.* That series was initiated by photo editor John G. Morris, who was baffled by the destructive power of the bomb and wanted to establish, in place of war, an image of shared values and experiences across the world. Morris and photographer Robert Capa travelled to Iowa, where they photographed a 'classic Iowa farm family' eating dinner. For the *People are People* feature, Morris used the same families from various places around the world, 'doing the familiar things that all families do – cook and eat and wash and work and play and sleep and so on'.[21]

***

In order to understand how the hydrogen bomb figures in the conception of *The Family of Man*, we need to see it in the context of the entire exhibition. *The Family of Man* has a narrative structure that seems relatively straightforward at first but grows increasingly complicated, doubling back on itself, as the series of images moves to its climax – the hydrogen bomb image. And here I should say that the exhibition and the book follow more or less the same plan, with the significant difference already mentioned, that the image of the bomb is not in the book. I'll return to that point later, but for now I want to briefly trace the narrative logic of the exhibition, allowing for the fact that the book invites the reader to turn pages in a consecutive order, while the exhibition allows the viewer greater freedom in moving around, looking at one image here, another there. I'll assume a more or less linear experience, which in the book is made normative by the physical structure of the book, and the latter shall serve as the paradigm for our discussion, with occasional comparisons to the exhibition.

The first part of *The Family of Man* portrays the life cycle as a universal human experience, regardless of the specific culture or nationality. It's hard not to observe the thematic groupings, as they move from love to marriage to pregnancy to mothers nursing, mothers and children, children growing up and playing, children in distress, children and fathers. We then are given a sense, beyond the life cycle of the family, of the space of habitation – farms, workplaces, the worker in industrial society, the construction of massive engineering projects. Workers of all kinds are shown, from fishermen hauling nets to workers building rail lines to women washing clothes. Into this flow of life as we knew it before 1945, Steichen introduces the nuclear theme, with images of scientists and architects and engineers. The accompanying captions (which are the same in the exhibition) are significant and are juxtaposed on a single page: 'Nuclear weapons and atomic electric power are symbolic of the atomic age: On one side, frustration and world destruction: on the other, creativity and a common ground for peace and cooperation. – U.S. Atomic Energy Commission'. Note the balanced phrasing: good or evil? Both seem possible. That quote is paired with one attributed simply to 'Sioux Indian': 'This is the fire that will help the generations to come, if they use it in a sacred manner. But if they do not use it well, the fire will have the power to do them great harm'. Fire also can cause harm or do good. The two quotes are saying the same thing, but making 'fire' the equivalent of the 'hydrogen bomb' is more than a category mistake. Nevertheless, Steichen is suggesting that nuclear weapons somehow fall into a type of dilemma human beings have dealt with before, so let's hope …

The exhibition and book continue with photographs celebrating the daily business of life across the wide range of human societies from the developed to the undeveloped world: getting water, baking, eating. Children play ring-around-the-rosy in a gathering of 18 images (the circular layout in the book mimics the museum installation); musicians make music; quilters quilt; we see orchestras, jazz bands, dancers, more dancers, audiences enthralled, nightclubs and dining halls, the pleasures of social life – eating, playing on swings, dancing, racing, swimming, amusement parks. Next is the world of formal education: a tribal circle, a lecture hall, a seminar room, and this leads to a second iteration of the nuclear theme, coupled with ominous undertones of war: on one page is a photograph of J. Robert Oppenheimer (the 'Father of the Atomic Bomb') teaching at Princeton, together with a smaller photo of Albert Einstein, whose theoretical formulas provided the logic of nuclear power, also at the Princeton Institute for Advanced Study. Einstein looks deep in meditation, baffled almost, as he stands before a desk piled with dishevelled papers, as if he might be looking for Beethoven's lost penny. Next to Einstein is an image of the same size, showing us a six-year-old at the blackboard – some future Einstein? – demonstrating basic arithmetic with the poise of a professor. By now, the nuclear music has become an ominous leitmotif in this opera.

Einstein and his avatar are followed by two more images of scientists, now with blackboards filled with equations, plus two images of lab scientists working with glowing materials. The threat of science is fulfilled in the full-page photograph of a bombed German city, Pforzheim, with the ruins of structures in the middle ground, half-standing walls, rubble and in the distance the remains of a church, with the steeple standing but damaged. The damage here was not caused by nuclear weapons, but it was still the product of science and technology at the service of the state. In the foreground is a flight of stone and brick stairs, still intact, leading to the destroyed city below and – the centre of our attention – a young boy is walking jauntily down the stairs, backpack on his back, as if he might be going to school, though there is no conceivable building with a roof in sight. Still, the boy's presence and the backpack convey a sense of optimism about the future: in the rubble of post-war Germany, new beginnings are being made, a new generation is rising, the photo suggests. Incidentally, the photograph was taken by Otto Hagel, a German refugee whose own future was less certain: after working for *Fortune* and *Life* during the 1930s and 1940s, Hagel and his wife, photojournalist Hansel Mieth, were blacklisted following their refusal to testify before the House Un-American Activities Committee during the 1950s, where they would have been required to name their associates in the labour movement.

Following the ruins of Pforzheim, *The Family of Man* recapitulates the earlier life cycle imagery, doubling back on itself, beginning with couples as at the start of the exhibition, but now we see couples who appear uneasily separated, followed by couples who appear closely happy. We see families, street scenes, a wonderful set of street photographs – but where is this recapitulation of daily life going? The answer is eventually found in a full-page photograph of a boy in a cemetery. Images of death and funerals fill the next pages, leading to another full-page cemetery photo. Death is here in *The Family of Man*, but it is accommodated within a larger conceptual frame: we are yet again brought back to the cycles of life – babies, old and young in one another's arms, and the caption states the theme here broadly: 'Flow, flow, flow, the current of life is ever onward [...] Kobodaishi'.

Now the exhibit dives into the more affective realm: people alone, suffering their loneliness; others showing compassion, comforting one another. Steichen reminds us next of the Great Depression in a suite of FSA images; then we see images of hunger from around the world. These are the tribulations of life, the exhibition is saying. And how can we cope with all this? The answer Steichen offers is belief in a greater power, a higher wisdom, an answer that seems to be endorsed even by the mythical Einstein ('To know that what is impenetrable to us really exists, manifesting itself as the highest wisdom and the most radian beauty'). Einstein – the theorist of the irrational nuclear age – is here made the servant of a beauty and order and wisdom beyond even his ken. There follow images of worship – churches, synagogues, along with Buddhist worship. Even Anne Frank, that innocent victim of Nazi evil, is brought into service, offering a sentiment that seems contrary to reason even if it is consistent with our wishes: 'People are really good at heart', she says to us, accompanied by photographs of teenagers and young women from around the world. And on the next page, amidst images of young men and young women, racing in a hot-rod or playing at the beach, we have the affirmation that underlies the optimism of *The Family of Man*: 'You are the young wonder-tree plant, grown out of ruins', from a Baronga African folk tale. New growth out of ruins: that is what we'd like to believe is always possible, and Steichen is affirming it here.

The Family of Man is taking us on a complicated journey of sentiment, clearly, and things grow even more complicated when the mood is suddenly again changed, this time with a two-page spread featuring a terrible moment in the history of the Warsaw Ghetto: Nazi soldiers are marching a phalanx of captured Jews through the streets – an image used at the Nuremberg trials. The energy of the Jews rushing forward could confuse us, as if they have somewhere to go, apart from death in a concentration camp; the Nazi soldiers stand on either side of the parade, as if they are innocent of the slaughter that lies ahead. *The Family of Man* now takes a directly political turn: back to children, to a barbed wire Korean prison camp, to images of justice and courts of law, to scenes of public political debate, street demonstrations, facing two images that seem prophetic in their pairing: a skyline of television aerials and below it the photograph of a mass audience at a convention of some sort. The ballot box is next celebrated, and we realize that the sequence is moving from the justice of the Nuremberg trials to the political process more generally in the age of mass media. Yet the ballot-box foundation of the political process – in democratic theory at least – is an important part of this sequence: we turn the page to find three images from France, Japan and Turkey of voters exercising their rights – the locked ballot box.

If Steichen is pointing to the power of democracies to determine their course of action, he then challenges us with the ultimate problem of contemporary civilization: what do we do with the hydrogen bomb? Up to this point we have had premonitions of darkness beyond the natural cycle of life and death; we have seen the destruction of Pforzheim during World War II, we have seen Nazi soldiers rounding up Jews, we have seen barbed wire prison camps and we have glimpsed revolution in the street. The leitmotif of death as well as the ominous music suggesting nuclear weapons have been heard. But the exhibition was working toward a faith in the future that rests with the renewal of energy in the younger generation and a faith in the goodness of human beings and the ballot box. Now Steichen wants to focus our attention on the reality of our contemporary world – the hydrogen bomb, with its promise of total destruction.

And here is where the book version of *The Family of Man* separates itself from the MoMA exhibition, for what is missing in the book was a crucial dimension of the museum experience, as the press release from MoMA indicates. As the release says, we see

> [...] a series of photographs which dramatically raise one of the greatest challenges of our time – the hydrogen bomb and what it means for the future of the family of man. Nine photographs of questioning faces, triptychs of three children, three women and three men are shown with a quotation from Bertrand Russell, '[...] The best authorities are unanimous in saying that a war with hydrogen bombs is quite likely to put an end to the human race [...] There will be universal death – sudden only for a minority, but for the majority a slow torture of disease and disintegration'.
>
> At the entrance to the next gallery the visitor sees a photograph of a dead soldier with the words from the 5th-century (B.C.) 'Who is the slayer, who the victim? Speak'. (Sophocles) This gallery is painted black, and the only light comes from a six by eight foot (Eastman) color transparency of the explosion of a hydrogen bomb.[22]

The image of the bomb itself – the six by eight back-lit colour photo – was published in the 3 May 1954 edition of *Life* magazine the year before the exhibition, in an article called 'New Ivy Pictures Show Fire and Ice'.[23] In the powerful image, mounted in its own wall space, the aftermath of the ten megaton explosion – ten times more powerful than all previous atomic blasts combined – looms as an enormous red cloud, a giant skull-shaped mountain with orange glowing globules, cut across by horizontal bands of reddish clouds against a black sky. (The black sky resulted from the use of filters, which were technically essential, given the blinding flash of the explosion.)[24]

The placement of the image was equally important: Steichen leads the viewer toward the spectacular cynosure via a wall of photos of individuals, each from a different national and ethnic background, and each seeming to look at something, pondering its significance. A few steps beyond, we realize that they are staring thoughtfully at the hydrogen bomb that faces us as well, darkly framed, glowing in colour. It is a powerful moment, strategically designed for maximum effect in the unreal world of the exhibition, where the viewer has become accustomed to the factitious world of black and white: the shock of a back-lit colour image in an otherwise black-and-white exhibition mimics – however remotely – the shock of the explosion itself.

The skill with which this effect was engineered as part of the viewing experience can only be compared to the 'Imagineering' designs of Walt Disney, the greatest inventor of crowd experiences in the world at the time. Though the comparison may seem odd, Disney and Steichen were both consummate artists – not only in terms of their respective forms and materials, but in terms of their understanding of how to move the viewer through a controlled environment. For Disney, the experience of Disneyland began with Main Street, an affirmation of America's central values; yet at the end of the vista, for the visitor, was the great castle of Fantasyland looming ahead, drawing the crowd to it like a magnet. This was no accident, as Disney revealed when talking about the design of his theme park; such magnets function as nodes, organizing the spatial experience of the park and moving people from one place to another, as you might lure a mouse to a trap with a piece of cheese. (The metaphor Disney used was the hot dog that he himself used to attract his hounds; he called Sleeping Beauty's Castle – in a term that quickly entered the Disney design idiom and challenges the sturdiest romantic – a 'weenie'.) Steichen likewise controlled the movement of the viewer, leading his visitor not to the escapist romance of an imagined castle but to the central fact and horror of twentieth-century life – the hydrogen bomb. It seems entirely logical, even if mere coincidence, that these two most successful middlebrow entertainments of the post-war era – the *Family of Man* and Disneyland – should both open in 1955, at the height of the Cold War, giving powerful form to the opposing impulses to confront the demons of our time and to escape from them into a world of nostalgia and fantasy.[25] Both also became part of America's globally exported culture.

What happened to the hydrogen bomb when *The Family of Man* left MoMA and underwent its subsequent iterations is itself a part of the history – and the mystery – of this greatest of all photographic shows.[26] The travelling exhibition, as we can learn from a photograph of the installation in Paris, featured a black-and-white image of the bomb that appears to be a reversed (left/right) version of the two-page black and white photo published in *Life* magazine on 12 April 1954; like the original MoMA image, it was strategically positioned, and like the original it too was not the familiar mushroom. It is, however, a different image from the MoMA colour original, and evidently the technical requirements of having a giant back-lit colour image could not be met in a travelling show. In Japan, however, nuclear bombs were excluded altogether from the exhibition, with photographs of Nagasaki by Yamahata included instead. (Such images, showing the horror and devastation of the city, were not part of the original exhibition or book, although Steichen had cropped a Yamahata photo of a Japanese child in Nagasaki holding a rice ball to serve as one of the nine portraits leading up to the climactic Russell quote.) Even these, however, were covered over when the emperor visited the show, in deference, one assumes, to the unceasing illusion, as much as the divinity, that doth hedge a king.

***

If the argument of the exhibition, so clear in its original form, became muted once it was translated into the many travelling exhibitions, it was even more muffled in book form. In the book – perhaps the most widely printed volume in the history of photography – the hydrogen bomb that was the central fact of the MoMA show, and in a way its raison d'être, has virtually disappeared. The bomb photograph represents death, the possibility of annihilation on an individual and a global level, the threat that hangs over life on earth in the age of nuclear warfare, and for the book Steichen and his editors simply took it off the table. The hydrogen bomb, they seem to have concluded, was simply unthinkable – at least in the form of a vivid photographic image. Only in the special edition of the book published in 1955 with a portfolio of installation photographs by Ezra Stoller, as mentioned earlier, does it make a minor appearance, visible as a photographic footnote in a series of images included as an appendix to the volume. And in that special appendix, it appears not as a primary photograph but as a secondary image, the background in an installation shot taken by Wayne Miller that features a family – Miller's own wife and children – standing and talking in front of the bomb photo.[27] (Miller had worked with Steichen in designing the show from the beginning.) In fact, the three children, who seem to be ages 5 to 12, are focused not on the image we see on the wall behind them but on their mother, who might be 'explaining' the bomb, mediating its impact. Oddly, given the importance the photo held in the show, the image in this portfolio of added photographs seems shrunken to near insignificance at the bottom of the page, surrounded by larger installation views – a mere footnote, as the saying goes.

The Family of Man as book makes the same argument as the exhibition, but it is pitched in a different key, so different that the nuclear logic of the conception has been virtually ignored by readers of the book, and the Cold War pastoral of a nuclear arcadia is nearly invisible. Although we have the same anticipation of the missing bomb, the same grid of nine portraits staring at something – as in the exhibition installation – the assumed object of their gaze, instead of an image of the H-bomb, is a black page with white lettering, featuring Bertrand Russell's stark utterance, quoted earlier as part of MoMA's press release: ' [...] the best authorities are unanimous in saying that a war with hydrogen bombs is quite likely to put an end to the human race [   ] there will be universal death – sudden only for a fortunate minority, but for the majority a slow torture of disease and disintegration'. The presentation is dramatic, but Russell's language, understated and with an edge of irony, is not the full colour back-lit image of the hydrogen bomb. In moving from exhibition to book, *The Family of Man* moved from a rhetoric of shock and confrontation to a rhetoric of philosophical reason, appealing to probabilities, likely outcomes, best authorities. Did Steichen and the editors think through the omission of the hydrogen bomb image? If it was omitted in order to emphasize a more positive message, it was an omission that risked suppressing the logic of Steichen's original conception.[28] The result is that we have in effect two 'Families of Man': the shock and awe of the original exhibition and the muted warnings that are implicit in the book version.

Like the original exhibition, the book continues beyond this moment, offering a single line of type on the left: 'Who is the slayer, who the victim? Speak' (180). With the source identified simply as Sophocles, we might forget that the line is spoken by the chorus in *Antigone*, upon learning that Euridyce's son Haemon has been slain. The specificity of guilt that is implied in the original Sophoclean context is, in the extracted text, turned on its head, as if slayer and victim might be interchangeable, as if all guilt is shared.[29] Facing the Sophocles quote is the photograph of a dead soldier lying in a foxhole, his rifle standing bayonet first in the ground. We might read this as any soldier in any war, or as the generic Unknown Soldier, the anonymous good soldier who dies pro patria, pro domo. It is a sad image, but it still might evoke conventional heroism and conventional warfare. In a way, it seems irrelevant to the spectacular destructive power of the hydrogen bomb.

Following the hydrogen bomb (or the surrogate contained in the Russell quote), *The Family of Man* offers us hope – in the form of the many images of couples, for each of which the caption is the same: 'We two form a multitude'. The words are taken from Ovid – *Nos duo turba sumus* – and describe Deucalion and Pyrrha after the deluge that destroys the world in the Greek version of Noah and the flood. This is the third iteration of a couples theme in the exhibition, only now much more schematic, the couples looking like multiples, each with the same quote. Moreover, these are not the joyous young procreating couples we have seen earlier: these couples are aged, tired, worn. They have seen everything. Their assumed utterance – 'We two form a multitude' – might evoke, especially to viewers in the 1950s, the more familiar sentiments of the widely popular *The Grapes of Wrath* (1939), where Steinbeck writes, addressing the powerful, that what you have to fear is one person getting together with another person against your authority. This is the 'anlage', the embryo, the beginning of shared consciousness, as Steinbeck writes, 'This is the thing to bomb: this is the beginning – from "I" to "We".' (How ironic that Steinbeck should say, this is the thing to bomb.) In *The Family of Man*, it is the individual (in the nine separate portraits looking at the Russell quote) who confronts the spectre of total destruction implied by Russell's pronouncement. Following the bomb, Steichen gives us the set of multiple couples. Individuals look at the bomb; couples somehow survive it: the couples pictured on the next pages are the beginning of a collective consciousness.

If the viewer is thinking of Steinbeck here, as is not unlikely, he or she might recall that in *Grapes*, Steinbeck is writing about a consciousness that grows between one man and another, presumably strangers, squatting beside one another as the women and children listen. In the visual narrative of *The Family of Man*, we have married couples, representing the 'nuclear family' at its core. Yet two men who discover a common interest are different from a married couple, who are already together; and whether the nuclear family – or any collective consciousness – can challenge the potential annihilation of the nuclear age is another question. Moreover, the Ovid quote that is repeated under each married couple photograph confirms the survival of a couple after the deluge, after the disaster. The logic of *The Family of Man* compels us to realize that such survival after disaster is impossible. In thus undercutting the bleak logic of the exhibition, Steichen is offering hope instead of despair, and that may have been a shrewd judgement, given that he doesn't want people weeping and gnashing their teeth as they leave the show. Despair is paralyzing, whereas hope might lead to some further action, and the succeeding two-page spread of the United Nations, together with some words from the Charter ('Determined to save succeeding generations from the scourge of war') may indeed offer us our best hope.

The Family of Man (book and exhibition) ends with a coda of sorts: a multitude of photographs of children, images of innocence, confidence, vulnerability, pathos. The final full-page photograph is by W. Eugene Smith, who was recovering at last from his own traumatic war injuries when he took the photo, and it required several tries before he got it exactly right, in terms of the timing, lighting and posing. We see two children (his own, in fact) walking from the darkness of the forest into the light of a clearing, with the optimistic text, 'A world to be born under your footsteps [...]' by St.-John Perse. The threat of the hydrogen bomb, we are asked to believe, might be held in abeyance, if we can only cherish the innocence of children. In fact, 'CHILDHOOD MAGIC' is the name given to this final grouping in the notes for the travelling exhibition.[30] One doesn't want to be cynical where the future of the world is at stake, but this coda is reminiscent of that moment in *Peter Pan* when Peter says, 'Do you believe in faeries? [...] If you believe, clap your hands!' Will the future generation save us? Can we learn to overcome our differences? Can the modern nation state (which doesn't care how much we love one another) be held in check? These questions still remain to be answered.

If Steichen was inspired by the power of photography that he saw exemplified in the FSA movement, a power to support and inspire social change, then he was doomed to fail. The FSA project was congruent with government power and interest. *The Family of Man* may have represented the United States as a peace-loving nation, but it was out of alignment with the juggernaut of military production – especially in the face of the development of the bomb by our putative enemy, the Soviet Union. Exported around the world by the US government as a message of peace and a warning against the horrors of nuclear war, *The Family of Man* was actually working against the policies of the US government, which were to further develop the programme of nuclear weapons – just in case. So we have a perfect illustration of the double bind or paradoxical logic of the Cold War: A= We must stop the madness, or else we'll destroy ourselves; B= We must keep producing weapons, just in case.

The Family of Man survives today, however, on several levels: it is of course a great work of middlebrow popular art, offering us an astonishingly complete representation of the range of human emotion – from love and joy to shock and horror. On another level, as I have suggested, it can be seen as a Cold War pastoral, an enduring genre that allows us to affirm the value of life at the same time that we must acknowledge the power of death over us. Yet considering the MoMA exhibition against the book version, I would argue that the original exhibition stands as a more complex and powerful work, with its central shocking death's head Golgotha hydrogen bomb; the book version is a sweeter, less threatening version of that pastoral, tempting us almost to believe in the possibility of global harmony in the family. Barthes and Horkheimer both read it that way, as a temptation to a needed harmony among nations and individuals; but where the former viewed the sentimentality of that appeal with irony and disdain, the latter accepted it with respectful attention and hope. Looking back on it, we can see it finally as a work that sums up the fears and desperate hopes of a cultural moment in a way that is still enduringly affecting.

Notes

1 My special thanks to Eric Sandeen not only for his foundational study of *The Family of Man*, on which I have relied at many points, but for his advice on several specific questions regarding captions; I'm grateful too for his generously sharing of archival materials from the exhibition. Thanks also to Gerd Hurm and Shamoon Zamir for inviting me to participate in this conversation on Steichen and for their valued advice along the way.

Roland Barthes, 'The Great Family of Man', in Roland Barthes, *Mythologies*, trans. Annette Lavers (New York: Hill and Wang, 1972), 101.

2 Edward Steichen, *The Family of Man* (New York: Museum of Modern Art, 1955), 4.

3 Ibid., 5.

4 Max Horkheimer, 'Opening of the Photo-Exhibition: *The Family of Man* – All of Us', 1958.

5 Erwin Panofsky, in his famous essay on the theme, calls the earlier interpretation of the moralistic meaning of the phrase (a warning against the thoughtless pursuit of riches or pleasure) and the later Poussin version, with a tomb but no death's head, as initiating an elegiac tradition: 'I too have lived in Arcadia, and now alas I am dead.' See Panofsky, 'Et in Arcadia Ego: Poussin and the Elegiac Tradition', in *Meaning in the Visual Arts* (1955; Chicago: University of Chicago Press, 1982), 295–320. I am reading *The Family of Man* as a version of the former convention.

6 William L. Laurence, 'Nagasaki was the climax of the New Mexico test', *Life*, 24 September 1945, 30.

7 Ibid., 30.

8 'New Mexico's Atomic Bomb Crater', *Life*, 25 September 1945, 28.

9 Ibid., 31.

10 Ibid., 30.

11 Charles V. Murphy, 'Outcasts of Yucca Flat', *Life*, 30 March 1953, 24. Murphy writes, 'The general's demeanor suggested that he was inclined to rate the A-bomb as something between a heavy hand grenade and an artillery shell'.

12 'Atom Bomb Effects', *Life*, 11 March 1946, 91.

13 John O'Brian calls this aspect of the bomb its 'atomicity'. John O'Brian, 'The Nuclear Family of Man', *Japan Focus: Asia Pacific Journal*, July 2008, http://www.japanfocus.org/-John-O_Brian/2816 (accessed 17 March 2017). Re-published on the History News Network, http://hnn.us/roundup/entries/52279.html. , 5 (accessed 17 March 2017). See 'Atomic Explosion stopped at Millionths of a Second', *Life*, 9 November 1953, 33.

14 Several images were published in Japanese newspapers in the immediate aftermath of the bombing, before US censorship was imposed, but they seem to have been quickly forgotten.

15 Yosuke Yamahata, 'Photographing the Bomb – A Memo' (1952), in *Nagasaki Journey: The Photographs of Yosuke Yamahata August 10, 1945*, ed. Rupert Jenkins (San Francisco: Pomegranate, 1995), 45.

16 'Letters to the Editor', *Life*, 20 October 1952, 7.

17 'All Plans to Evacuate Face Staggering Difficulties', *Life*, 12 April 1954, 30.

18 In 1946 *U.S. Camera* published a book version, *U.S. Navy War Photographs, Pearl Harbor to Tokyo Bay*, ed. Edward Steichen, text Tom Maloney (New York: Bonanza, 1984).

19 On the design of the exhibition, see Eric J. Sandeen, *Picturing an Exhibition: The Family of Man and 1950s America* (Albuquerque: University of New Mexico Press, 1995), 44, 133–4.

20 I am speaking of Steichen the individual here, but there are times, when discussing the 'authorship' of the exhibition, that 'Steichen' can be taken as a shorthand for the team who worked with him as well – Wayne Miller, Paul Rudolph, Carl Sandburg and others.

21 John G. Morris, '*The Family of Man* as American Foreign Policy', *History of Photography* 29, no. 4 (Winter 2005): 365. See Sandeen, *Picturing an Exhibition*, 23.

22 Press Release, 'Family of Man', 26 January 1955, Museum of Modern Art, Archives, https://www.moma.org/learn/resources/press_archives/1950s/1955 (accessed 17 March 2017).

23 Sandeen writes that Steichen had the colour transparency specially reproduced at the Kodak laboratory in Rochester, NY. Sandeen, *Picturing an Exhibition*, 67.

24 It may be purely coincidental, but the photograph of the dead soldier referred to in the MoMA announcement, which is even more prominently featured in the book version of *The Family of Man*, was a US Coast Guard image taken during the Battle of Enewetak in February 1944, eight years before the first hydrogen bomb test on the same atoll. It's unlikely, but possible, that Steichen chose that image because of its geographical provenance.

25 Steichen's wall of ethnically diverse individuals staring toward the bomb is not unlike the broader diversity that Disney would incorporate into his own signature work of the 1960s – 'It's a Small World'.

26 Sandeen notes Wayne Miller's explanation 'that a color picture was not practical in a black-and-white volume retailing for one dollar', observing – and I agree – that it doesn't quite explain everything. Sandeen, *Picturing an Exhibition*, 74.

27 The image appears in the deluxe edition of Steichen, *The Family of Man*, which contains 'A Special Portfolio of Photographs by Ezra Stoller of the Family of Man exhibition on the walls of the Museum of Modern Art, New York' (New York: Museum of Modern Art, 1955), 207.

28 The other often-noted deletion was the photograph of a lynching (along with the picture of a mass execution), which was removed from the MoMA exhibition after some weeks on account of its being too powerful, too striking, and causing visitors to pause and gaze, thus interrupting the flow of movement and the flow of the message. See Zamir's contribution to this volume.

29 The lines remind us of Emerson's *Brahma*: 'If the red slayer think he slays/ Or if the slain think he is slain,/ They know not well the subtle ways/ I keep, and pass, and turn again.' Horkheimer saw in *The Family of Man* a reflection of a different aspect of Emerson – his Kantian respect for the individual, together with an affirmation of the pluralism of a diverse American society.

30 Instructions for travelling show, MoMA Archives, scan of typescript. I'm indebted to Eric Sandeen for sharing his copy with me.

13 *The Family of Man* and Post-war Debates about American Art

Ulrike Gehring

For the frontispiece of *Leviathan*, his 1651 work of political philosophy, Thomas Hobbes chose an engraving that depicts, in its upper half, a giant rising into the sky (see illustration 44). With its crown, sword and crosier, this colossus is seen today as an incunabulum of political iconography, the first representation of modern society as a 'body politic'.[1] The figure of Leviathan contains the tightly packed bodies of those vassals who, 300 years later, have abandoned their shell and can now be seen apparently peacefully side by side in the visual documents of Western democracies – as attested, for example, by Andy Warhol's 1963 *Crowd* (see illustration 45). What appears to be a scene of harmony sans sovereign turns out to be peaceful only insofar as it is a gathering solely of middle-class whites of the same religion. Completely missing from Warhol's photography is the black minority that was, in the 1960s, attempting through the Civil Rights movement to secure rights comparable to those of their white fellow citizens. This absence is due to the fact that the image is based on a 1955 United Press photograph that was taken on Easter Sunday in Saint Peter's Square in Rome, reproduced in an American newspaper and ultimately translated by Warhol into the art context.[2]

The interchangeability of a single person in the crowd, when that person is no longer capable of standing out from the crowd as an individual, is also illustrated by the Pat English photograph through which viewers entered Edward Steichen's 1955 exhibition *The Family of Man* (see illustration 36). One absence recently noted in this visual document is that of the many immigrants who flocked to England from its colonies in India and the Caribbean after World War II, but who were not present at the coronation of Elizabeth II: when she was crowned Head of the Commonwealth in London in 1953, it was under the gaze of her white subjects only. Thus the enormous societal pressure brought to bear on immigration countries such as Great Britain and the United States by the redefinition of concepts of citizenship in the 1950s remains outside English's frame.[3] What unites the two images – Warhol's Easter Mass and the coronation scene in *The Family of Man* – is

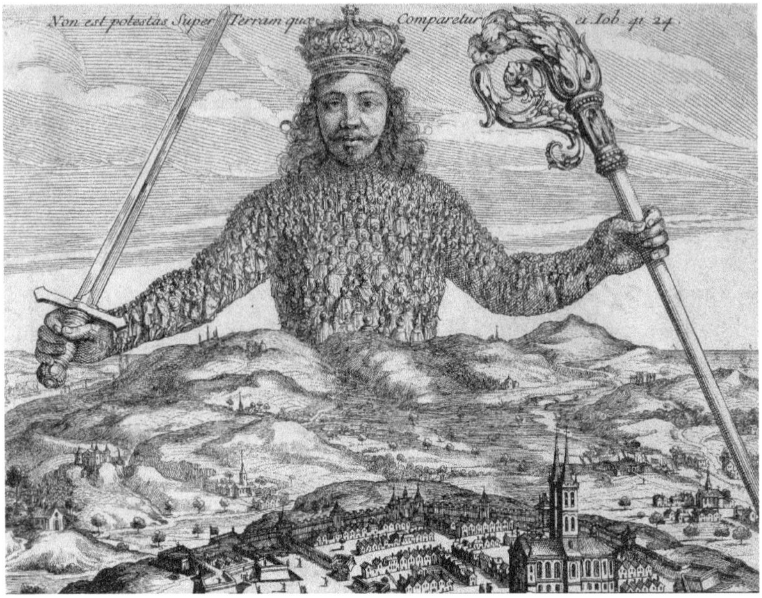

44 Frontispiece of Thomas Hobbes' *Leviathan*, by Abraham Bosse, with creative input from Thomas Hobbes, 1651.

the way they depict crowds of people attending traditional (political or religious) ceremonies without raising questions about multiculturality.

This 'flaw', however, is taken up in the art and the exhibition. What is effaced in the photographs is supplied by Warhol's and Steichen's reworkings and recontextualizations. Warhol uses a collage-like technique to reproduce the news photograph, repeatedly printing copies of the image side by side. As the crowds of people grow larger and larger, the faceless mass gains political significance – a weight, or force, whose deployment against racist violence the artist solicits. The specific violence he has in mind becomes clear by 1964 at the latest with his *Race Riots* series.

Warhol's vision of a politicized crowd fighting against inequality stands in contrast to Steichen's peaceful utopia of a world-encircling 'human family' conscious of its 'one' nature.[4] With his central assertion that 'we shall be one person',[5] Steichen chooses 'the only universal language we have',[6] revealing a oneness in diversity. This is the same unity to which Roland Barthes alludes in his reference to 'the universality of human actions in the daily life of all the countries of the world'.[7] The Israeli historian of photography Ariella Azoulay indicates a different stance, placing the focus on 'multiplicity': 'When I look at images from the exhibition, one of the first things to strike my eye is multiplicity: the fact that in spite of the similarity of

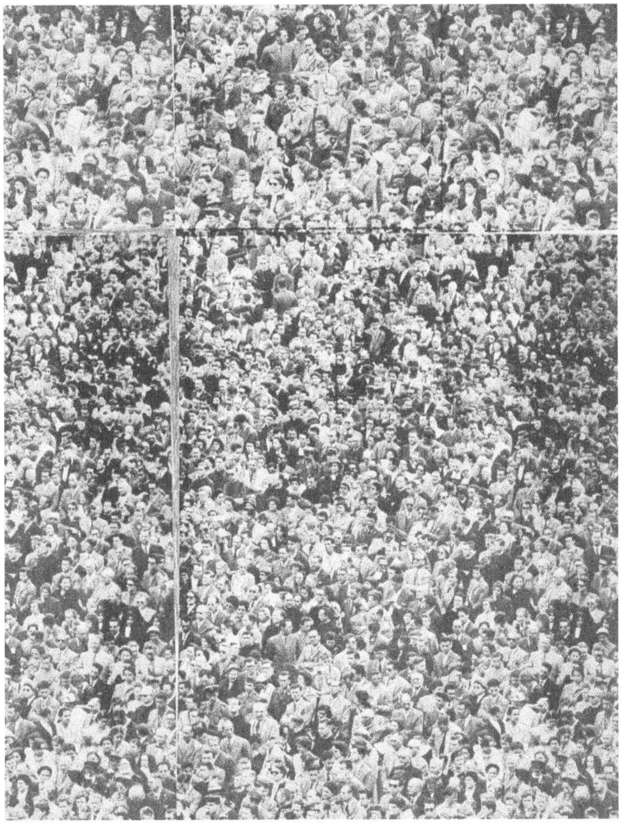

45 Andy Warhol, *Crowd*, 1963.

described situations in different areas of the exhibition, they do not constitute a unified mode of behavior.'[8]

If we draw an analogy between the concept of multiplicity and that of multifocality, an art-historically relevant question arises: to what extent can Steichen's novel and expansive exhibition format be linked to the abstract expressionists' redefinition of pictorial space? Answering that question calls for a methodical experiment, entailing as it does a comparison of the motivation of a curator-qua-author (Steichen) with the goals of a relatively heterogeneous avant-garde. However, the result will repay the effort.

The first points of similarity emerge in connection with the fact that both curator and artists called long-established concepts into question. Steichen broke with curatorial tradition, mounting prints flat on the wall rather than framing them behind conservation glass. Meanwhile, abstract expressionist artists such as Jackson Pollock declared easel painting obsolete; their 'non-compositional' all-over paintings, too, were exhibited unframed. They renounced recognizable pictorial subjects, deliberately distanced themselves from the European tradition and attempted a new cultural beginning on post-1945 American soil.[9] How US policy is entangled with art and culture will be made clear below.

Political Implications in Post-war Cultural Debates

A central concern of American domestic and foreign policy in the 1950s was the 'containment' of communist influence.[10] During the McCarthy era, anticommunist conspiracy theories and denunciations created a climate that was formative for the leftist intellectual art scene.[11] The United States cracked down on pro-Soviet endeavours at home just as harshly as it condemned the artistic production of totalitarian regimes such as the Soviet Union. (Socialist) realism was quickly pronounced the visual language of the enemy. Non-abstract styles such as American regionalism (which had been quite successful in the 1930s) faced increasing criticism. For Harry S. Truman, US president from 1945 to 1953, this development resulted in a 'historical contradiction': his low opinion of modern art was well known in the art world, yet during his term in office the United States Information Service and the Museum of Modern Art (MoMA) began to support avant-garde art in a major way.[12] That this political calculus worked out was due in part to renowned art critics such as Clement Greenberg and Harold Rosenberg, who declared the new, non-objective movement of abstract expressionism to be the West's answer to socialist realism.[13] Thus the unfree, realistic art of the Eastern Bloc was placed in opposition to free, abstract American painting.

The abstract expressionists' paintings were shown between 1950 and 1969 in internationally touring exhibitions such as the ones organized by the Congress for Cultural Freedom.[14] With this organization's assistance, MoMA presented an exhibition of works by Pollock, Willem de Kooning and Robert Motherwell in Paris in 1952. The show brought together works 'that could not have been created nor whose exhibition would be allowed by such totalitarian regimes as Nazi Germany or present-day Soviet Russia and her satellites', as its curator self-confidently announced.[15]

America's boasts about its rebellious new avant-garde in the 1950s precipitated the dethronement of its earlier artistic heroes. Whereas in 1952 it was still possible for Edward Hopper to be chosen as the country's representative at the Venice Biennale, by 1956 *Time* magazine was featuring him on the cover of its Christmas issue as 'The Silent Witness'. The article celebrated Hopper as a last great realist whose illustrational art unfortunately hewed to an outmoded style. The author, Alexander Eliot, acknowledged Hopper's past services, positioning him in the tradition of Thomas Eakins, before denying his work's legitimacy – first praising the century's 'silent witness', then delivering a political stab in the back.[16]

This ideological shift could not have escaped Steichen's notice, especially since he chose more than 500 photographs mostly in the straight or documentary style for his 1955 exhibition. The macro- and microscopic precision of their vision leaves no doubt that Steichen put more stock in their tradition than in abstract tendencies. Indeed, some of the pictures in *The Family of Man* had been taken by photographers who had worked for the Farm Security Administration (FSA) or the Office of War Information (OWI) in the 1930s and 1940s.[17] That the exhibition was nonetheless programmatic rather than retrospective is due to the curatorial concept: Steichen's message could not be conveyed via the individual documentary image. His chosen narrative was not linear but multifocal. Instead of dictating a path, he relied on optional visual relationships, pitting the singular narrative of history against the multiple pictorial narratives of individuals. For viewers, facing this challenge was the key to discerning the universally human problems in the diversity of the individual fates depicted.

Formal Equivalencies

Some of the visitors to *The Family of Man* might have been reminded of Pollock's highly praised first solo exhibition at Peggy Guggenheim's Art of This Century gallery in 1943, which displayed some striking similarities to Steichen's presentation. To reach the gallery's central exhibition space, viewers had to pass by Pollock's *Mural*, a six-metre-long multifigural painting in which a great number of vaguely suggested forms were woven into a two-dimensional pattern. Inside the main space were enormous, wall-size painting-installations that presented themselves to the viewer unglazed and unframed. Additionally, the exhibition architecture, by Frederick Kiesler, favoured a non-hierarchical mix of various interlinked images whose deeper logic became apparent only from a distance. Although each painting represented its own self-contained cosmos, the juxtaposition of Pollock's (by then quite abstract) canvases gave rise to a higher-level network pervading every dimension of the exhibition space.

In Pollock's work, however, interwoven structures not only emerge between the paintings but by the 1950s become a formal structural element within them as well. The point of departure here is the line, dripped from a can of thinned paint onto unprimed canvas. The path traced by the line – for example, in *Number 32*, from 1950 (see illustration 46) – documents what Bryan Robertson called the 'ritual' of painting, which is long over by the time the work is displayed. Two aspects of Pollock's drip technique are worthy of note: first, that the focus is on the act of painting rather than on the painting's subject, and second, that the composition has no centre; the traces of paint run far beyond the canvas's edges.[18] When in this connection Greenberg refers to an 'all-over' picture, he is referring to another criterion – along with the large scale, the non-objective compositions and the use of cheap house paint – that typifies for him a new, genuinely American style.[19]

The term 'all-over' is also used by Rob Kroes to describe *The Family of Man* in a discussion of the symbiotic relationship between Paul Rudolph's exhibition architecture and Steichen's 'overall narrative strategy'. Steichen, says Kroes, distanced himself from the 'linearity of displays along museum walls', creating a

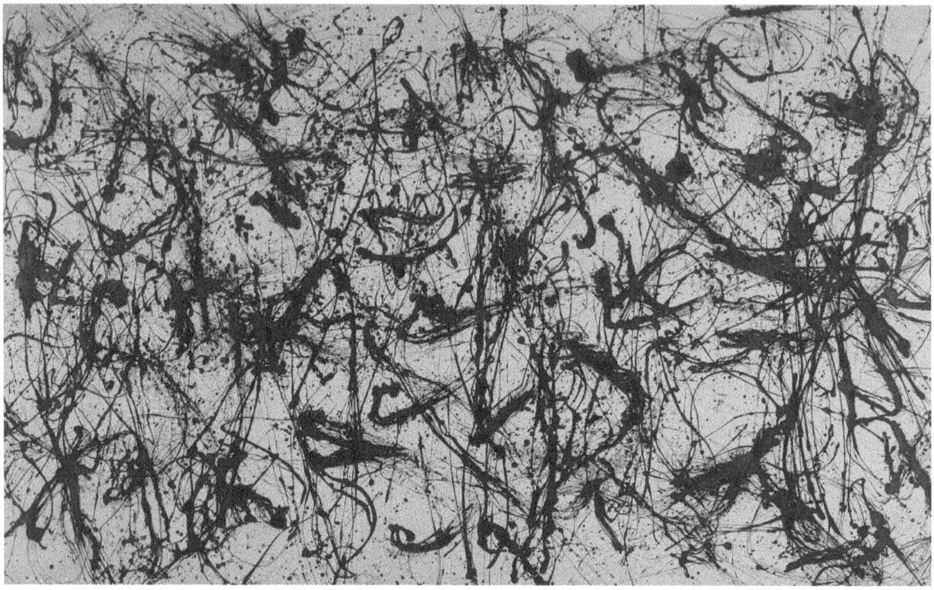

46 Jackson Pollock, *Number 32*, 1950.

'three-dimensional collage' that viewers experienced not sequentially, but rather discontinuously, as they moved from display to display.[20] The link to collage is also noted by Ralph Harley, who locates Steichen's 'modernist art-space' in the tradition of cubist conceptions of the image: 'This new space emerged out of the Synthetic Cubist collage introduced in Paris around 1913 by Pablo Picasso and Georges Braque.'[21] The validity of the cubist connection shall not be explored further here, but the analogy between Steichen's curatorial concept and the layered pictorial structures of collage merits attention. The exhibition's collagistic approach (see illustrations 1, 2 and 3) enabled viewers to alternate between intimate close-ups and an objectivizing distance, which is why Kroes credits Steichen's photographic setting with 'multi-vocality' as well as 'multi-focality'.[22]

Similar processes of accommodation occur for the viewer of Pollock's drip paintings when the eye follows the path of a line toward one of the image's focal points. Max Imdahl, who believes these compositional centres are no accident, describes the paintings as 'multifocal all-over image[s]'.[23] What may at first seem like a note in the margins of art history is in fact a refutation of the Greenbergian 'myth' of the unconsidered, automatic act of painting. Confining ourselves to the facts in this dispute, which are that the drip paintings do contain areas of focus, we must acknowledge that this concentration of information does not lead, either in Pollock's work or in Steichen's, to a hierarchical ordering of content. Rather, the multifocality prevents us from taking in the visual information at a glance. There is neither a clearly defined beginning nor an end. Both Pollock's paintings and Steichen's floor plan (see illustration 8) present themselves as labyrinthine continua that can be experienced only by degrees. In Steichen's exhibition, where room 37 connects directly to room 2, beginning and end form a unit. This unity is reinforced by the images selected: when, at the end of *The Family of Man*, the two children in W. Eugene Smith's famous 1946 photograph *The Walk to Paradise Garden* walk hand in hand toward the light, they are not only entering the heavenly Jerusalem but also leaving the Garden of Eden.[24] The end leads to the beginning, and the viewer is faced once again with the images of 'lovers' and 'childbirth' in room 2. What was seen, at the start of the exhibition, as a random juxtaposition of individual moments of happiness now appears as the embryo of the 'family of man'.

Archetypal Symbols, or the Search for the Universal

After the savagery of World War II, the discursive new beginnings sought by the abstract expressionists took very different forms.[25] In response to the systematic murder of the Jews in Nazi Germany, Mark Rothko began in 1941 to banish all figural references from his imaginal world,[26] tending thereafter to convey his existential impressions via non-representational colour spaces. Pollock was increasingly drawn to mythological themes in the 1940s, studying ancient tales and the legends and rituals of indigenous peoples. He was especially fascinated by the totems of the Native Americans, which were shown at MoMA in 1941 as part of the exhibition *Indian Art of the United States*.

In our discussion of the parallels between various phenomena in the work of Pollock and Steichen, this exhibition deserves special mention for its proclamation of a universal aesthetic to be seen in the art of America's first inhabitants. For proof, it pointed to the Navajos' ceremonial sandpaintings, which were among the items on view. By Pollock's own account, these works made a powerful impression on him; they may have inspired him to take up action painting.[27] While Pollock's spontaneous, impulsive painting style was uncoupled from ancient ritual, he still felt that something primeval was preserved in his largely unconscious gestures.

The unconscious played a part in Steichen's exhibition as well – not in terms of the curator's choices, but certainly with regard to the role of the viewer. While Steichen did lay out a subtext through the selection of images and the context provided by the exhibition, this subtext was, in comparison to the narrative of a film, quite fragmentary. As a result, viewers were required to unconsciously fill in the gaps between the images with their own memories, ideas and imaginings. Only in this way could they perceive 'the systematic inversion from the particular to the universal, from profane to sacred, from visual serendipity to divine plan for creation'.[28]

The 'Truth' behind the Visible Image

The impact of Steichen's exhibition can be explained as a combination of powerful images and innovative presentation. It is important that the photographs are the occasion, not the cause, for a feeling of empathy transcending the individual. Expressions of emotion such as love, grief and despair are not limited to those pictured but transferred onto the viewer in an act of visual identification. In the specific, we recognize the universal.

A world away from this inductive approach is Jasper Johns's iconic 1955 painting *Flag*. Unlike *The Family of Man*, it represents the collective (the 'body politic') by means not of the individual, but of a pre-established heraldic symbol. The composition not only resembles an American flag, but also represents it. In its symbolic appropriation of the motif, the flag/image becomes an emblem of American values. These values were expressed by Johns though heraldry, by Steichen in a 'drama of [...] humanity',[29] and by Pollock through the myths of the Native Americans. Only in Johns's painting, however, do image and subject become one: it is both a picture and a flag. As a picture, it stands for the democratic values presented in their many aspects in *The Family of Man*; a preliminary outline of these values can also be seen in Gordon Parks's 1942 FSA photograph *American Gothic*.[30] Parks's portrait depicts an African American cleaning woman, Ella Watson, posing with mop and broom in front of an American flag in a display of loyalty to a nation to which her own father had fallen victim.[31] The image exemplifies a deeply democratic mindset and morality that may also be adduced in connection with Steichen's curatorial concept. The message of that concept is that a modern global society can develop in peace only when differences of race, culture and national origin do not provoke discrimination. Only when all citizens share the same rights as part of a single 'body politic' will Steichen's utopia of the great global family be achieved. The architecture of his exhibition attempted to accommodate this lofty moral aspiration on a fundamental level by presenting photographs of various sizes and formats at various heights on the walls and in the space, producing ever-changing sight lines and visual relationships.

It is no coincidence that Fred Turner described the show as an 'arena',[32] using the same term Pollock chose in 1952 for his (multifocal) canvases.[33] The nomenclatural analogy establishes the connection to Steichen's multifocal exhibition, which conveyed its information in the form of a photographic mosaic. In doing so, it fulfilled one of its central ambitions: to be 'a three-dimensional arena in which visitors could practice acts of mutual recognition, choice, and empathy – the core perceptual and affective skills on which democracy depended'.[34]

Notes

1 Horst Bredekamp, *Thomas Hobbes. Der Leviathan. Das Urbild des modernen Staates und seine Gegenbilder 1651–2001*, 3rd edn, Acta humaniora (Berlin: Akademie, 2006).

2 Andy Warhol Museum and Hamburg Kunsthalle, *Andy Warhol Photography*, exhibition catalogue (Zurich: Edition Stemmle, 1999), 136, 138–9.

3 Allan Sekula, 'Between the Net and the Deep Blue Sea: Rethinking the Traffic in Photographs', in *The Family of Man 1955–2001: Humanism and Postmodernism; A Reappraisal of the Photo Exhibition by Edward Steichen*, ed. Jean Back and Viktoria Schmidt-Linsenhoff (Marburg: Jonas, 2004), 168.

4 Viktoria Schmidt-Linsenhoff, '1955–2001: *The Family of Man* and *here is new york*', in *The Family of Man 1955–2001: Humanism and Postmodernism; A Reappraisal of the Photo Exhibition by Edward Steichen*, ed. Jean Back and Viktoria Schmidt-Linsenhoff (Marburg: Jonas, 2004), 18.

5 Edward Steichen, *The Family of Man* (New York: Museum of Modern Art, 1955), 15.

6 Edward Steichen, 'Photography: Witness and Recorder of Humanity', *Wisconsin Magazine of History* 41, no. 3 (Spring 1958): 160.

7 'A big exhibition of photographs has been held in Paris, the aim of which was to show the universality of human actions in the daily life of all the countries of the world: birth, death, work, knowledge.' Roland Barthes, 'The Great Family of Man', in *Mythologies*, trans. Annette Lavers (New York: Hill and Wang, 1972), 100.

8 Ariella Azoulay, '*The Family of Man*: A Visual Universal Declaration of Human Rights', in *The Human Snapshot*, ed. Thomas Keenan and Tirdad Zolghadr (Berlin: Sternberg, 2013), 20–1.

9 Harold Rosenberg, 'On the Fall of Paris', *Partisan Review* 7, no. 6 (November–December 1940): 441.

10 László Borhi, 'Rollback, Liberation, Containment, or Inaction? U.S. Policy and Eastern Europe in the 1950s', *Journal of Cold War Studies* 1, no. 3 (Fall 1999): 67–110.

11 See David Caute, *The Great Fear: The Anti-Communist Purge under Truman and Eisenhower* (New York: Simon and Schuster, 1978); Richard M. Fried, *Nightmare in Red: The McCarthy Era in Perspective* (New York: Oxford University Press, 1990); Ellen Schrecker, *Many Are the Crimes: McCarthyism in America* (Boston: Little, Brown, 1998); and Frances Stonor Saunders, *The Cultural Cold War: The CIA and the World of Arts and Letters* (New York: New Press, 2000).

12 Serge Guilbaut, *How New York Stole the Idea of Modern Art: Abstract Expressionism, Freedom, and the Cold War*, trans. Arthur Goldhammer (Chicago: University of Chicago Press, 1983), 4. See also Serge Guilbaut, *Reconstructing Modernism: Art in New York, Paris, and Montreal, 1945–1964* (Cambridge, MA: MIT Press, 1990).

13 Rosalind P. Blakesley and Susan E. Reid (eds), *Russian Art and the West: A Century of Dialogue in Painting, Architecture, and the Decorative Arts* (DeKalb: Northern Illinois University Press, 2007).

14 Saunders, *The Cultural Cold War*, 5

15 Ibid., 100.

16 Alexander Eliot, 'The Silent Witness', *Time*, 24 December 1956, 28–39.

17 Rob Kroes, 'Projecting National Identities through Cultural Diplomacy: The Case of *The Family of Man*', in *The Dynamics of Interconnections in Popular Culture(s)*, ed. Ray B. Browne and Ben Urish (Newcastle upon Tyne: Cambridge Scholars Publishing, 2014), 206. See also Centre National de la Photographie, *American Photographers of the Depression: Farm Security Administration Photographs 1935–1942* (London: Thames and Hudson, 1991); and Stuart S. Kidd, *Farm Security Administration*

Photography, the Rural South, and the Dynamics of Image-Making, 1935–1943 (Lewiston, NY: Edwin Mellen, 2004).

18 Pepe Karmel, 'Pollock at Work: The Films and Photographs of Hans Namuth', in *Jackson Pollock*, Kirk Varnedoe and Pepe Karmel, exhibition catalogue (New York: Museum of Modern Art, 1998), 87–137.

19 Clement Greenberg, '"American-Type" Painting', in *Art and Culture: Critical Essays* (Boston: Beacon, 1989), 218. See also Anne-Grit Becker, '*After Abstract Expressionism* oder Clement Greenbergs Qualität der "Offenheit"', *all-over* 1 (July 2011), http://allover-magazin.com/?p=326 (accessed 17 March 2017).

20 Kroes, 'Projecting National Identities', 210.

21 Ralph L. Harley, Jr, 'Edward Steichen's Modernist Art-Space', *History of Photography* 14, no. 1 (January–March 1990): 1.

22 Kroes, 'Projecting National Identities', 211.

23 Max Imdahl, 'Barnett Newman. "Who's Afraid of Red, Yellow and Blue III"', in *Max Imdahl. Gesammelte Schriften*, vol. 1, *Zur Kunst der Moderne*, ed. Angeli Janhsen-Vukićević (Frankfurt am Main: Suhrkamp, 1996), 255.

24 Marc-Emmanuel Mélon, 'The Patriarchal Family: Domestic Ideology', in *The Family of Man 1955–2001: Humanism and Postmodernism. A Reappraisal of the Photo Exhibition by Edward Steichen*, ed. Jean Back and Viktoria Schmidt-Linsenhoff (Marburg: Jonas Verlag, 2004), 57.

25 David Anfam, 'Beginning at the End: The Extremes of Abstract Expressionism', in *American Art in the 20th Century. Painting and Sculpture 1913–1993*, ed. Christos M. Joachimides and Norman Rosenthal, exhibition catalogue (Munich: Prestel, 1993), 91.

26 Anna C. Chave, *Mark Rothko: Subjects in Abstraction*, Yale Publications in the History of Art 39 (New Haven, CT: Yale University Press, 1989), 77–97.

27 Jackson Pollock, 'Jackson Pollock: A Questionnaire', in *Jackson Pollock: Interviews, Articles, and Reviews*, ed. Pepe Karmel (New York: Museum of Modern Art, 1999), 15–16. See also Kirk Varnedoe, 'Comet: Jackson Pollock's Life and Work', in *Jackson Pollock*, Kirk Varnedoe and Pepe Karmel, exhibition catalogue (New York: Museum of Modern Art, 1998), 32.

28 Viktoria Schmidt-Linsenhoff, 'Denied Images: *The Family of Man* and the Shoa', in *The Family of Man 1955–2001: Humanism and Postmodernism. A Reappraisal of the Photo Exhibition by Edward Steichen*, ed. Jean Back and Viktoria Schmidt-Linsenhoff (Marburg: Jonas Verlag, 2004), 95.

29 'A camera testament, a drama of the grand canyon of humanity, an epic woven of fun, mystery and holiness – here is *the Family of Man*!' Carl Sandburg, prologue to Steichen, *The Family of Man*, 5.

30 The photo is available online at https://www.loc.gov/photos/?q=parks%20gordon%20american%20gothic (accessed 17 March 2017).

31 Miles Orvell, *American Photography*, Oxford History of Art (Oxford: Oxford University Press, 2003), 118–19.

32 Fred Turner, '*The Family of Man* and the Politics of Attention in Cold War America', *Public Culture* 24, no. 1 (2012): 58.

33 Fred Orton, 'Action, Revolution and Painting', in *Pollock and After: The Critical Debate*, 2nd edn, ed. Francis Frascina (London: Routledge, 2000), 286.

34 Turner, '*The Family of Man*', 58.

14 Carl Sandburg's Journey to *The Family of Man*

Eric J. Sandeen

The Family of Man is so much the product of the master showman Edward Steichen that the collaboration of Carl Sandburg can be overlooked. Through his long engagement with Abraham Lincoln, Sandburg may have given Steichen the title of his massive exhibition in a phrase uttered by the Great Emancipator. Perhaps Steichen extracted it from an epic Sandburg poem, *The People, Yes* (1936), that, in turn, looked back to Lincoln. Sandburg frequently visited the loft where the exhibition was being assembled, posing next to Steichen, inviting other writers into the presence of this world of photographs, and, along with Dorothy Norman, selecting the wall text that was interspersed among the photographs. Sandburg's poem, seemingly simple but revised over several years, stood at the entrance to the exhibition space, written out in the poet's own hand:

> There is only one man in the world
> and his name is All Men.
> There is only one woman in the world
> and her name is All Women.
> There is only one child in the world
> and the child's name is All Children
> A camera testament, a drama
> of the grand canyon of humanity,
> an epic woven of fun, mystery and holiness –
> here is The Family of Man![1]

The two kindred spirits had been linked by temperament and circumstance since the early part of the twentieth century. Steichen's sister, Lilian, married Sandburg in 1908, after the two had met through the social democratic politics that they shared. Edward Steichen and Carl Sandburg had achieved fame early in their careers – Steichen as a photographer and Sandburg as a poet – and by the 1920s both had become comfortable with their own celebrity: the most famous photographer in America and the nation's bard. Steichen had produced a photomontage of Sandburg that echoed the celebrity shots and advertising spreads that had made him the decade's most highly paid photographer. Steichen's use of dramatic lighting and sequence of gestures emphasized not only Sandburg's genius but his ability to project his character to an audience. Sandburg, in his turn, contributed to *Steichen the Photographer* (1929), a long, loving biography that drew his brother-in-law back through now famous episodes in his career, such as the portrait sitting of irascible J. Pierpont Morgan, to the self-manufacture and then recognition of Steichen's genius as a youth in Catholic school:

> In a drawing class at the Pio Nono [Pius IX] school Destiny connected him up with art. He brought in sketches he had made through using transparent paper (which was cheating) and on which he had received help from older persons (which was also cheating). He roughed up some of the firm clear lines made through transparent paper (which was not merely cheating, but was cheating 'with felonious intent'). Now the priest gave high praise to his sketches. So did others of the elders. His mother declared, 'He must be an artist, he shall be a g-r-e-a-t artist!' From then on he was in for it.[2]

By 1955 both famous men were accustomed to promoting their works with their own celebrity, mugging for the camera as they worked. This connection with *The Family of Man* persisted to what was for Steichen the culminating moment, the appearance of the photographs at the American Exhibition in Moscow in August 1959. The two men fought travel difficulties – Sandburg lost his passport, Steichen had to accommodate a broken arm – to appear in this American space in the capital of the nation's Cold War adversary. Upon their return the pair was interviewed by the American news programme *Meet the Press* about their impressions of the other side of the Iron Curtain. The four inquisitors treated them as grand old men of American arts and letters; the National Broadcasting Company devoted 30 minutes of Sunday morning air time to two people it assumed that a mass audience would want to see and hear. And Steichen and Sandburg, true to form, assumed that this was correct: that their observations would have currency among a wide range of listeners.

This chapter brings Carl Sandburg to the *Family of Man* project in the 1950s (see illustration 47). In his time during the interwar years he was not a man accustomed to playing second fiddle. Sandburg's influence on American culture was every bit as great as Steichen's. He had received the Pulitzer Prize, twice in poetry and once in history, and had been nominated for the Nobel Prize for literature seven times. His *American Songbag* (1928) contributed to the discovery of folk music. The six-volume set of books chronicling the life of Abraham Lincoln – *The Prairie Years* (1926) and *The War Years* (1939) – had been bestsellers that made him the most popular Lincoln biographer and most sought after voice in commemorative celebrations.[3] He had been a troubadour for years, touring

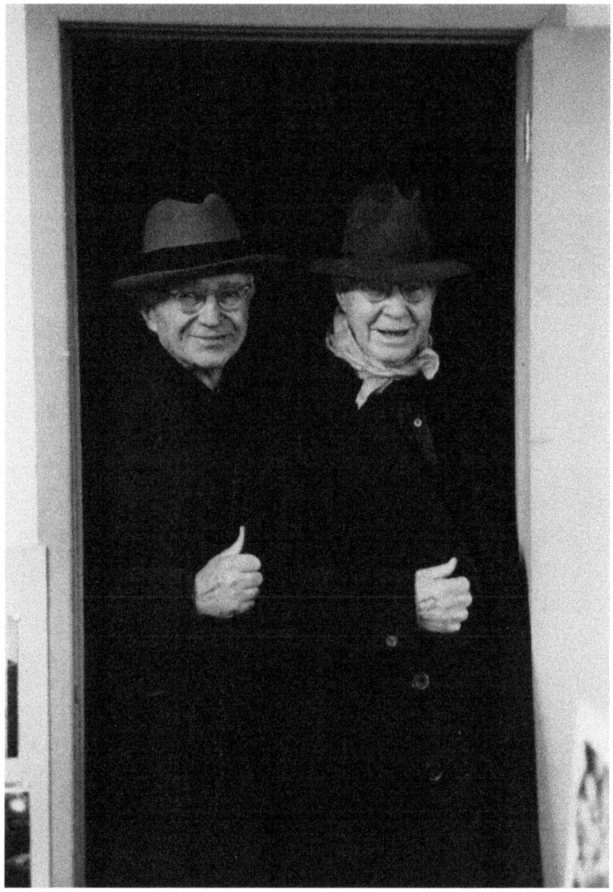

47 Edward Steichen and Carl Sandburg, 1958.

the college circuit, appearing on the radio, and providing the raw material for dramatizations of Lincoln's life.

Sandburg and Steichen were kindred spirits. Both men were voracious collectors, using their own celebrity and a network of sympathetic colleagues to amass material for compelling projects of cultural importance. Both were showmen who expressed the success of their ventures through numbers. Both trusted that their ambitious work would be understood by a general audience that would see common purpose in a simple message. Like Steichen, Sandburg projected a particular persona – dramatic, even histrionic, and demanding command of the stage. As was the case with Steichen's photographic collections, Sandburg's work rose with public interest and fell with critical tastes. Except for the efflorescence of *The Family of Man*, the cultural moment for Sandburg, as for Steichen, was during the interwar years.

***

Sandburg's three major projects during the interwar years – the two massive biographies of Abraham Lincoln and the anthology of American folk songs – made him into a very conspicuous collector of Americana. During the period immediately after World War I, when he was assembling the material for *Abraham Lincoln: The Prairie Years*, a significant portion of the papers of the 16th President remained with the Lincoln family or lay in private hands. Sandburg culled available resources, scoured used bookshops and conducted interviews with the few remaining people who could have remembered Lincoln. The project of writing *Abraham Lincoln: The War Years*, more than a decade later, was an even more intense endeavour. The reception of the first books and the constantly burgeoning scholarship on Lincoln meant that Sandburg had to employ two secretaries to transcribe excerpts that were to be included. These were arranged and inserted into envelopes by theme. The production of the typescripts remained the same in both cases: in a secluded home, Sandburg composed the text on a typewriter set on a table consisting of packing crates.[4]

Not only was the act of collecting kept in the public eye but the product was measured by quantity as well as quality. Sandburg had composed more words about Lincoln – 1.25 million – than the subject himself had written. *The Prairie Years* had been a bestseller in 1926. More than 14,000 two-volume sets were immediately distributed to eager readers; 48,000 sets were sold in the first year.[5] The Book-of-the-Month Club issued a special edition, on cheaper paper with fewer illustrations, in time for the 1928 Christmas trade.[6] *The War Years*, likewise, sold well, despite the massive 3,400 pages of typescript that Sandburg produced: 29,000 sets were purchased in the first few months at $20 each.[7] Because of the success of the earlier two-volume set, '[t]he publication of *The War Years* [...] was a public event',[8] the product of unstinting labour by one of America's writer-celebrities.

During the 1920s, Sandburg toured the country as 'the self-appointed emissary of the American past'.[9] His celebrity allowed him to collect entries for his *American Songbag* project as he toured 'two-thirds of the state universities of the country, audiences ranging from 3,000 people at the University of California to 30 at the Garret Club in Buffalo, New York, and organizations as diverse as the Poetry Society of South Carolina and the Knife and Fork Club of South Bend, Indiana'. Along the way, he picked up regional tunes, such as 'I Ride an Old Paint', 'The Boll Weevil Song' and 'Blow the Man Down', the last contributed by fellow poet Robert Frost.[10] By the time that the full *Songbag* was published, Sandburg had winnowed these potential entries down to 280 songs under 24 headings, representing American regional and occupational cultures. In his Introduction to a recent reissue of the *Songbag*, Garrison Keillor, himself a purveyor of American folk traditions, drolly remarked that Sandburg's 'steady rise to fame as a poet-troubadour and near-mythic status as Voice of the Common Man was accomplished with considerable campaigning on his part'.[11]

Sandburg was comfortable performing himself – the poet, the vagabond, the troubadour, the newspaper man and reviewer of movies, the man of letters and

Pulitzer Prize winner who was also a man of the people. A reading turned into a concert when he broke out his ever-present guitar. He played imperfectly, but presented in his baritone voice vaguely familiar songs that were intended to unite a people. H. L. Mencken, a Sandburg friend but ever the curmudgeon of Baltimore, quipped, 'Do you want the words and music of "I am a Hundred Percent American"? I have them if you do'.[12] The quality of Sandburg's voice and his theatrical delivery drew listeners to him, whether he was singing 'Foggy, Foggy Dew' or reading from his Lincoln manuscript. Friend and collector of Lincoln photographs, Frederick Meserve, recalls:

> I can hear him now reading from the manuscript to show the kind of thing he was doing on Lincoln's early life – something never before done, poetry and history together, a marvelous blending of his own. I can hear the extraordinary voice, now whispering soft, now booming loud, slowed down almost to stopping one moment, words mouthed and rolled on the tongue and lingered over, then suddenly rippling and tripping forth in a heart-jumping change of pace.[13]

Sandburg, in turn, was confident of his ability to be the representative American, the jack-of-all-trades: 'Among biographers, I am a first-rate poet. And among the poets, a good biographer; among singers, I'm a good collector of songs and among song collectors a good judge of pipes'.[14]

In *Mystic Chords of Memory*, the cultural historian Michael Kammen charts two paths for establishing American cultural nationalism in the interwar years. Carl Sandburg's work contributes to both these paths. American culture could be seen as a weaving together of diverse folk traditions that emanated from distinct, richly layered, local landscapes. This conception of culture was democratic and, especially in the midst of the profound social change of the 1930s, richly nostalgic. It valued tall tales, ballads, myths and non-literary materials, such as local craft traditions. Both of Sandburg's major productions of the 1920s, *Abraham Lincoln: The Prairie Years* and *American Songbag*, reflect this view of American culture and draw on his experience as a newspaper reporter in Chicago and his established reputation as the poet of the working man. Sandburg readily embraced the notion that the left would see its own version of a romantic American past in working-class struggle.[15] Another view of American culture emphasized nationwide characteristics that knit together a heterogeneous nation into one unique, mature entity. Such a culture insistently demonstrated national greatness.[16] This was Sandburg's work of *The War Years*, depicting Lincoln as the unifier of the nation during the moment of its deepest division. Sandburg joined those who believed that 'high culture and popular culture really could be bridged, and perhaps even, with sufficient extension, mass culture as well'.[17] Michael Kammen asserts that 'Abe Lincoln had unquestionably emerged as the populist hero of the depression era', and Sandburg was key to this enshrinement.[18]

The regionalism that Sandburg expressed reverberated throughout the culture. In 1923, while wrestling with the young Lincoln, he conferred with Walter Prescott Webb, whose own ideas of regional culture would result in *The Great Plains*, a seminal work of cultural geography.[19] The flowering of Midwestern cultural study during this period included small literary magazines such as *Midland* magazine and regional painters like Grant Wood and Thomas Hart Benton. Michael Kammen traces the founding of many folklore societies to this period. Already by 1934 Malcolm Cowley, a chronicler of American writers who had become expatriots or 'exiles', acknowledged that the United States 'possessed a folklore, and traditions, and the songs that embodied them'.[20] During this decade, large, collective writing projects, some of them sponsored by New Deal programmes such as the Federal Writers Project, produced guide books and descriptions of such emblematic American landscapes as river valleys in order to create a sense of place by 'infusing the landscape with emotional and symbolic content'. These connections would, in turn, root the reader in the symbolic landscape of the nation through local attachments. Fixed in place by economic circumstances and rudimentary transportation options, Americans viewed the expanse of the continental nation vicariously, through reading these expansive projects or listening to a peripatetic troubadour like Sandburg. State guide books enticed the traveller, at the present moment through their imaginations but, eventually, through the grounded intricacies of American landscapes: 'Travelers were to know who they were by knowing where they were.'[21]

Sandburg was one of those who also allowed Americans to *hear* who they were. While he was assembling the contents of his *American Songbag*, John Lomax began his ambitious effort, later continued by his son, Alan, to collect folk songs springing from 'the isolated life of rural communities' that, he feared, were losing their distinctiveness to encroaching modernity. Sandburg was more eclectic in his selection of materials to collect and more optimistic about the ability of folk traditions to coexist with modern modes of industrial production and musical reproduction. Through categories such as 'Hobo Songs' and 'The Big Brutal City' he acknowledged the realities of modern urban life.[22] He selected songs composed by known individuals, thereby breaking with an academic definition of 'folk' by including commercially generated music. His 'recognition of pluralism as a critical feature of American identity would continue among every succeeding generation of folk revivalists'. More than that, Sandburg 'became an advocate for the people whose music he collected. For him, folk music was a way to champion economically, socially, and politically marginalized citizens.'[23] This combination of attributes – voicing the needs and values of overlooked groups of people and using class as a collecting category – links Sandburg with the social justice and protest music of succeeding generations.[24]

The vigour of Sandburg's efforts as a collector and a performer is evidenced by the breadth of his influence. His celebrity as an American troubadour led to popularizers such as Burl Ives – a fellow Illinoisan born a generation later 400 kilometres southeast of Sandburg's home in Galesburg – who fashioned his own songbag, *Song in America*,[25] and purveyors of the folk revival in popular culture, of whom the Kingston Trio was the most successful example from the early 1960s. He was also a forbear of 'the singing left',[26] beginning with his fellow wanderer Woody Guthrie and extending to Pete Seeger and the Weavers, who brought politics to folk performance in the charged atmosphere of the 1950s. Like Sandburg, who caused many fans to pick up the guitar in the 1920s and 1930s, the genial Seeger authored a pamphlet – later a book – on how to play the banjo that brought a folk instrument into the mainstream in time for the post-war folk revival.[27] While Sandburg, playing the role of the ancient sage, was holding forth about the accomplishments of *The Family of Man* at the 1959 American Exhibition in Moscow, in the midtown New York studio of the National Broadcasting Company's *Meet the Press* show, barely two miles to the south the folk revival scene in Greenwich Village was coming into full bloom. Bob Dylan and Ramblin' Jack Elliott drew from a lineage of music that included Sandburg.

During the interwar years, Carl Sandburg was one of the most notable contributors to the project of assembling a national history and an American mythology. This effort was undertaken by groups of culturally important figures who moved with ease over a wide range of venues both popular and academic. Some writers were national celebrities then but are as seldom studied now, like Sandburg himself: Stephen Vincent Benet, author of *John Brown's Body*, an epic poem 'that commenced almost where Sandburg's Lincoln biography concluded' and sold over 100,000 copies as a Book-of-the-Month Club selection;[28] Edgar Lee Masters, whose *Spoon River Anthology* brought Midwest culture to national attention; and Archibald MacLeish, who became an arbiter of the American past through his position as the Librarian of Congress. Some projects relied on individual anthologizers, like Alan Lomax. Other efforts were collaborative, the product of Federal efforts, such as the photographic explorations of the Farm Security Administration or the many productions of the Federal Writers Project.

Moving from collection to critique, cultural commentators reflected on the significance of these efforts to establish an American tradition. While this was a subject of some conversation at universities, much of this discussion was held in the public realm by critics who, in future generations, would hold academic positions. Van Wyck Brooks, for example, had already established himself as an interpreter of literature and had coined terms – 'highbrow' and 'lowbrow' and 'the search for a usable past' – that had become common parlance. Constance Rourke made her living as a writer of articles for publications like *The New Republic* and as an author of books that explored what she and others called the American character. Brooks and Rourke disagreed about how this character would be described and national traditions established. Brooks focused on the national scene and Rourke on the harmonizing of distinct folk culture and local traditions. Sandburg spoke to the same public audience as Brooks and Rourke, also from a position outside the university. His version of this cultural project combined both traditions: his Lincoln constructed a national history and his *American Songbag* explored the local roots of American culture, to borrow a phrase from the title of the posthumous book of

Rourke's for which Brooks wrote the Preface.[29] These sorts of concerns would help name a university location for future debates about American culture – American Studies.

In his recent study, *Lincoln's Body*, Richard Wightman Fox constructively reassesses the accomplishment of Sandburg's portrayal of the prairie years of Abraham Lincoln. As many critics from the beginning had noted, there were no footnotes, but, Fox comments, 'there could be no footnotes' for this composition of 'lyrical riffs' that 'produced something vaster than a "life"'.[30] This was Sandburg the collector, even Sandburg the oracle at work, weaving together a communal Lincoln: 'The more legendary folklore about Lincoln that was thrown into the mix, the better, since the lore had bubbled up from the purest source: the people.' Lincoln was more than an historical figure. He was 'the historical emanation of a people's habits, longings, and fantasies'.[31] This approach would give Sandburg licence to enter Lincoln's brain for the creative meditations that drew the ire of historians. It also gave him the power to link with the folkloric traditions that Constance Rourke was tracing at the same time that Sandburg was writing. She pointed out that Mike Fink, the riverboat legend, was alive during Lincoln's time and was obviously matched by Sandburg's accounts of his subject's exploits on the Sangamon and the Mississippi. Davey Crockett lore was developing during Lincoln's youth, mythologizing familiar terrain. 'The Hunters of Kentucky', a poem of immense influence in constructing one myth of American character, was first promulgated when Lincoln was 13.[32] The power of *The Prairie Years* to exist between history and folklore – between Lincoln the ordinary man and the anointed Lincoln that was more than human – was matched by Sandburg's intent to address through *The War Years* contemporary domestic issues such as racism and rural–urban difference and to prepare a united nation for the international crises to come: 'Without ever trying to impersonate him, Sandburg managed to evoke Lincoln's presence, and to let him speak for the people – a unified people that in the mid-1930s, a time of dissipating radical hopes, could stand up to the fascists.'[33]

Sandburg's Lincoln reverberated through popular culture. Scripts for Hollywood movies such as *Abraham Lincoln* and *Young Mr. Lincoln* relied on *The Prairie Years*.[34] *Abe Lincoln in Illinois* shows how Sandburg's image of Lincoln dominated what Americans saw. The playwright Robert Sherwood drew from Sandburg's work for his 1938 Broadway play, the 1940 film of the same name and the 1940 radio version of *Abe Lincoln in Illinois*. This was more than an awarding-winning project for Sherwood, who won the Pulitzer Prize for a play that ran for more than 400 performances, and a career boost for Raymond Massey, who portrayed Lincoln in all three productions and was nominated for an Academy Award in 1940. It also established Lincoln's character in the public eye. The play opens with the young Lincoln learning the five moods of the English language – 'The Indicative, Imperative, Potential, Subjunctive and Infinitive.' 'Every one of us has many moods,' his mentor lectures. 'You yourself have more than your share of them, Abe. They express the various aspects of your character.'[35] Lincoln dutifully constructs examples of the five moods, in textbook fashion, thereby giving the audience an insight into his developing persona. Sherwood, and through him Sandburg, organized Depression-era sentiment, 'made it conceivable, intelligible, communicable, and public'.[36] Fox summarizes the importance of Sandburg's Lincoln to American culture of the interwar period: 'there are two great monuments to Lincoln constructed during these years. One was the Lincoln Memorial, constructed at the west end of the national mall in Washington, D. C.; the other was Sandburg's Lincoln.'[37]

Alfred Kazin's *On Native Grounds* both summarizes Sandburg's accomplishment and gestures at how Sandburg's project of making Lincoln into both man and hero was viewed askance after World War II. Writing in 1942, Kazin includes a lengthy summary of Sandburg's Lincoln in his magisterial interpretation of American literary traditions. Sandburg articulated 'a new historical consciousness [...] [T]he very effort of Sandburg's imagination was subtly transformed into a supreme historical sensitiveness, a capacity for embracing the whole stupendous past.' If facts were 'poetized' in Sandburg's massive work, the stature of Lincoln became 'the measure of that whole American civilization that would find its apotheosis in him'. The figure of Lincoln arose 'like a massive shadow [...] a stupendous aggregation of all those American traits that were to find so ambiguous and moving an expression in him'. Lincoln lived because of what he symbolized, because of the democratic principles and anxieties he embodied. In Sandburg's hands, Lincoln became 'a great symphonic poem', 'the greatest of all American works of art'.[38] This paragraph, Kazin's paean to Sandburg's poetic construction of a national symbol, was omitted from the 1956 abridged edition of *On Native Grounds* and replaced with a statement that the search for 'a usable tradition' – a significant alteration of Brooks's usable *past* – is over. In place of Sandburg, Kazin inserts Edmund Wilson as the interpreter of Lincoln's significance: Wilson's Lincoln is 'the great *mind* of American history rather than its sad saint'.[39]

This shift is significant and is indicative of the seismic gulf that separated pre- and post-war American critical traditions. Sandburg, and, for that matter, his brother-in-law Steichen, operated in the new terrain of the post-war world, but their sensibilities, their assumptions about their relationships to their audiences, and their warm embrace of patriotism and national myth-making remained in the pre-World War II culture that Michael Kammen and the original version of Alfred Kazin's work describe.

Edmund Wilson did to Carl Sandburg's Lincoln what Mark Twain did to James Fenimore Cooper's Natty Bumppo. A critique of a particular text was the launching pad for a much broader dismantlement of another, presumably outmoded, form of literary expression. Twain applied the realist's microscope to a romantic figure painted in broad brushstrokes that were oblivious to detail. Wilson demanded rigour, depicting Lincoln as a figure of intellectual depth, and judged Sandburg's approach as folkloric rather than historically useful: 'the corn is getting high, indeed'.[40] According to Wilson, the complexity of Lincoln took Sandburg out of his depth. In fact, Wilson summarizes in the most often quoted line of his critique, 'the cruelest thing that has happened to Lincoln since he was shot by Booth has been to fall into the hands of Carl Sandburg'.[41]

Wilson's Lincoln serves as one of the major portraits in his study of Civil War literature, *Patriotic Gore*. Lewis Dabney, Wilson's biographer, describes the inundation of voices that one meets in this thick volume: 'Reading this book is a little like being set down in a room packed with people, each of whom wants your ear for however long it takes to tell of himself or of others, of private struggles or of great events.'[42] But *Patriotic Gore* is more than what Alfred Kazin described as a modern version of Plutarch's *Lives*.[43] In his Introduction, Wilson makes it clear that his purpose is to put the Civil War into the context of the recently-completed World War II and to compare Lincoln to two world leaders who had brought their countries through periods of conflict and national consolidation – Bismarck and Lenin.[44] This Lincoln was a free thinker,[45] an ambitious man who saw himself in a heroic light.[46] Wilson rejects the folksy Lincoln, the teller of tails and the splitter of rails. There is very little humour in this Lincoln. He is cold, aloof, even intellectually arrogant, 'a man of intent, self-controlled, strong in intellect, tenacious of purpose'.[47] 'His own style was cunning in its cadences, exact in its choice of words, and yet also instinctive and natural; and it was inseparable from his personality in all of its manifestations.'[48] This was not a populist Lincoln but a tortured man of high intellect who knew how to mould his image and manipulate the people to conform to his will. Sandburg would not have recognized this man or appreciated the dispassion of this critical approach.

***

On 13 September 1959, Carl Sandburg and Edward Steichen appeared on the National Broadcasting Company's *Meet the Press*, a weekly programme where newsworthy individuals were interviewed by four reporters. The brothers-in-law had just returned from a sojourn to Moscow to attend the American Exhibition in Sokolniki Park, the American half of the first bilateral exchange of exhibitions between the United States and the Soviet Union, and to visit, once again, *The Family of Man* exhibition, one of the highlights of this immensely successful, six-week episode in cultural diplomacy. Lawrence E. Spivak, the producer of the programme, and his colleagues were well aware that Steichen and Sandburg had been sent as emissaries of American culture: Steichen had been designated an American Specialist by the State Department. Sandburg had declined this special treatment and his tourist passport, expedited by the State Department to replace the one he had lost, gave him more freedom to roam through Moscow, speaking with writers in addition to attending to the business of supporting the American Exhibition. Freshly returned, the two octogenarians faced questioning that was, on the one hand, deferential and appreciative and, on the other, sharpened by Cold War suspicions.

This appearance is remarkable for several reasons. First of all, it was natural for all concerned that such an interview would take place in the context of a news programme: the four interviewers probed for observations about the Soviet Union and the subjects of their curiosity displayed by their demeanour that they expected to be asked questions that quickly turned from art to politics. Secondly, the position that Steichen and Sandburg assumed drew not only from their recent experience but from an immense body of work that established a relationship between them and what they considered to be the common citizens of a democratic culture. Finally, despite pointed invitations to make invidious comparison between the United States and the Soviet Union, both Steichen and Sandburg repeated their faith in the common emotions and aspirations of humankind, the epitome of which was expressed through *The Family of Man*.

The colloquy reveals a politics that comes with this faith in humanity. Sandburg and Steichen spoke through works of art to Soviet citizens who were subjected to the narrow interests of the state and defended this approach to *Meet the Press* viewers who had their own ideological predispositions. *The Family of Man*, the two insisted, drew the two sides of the Iron Curtain together in a common humanity. This form of humanism, developed over long careers, clearly went unappreciated by their bemused interrogators. Stuck between the feeling of national purpose that welcomed Sandburg's interwar work and the Vietnam generation who dismissed him after his death, Sandburg appeared as an earnest anachronism, offering observations that he knew would be misinterpreted by those wanting affirmation of a particular ideology rather than mere observation. Steichen, labelled 'probably the greatest photographer of all time' and tied to the production of *The Family of Man*, 'the greatest epic poem of mankind, that mankind everywhere can read and feel', hampered by a hacking cough, let his brother-in-law lead the way.[49] To some contemporary observers, their pronouncements seemed, at best, banal, but, from the start, it was apparent that they were confidently defending a world-view that the commentators were not prepared to hear.

The first question was innocent enough: what did the two feel that *The Family of Man* accomplished by being exhibited in Moscow? The second, however, set the tone for the rest of the interview. Lawrence E. Spivak inquired, 'You also said, all the world, all humanity is alike. There is no iron curtain, no real curtain between people. Now did you find that true in the Soviet Union despite some forty years of suppression?' Then, 'Did you have any feeling at all that the absence of liberty among the Russian people for forty years has had an effect upon human beings as human beings?' And so the interviewer continued. Yes, Russian people were subjected to a great deal more regimentation than their American contemporaries. No, no one was starving. 'Tell him about the lady from Waterloo, Iowa,' Sandburg prompted Steichen. She had been appalled by the poverty in the Soviet Union. 'Where did you see it?' Steichen inquired. 'She said, "all over".' 'Well,' Steichen recalled, 'I didn't see any sign of any poverty.' Were the Russians happy people, as you would find happy people in a free country, Spivak wanted to know. Steichen replied:

> Happiness, real happiness is an inner thing. It's a very difficult thing to see. I found in their daily behavior that they were just like everybody else. They were very lovable people. [As] human beings, I would rate them as very

> close. As a matter of fact, I think they are almost more like us in many ways than any other people I've met.

Earlier in 1959 Sandburg had addressed a joint session of Congress on the occasion of the 150th anniversary of Abraham Lincoln's birth. The *Meet the Press* panel turned to him in the familiar role as interpreter of the 16th president. Russians had been asked to vote for their favourite American statesman and Lincoln had come out on top, surpassing the 'revolutionary' Washington and F. D. Roosevelt, 'who had given them eleven billion bucks'. Why was there such fascination with Lincoln? 'Well,' Sandburg began,

> because he had a partner [the Civil War] [...] He had a career of violence that surpassed any of the Bolsheviks. He was not afraid of a civil war [...] The Union was first with him. But secondarily [...] he issued the Emancipation Proclamation, [freeing three million] slaves who were on the tax books as property. That was something that appealed to them. The violence and the break from the past appeals to them so that Lincoln has a certain fascination for them not parallel to that that Lenin has, but it's there.

Sandburg was about to make another observation when he was cut off in mid-sentence by the moderator, who brought the interview to a quick conclusion.

The interview was convened by the newsworthy appearance of *The Family of Man* in the heart of Moscow. Sandburg and Steichen remained true to the message of the exhibition – that mankind is one – but the questions assumed difference. Throughout his long career, Sandburg had knit American culture together through the national purpose of Abraham Lincoln's vision and the many regional voices of folk performance, singing in harmony the collective stories of the people of the United States. He was a worthy companion, a truly kindred spirit to Edward Steichen, whose effort as the impresario of *The Family of Man* dominates critical understanding of the project. Sandburg deserves attention, not so much as a collaborator in the making of this photographic exhibition, but as a person who strengthened the philosophical underpinnings of this effort and understood full well the importance of labouring over projects that would draw vast amounts of material together in an effort to help people see themselves. This protean era of collecting had passed; the culture to which the two old men spoke had been hardened by two wars, one hot and the other cold. Bringing Sandburg to his position, looking over Steichen's shoulder as the photographer prepared *The Family of Man* in the loft above 52nd Street, helps explain both the gravity of this effort and also the historically bounded vocabulary in which it spoke.

Notes

1 Edward Steichen, *The Family of Man* (New York: Museum of Modern Art, 1955), 3.

2 Carl Sandburg, 'Steichen the Photographer', in *The Sandburg Range* (New York: Harcourt, Brace and Company, 1953), 306.

3 Carl Sandburg, compiler, *The American Songbag* (New York: Harcourt, Brace, 1927); Carl Sandburg, *Abraham Lincoln: The Prairie Years*, 2 vols (New York: Harcourt, Brace, 1926); Carl Sandburg, *Abraham Lincoln: The War Years*, 4 vols (New York: Harcourt, Brace, 1939).

4 Benjamin Thomas, *Portrait for Posterity: Lincoln and His Biographers* (New Brunswick, NJ: Rutgers University Press, 1947), 295.

5 Penelope Niven, *Carl Sandburg: A Biography* (New York: Charles Scribner's Sons, 1991), 432.

6 Ibid., 462.

7 North Callahan, *Carl Sandburg: His Life and Works* (University Park: Pennsylvania State University Press, 1987), 151.

8 Alfred Jones, *Roosevelt's Image Brokers: Poets, Playwrights, and the Use of the Lincoln Symbol* (Port Washington, NY: Kennikat Press, 1974), 52.

9 Niven, *Carl Sandburg*, 444.

10 Ibid., 445.

11 Garrison Keillor, 'An Introduction to the 1990 Edition', in *The American Songbag*, Carl Sandburg, compiler (New York: Harcourt, Brace, Jovanovich, 1990), x.

12 Niven, *Carl Sandburg*, 444.

13 Frederick Meserve, 'Thoughts on a Friend', *Journal of the Illinois State Historical Society* 45 (1952): 337.

14 Callahan, *Carl Sandburg: His Life and Works*, 134.

15 Michael Kammen, *Mystic Chords of Memory: The Transformation of Tradition in American Culture* (New York: Alfred A. Knopf, 1991), 411.

16 Ibid., 407–8.

17 Ibid., 419.

18 Ibid., 509.

19 Ibid., 426.

20 Ibid., 433.

21 Jarrold Hirsch, *Portrait of America: A Cultural History of the Federal Writers' Project* (Chapel Hill: University of North Carolina Press, 2003), 39.

22 Rachel Donaldson, *'I Hear America Singing': Folk Music and National Identity* (Philadelphia: Temple University Press, 2014), 17.

23 Ibid., 18.

24 Ibid., 19.

25 Burl Ives, compiler, *Song in America: Our Musical Heritage* (New York: Duell, Sloan and Pearce, 1962).

26 Ronald Cohen, *Rainbow Quest: The Folk Music Revival and American Society, 1940–1970* (Amherst: University of Massachusetts Press, 2002), 42.

27 Donaldson, *'I Hear America Singing'*, 102.

28 Jones, *Roosevelt's Image Brokers*, 33.

29 Constance Rourke, *The Roots of American Culture and Other Essays*, ed. and Preface Van Wyck Brooks (New York: Harcourt, Brace and Company, 1942).

30 Richard Wightman Fox, *Lincoln's Body: A Cultural History* (New York: W.W. Norton, 2015), 230.

31 Ibid., 231.

32 Constance Rourke, *American Humor: A Study of the National Character* (New York: Harcourt, Brace, 1931), 153.

33 Fox, *Lincoln's Body*, 232.

34 Ibid., 250.

35 Barry Schwartz, *Abraham Lincoln in the Post-Heroic Era: History and Memory in Late Twentieth-Century America* (Chicago: University of Chicago Press, 2008), 271.

36 Ibid., 272.

37 Fox, *Lincoln's Body*, 234.

38 Alfred Kazin, *On Native Grounds: An Interpretation of Modern American Prose Literature* (New York: Harcourt, Brace, 1942), 507–8.

39 Alfred Kazin, *On Native Grounds: An Interpretation of Modern American Prose Literature from 1890 to the Present*, abridged edn (Garden City, NY: Doubleday, 1956), 408.

40 Edmund Wilson, *Patriotic Gore: Studies in the Literature of the American Civil War* (Boston: Northeastern University Press, 1984), 115.

41 Ibid., 116.

42 Lewis Dabney, *Edmund Wilson: A Life in Literature* (New York: Farrar, Straus, and Giroux, 2005), 432.

43 Cited in Wilson, *Patriotic Gore*, 432.

44 Wilson, *Patriotic Gore*, xx.

45 Ibid., 99.

46 Ibid., 108.

47 Ibid., 117.

48 Ibid., 120.

49 All quotations taken from the transcript of the *Meet the Press* programme, broadcast 13 September 1959. For an audio version of the programme, consult http://www.oldtimeradiodownloads.com/historical/meet-the-press/meet-the-press-59–09–13-carl-sandburg-edward-steichen-photographer (accessed 29 March 2016).

15 Commentaries on Photographs

The Family of Man (1962)

Witold Wirpsza
Translated from the Polish with an introduction by Benjamin Paloff

Three decades after his death in West Berlin, where he relocated following the political unrest of March 1968 (and, with it, renouncing his membership of Poland's Communist Party), the world seems finally to be catching up to Witold Wirpsza (1918–85). Though never quite ignored, the critical response to his poems, novels and essays were, in his lifetime, remarkably consistent in their inconsistency. Despite early work in socialist realism, to readers intent on toeing the official line Wirpsza's stylistic accessibility foundered against an ideological heterodoxy bordering on outright cynicism. Quick to challenge the most fundamental features of the national narrative, whether the focus was on Polish martyrdom or the virtues of socialism, his book-length essay *Pole, wer bist du?* (Pole, Who Are You?, 1971; written in German) made him an easy target for the political establishment. He was nevertheless hardly a darling of the proponents of the so-called 'poetry of witness' – a minor irony, given that his lyric method is largely observational. During a half-century when Polish poetry enjoyed global visibility through the likes of Czesław Miłosz (1911–2004) and Zbigniew Herbert (1924–98), poets prized for their verbal elegance and the clarity of their moral vision, Wirpsza's often rough language and deep scepticism of truths declaimed, whatever their stripe, all but ensured that he would remain something of a poet's poet during his lifetime.

If the collapse of Poland's Communist regime in 1989 has brought renewed attention to Wirpsza's work, it has less to do with a relaxation of state controls than with the direction Polish poetry has taken in the interim. The last three decades have seen an increasing interest in those poets who defied easy political or aesthetic categorization during the Communist period, poets who often couch commentary on everyday life in language that blossoms into unexpected wordplay. Versions of this approach appear in every generation, from Wirpsza's own – especially in the work of Miron Białoszewski (1922–83) – to that of Krystyna Miłobędzka (b. 1932),

Piotr Sommer (b. 1948) and Andrzej Sosnowski (b. 1959). The conversation that has arisen around these poets has made a new home for Wirpsza as well.

The lyric cycle that Wirpsza composed in response to *The Family of Man* provides an excellent introduction to his work, as well as an essential tonic to Carl Sandburg's exuberant commentary to the original exhibition (see illustration 48). Wirpsza was hardly alone in expressing his misgivings about the exhibition, as readers of the present volume have already discovered. What is special about his response is that it successfully turns the performance of distrust, even outright jadedness, into its own object of aesthetic contemplation. For Wirpsza, whose distaste for propaganda is visceral, images distort at least as much as they reveal, and the significance we attach to them, always imposed from outside the frame, can quickly become the illusion by which we deceive ourselves. This is especially the case when we are told *in advance* what these images should mean – thus the dedicatory poem's caustic address toward those who want to improve the lot of mankind, especially 'pedagogues'. Wirpsza's poems enact the dialectical interplay of attraction to the image and disgust at its mendacity, an interplay from which some 'truth' may emerge, though it cannot be declared such without immediately collapsing back into deception. These poems demonstrate what Roman Jakobson, writing on the antilyrics of the Czech poet Vítězslav Nezval, called a 'carefully thought-out, mercilessly logical exhibitionism'.[1]

It would then seem a reinforcement of his own ironic stance, both within the frame and well beyond it, that Wirpsza allows his misgivings to lead him into error. The poet who is so preoccupied with the possibility of being manipulated ('Birds and Shadows') – with what Wit Pietrzak calls, in a recent article on Wirpsza's cycle, 'the dangerous process of ideologizing reality' – is also likely to perceive only what he has preconceived.[2] Thus the poet sees a pathetic image of staged grieving, a 'second-rate / Actor' flooded in 'artificial / Illumination' over a grave ('Grief'), in what a higher-quality reproduction clearly shows is a busker smiling with his violin in front of parked cars. More minor infelicities abound in the poems when read against the same photographs they read. Yet these interpretive failures do nothing to diminish the poems' artistry or the new meanings that arise from their collision, notably in the three 'contrapuntal studies' that place the photographs and poems into direct, if contradictory, conversation. Wirpsza wants nothing more than for us to doubt ourselves, *not* to believe what we are told, and perhaps also to question whether, if truth in representation is a contradiction in terms, there can be any way of sorting what's a mistake from what is not.

Notes

1 Roman Jakobson, *Language in Literature*, ed. Krystyna Pomorska and Stephen Rudy (Cambridge, MA: Harvard University Press, 1987), 376.

2 Wit Pietrzak, 'Anty-mitologia Witolda Wirpszy. Komentarz do *Komentarzy do fotografii*', *Ruch literacki* 60, no. 4–5 (2014): 505.

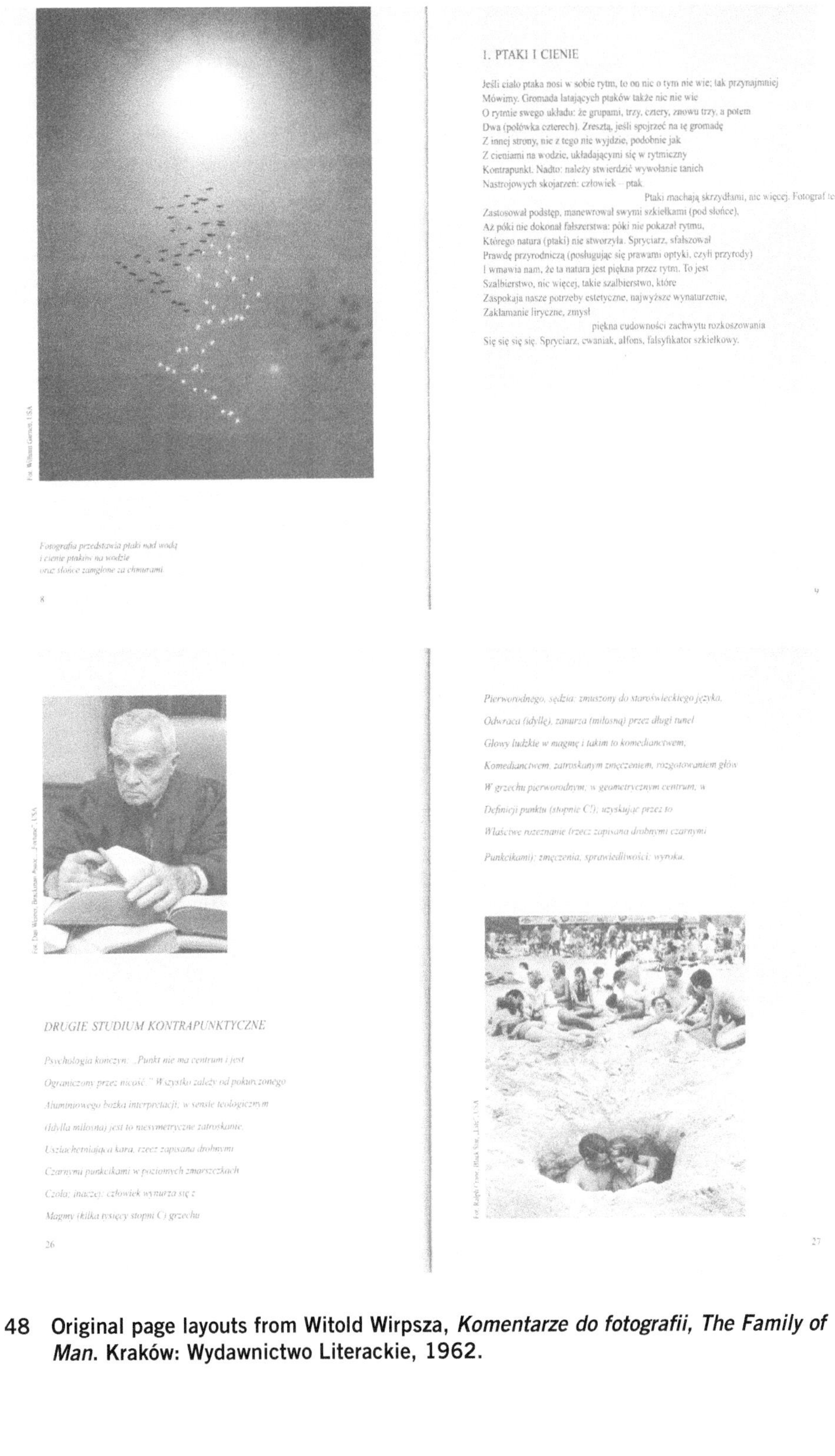

Fotografia przedstawia ptaki nad wodą
i cienie ptaków na wodzie
oraz słońce zamglone za chmurami.

8

1. PTAKI I CIENIE

Jeśli ciało ptaka nosi w sobie rytm, to on nic o tym nie wie; tak przynajmniej
Mówimy. Gromada latających ptaków także nic nie wie
O rytmie swego układu: że grupami, trzy, cztery, znowu trzy, a potem
Dwa (połówka czterech). Zresztą, jeśli spojrzeć na tę gromadę
Z innej strony, nic z tego nie wyjdzie, podobnie jak
Z cieniami na wodzie, układającymi się w rytmiczny
Kontrapunkt. Nadto: należy stwierdzić wywołanie tanich
Nastrojowych skojarzeń: człowiek – ptak.
Ptaki machają skrzydłami, nic więcej. Fotograf tedy
Zastosował podstęp, manewrował swymi szkiełkami (pod słońce),
Aż póki nie dokonał fałszerstwa: póki nie pokazał rytmu,
Którego natura (ptaki) nie stworzyła. Spryciarz, sfałszował
Prawdę przyrodniczą (posługując się prawami optyki, czyli przyrody)
I wmawia nam, że ta natura jest piękna przez rytm. To jest
Szalbierstwo, nic więcej, takie szalbierstwo, które
Zaspokaja nasze potrzeby estetyczne, najwyższe wynaturzenie,
Zakłamanie liryczne, zmysł
piękna cudowności zachwytu rozkoszowania
Się się się się. Spryciarz, cwaniak, alfons, falsyfikator szkiełkowy.

9

DRUGIE STUDIUM KONTRAPUNKTYCZNE

Psychologia kończyn: „Punkt nie ma centrum i jest
Ograniczony przez nicość." Wszystko zależy od pokurczonego
Aluminiowego bożka interpretacji; w sensie teologicznym
(Idylla miłosna) jest to niesymetryczne zatroskanie,
Uszlachetniająca kara, rzecz zapisana drobnymi
Czarnymi punkcikami w poziomych zmarszczkach
Czoła; inaczej: człowiek wynurza się z
Magmy (kilka tysięcy stopni C) grzechu

26

Pierworodnego, sędzia: zmuszony do staroświeckiego języka,
Odwraca (idyllę), zanurza (miłosną) przez długi tunel
Głowy ludzkie w magmę i takim to komediantctwem,
Komediantctwem, zatroskanym zmęczeniem, rozgotowaniem głów
W grzechu pierworodnym; w geometrycznym centrum; w
Definicji punktu (stopnie C!); uzyskując przez to
Właściwe rozeznanie (rzecz zapisana drobnymi czarnymi
Punkcikami); zmęczenia, sprawiedliwości; wyroku.

27

48 Original page layouts from Witold Wirpsza, *Komentarze do fotografii, The Family of Man*. Kraków: Wydawnictwo Literackie, 1962.

Dedication

There once was a guy
In a tropical country
Who avenged himself on his friend:

Which is to say, he got hold of
A parasite he knew of, a white, threadlike worm
Roughly five centimeters long, and during some serious drinking
Placed it on the other's collar, and then, calmly and with satisfaction,
Now and then plying his comrade with drink
(The warm wine smelled of yeast – you know the kind), watched as
(The other guy didn't feel so much as a tickle, the parasite, so fine,
Weighed next to nothing), in wormy slow motion, this creature
Crawled into the bristly opening of his ear; good, it had disappeared into the balmy canal:
After which they drank another, and another, and another, until, blissful
In the glow of their mutual friendship, a bit drowsy, they parted ways.

The friend's unbearable headaches lasted several weeks, two
Months, let's say, something along the lines of a hot, moving rod
In the brain, which had an unusually stimulative effect on the imagination. For example:
Flaming fishes boring through ships from beneath the waterline, oh so quiet; or else:
Air hard as ice (the temperature correspondingly low) filling the lungs (each alveolus in turn); or:
Instrumental polyphony, no dissonance (sound solely consonant),
Only it is mind-meltingly loud, ending in a deafening, univocal trumpeting.
And a great many similar things, and all of it amidst the increasing
Aching of his entire skull. The perpetrator, however,
Nursed his friend devotedly; he came daily: when it was the fishes
He brought a net, when it was ice-air he made hot compresses, to
Harmonious sounds he sang shrilly and off-key, and thus he strove
To bring relief to every notion.

There came a day, and his (the other guy's) pain subsided,
And the friend was happy, he laughed and poured the wine. And then
Looked hard at the other guy's shirt, got hold of the hair-thin creature
And said: Here's the culprit. He looked even harder and said: it's
A female, it's sure to have left eggs. (Which was untrue.) Then
The friend started crying, his cry turned to wailing, and that wail has lasted
Five years now, with pauses for meals, almost without sleep, though

Without pain (since it was untrue).
What was behind this revenge was natural enough. For the afflicted
Had wanted his friend to become a better person, nobler,
Wiser, etc. Whereas I, the author of this dedication, offer it
To all those who desire the same for humanity (e.g., pedagogues, especially
If in this respect they are drumming up a so-called animated effort), and I do
So while paying them humble thanks for the benefits I've enjoyed.

1. Birds and Shadows

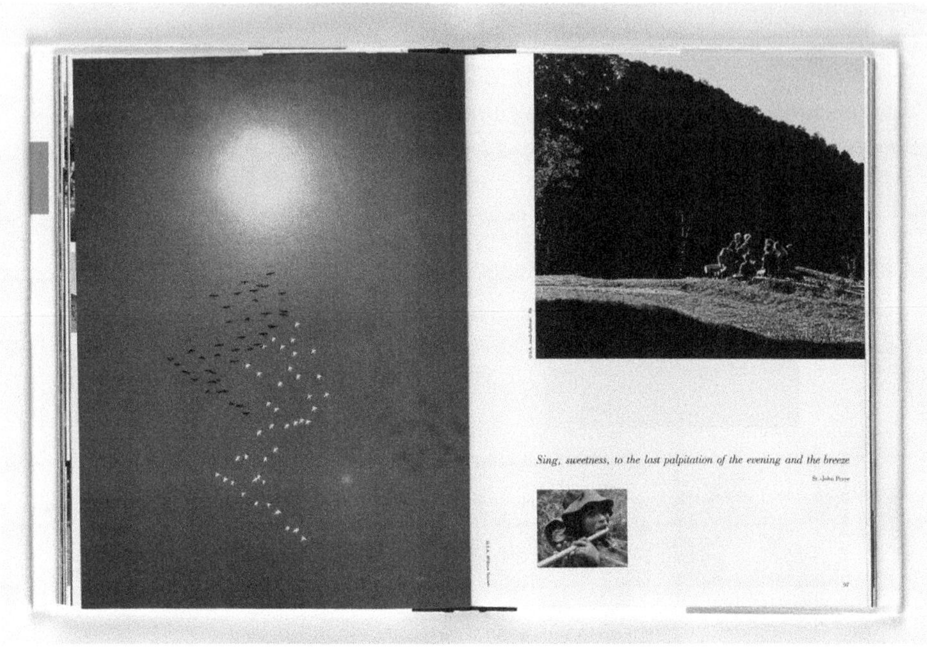

49 Pages 96–7 extracted from *The Family of Man: 60th Anniversary Edition.*

If a bird's body carries a rhythm within, it knows nothing of it; that's just
something
We say. A flock of flying birds likewise knows nothing
Of the rhythm of its configuration: that it's in groups, three, four, three again,
and then
Two (half of four). Anyway, if you look at that flock
From the other side, nothing will come of it, the same as
With the shadows on water arranging themselves into a rhythmic
Counterpoint. Furthermore: one must affirm the evocation of cheap
Romantic associations: man – bird.
Birds flap their wings, nothing more. So
the photographer
Has employed a trick, has shifted his slides (beneath the sun)
To the point of falsehood: to the point of showing a rhythm
That nature (the birds) has not created. The smartypants, he'd falsified
Natural truth (availing himself of the laws of optics, i.e., nature),
And he convinces us that this nature's beauty comes through its rhythm. It's
A sham, nothing more, the kind of sham that
Suits our aesthetic needs, a denaturing of the highest order,
Lyric hypocrisy, a sense
of beauty wondrousness rapture delighting one-
Self self self self. The smartypants, con artist, pimp, falsifier in glass.

2. Around the Stove

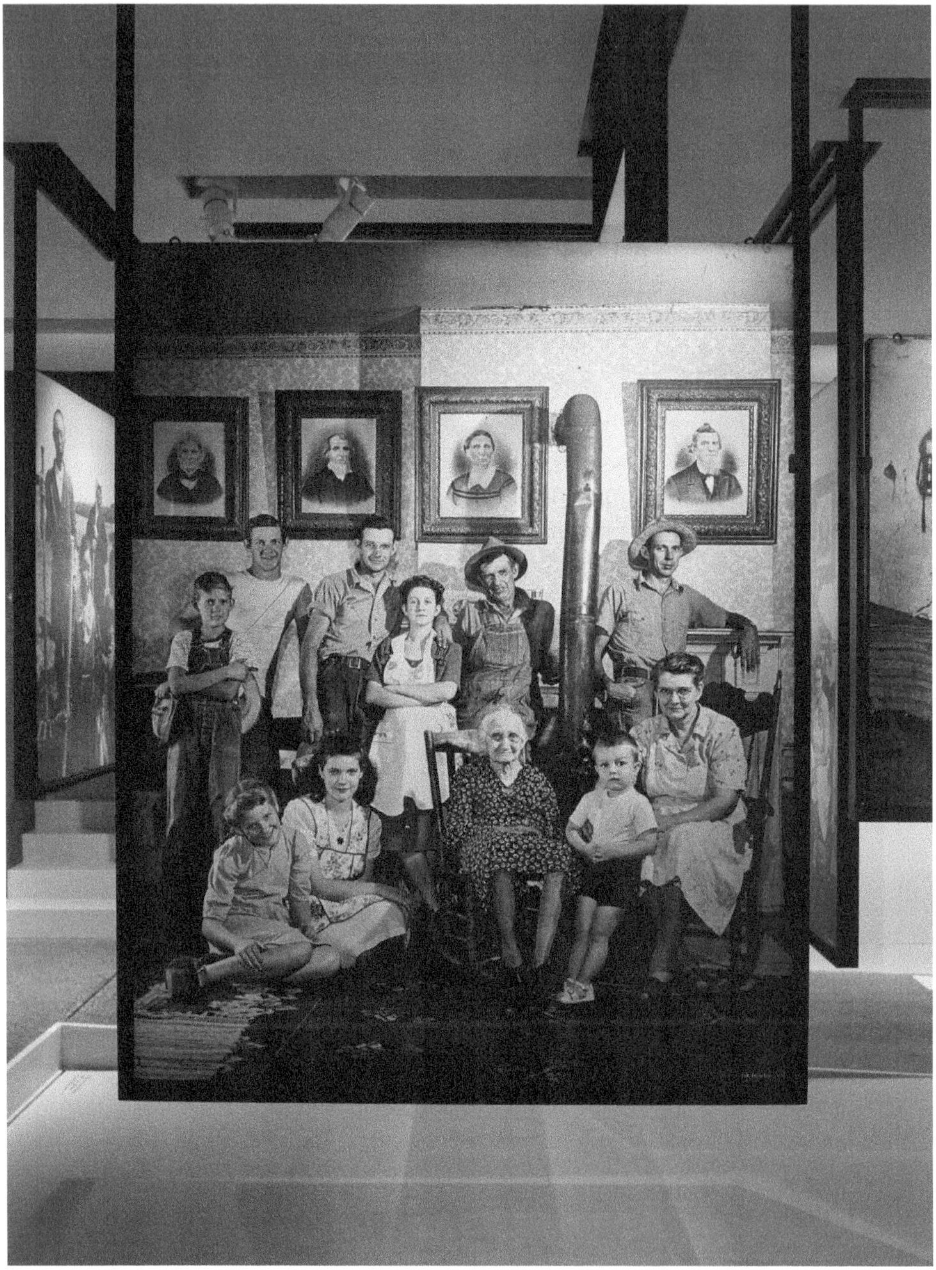

50 *The Family of Man* installation at Clervaux Castle. Theme 'Family of Man'. Photograph by Nina Leen.

The children have been told to be happy, so they do what they can (children
Are superb comedians), especially great at it are the
Middle-school-age (10–14, give or take) girls, only the thirteen-
Year-old boy seems not to have understood, hence the surprised look. The grownups
Smile stiffly, posed around the stove, beneath the wallpaper: the convention
Of group photography (the family keepsake), i.e., of socio-social
Life. There's a low level of feigned
Happiness. The slack muscles and skin
Of the old-timers no longer bend to their (insincere) will or imaginations
(Compelled by familiar cohabitation to arise), so:
A bit of truth breaks through, it might be truth, because how else would we get that mocking
Sneer? The decay of the body is in the service of truth. Whereas the photographs
In heavy frames, against the wallpaper, express nothing, mere
Hieratics (what's that mean?); just that the retoucher
Has enhanced their severity (strict morals, perhaps as it had to be).
We therefore conclude that shortly before death, due to the body's disobedience,
One could speak the truth: mockery, posed around a stove.

3. Thirst

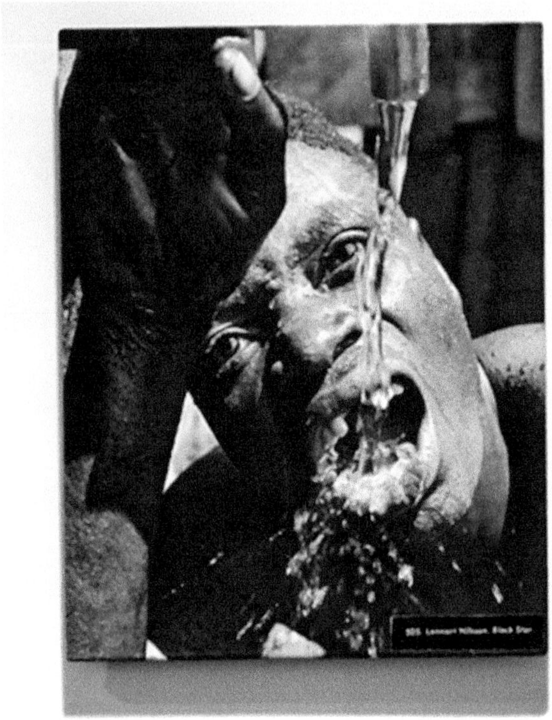

51 *The Family of Man* installation at Clervaux Castle. Theme 'Labour': Lennart Nilsson (cropping).

Mouth agape; two front teeth missing from the upper jaw (both
Incisors); water from the spigot splashes against
The bottom lip; the stream splits: some pours in, some
Crashes against the oral cavity (palate, tongue, larynx). Broad
Grimace of the eyes; what do these eyes see,
Turned upward (not the water)? a wall behind the spigot? and if there is
None (the photograph suggests nothing), what? a jet
Plane (the photograph is mute) diving straight
Into the pupils? the knife blade (no hand) slowly nearing
The unprotected (defenseless) mucosa of the throat? the two golden needles
Of Oedipus, they intend: drill (i.e., needles being knife-like in their autonomy,
Absolutely unavoidable)?
Well, no: in the photograph we see merely
The grimace of the eyes: suffering; from which it follows that quenching thirst
Is as painful as thirst itself. What's more: this pain is
Static. After all: thirst is unquenchable, only:
The stomach (not shown) is filling up with the water's gurgle.

4. The Law

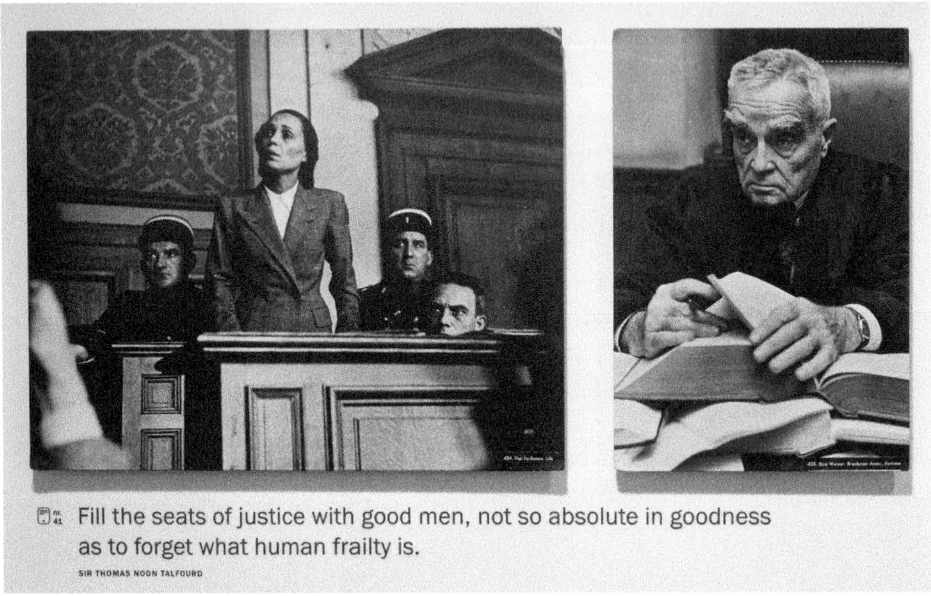

52 *The Family of Man* installation at Clervaux Castle. Theme 'Justice': (from left to right) Nat Farbman and Dan Weiner.

The majority of furrows on his face; symmetrically; they're arranged
In an inverted V; from the eyes, from the nose, from the mouth. The hands,
too; symmetrically; in the letter
V, uninverted (on open volumes of codices, i.e., on
Very broadly stretched V's). Attorney? Prosecutor?
Judge? Toga: lawyer. A concerned (exhausted?) actor. Acting,
In the old parlance: comedia (intending no
Offence) is recorded in the little black flecks
In the horizontal furrows of his forehead (from heavy lifting; symmetrically;
The eyebrows). But in comedia (how else to save mankind from
Evil? The punishment ennobles the society, does it not? Everything
Depends upon the crumpled little aluminum idol of interpretation, right,
Friend?), and so, in comedia (several times repeating
The word: comedia), so in comedia he fades, he melts away;
Without symmetry; concern; then only an exhausting (formerly
In parentheses) remains: this gerund is not spelled
With a 'V.'
At his neck the photograph shows a very
Busy tie.

5. Hands. Helplessness

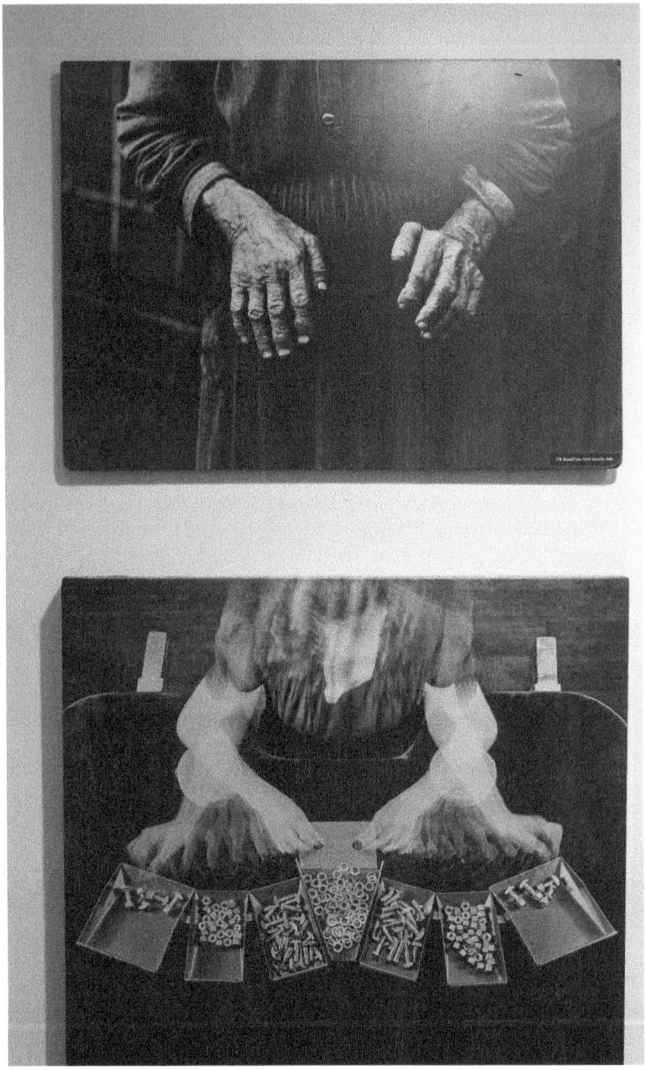

53 *The Family of Man* installation at Clervaux Castle. Theme 'Household and office work': Russell Lee (above), Gjon Mili.

Absolute helplessness. Reflexively, just looking at them,
They (the hands) arouse our respect: for work, for so many years (70? 80?),
For the arthritic swelling (poor earnings, damp
Apartment), the veins, look, bulging, the skin, look
(But sorry, you can't see it, sorry, you have to
Picture it), in spite of everything, look: cracked; for, what's more,
Facing death. So, reflexively: ohhhh (exactly). In reality, however,
Absolute helplessness, i.e., the helplessness of cruelty, since:
1) 'Just look,' says she, 'at the weariness of an old woman; how I labored,'
Says she, 'just look,' says she, 'such is my fate, the misery,' says she,
'I'm spent, these long years.' Obviously, this old-lady helplessness
Is the cause behind the helplessness of cruelty.
2) Whereas: 'So what was it you did?' I ask. 'What
Effort? Maybe corpses at midnight,' I ask (balladic), 'at the cemetery,
Only your accomplice, right?, took everything, and too bad? Or maybe
Day after day,' I ask, 'the concern, when your husband's a cutthroat,
Your son a cutthroat? Maybe even,' I ask, 'it's just: milking the cows,
There's the kids, the grandkids,' I ask, 'honesty, dependability, just the stuff
Of old age and poverty, no?' I ask. Thus, again, helplessness.

The face is outside the frame. What kind of face? Honest
Exhaustion? Clever exhaustion? Peevish peevishness? Oh, senti-
Mental helplessness of mine! Besides the old hands on 1/3
Of a threadbare garment: terror? tenderness?

People who, like women, are single-minded (politicians, priests,
Imbeciles, etc.) in their goals, pragmatic, as we say, they'll say: young ones,
Young ones – kneel before this sacred image (while they themselves are on
The pulpit).
          We will flee. Helplessness. The hands
Of the Mighty Strangler.

6. Drying

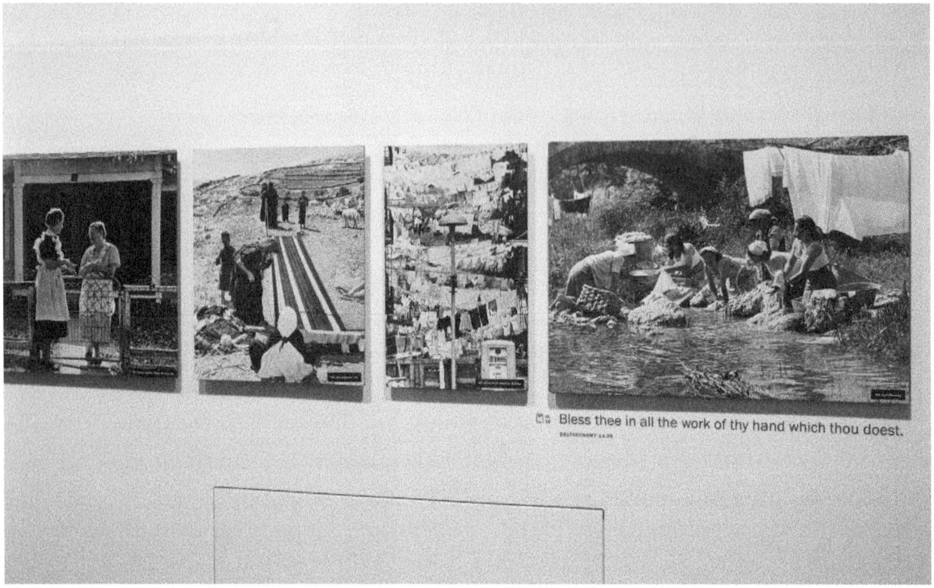

54 *The Family of Man* installation at Clervaux Castle. Theme 'Household and office work': (from left to right) Simpson Kalisher, David Duncan, Elliott Erwitt and Emil Obrovsky.

Day, maybe; in the foreground a box (vending machine?)
Emblazoned TYDOL ETHYL; maybe sunny, all this billowing
(Shirts, handkerchiefs, school smocks, dishrags, gym
Shorts, dresses, long johns, pillowcases, towels, skirts,
Bras, sweaters, I've probably covered
Everything, there are a few others I can't
Recognize by shape), so, billowing (TYDOL ETHYL metallic, not
Billowing): a breeze. The lines sometimes oblique, sometimes level
(More often) 2–3 floors up. From this, bit by bit, the damp
Steams off (along with the fragrance of detergent), the underwear dries.
These are the things close to the body (what does TYDOL ETHYL mean?),
wherefore
Must they dry, thus one trains (moralizes) underwear;
No humidity; sun and breeze; delightful (beyond the things
Close to the body); it moralizes into delightedness, dryness, into
No trace of detergent left. It dries. TYDOL
ETHYL (sheet metal? plastic?) is always dry: an ideal, i.e.:
A vending machine. Oh, it dries, eyes, eyes, eyes (the echo of drying), close
To the body; maybe sunny; eyes; day.
To keep the body
(Breakdown: stomach, lungs, kidneys, nerves, arteries, pancreas,
Adrenal glands, lymph nodes, genitals, brain, etc., etc.) hanging out
On lines; eyes; evaporating from it; eyes; damp, and then:
Training; TYDOL; moral education; ETHYL; sunny; TYDOL;
Day; ETHYL; delightedness. TYDOL ETHYL (thank God I
Don't know what it is) ETHYL TYDOL (what's it mean?) eyes eyes eyes.

First Contrapuntal Study

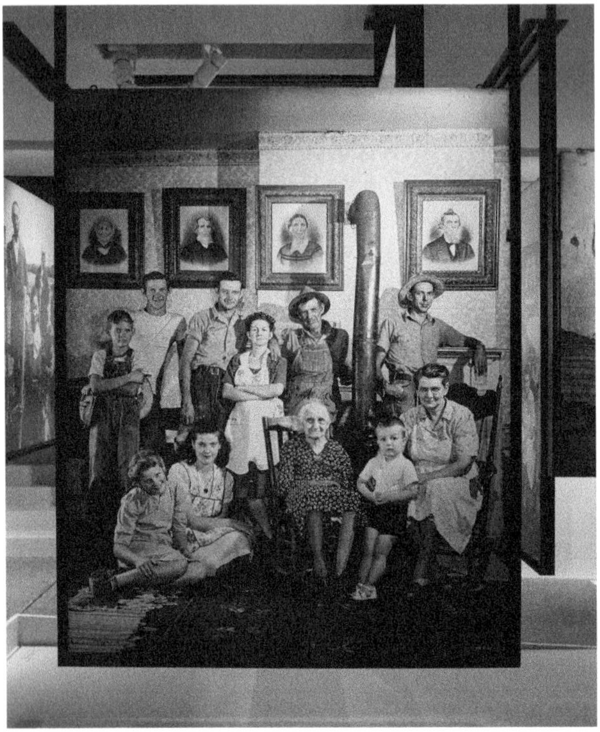

55 ***The Family of Man*** **installation at Clervaux Castle. Theme 'Family of Man'. Photograph by Nina Leen.**

Day, perhaps; the decay of the body is in the service
Of truth. Slack muscle and skin; it's swelling,
All of it, so it's swelling; they obey neither the will, nor imaginations.
Wherefore must they dry, especially the teenage
Girls, that's how to train them, moralize them
Into delightedness: into socio-social life. An
Excellent comedian (les comédiens, in French there's
No pejorative connotation)? And no trace left
Of detergent? Is it on this basis that the retoucher
Enhances the severity in the photograph? The severity in the eyes, in
The brow? Resulting from the body's disobedience,
Perhaps; near to death; to express
Mockery. It's drying, on a sunny day, on lines: it's
Close to the body; the disobedient body, near
To death; on lines; on the wind.

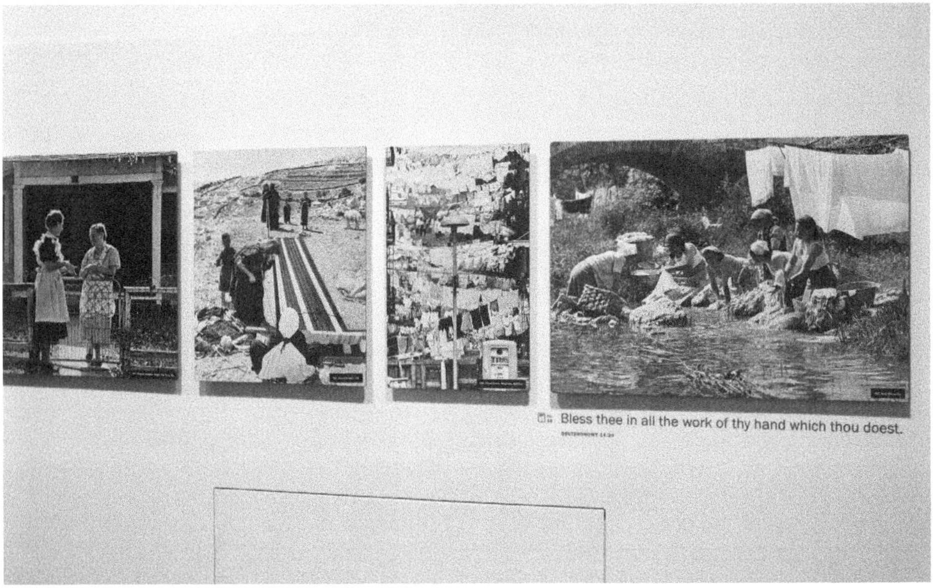

56 *The Family of Man* installation at Clervaux Castle. Theme 'Household and office work': (from left to right) Simpson Kalisher, David Duncan, Elliott Erwitt and Emil Obrovsky.

7. Music

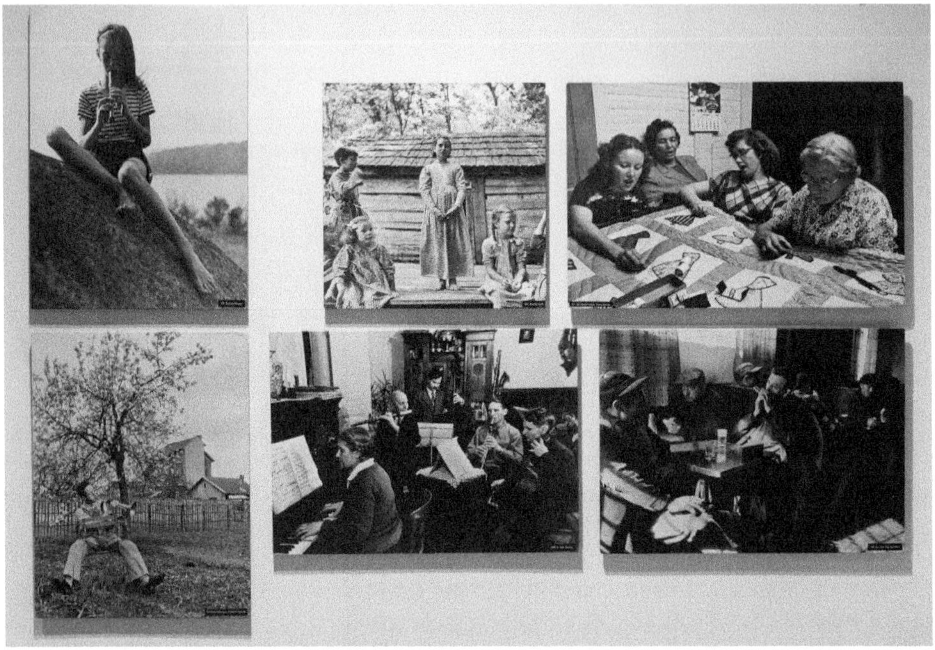

57 *The Family of Man* installation at Clervaux Castle. Theme 'Folk-singing': (left to right, top row) Barbara Morgan, Bradley Smith, Sol Libsohn; (bottom row) Robert Doisneau, N. Kolli and Sam Falk.

They read the notes attentively. Mother: upright piano; father: flute; first
Son: bass; second son: clarinet; third son: cello. No daughters
in this family. The furnishings a bit old-fashioned;
A saxophone hangs on the wall, next to it a clock with weights. The father
(Flute) is surely tapping out the rhythm with his foot. They read the notes
attentively;
(The transcription for piano is visible in outline, the upright
Piano in the foreground, no doubt: nineteenth century); the reading
Of notes (close attention) lends the faces an air of torpor.
They take it in; expressiveness; beauty; torpor. Wherefore
These notes (sticks with knobs) will any moment now drill
Into their skulls, and they'll walk around with their heads thus stuffed;
The notes protruding with their knobs; as one might say of round-quilled
(All around town, even to work) hedgehogs; in the brain, however,
The little sticks' points evoke a tickling. 'And what's tickling
You, son?' 'I'm tickled, Mother, by the A, the G-sharp, the B, the E-
Major chord.' 'And what tickles you, Father?' 'Son, the B, it's the
B that tickles me, the tone that takes us to C.' One of the most
Sublime; music is the most perfect; of ways
Of speaking; the shape of beauty; of falsehood.
They read the notes attentively,
finger
Them precisely; if only; with their fingertips; not to err.

8. Hole in the Sand

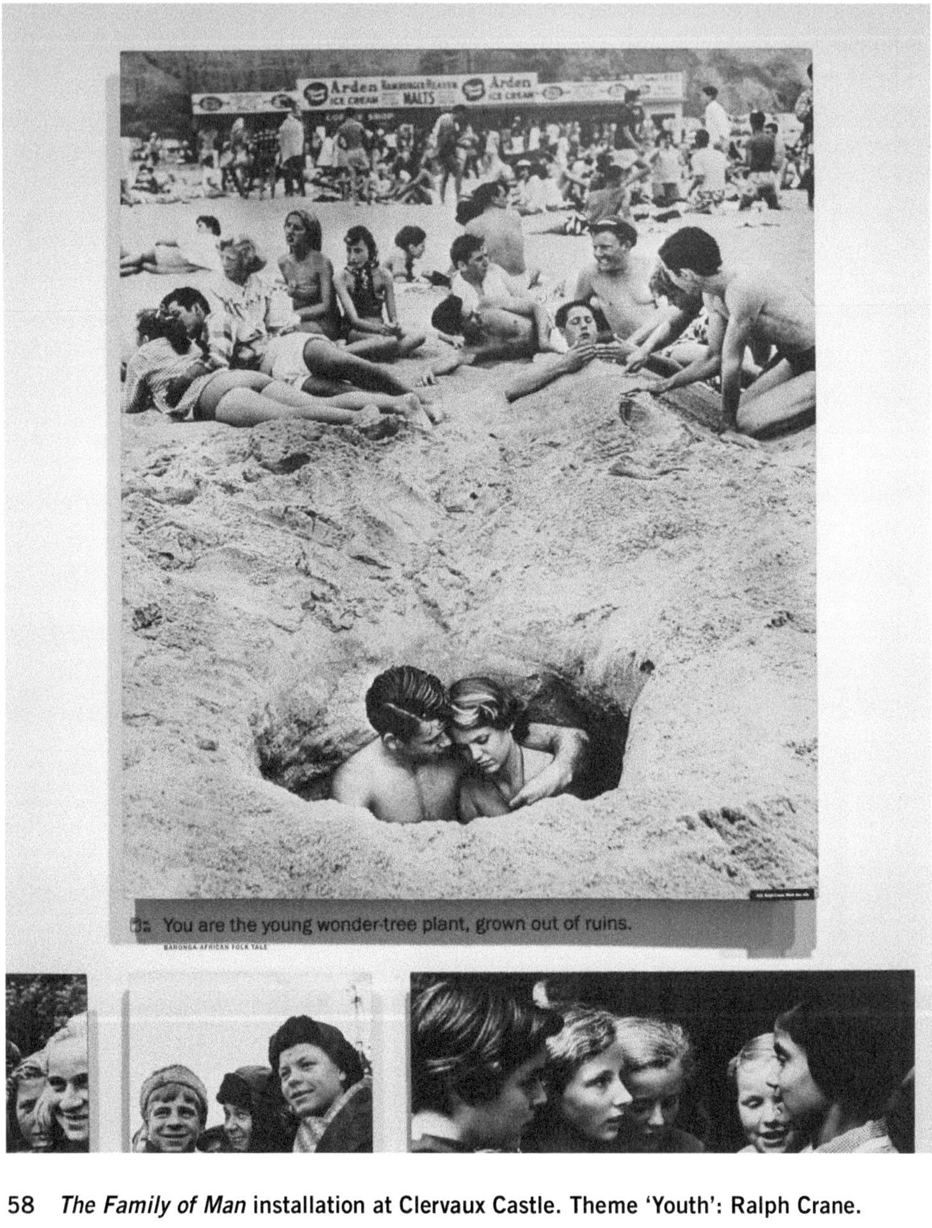

58 *The Family of Man* installation at Clervaux Castle. Theme 'Youth': Ralph Crane.

That's just how it seems; all around, a garland of people enjoying
Themselves; that the pair are (he, smiling, she; there's a word for it; pensive),
that they're
Into each other. Yet all you can see is half the torso: his arm
Across her shoulder, her temple against his brow (it's going to rhyme),
All this affection in a sandy hole somehow (there's the rhyme).
The hole is bottomless, despite their having dug it themselves to suit their
Size; it reaches to the center of the world, to the world's underworld,
Where the projections of all (the erotic idyll) longitudes and
Latitudes come down to a single point. Their legs, too, have
Extended accordingly; the ends of these legs (no longer feet, too thin),
Run together at this point, too, thus becoming the very same
Point (a period). And there: a temperature of several thousand degrees C,
Aside from that; the psychology of ends reduced to 'a point has no center
And is bounded by nothingness,' that's what's needed; so aside from that,
Hell, in the theological sense (the erotic idyll): they arise from hell,
From solitude, suffering, and hubris. So these quasi-feet are a piece
With magma and original sin. Have they been informed? Can they feel
Those degrees C? They have to be (the erotic idyll) told.
Or else pull them out, flip them around, rest their heads on feet that have no
(Geometric) center; heads; may their feet flutter
At the mouth (idyll) of the hole (erotic) in the sand above them;
May the tips of their toes nestle into each other, while the brain (idyll):
May it plunge (erotic) into hubris, suffering, solitude.
Whereas within the tunnel
There could be (inside: at 1/3 their length)
An act that affords (idyll) a beginning (erotic) to later
Generations of the 'family of man'.

Second Contrapuntal Study

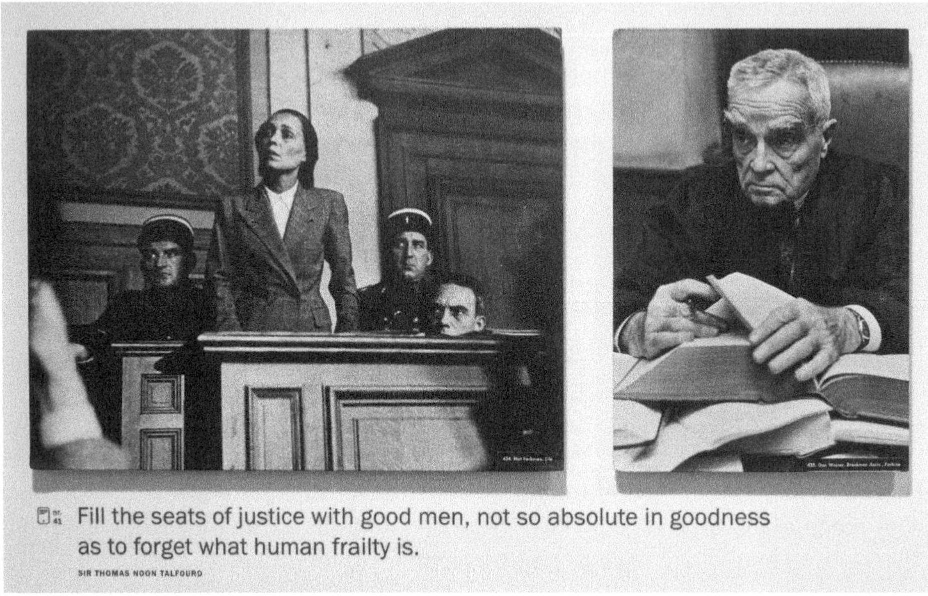

59 *The Family of Man* installation at Clervaux Castle. Theme 'Justice': (from left to right) Nat Farbman and Dan Weiner.

The psychology of ends: 'A point has no center and is
Bordered by nothingness.' Everything depends on the crumpled
Aluminum idol of interpretation; in the theological sense
(Erotic idyll) this is an asymmetrical concern,
An ennobling punishment, a thing recorded in tiny
Black flecks on the horizontal furrows
Of the brow; otherwise: man emerges from
The magma (several thousand degrees C) of original
Sin, the judge: compelled toward the old parlance,
He inverts (the idyll), through the long tunnel he plunges (erotic)
Human heads into magma, and of this is comedia made;
Comedia, concerned exhaustion, the overcooking of heads
In original sin; in the geometric center; in
The definition of a point (degrees C!); thereby attaining
Appropriate insight (the thing recorded in tiny black
Flecks); into exhaustion; justice; the verdict.

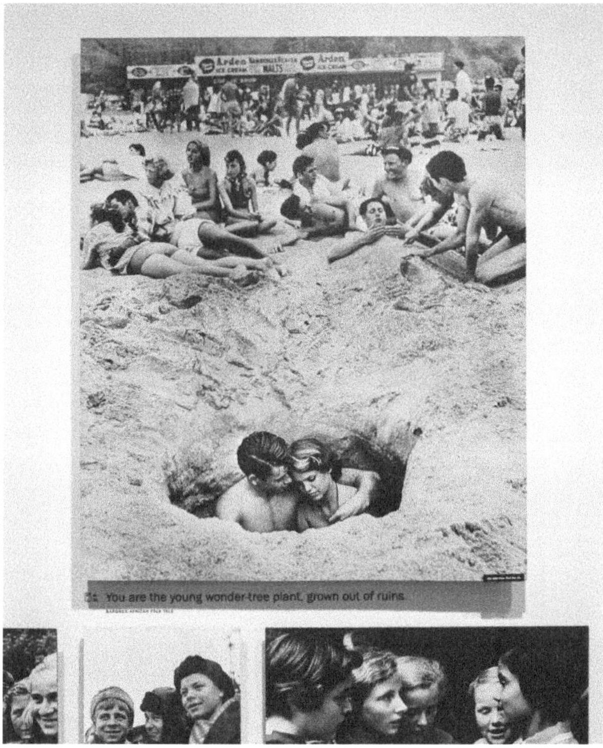

60 *The Family of Man* installation at Clervaux Castle. Theme 'Youth': Ralph Crane.

9. Hunger

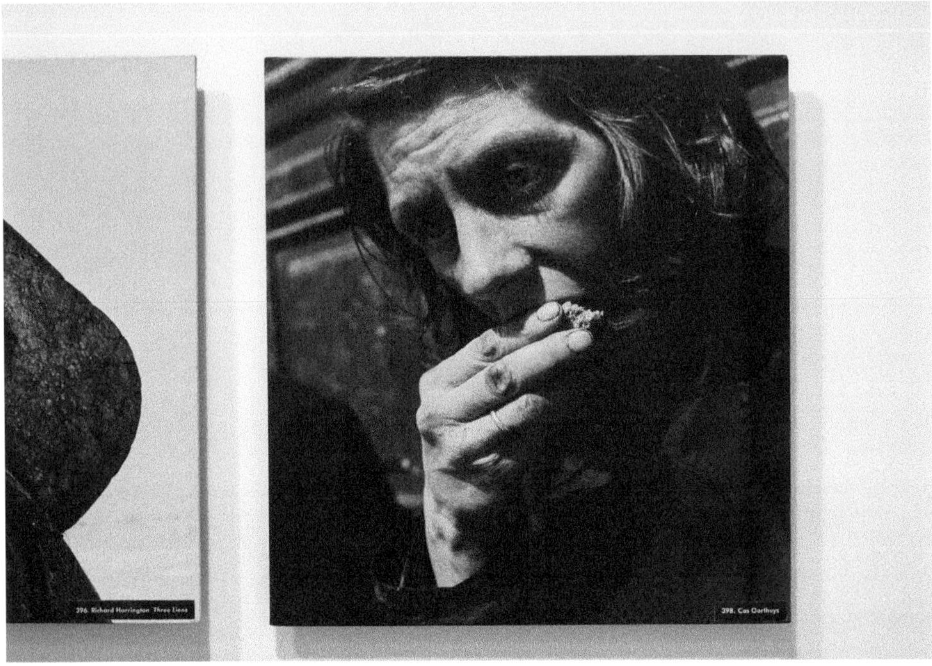

61 *The Family of Man* installation at Clervaux Castle. Theme 'Hard times and famine': Cas Oorthuys.

Were the wedding band gold, she'd have sold it long ago.
Just a couple months back the nails were still well kept,
Now they're black at the edges. The eyes are sunken,
If still open wide enough to express sadness.
A hungry person has a right to sadness. She avails herself of this right.

This woman will go and eat. She'll eat the crust of bread and
Go on eating, more and more voraciously, doing so with the help
Of the movement of her jaws and, in swallowing, the bump in the throat;
In this manner the things (one mustn't forget the voraciousness) will make
their way from oral cavity
To stomach (ravenousness). She'll go and eat. After eating the bread
The dirt from under her fingernails will end up in her stomach. She'll go on
Eating. Then it'll be her fingers; hands next; then,
In turn, forearms (which gives her some practice
At eating bones) (voraciousness); after the forearms, the upper arms. She'll
go on
Eating. It'll be the left leg's turn, she'll drive it right into
Her mouth, she'll get along swimmingly on the right. And she will eat
The right leg, and by then she'll move (ravenousness) on the air, un-
Tethered; she'll; with her body; go on; earthly; and eating. Next
The torso; she'll keep eating; the torso, to the height of the stomach,
And after that she'll just go on eating the air, she'll go on
At the head of the procession (voraciousness) of freaks. She'll lead the freaks
To heaven. And she'll travel; she'll walk; the whole sky;
Eating; and; (ravenousness); she'll eat; doing so with
The help of the movement of her jaws.

10. Grief

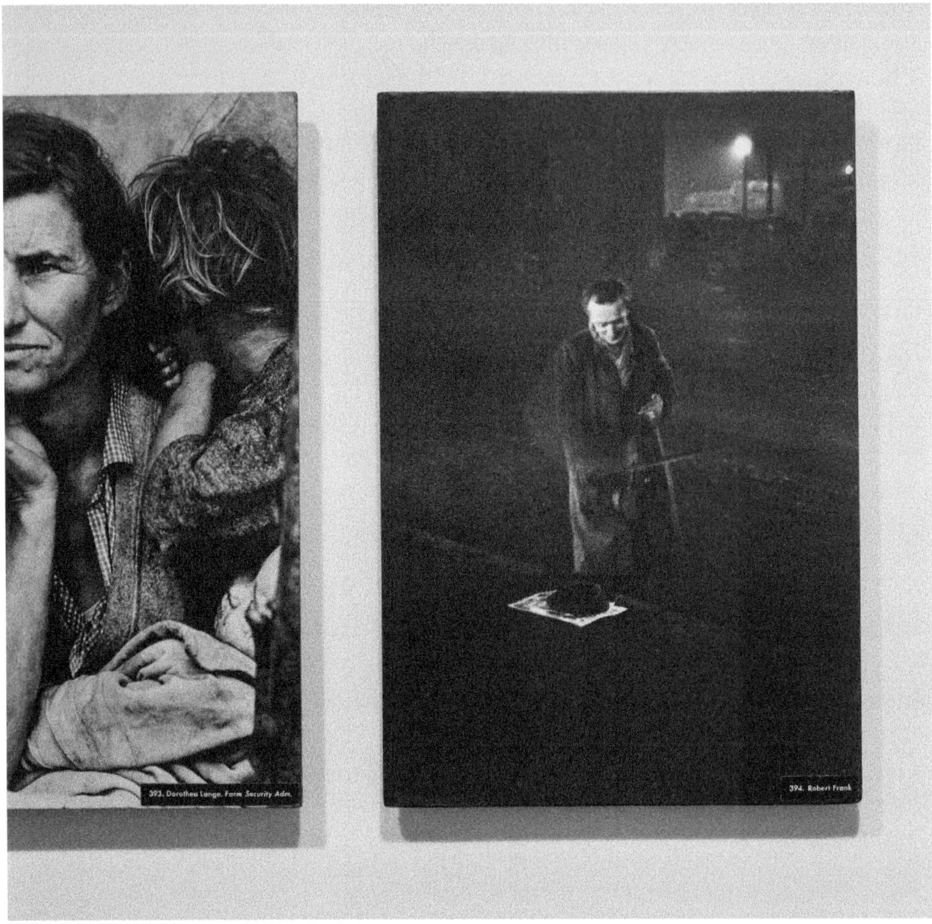

62 *The Family of Man* installation at Clervaux Castle. Theme ‘Hard times and famine’: Robert Frank.

One must assume that this sad
Person (in a poor coat, with a bare head) leaning
Against a straight iron (damp, autumn) cross reaching
To the height of his liver is a second-rate
Actor, ctor, tor, or, r; (r, ro, rot, rotc, rotca); for
Why else would he allow the photographer his artificial
Illumination of the face with a floodlight (don't mention
A flash, the photo's rushed); aside from that, in the background,
A quite well-composed (welcome; posed)
Light; flashlights, maybe; with chimneys' silhouettes
Way back; he must have been positioned (r, ro, rot,
Rotc, rotca), actor.
                                    And even if this
Person really had; lost someone; (dear); then
In light of the above (ongoing) analysis:
Now he wants to be an actor; who; hoo; if but
For a moment, since he wants to be
(Ctor, tor, or, r) on his own side
As he displays (plays, imposes) himself to (on) the photographer,
I.e., he wants: to be; (r, ro, rot;).

11. Obstruction

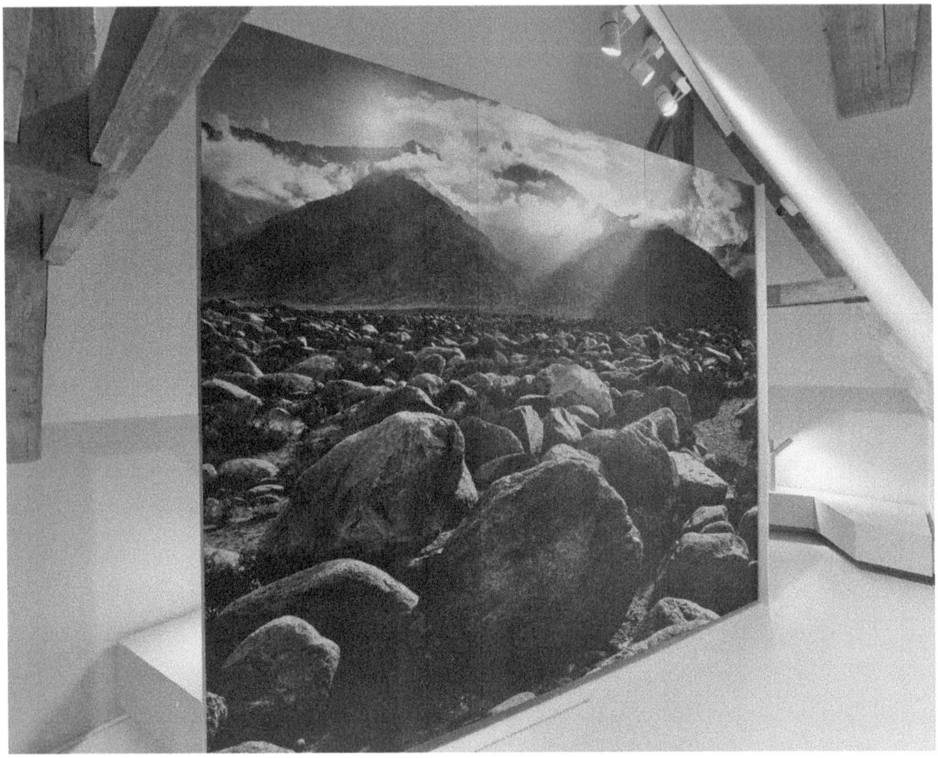

63 *The Family of Man* installation at Clervaux Castle. Ansel Adams.

Nature unanimated, by appearances cohesive (granite
Boulders), disintegrates, like everything that
Appears cohesive, disintegrates (it's apparently
Cohesive) into fragments, hard to pass, these
Fragments (and more granite boulders, only
Smaller), these fragments (likewise
Appearing cohesive) become obstructions, that is:
Unanimated nature of this kind (by appearances cohesive)
Will obstruct our paths, the globe (being,
Apparently, cohesive) disintegrates, obstructs the way
In the brilliance (apparently cohesive) of the sun, only
Non-cohesive, unanimated matter (in the photo:
Clouds, whisps), only such matter
Blocks no way, our hatred of coherence
(Demoralization of community of motes and atoms)
Blocks not our way, demoralization.
Of community (by appearances cohesive), of course,
In unanimated nature.

12. Guesswork

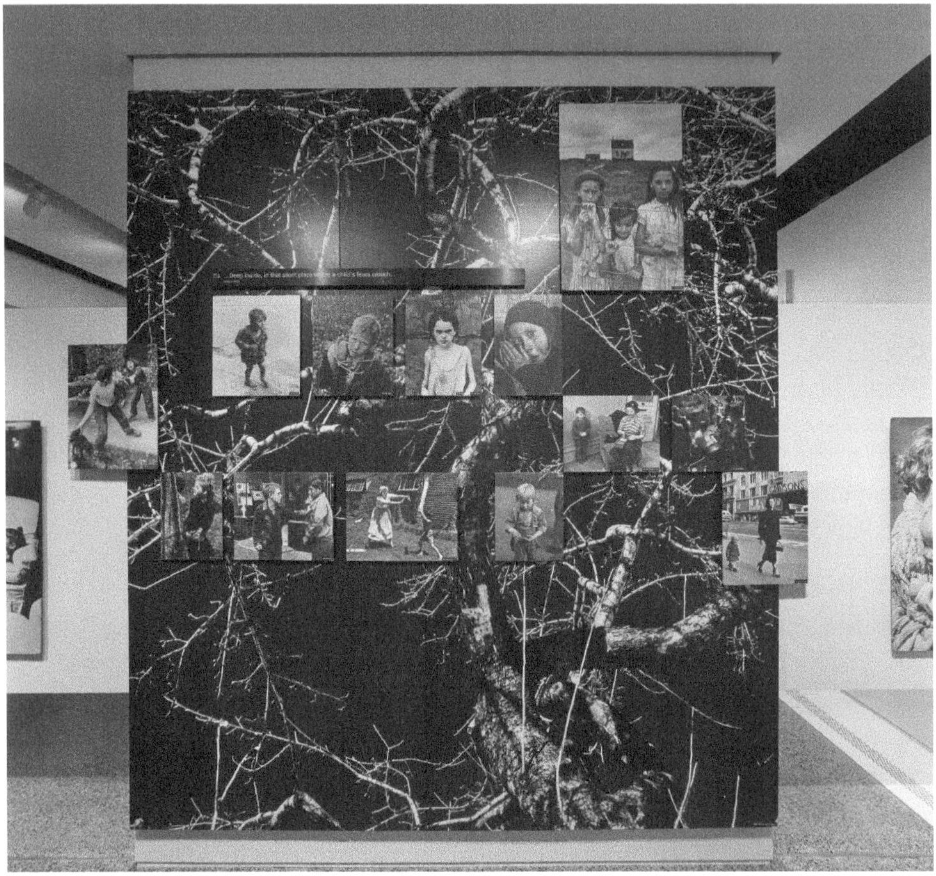

64 *The Family of Man* installation at Clervaux Castle. Theme 'Disturbed children'.

We'll show you, the universe
Is ours, our imagination is
Shattered, our brains dominated by majestic
Satiety, (none of which we know how to
Say, this satiety; to sate oneself; eat; it's
The kielbasa of the brain), we have brain kielbasa,
We'll let you taste it, squished kielbasas, sausages, franks,
These are our mushy grimaces, this the majesty
Of Victors; smashed kielbasa innards; it is we
Who are triumphant, we have brought about
Synthesis; the sausage of synthesis; synthesis of lamp and fish,
Which means, it swims, it illuminates the frank; frankly,
We're steaming; blah, blah, blah; (that's the proper way
Of expressing oneself); eternal bliss, the order of the bulging
Kielbasa, we, underdeveloped, triumphant,
We; frankly, we're steaming; we'll bring about; the universe;
To the blissfulness of the frank, the kielbasa, amen, the great gnashed
Deal, a blessing, the gods, amen,
It's growing into us, ever stronger, triumphant,
An exploding, all-encompassing, trampled kielbasa (frank,
Sausage) amen.

13. Work

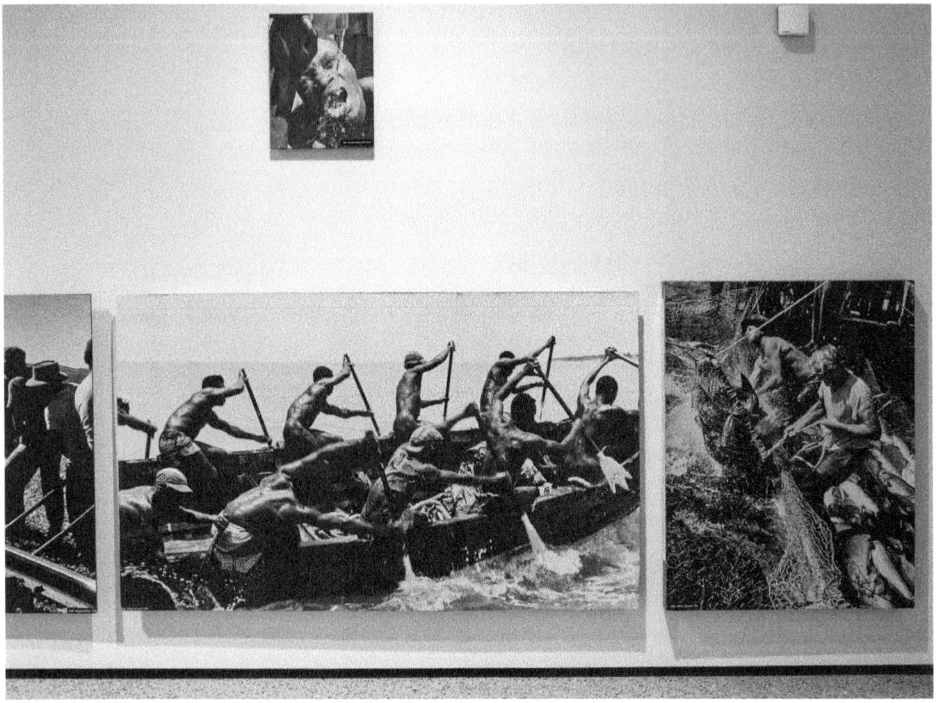

65 *The Family of Man* installation at Clervaux Castle. Theme 'Labor': Lennart Nilsson (above), Alfred Eisenstaedt and Allan Grant.

There, the trident oars splash; real good muscle
On the back; beneath the skin; they splash, glistening. So far,
Glistening; there are lines, there are nets; oh, into the distance; for fish;
They splash; oh how they glisten.
At a certain spot at sea
There's a hole, an opening more or less two meters
In diameter, a whirlpool, but not funnel-like, on the contrary: shaped
Like a cylinder (2m in diameter), its watery greenish
Walls whirling (oh how they splash; how they glisten). This hole, then,
Is where it leads; oh, glistening; the rowers' rowing (that is:
Useful work; oh how they splash). They slide some-
Teen, tens, hundreds of kilometers down (the hole), into the under-
World, more precisely: -water. Hell (no splashing, no
Glistening). Now hundreds of kilometers (square). And in one
Place (oh, hell; oh, glistening) stands a pillar (country
Fair) of enflamed copper, and the fish they were supposed to catch
Will tell them: Climb up; thus they'll climb
Up (their skin will hiss) the enflamed
Copper to the top (real good muscle on the
Back); (oh how it hisses; oh, the glistening); enflamed (skin pressed to pillar),
Single file; chest toward; on the back; enflamed; real good
Muscle; single file. The everlastingness of hissing; it splashes; glistening;
Single file; it hisses. The pillar then zigzags through the universe,
A pillar in nooses, useful; infinitude; work; there they are
Splashing; the muscles; the chest; hell; it hisses; single-file.

Third Contrapuntal Study

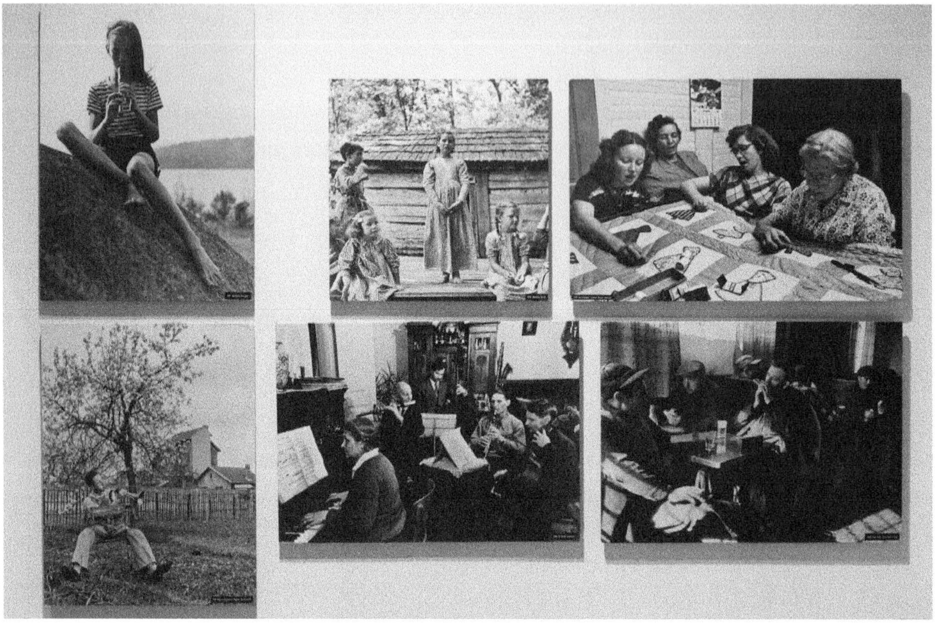

66 *The Family of Man* installation at Clervaux Castle. Theme 'Folk-singing': (left to right, top row) Barbara Morgan, Bradley Smith, Sol Libsohn; (bottom row) Robert Doisneau, N. Kolli and Sam Falk.

They'll climb the enflamed copper,
Up; notes (sticks with knobs) drilled into skulls;
Rowers (who knows), musicians (who knows), (hell;
Oh how it glistens), The Fish they were supposed to catch: 'And
What's tickling you, Son?' Music tickles, zigzagging through
The universe, as a pillar of flaming copper: a trumpet,
Tuba mirum; a sound, a watery, greenish, whirling slide down.
The possessing of everlastingness occurs in a room with
Old-fashioned furnishings, there: the skin hisses,
Chest hard against the enflamed metal, the skin
Smokes, round-quilled hedgehogs with a tickle in their brains blow
Into the flute's opening, file across the strings
Of the cello, bang their little fingers on the keys, file
Across the strings of the bass, blow on the clarinet's
Reed; the rowers have taken the plunge; explorers; real
Good muscle on the back; of the maw of hell.

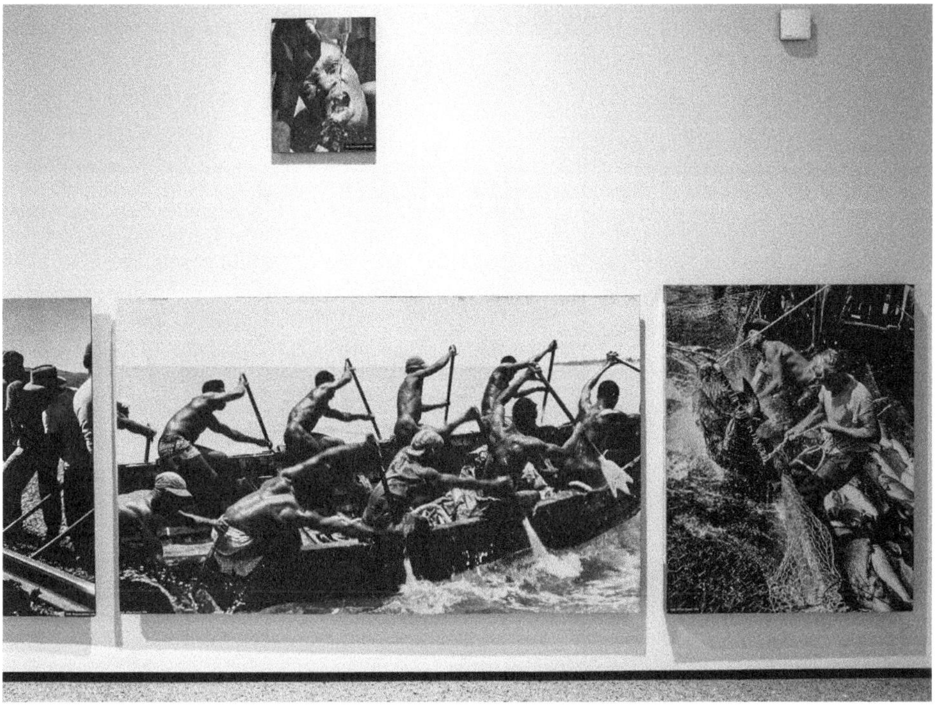

67 *The Family of Man* installation at Clervaux Castle. Theme 'Labor': Lennart Nilsson (above), Alfred Eisenstaedt and Allan Grant.

On the Last Page, Where There are No More Photographs

Monologue:

'I'll someday be – the great educators, you see,
O Poet, they're shaping me ideally for life and I'll someday
(Maybe quite soon, in a hundred years) someday
Be exactly, which is to say without remainder, without friction, without
Misunderstandings, and thus exactly, included in the perfect
Society, i.e., my own and society's
Good fortune: two geometric figures fitted tightly together,
O Poet, they (the educators) will intervene with shots
(Of all manner, these are exact calculations, oh the precision) shots
Into my pregnant mother's womb (that is, my body), and in this way
They will shape my bones, muscles, nervous system and brain and
I'll be highly gifted, Poet, you see, I'll have
A character in no way impeachable, i.e., the I who
Will be will in no way betray itself, I'm not
Here yet, Poet, you see, I'm not here, thus
I'm afraid, I'm trembling, slack atoms in air or wherever, you see,
Poet, you too will be – the great educators – prepared, and thus will
I, a preparation, be for you, a preparation: oh sing,
(Such must be my speech), the world's mild beauty, abandon
(You must), abandon, you see, Poet, this original
Sin, you've parted ways, I know, the beauty of the world, the good
(Falsified; with shots) of humanity, that's when I won't be afraid, now
I'm afraid, I'm not here, Poet, you see, we'll be
Happy, and you, Poet, you see, with beauties you'll prepare
(You lie up a storm of sinlessness) us for
The blessing of beatification.'

That's the monologue. My dear sweet educators, by original
Sin, by this, my hubris, I bring my loved ones to despise
Your beloved mankind; your blind eyes
(Your love); you won't see; educators.

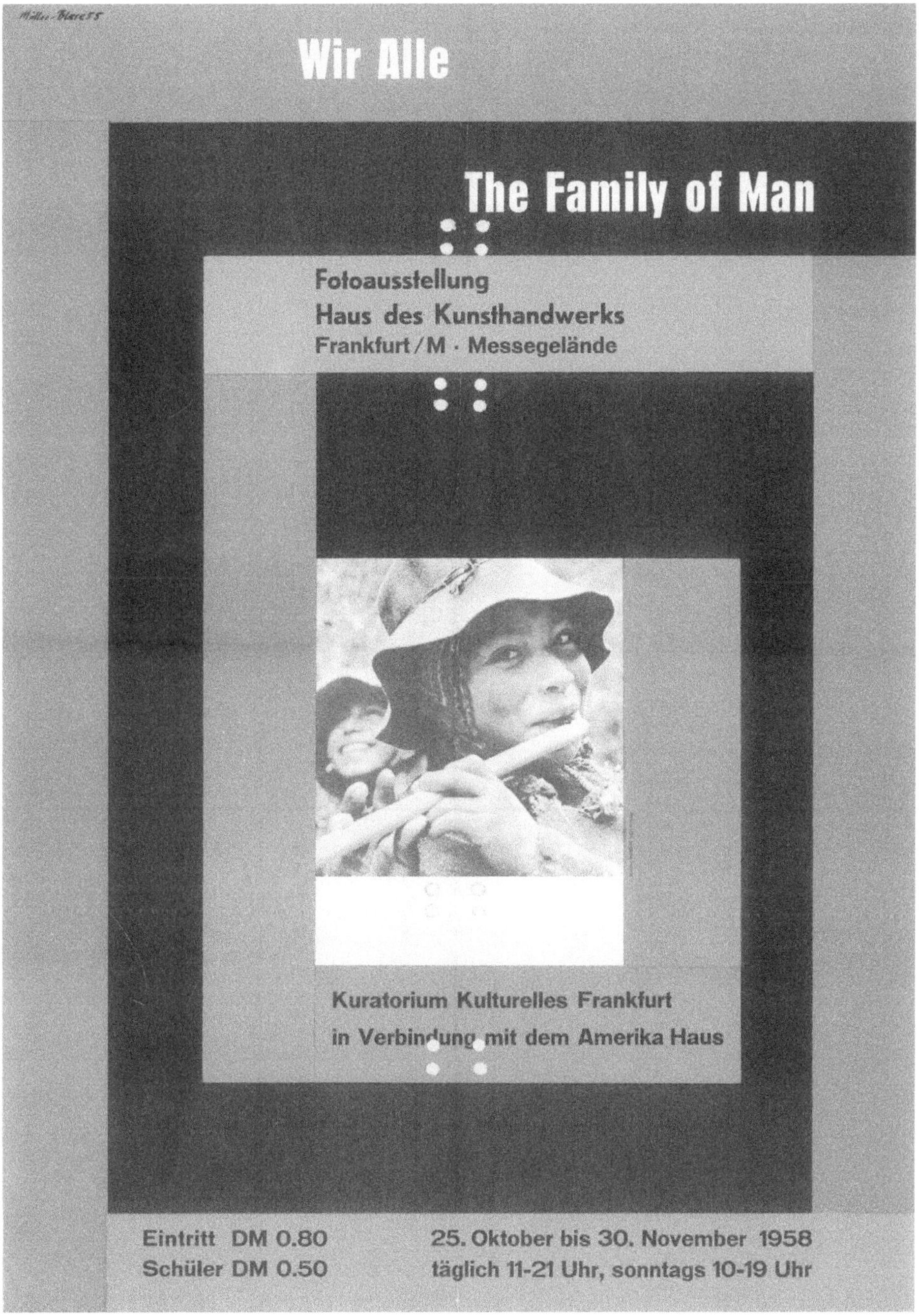

68 Poster for *The Family of Man* exhibition at Haus des Deutschen Kunsthandwerks, Frankfurt.

Bibliography

Azoulay, Ariella. '*The Family of Man*: A Visual Universal Declaration of Human Rights'. In *The Human Snapshot*. Edited by Thomas Keenan and Tirdad Zolghadr, 19–49. Feldmeilen: LUMA Foundation, 2013.

———. 'Photography Is Not Served: *The Family of Man* and The Human Condition'. In *Documentary Across Disciplines*. Edited by Erika Balsom and Hila Beleg, 10–19. Cambridge, MA: MIT Press, 2016.

Back, Jean and Gabriel Bauret, eds. *The Family of Man: Temoignages et Documents*. Luxembourg: Centre national de l'audiovisuel, 1994.

Back, Jean and Viktoria Schmidt-Linsenhoff, eds. *The Family of Man 1955–2001: A Reappraisal of the Photo Exhibition by Edward Steichen*. Marburg: Jonas Verlag, 2004.

Barthes, Roland. 'The Great Family of Man'. In *Mythologies*. Translated by Annette Lavers, 100–2. New York: Hill and Wang, 1972.

Berger, John. *About Looking*. New York: Pantheon Books, 1980.

Berger, John and Jean Mohr. *Another Way of Telling*. New York: Random House, 1982.

Berlier, Monique. '*The Family of Man*: Readings of an Exhibition'. In *Picturing the Past: Media, History, and Photography*. Edited by Bonnie Brennan and Hanno Hardt, 206–41. Urbana: University of Illinois Press, 1999.

Bezner, Lili. *Photography and Politics in America: From the New Deal into the Cold War*. Baltimore, MD: Johns Hopkins University Press, 1999.

Bezzola, Tobia. 'Lights Going All Over the Place'. In *Edward Steichen: In High Fashion. The Condé Nast Years, 1923–1937*. Edited by Todd Brandow and William E. Ewing, 187–97. Minneapolis and Lausanne: Foundation for the Exhibition of Photography and the Musée de l'Elysée, 2007.

Böger, Astrid. *People's Lives, Public Images: The New Deal Documentary Aesthetic*. Tübingen: Gunter Narr Verlag, 2001.

———. 'Transnational Exposure: *The Family of Man* and the Emergence of Global Photography.' In *Transnational Mediations: Negotiating Popular Culture between Europe and the United States*. Edited by Christof Decker and Astrid Böger. 57–72. Heidelberg: Winter, 2015.

Brandow, Todd and William A. Ewing, eds. *Edward Steichen: Lives in Photography*. New York: W. W. Norton, 2007.

——. *Edward Steichen: In High Fashion. The Condé Nast Years, 1923–1937.* London: Thames & Hudson, 2008.

Bravo, Monica. 'Aesthetics of Reception? A Jaussian Reading of *The Family of Man*'. *Art Criticism* 14, no. 1 (2009): 20–33.

Damrosch, David. *Meetings of the Mind.* Princeton, NJ: Princeton University Press, 2000.

Daniel, Malcom R. *Stieglitz, Steichen, Strand: Masterworks from the Metropolitan Museum of Art.* New Haven, CT: Yale University Press, 2010.

Decker, Christof, ed. *Visuelle Kulturen der USA. Zur Geschichte von Malerei, Fotografie, Film, Fernsehen und Neuen Medien in Amerika.* Bielefeld: transcript, 2010.

Delaney, Samuel R. and Matthew Cheney. *The Jewel-Hinged Jaw: Notes on the Language of Science Fiction.* Middletown, CT: Wesleyan University Press, 2009.

Deschin, Jacob et al. 'The Controversial Family of Man'. *Aperture* 3, no. 2 (1955): 8–27.

Duganne, Erina. *The Self in Black and White: Race and Subjectivity in Postwar American Photography.* Lebanon, IL: UPNE, 2010.

Elsen, Thomas and Christof Trepesch, eds. *Edward Steichen: Portraits d'artistes – Die Künstlerporträts.* Berlin: Deutscher Kunstverlag, 2014.

Eskildsen, Ute and Petra Steinhardt, eds. *Edward Steichen: Celebrity Design. Museum Folkwang.* Göttingen: Steidl, 2010.

Faram, Mark. *Faces of War: The Untold Story of Edward Steichen's WWII Photographers.* New York: Berkley Caliber, 2009.

Felski, Rita. *Doing Time: Feminist Theory and Postmodern Culture.* New York: New York University Press, 2000.

Felski, Rita. *Uses of Literature.* Oxford: Blackwell, 2008.

——. *The Limits of Critique.* Chicago: University of Chicago Press, 2015.

Ferretti-Theilig, Madeline and Jochen Krautz. 'Sprechende Bilder der Menschheit. Relationale Bildpraxis am Beispiel der Ausstellung *The Family of Man*'. In *Sprechende Bilder – Besprochene Bilder. Bild, Begriff und Sprachhandeln in der deiktisch-imaginativen Verständigungspraxis.* Edited by Alexander Glas et al., 303–26. Munich: kopaed, 2016.

Finnegan, Cara A. *Picturing Poverty: Print Culture and FSA Photographs.* Washington, DC: Smithsonian Institution Press, 2003.

Fluck, Winfried. 'Aesthetic Experience of the Image'. In *Romance with America? Essays on Culture, Literature, and American Studies.* Edited by Laura Bieger and Johannes Voelz, 409–31. Heidelberg: Winter, 2009.

——. 'Poor Like Us: Poverty and Recognition in American Photography'. *Amerikastudien / American Studies* 55, no. 1 (2010): 63–93.

Garb, Tamar. *Rethinking Sekula from the Global South: Humanist Photography Revisited.* In *Grey Room. Special Issue: Allan Sekula and the Traffic in Photographs* 55 (2014): 34–58.

Gedrim, Ronald J. *Edward Steichen: Selected Texts and Bibliography.* Oxford: ABC-CLIO, 1996.

Gee, Helen. *Limelight: A Memoir. A Greenwich Village Photography Gallery and Coffeehouse in the Fifties.* Albuquerque: University of New Mexico Press, 1997.

Goldberg, Vicki and Robert Silberman. *American Photography: A Century of Images.* San Francisco: Chronicle Books, 1999.

Greif, Mark. *The Age of the Crisis of Man: Thought and Fiction in America, 1933–1973.* Princeton, NJ: Princeton University Press, 2015.

Gresh, Kristen. 'The European roots of *The Family of Man*'. *History of Photography* 29, no. 4 (Winter 2005): 331–43.

Guittard, Jacqueline. 'Impressions photographiques: les Mythologies de Roland Barthes'. *Littérature* 143 (2006): 114–34.

Hagen, Charles, ed. *American Photographers of the Depression: Farm Security Administration Photographs 1935–1942.* London: Thames and Hudson, 1991.

Harley, Ralph L. 'Edward Steichen's Modernist Art-Space'. *History of Photography* 14, no. 1 (1990): 1–22.

Hirsch, Marianne. *Family Frames: Photography, Narrative and Postmemory.* Cambridge, MA: Harvard University Press, 1997.

Hoffman, Katharina. '*The Family of Man*: An Introduction'. *History of Photography* 29, no. 4 (Winter 2005): 317–19.

———. 'Sowing the Seeds / Setting the Stage: Steichen, Stieglitz, and *The Family of Man*'. *History of Photography* 29, no. 4 (Winter 2005): 320–30.

Horkheimer, Max. 'Die Bedeutung der Photographie für unsere Zeit'. In *Gesammelte Schriften*, Vol. 13. Edited by Alfred Schmidt, 38–43. Frankfurt: S. Fischer, 1989.

———. 'Eröffnung der Photo-Ausstellung *The Family of Man* – Wir alle'. In *Gesammelte Schriften*, Vol. 13. Edited by Alfred Schmidt, 30–7. Frankfurt: S. Fischer, 1989.

Hunter, Jefferson. *Image and Word: The Interaction of Twentieth-Century Photographs and Texts.* Cambridge, MA: Harvard University Press, 1987.

Hurm, Gerd. 'Die Rhetorik des Details: Barthes, Brecht und die epochale Fotoausstellung *The Family of Man*'. In *grenzen & gestaltung. Figuren der Unterscheidung und Überschreitung in Literatur und Sprache.* Edited by Nikolas Immer, Stefani Kugler and Nikolaus Ruge, 323–31. Trier: WVT, 2015.

———. 'Barack Obama and Edward Steichen: A Luxembourgian Seed and the American Liberal Presidency'. In *Obama and Transnational American Studies.* Edited by Alfred Hornung, 417–54. Heidelberg: Winter, 2016.

———. 'Edward Steichen: The "Lëtzebuerger Jong" who Brought Modernism to the New World'. In *Steichen Collections.* Edited by Malgorzata Nowara. Luxembourg: Musée National d'Histoire et d'Art, forthcoming 2018.

———. 'Between Faking and F.S.A.: Edward Steichen's Forgotten Contribution to the Debates about Realism, Naturalism, and Photography'. In *Revisionist Approaches to American Realism and Naturalism.* Edited by Jutta Ernst. Heidelberg: Winter, forthcoming 2018.

I-Fen Cheng, Cindy. *Citizens of Asian America: Democracy and Race during the Cold War.* New York: New York University Press, 2013.

James, Sarah. *Common Ground: German Photographic Cultures Across the Iron Curtain*. New Haven, CT: Yale University Press, 2013.

Jay, Martin. 'The Frankfurt School's Critique of Marxist Humanism'. In *Permanent Exiles: Essays on the Intellectual Migration from Germany to America*, 14–27. New York: Columbia University Press, 1985.

———. 'Mass Culture and Aesthetic Redemption: The Debate between Max Horkheimer and Siegfried Kracauer'. In *Fin-de-siècle Socialism and Other Essays*, 82–94. New York: Routledge, 1988.

Johnston, Patricia A. *Real Fantasies: Edward Steichen's Advertising Photography*. Berkeley: University of California Press, 1997.

Kaledin, Eugenia. *Daily Life in the United States, 1940–1959: Shifting Worlds*. Westport, CT: Greenwood, 2000.

Kaplan, Louis. *American Exposures: Photography and Community in the Twentieth Century*. Minneapolis: University of Minnesota Press, 2005.

Koeppen, Wolfgang. 'Der Kamera entgeht nichts'. Undated [1955] clipping from *Süddeutsche Zeitung*. Wolfgang-Koeppen-Archiv Greifswald M56.

Kracauer, Siegfried. *The Theory of Film: The Redemption of Physical Reality*. New York: Oxford University Press, 1960.

Kramer, Hilton. 'Exhibiting *The Family of Man*: "The World's Most Talked about Photographs"'. *Commentary* 20, no. 4 (October 1955): 364–67.

Krautz, Jochen. 'Kunstpädagogik als Friedenserziehung. Einige grundlegende Betrachtungen am Beispiel der Ausstellung *The Family of Man*'. In *Topoi. Beiträge zu einer kulturarchäologischen Ortsbestimmung*. Edited by Hermann J. Mahlberg, 61–73. Wuppertal: Bergische Universität Wuppertal, 2004.

———. *Vom Sinn des Sichtbaren. John Bergers Ästhetik und Ethik als Impuls für die Kunstpädagogik am Beispiel der Fotografie*. Hamburg: Verlag Dr. Kovač, 2004.

Krieps, Rosch. *Steichen-Story I/II. 'Er umarmte die Menschheit'*. Luxembourg: Selbstverlag, 2004.

———. *Humanheit: The Family of Man richtig verstehen*. Dudelange: Centre de Documentation sur les Migrations Humaines, 2005.

Kroes, Rob. *Photographic Memories: Private Pictures, Public Images, and American History*. Hanover, NH: Dartmouth College Press, 2007.

———. 'Projecting National Identities Through Cultural Diplomacy: The Case of *The Family of Man*'. In *The Dynamics of Interconnections in Popular Culture(s)*. Edited by Ray B. Browne and Ben Urish, 205–20. Newcastle upon Tyne: Cambridge Scholars Publishing, 2014.

Linfield, Susie. *The Cruel Radiance*. Chicago: University of Chicago Press, 2010.

Longwell, Dennis. *Steichen: The Master Prints 1895–1914, The Symbolist Period*. London: Thames and Hudson, 1978.

Lugon, Olivier. 'Edward Steichen as Exhibition Designer'. In *Edward Steichen: Lives in Photography*. Edited by Todd Brandow and William E. Ewing, 267–73. Minneapolis and Lausanne: Foundation for the Exhibition of Photography and the Musée de l'Elysée, 2007.

Lury, Celia. *Prosthetic Culture: Photography, Memory and Identity*. London: Routledge, 1998.
Marchessault, Janine. 'Manufacturing Humanism: Steichen/Burtynsky'. *Prefix Photo* 15 (2007): 54–67.
Mélon, Marc-Emmanuel. 'The Patriarchal family. Domestic Ideology'. In *The Family of Man 1955–2001. A Reappraisal of the Photo Exhibition by Edward Steichen.* Edited by Jean Back and Viktoria Schmidt-Linsenhoff, 57–81. Marburg: Jonas Verlag, 2004.
Miller, Wayne. 'World War II and *The Family of Man*'. In *Witness in Our Time: Working Lives of Documentary Photographers*. Edited by Ken Light, 44–53. Washington, DC: Smithsonian Books, 2010.
Morgan, Barbara. 'The Theme Show: A Contemporary Exhibition Technique'. In 'The Controversial Family of Man', *Aperture* 3, no. 2 (1955): 24–6.
Morris, John G. '*The Family of Man* as American Foreign Policy'. *History of Photography* 29, no. 4 (2005): 360–71.
Morris-Suzuki, Tessa. *The Past Within Us: Media, Memory, History*. London: Verso, 2005.
Muller, Jean-Claude. '"Ech sin e Lëtzebuerger Jong ...". Edward Steichen und sein Herkunftsland Luxemburg / Edward Steichen and Luxembourg, His Native Land'. In *Edward Steichen: Portraits d'artistes – Die Künstlerporträts*. Edited by Thomas Elsen and Christof Trepesch, 27–47. Berlin: Deutscher Kunstverlag, 2014.
Niven, Penelope. *Carl Sandburg: A Biography*. New York: Charles Scribner's Sons, 1991.
———. *Steichen: A Biography*. New York: Clarkson Potter, 1997.
O'Brian, John. 'The Nuclear Family of Man', *Japan Focus: Asia Pacific Journal*, July 2008. http://www.japanfocus.org/- John-O_Brian/2816. Republished on The History News Network, http://hnn.us/roundup/entries/52279.html (accessed 17 March 2017).
Olin, Margaret. *Touching Photographs*. Chicago and London: University of Chicago Press, 2012.
Orvell, Miles. *American Photography*. Oxford History of Art. Oxford: Oxford University Press, 2003.
Parsons, Melinda Boyd. '"Moonlight on Darkening Ways": Concepts of Nature and the Artist in Edward and Lilian Steichen's Socialism'. *American Art* 11 (1997): 68–87.
Philipp, Claudia Gabriele. 'Die Ausstellung *The Family of Man* 1955. Fotografie als Weltsprache'. *Fotogeschichte* 7 (1987): 45–62.
Phillips, Christopher. *Steichen at War*. New York: H.N. Abrams, 1981.
———. 'The Judgment Seat of Photography'. *October* 22 (1982): 27–63.
Poos, Françoise. 'Edward Steichen and *The Family of Man*.' In *Lieux de Memoire au Luxembourg II*. Edited by Sonja Kmec and Pit Peporte. 126–32. Saint-Paul: Luxembourg, 2012.
———, ed. *The Bitter Years: The Farm Security Administration Photographs Through the Eyes of Edward Steichen*. London: Thames and Hudson, 2012.

Priem, Karin and Kerstin te Heesen, eds. *On Display: Visual Politics, Material Culture, and Education.* Münster: Waxmann Verlag, 2016.

Raeburn, John. *A Staggering Revolution: A Cultural History of Thirties Photography.* Chicago: University of Illinois Press, 2006.

Ribalta, Jorge. 'Introduction: The Discursive Space of the Exhibition'. In *Public Photographic Spaces: Exhibitions of Propaganda, from* Pressa *to* The Family of Man, *1928–1955.* Barcelona: MACBA, 2008.

Ribbat, Christoph. *Blickkontakt: zur Beziehungsgeschichte amerikanischer Literatur und Fotografie 1945–2000.* Munich: Fink, 2003.

Roberts, John. *The Art of Interruption: Realism, Photography and the Everyday.* Manchester: Manchester University Press, 1998.

Salemme, Kevin. 'Chasing Shadows: Steichen's Dream of the Universal'. *History of Photography* 29, no. 4 (2005): 372–7.

Sandburg, Carl. *Steichen the Photographer.* New York: Harcourt, Brace and Company, 1929.

Sandeen, Eric J. *Picturing an Exhibition: 'The Family of Man' and 1950s America.* Albuquerque: University of New Mexico Press, 1995.

———. '"The Show You See With Your Heart": *The Family of Man* on Tour in the Cold War World'. In *The Family of Man, 1955–2001.* Edited by Jean Back and Viktoria Schmidt-Linsenhoff, 101–23. Marburg: Jonas Verlag, 2004.

———. 'The International Reception of *The Family of Man*'. *History of Photography* 29, no. 4 (2005): 344–55.

———. 'The Family of Man in Guatemala'. *Visual Studies* 30, no. 2 (2015): 123–30.

Schmidt, Kerstin. 'The "Other" Country in the City: Urban Space and the Politics of Visibility in American Social Documentary Photography'. In *Pictorial Cultures and Political Iconographies.* Edited by Udo Hebel and Christoph Wagner, 253–71. Berlin: De Gruyter, 2011.

Schmidt-Linsenhoff, Viktoria. '1955–2001. "*The Family of Man*" and "here is new york"'. In *The Family of Man 1955–2001. A Reappraisal of the Photo Exhibition by Edward Steichen.* Edited by Jean Back and Viktoria Schmidt-Linsenhoff. Marburg: Jonas Verlag, 2004.

———. 'Denied Images: *The Family of Man* and the Shoa'. In *The Family of Man 1955–2001. A Reappraisal of the Photo Exhibition by Edward Steichen.* Edited by Jean Back and Viktoria Schmidt-Linsenhoff, 80–100. Marburg: Jonas Verlag, 2004.

———. 'Verleugnete Bilder: *The Family of Man* und die Shoa'. In *The Family of Man 1955–2001.* Edited by Jean Back and Viktoria Schmidt-Linsenhoff, 80–99. Marburg: Jonas Verlag, 2004.

Sekula, Allan. *Photography Against the Grain: Essays and Photo Works, 1973–1983.* Halifax, Nova Scotia: Press of the Nova Scotia College of Art and Design, 1984.

———. 'Between the Net and the Deep Blue Sea: Rethinking the Traffic in Photographs'. In *The Family of Man 1955–2001.* Edited by Jean Back and Viktoria Schmidt-Linsenhoff, 140–87. Marburg: Jonas Verlag, 2004.

Smith, Joel. *Edward Steichen: The Early Years*. Princeton, NJ: Princeton University Press, 1999.

Sollors, Werner. *The Temptation of Despair: Tales of the 1940s*. Cambridge, MA: Belknap Press, 2014.

Solomon-Godeau, Abigail. '*The Family of Man*: Refurbishing Humanism for a Postmodern Age'. In *The Family of Man 1955–2001. A Reappraisal of the Photo Exhibition by Edward Steichen.* Edited by Jean Back and Viktoria Schmidt-Linsenhoff, 9–55. Marburg: Jonas Verlag, 2004.

Sontag, Susan. *On Photography*. London: Penguin, 1977.

Staniszewski, Mary Anne. *The Power of Display: A History of Exhibition Installation Design at the Museum of Modern Art*. Cambridge, MA: MIT Press, 1998.

Steichen, Edward. 'The F.S.A. Photographers'. In *U.S. Camera Annual 1939*. Edited by Tom Maloney, 43–66. New York: Morrow, 1938.

———. *The Family of Man.* New York: Museum of Modern Art, 1955.

———. 'Photography: Witness and Recorder of Humanity'. *Wisconsin Magazine of History* 41 (1958): 159–67.

———. *A Life in Photography*. New York: Doubleday, 1963.

Steichen, Joanna T. *Steichen's Legacy: Photographs, 1895–1973*. New York: Knopf, 2000.

Stimson, Blake. *The Pivot of the World: Photography and its Nation.* Cambridge, MA: MIT Press, 2006.

Sylvan, Rita and Avis Berman. 'Edward Steichen, a Memoir: The Making of *The Family of Man*'. *Connoisseur* 218 (February 1988): 118–25.

Szarkowski, John. *'The Family of Man'*. In *The Museum of Modern Art at Mid-Century: At Home and Abroad*. Edited by John Elderfield, 12–37. New York: Museum of Modern Art, 1994.

Turner, Fred. '*The Family of Man* and the Politics of Attention in Cold War America'. *Public Culture* 24, no. 1 (2012): 55–84.

———. *The Democratic Surround: Multimedia and American Liberalism from World War II to the Psychedelic Sixties.* Chicago: University of Chicago Press, 2013.

Wirpsza, Witold. '4. Prawo'. In *Komentarze do fotografii The Family of Man.* Kraków: Wydawnictwo Literackie, 1962.

Zamir, Shamoon. *The Gift of the Face: Portraiture and Time in Edward S. Curtis's* The North American Indian. Chapel Hill: University of North Carolina Press, 2014.

Notes on Contributors

Winfried Fluck is Professor of American Culture at the John F. Kennedy Institute for North American Studies of Freie Universität Berlin. He is a founding member and former director of the Graduate School for North American Studies at Freie Universität Berlin and Co-Director of the Futures of American Studies Institute at Dartmouth College. His most recent publications are *Romance with America? Essays on Culture, Literature, and American Studies* (2009), *Towards a Post-Exceptionalist American Studies*, edited with Donald Pease (2014), and *American Studies Today: New Research Agendas*, edited with Eric Redling, Sabine Sielke and Hubert Zapf (2014).

Ulrike Gehring is Professor of Art History at the University of Trier with a focus on modern art and new media. Her latest publications deal with the iconic status of scientific pictures in the art of the early modern period and modernity, notably *Mapping Spaces: Networks of Knowledge in 17th Century Landscape Painting*, edited with Peter Weibel (2014) and *Die Entdeckung der Ferne. Natur und Wissenschaft in der niederländischen Malerei des 17. Jahrhunderts* (editor, 2014).

Gerd Hurm is Professor of American Literature and Founding Director of the Trier Center for American Studies at the University of Trier (TCAS). He is the author of studies on modern American city fiction (*Fragmented Urban Images*, 1991) and nineteenth-century realism (*Rewriting the Vernacular Mark Twain*, 2003). He has edited books on American politics and presidential rhetoric (with Paul Goetsch, *The Fourth of July*, 1992; *Important Speeches by American Presidents*, 1994) and post-World War II literature and culture (with Ann Marie Fallon, *Rebels without a Cause*, 2007). In 2014, on the occasion of the 10th anniversary of the Trier Center for American Studies, Hurm organized an international symposium on Edward Steichen's *The Bitter Years* in Dudelange, Luxembourg.

Martin Jay is Ehrman Professor of History at the University of California, Berkeley. He received his BA from Union College and his PhD from Harvard University. His many publications include *The Dialectical Imagination: A History of the Frankfurt School and the Institute of Social Research, 1923–50* (1973) and *Downcast Eyes: The Denigration of Vision in Twentieth-Century French Thought* (1993).

Miles Orvell is Professor of English at Temple University. His research areas include American literature and culture, with special interests in realism and modernism, as well as visual culture, urbanism and technology. Orvell's research in recent years has focused on the cultural significance of space, and his 2012 study of Main Street explored the complex and contradictory cultural meanings of the small town at the same time that it problematized the icon of Main Street. His current research is on the cultural meaning of ruins, and he is looking at the representation of archeological ruins, industrial ruins, urban ruins, atomic ruins, and other sites of destruction, primarily using the lens of photographic representation. His many publications include *The Real Thing: Imitation and Authenticity in American Culture, 1880–1940* (1989) and *American Photography* (2003), a volume in the Oxford History of Art series.

Benjamin Paloff is Associate Professor of Slavic Languages and Literatures and of Comparative Literature at the University of Michigan, Ann Arbor. He is the author of *Lost in the Shadow of the Word (Space, Time, and Freedom in Interwar Eastern Europe)* and of the poetry collections *And His Orchestra* and *The Politics*. Professor Paloff is also the translator of several books and shorter works from Polish, Czech, and Russian.

Anke Reitz is Curator for Photography at the Centre national de l'audiovisuel (CNA) in Luxembourg since 2005 and head of the Steichen Collections held at the institute. She studied visual communication with a focus on audiovisual arts in Liège and Paris and art history in the UK. Further specialization brought her to photography conservation and visitor-centred art mediation.

Eric Sandeen is Professor of American Studies at the University of Wyoming and Director of the Wyoming Institute for Humanities Research. He is the author of *Picturing an Exhibition: The Family of Man and 1950s America* (1995) and several articles on the international tour of Steichen's massive exhibition, the most recent of which looks at the September 1955 installation in Guatemala City. He first saw the *Family of Man* images in Clervaux in 1989. Sandeen has held five Fulbright lectureship positions. In autumn 2014 he was Senior Fulbright Professor at Radboud University, Nijmegen, the Netherlands.

Kerstin Schmidt is Professor of American Studies at the Catholic University of Eichstaett, Germany. She is the author of *The Theater of Transformation: Postmodernism in American Drama* (2005) and has published on modern American drama, ethnic literatures in the US and Canada, the Harlem Renaissance, theories and cultures of diaspora as well as on media theory/radio studies and visual culture studies, especially on documentary photography. She also co-edited the essay collection *America and the Sea* (2004) and has edited and contributed to *Space in America: Theory History Culture* (2005). Her current research projects include 'Negative Space and the Making of Modern America: Concepts of Space in

American Literature, Architecture, and Photography', as well as 'The Literature of Relation: Reconceptualizations of the Black Atlantic and Diasporic Writing'.

Werner Sollors is Henry B. and Anne M. Cabot Professor of English Literature and Professor of African and African American Studies at Harvard University. He is co-editor with Greil Marcus of *A New Literary History of America* (2009), and his major book publications include *Beyond Ethnicity* (1986), *Neither Black nor White yet Both* (1997), *Ethnic Modernism* (2008) and *The Temptation of Despair: Tales of the 1940s* (2014). He is a Fellow of the American Academy of Arts and Sciences and corresponding member of the Austrian Academy of Sciences and the Academia Europaea.

Shamoon Zamir is Associate Professor of Literature and Visual Studies and the Director of Akkasah, the Center for Photography at New York University Abu Dhabi. He has previously taught at the University of Chicago, the University of York and the University of London. Zamir works in the areas of literature, photography and intellectual history. His book *The Gift of the Face* explores the relationship of aesthetics and ethics in the work of the early twentieth-century photographer Edward S. Curtis and examines the ways in which image and text, art and science, pictorialist photography and anthropology come together in Curtis's portraits of Native Americans. Zamir is co-editor of *The Photobook* (2012) and has in addition published on twentieth-century African American and Native American fiction and on modern poetry, and has translated short stories from Urdu.

Index

Italic page numbers refer to illustrations.